International GOSSIP

International GOSSIP

A History of High Society
1970-1980

Andrew Barrow

Hamish Hamilton · London

Design by Craig Dodd

First published in Great Britain 1983
by Hamish Hamilton Ltd
Garden House 57–59 Long Acre London WC2E 9JZ

Copyright © 1983 by Andrew Barrow

British Library Cataloguing in Publication Data

Barrow, Andrew
  International gossip.
  1. Upper classes—Great Britain—History
  —20th century.   2. Great Britain—
  Social life and customs—20th century
  I. Title
  941.085′7′0880621   SA566.4
  ISBN 0–241–10974–4

Printed in Great Britain by
Jolly & Barber Ltd, Rugby

For Isobel Strachey

INTRODUCTION

·This is a day-to-day record of the social and sporting activities, eating habits, births, deaths, love affairs and crimes of the international upper class over the ten year period 1970–1980.

I have concentrated on the activities of a headline-grabbing gang of globe-trotters such as Bianca Jagger, Lady Rothermere and others 'famous for being famous' who emerged during these years, but have also included the doings of less trendy characters, some of whom have been established for many decades, and I have not entirely ignored the politicians who have held the centre of the stage.

The story moves between London, New York, Washington, California, Riyadh, Paris, Moscow, Miami, the Mediterranean and other resorts. If a disproportionate number of events seem to happen in London, it is only because in my view, in spite of England's steady decline during the period, London remains the world's principal playground. A lot of the action takes place at airports, if not on aeroplanes themselves, though I have not ventured into outer space or attempted to obtain details of what the astronauts on the Apollo missions had for breakfast.

The narrative begins at the end of the Swinging Sixties and ends in the post-punk era in the midst of a recession of Great Depression proportions. In the pages that follow several long drawn out sagas are followed through from start to finish. The complete Watergate saga is contained here, along with the Jeremy Thorpe Affair, the rise and fall of General Idi Amin and the marriage and divorce of Mick and Bianca Jagger. I have dissected these stories into small bits and interwoven them with each other.

The events that follow have been placed in strict chronological order. It will be seen that sometimes three unconnected events occur the same day while occasionally a whole week goes by without anything happening. Hair transplants, riding mishaps and glittering social events will be found interspliced with suicides, hijackings and political upheavals.

As the years go by, the action gets more violent and socialites become more frenzied and wierder in their personal habits. Scenes at airports get uglier and more and more politicians are discredited as the power of the media increases. During this period, investigative journalists become increasingly intrusive and gossip columnists achieve a status they have never before enjoyed. Never before have celebrities' lives been laid so bare nor public life been made to look so absurd. For this reason I have noted the activities of gossip columnist Nigel Dempster, who hob-nobs with everyone throughout this period and ends up married to the daughter of a duke.

It is curious how those in the limelight often seem to escape the effects of the political and economic troubles of the time. As we will see, Claridge's restaurant remains packed out in the middle of Mr Heath's three day week. Behind the quicksilver fashionable façade, I have chosen items to show how a reactionary and traditional life continues undisturbed. Charity balls are held in the hotels of London and New York, Princess Anne takes up fox hunting, Conservative cabinet ministers still shoot grouse and ageless and dateless socialites still gather at Maxim's, Gstaad, Longchamps and Royal Ascot, apparently immune to the Age of the Common Man. As we will see, dukes and duchesses go on entertaining magnificently behind closed doors.

The years that see the rise of Nigel Dempster and Lady Falkender also see the fall of Jim Slater, Bernie Cornfeld, Jeremy Thorpe, Richard Nixon, Sir Anthony Blunt and others – though some of these people succeed in making partial comebacks before the end of the decade. Not all the 'old favourites' from the previous decades survive to the end of the period. The old Duke of Leinster commits suicide at the age of eighty-three, the Duchess of Windsor fades out of the scene with a major haemorrhage and Lord Mountbatten is one of thousands of victims of IRA violence.

I have drawn my material from the pages of *Woman's Wear Daily*, the *New York News*, *The Times*, *Daily Mail*, *Daily Express*, *Sunday Express*, *Sunday Times*, the *New York Times* and other publications. I have found Jennifer's Diary in *Harpers Queen* unexpectedly helpful and I have dared to use *Private Eye* as an occasional source. Books I have found specially useful include Allan Mayer's *Madam Prime Minister*, Bob Woodward and Carl Bernstein's *The Final Days*, Auberon Waugh's *The Last Word*, *Aristotle Onassis* by Nick Fraser and others, Sir Cecil Beaton's *The Parting Years*, Thomas Kiernan's *The Roman Polanski Story* and, with certain reservations, Nigel Dempster's *HRH Princess Margaret*. Mary Henderson's *Paris Embassy Cookbook* provided me with the recipe for the quail pie served to the Queen Mother in October 1976. Some of the material that follows has never been previously published. I am grateful to Hugo Vickers for giving me details of a secret visit to England by the Duchess of Windsor in 1973 which went entirely unnoticed in the press at the time.

I would also like to thank Sir Harold Wilson for answering a specific enquiry, Richard Ingrams for publishing extracts of this book in *Private Eye*, Liz Smith of the *New York News* for lending me her entire file of back numbers and Lady Olga Maitland of the *Sunday Express* for offering me the same privilege. I am grateful to Valerie Gold for going through back numbers of *Time* magazine, to Maureen Delany for re-typing my own untidy typescript, and to Caroline Tonson Rye for editing the final version and finding the photographs. Finally, I would like to thank Sonny Mehta who, over lunch at Waltons restaurant on Saturday 29 December 1979, first suggested that I write this book.

1970

The decade begins with London still swinging. The easy-going Mr Wilson is in his sixth year at 10 Downing Street and the nattily dressed, heavily moustachioed Dr Roy Strong is in his third year at the National Portrait Gallery. Pot-smoking young aristocratic 'drop-outs' still pursue a hedonistic life style, driving around Chelsea in blacked out Rolls-Royces or Aston Martins and appear almost undistinguishable from the pop stars with whom they mingle so easily. Over in America, the resourceful President Nixon is secure at the White House in spite of growing student unrest about Vietnam. On the international scene, unquestionably dominated by the legendary big spender Jackie Onassis, people like the Vicomtesse de Ribes, the Burtons, and the frail but active Duke and Duchess of Windsor still go about their endless social round. During the twelve months that follow, the impact of inflation, taxation and estate duty is keenly felt. High-flyer Bernie Cornfeld's fortunes go into a spin, causing anxiety throughout the investment business. The launching of the first jumbo jet is followed by a rash of hijackings. Aristocrats not already tax exiled make ends meet by selling jewellery and opening safari parks, while their trendy children begin to settle down at last. Meanwhile, Women's Lib makes its voice heard, throwing the Miss World Contest into confusion after twenty-three untroubled years. During this year, Mick Jagger and Marianne Faithfull finally break up, there are rumours of disharmony at Kensington Palace and the Beatles, who have done so much to bring about the Permissive Society, also go their separate ways. The year ends with John Lennon declaring that the dream is over and it's time we got down to so-called reality.

On New Year's day, Vice-President Spiro Agnew landed by helicopter in the jungles of Vietnam thirty-six miles north-west of Saigon. 'The people back home are pretty damned proud of what you are doing,' he told American troops. 'Don't be misled by what you see and read in certain publications.'

On Friday January 2, the British Prime Minister Harold Wilson returned to London after a short holiday at his three bedroom bungalow in the Scilly Isles.

Meanwhile, Mr Wilson's former colleague George Brown had set off on an unofficial tour of the Middle East. That weekend in Cairo, he caused consternation by calling President Nasser's adviser on foreign affairs, Dr Mahmoud Fawzi, 'You wily old bugger'.

Back in America on Monday January 5, the inquest opened at Martha's Vineyard on Miss Mary Jo Kopechne who had been drowned after an evening out with Senator Edward Kennedy. Senator Kennedy arrived looking bronzed and fit after a ski-ing holiday in the Rocky Mountains and gave evidence in camera for seventy-five minutes. Outside, pressmen pounded the pavement to keep warm and a Kennedy press secretary, Dick Drayne, snapped at a reporter with a microphone, 'Put that thing away. I'm no celebrity.'

The following day in New York, 27-year-old Muhammed Ali, who had been stripped of his world title after refusing to be called up for service in Vietnam, signed a contract to write his autobiography. 'Nobody knows about me really,' he said. 'I'm going to tell it just like it is.'

That night in London the post-Christmas depression was enlivened by a fancy dress party at Christie's organized by 37-year-old Lady Antonia Fraser and Lady Amabel Lindsay, and attended by fashion designer Michael Fish, critic Kenneth Tynan and other celebrities dressed in 'rich and royal robes'.

The following day Prime Minister Wilson visited a school near his birthplace in Yorkshire and ate a jam tart cooked by a six-year-old.

Back in America, on Thursday January 8, the inquest on Mary Jo Kopechne ended with evidence from the caretaker of the Chappaquiddick municipal rubbish dump. Judge James Boyle said he would prepare his report 'without undue delay', and Senator Edward Kennedy announced that he was confident he would be fully vindicated.

On Sunday January 11, bachelor Canadian Prime Minister Pierre Trudeau flew home to Ottawa after a skin-diving 'interlude' in the Caribbean to face questions about the alleged use of government aircraft for his private purposes.

On Tuesday January 13, 42-year-old Bernie Cornfeld, controversial head of IOS and reputedly worth £56 million, flew into London from Geneva where he occupied the house originally built by Napoleon for Empress Josephine. He was taken to his Belgravia home by Rolls-Royce accompanied by a bevy of young women.

That night, the Duke and Duchess of Windsor appeared on British television for the first time. In the course of a lengthy interview the 75-year-old Duke described America as 'one vast golfcourse' and the Duchess said of the mini-skirt, 'Well you certainly know what you're getting don't you?' and said she would have liked to run an advertising agency.

Meanwhile, George Brown's tour of the Middle East had caused more confusion. Arriving in Jerusalem he had greeted Israeli Premier Golda Meir with the words 'Hello, sister', and at a dinner party in Tel Aviv on Sunday January 18, he told General Herzog, 'Wipe that silly smile off your face.'

The following day the former Foreign Secretary was back in London. 'I am what

God made me. I don't propose to change at the age of fifty-five,' he said.

On Wednesday January 21, the first operational jumbo jet was launched by Mrs Nixon who pulled a lever unleashing a spray of red, white and blue liquid on the plane's nose. The first flight was however delayed by various technical difficulties – weak rivets and two serious in-flight turbine wheel disintegrations were later discovered – and did not eventually reach London until 2.14 p.m. on January 22. Later that day, the plane returned to New York, now seven hours behind schedule, with actress Raquel Welch in knee-length suede boots among the 150 people on board.

On Monday January 26, at Marlborough Street Court in London, Mick Jagger was fined £200 following the discovery of cannabis resin at his Chelsea home. His girl-friend, singer Marianne Faithfull, who appeared in court wearing a white maxi-dress, was found not guilty of possessing the drug and they drove off together in a chauffeur-driven white Bentley.

On Tuesday January 27, 77-year-old Lady Diana Cooper appeared at a memorial service at St James's Piccadilly for the Earl of Dudley upstaging others present, such as Lady Antonia Fraser and the Duke of Buccleuch, by wearing a fashionable black maxi coat.

On Wednesday January 28, it was revealed that Mrs Jackie Onassis had ordered £200 worth of seeds for her rockery on the island of Skorpios, including alyssum, campanula, thistle and lobelia.

That night in Paris, the beau-monde was out in force for the première of Maria Callas's first film *Medea* at the Paris Opera. Miss Callas was escorted by the film's director Pasolini and wore a simple dark blue dress. The singer's friend Aristotle Onassis had reserved a box for four, but cancelled it at the last moment. Miss Callas dined with him afterwards at an apartment on the Avenue Foch.

On Friday January 30, the British Shadow Cabinet under Opposition leader Edward Heath gathered at Selsdon Park Hotel, twenty miles south of London, to take part in a policy-making conference. On Saturday those present dined off smoked salmon and roast pheasant, and consumed twenty-four bottles of Château Haut Bages '59.

The same day in Hollywood, 65-year-old royal photographer Cecil Beaton went on an LSD 'trip' with a friend.

The following day, Sunday February 1, Mr Beaton attended a revivalist meeting at a local Methodist chapel and linked hands with other members of the congregation.

On Monday February 2, the death of 97-year-old Earl Russell drew tributes from across the world. 'He was one of the greatest men of the century,' said Labour minister Michael Foot. 'He was a great liberator, perhaps the greatest fashioner of the permissive or civilized society.'

The following morning, a military string ensemble pumped out show tunes in the ballroom of Buckingham Palace as 70-year-old Noël Coward knelt to receive his knighthood from the Queen. 'The Queen was absolutely charming. She always is. I've known her since she was a little girl,' he remarked before strolling off to the Savoy Hotel where he lunched off a silverside of beef from the trolley, with no starter and nothing to follow.

That night, police raided London's Open Space Theatre where Andy Warhol's film *Flesh* was showing to a packed house. Film censor John Trevelyan said afterwards: 'I cannot see why the police should object to the showing of this film under club licence. It is a film for a limited audience of intellectuals.'

Over in New York on Wednesday February 4, bearded tycoon Bernie Cornfeld told admiring institutional investors that his company, IOS, was experiencing a new cash flow of $100 million a month and made a wild and unjustified accusation that the Securities and Exchange Commission, who had suggested otherwise, were plotting to overthrow the Stock Exchange.

On Friday February 6, there was a party at the Iranian Embassy in Washington, at which Iranian caviare was served to guests seated at thirty-five candle-lit tables. 'The new Ambassador wants to be known as a terribly swinging jet-setter,' explained one of those present.

That weekend in New York, Noël Coward's knighthood was celebrated with a party at Raffles Club, attended by sun-tanned Douglas Fairbanks Jnr, Walter Lippmann, Cary Grant, Hermione Gingold and other Show Biz figures. After an informal supper, Sir Noël gave an impromptu cabaret.

Sir Noël Coward pauses for a cigarette after receiving his knighthood at Buckingham Palace. He left later for the Savoy Grill where he had a silverside of beef from the trolley

On Tuesday February 10, four affectionate letters written by Mrs Jackie Onassis to former Deputy Secretary of Defence Roswell Gilpatric, and stolen from his office safe, were published in the *Washington Post*.

Back in swinging London the following day, Prince Charles took his seat in the House of Lords for the first time. Dressed in a floppy black Cap of Maintenance and scarlet duke's mantle with four rows of ermine and gold, he strode into the historic chamber looking 'as if he owned the place'.

Meanwhile, a Buckingham Palace landau on its way to pick up the new German Ambassador to the Court of St James's had crashed before reaching the German Embassy.

On Tuesday February 17, Frank Sinatra appeared at a secret meeting at Trenton, New Jersey, to be quizzed by State officials investigating organized crime in Mafia-riddled New Jersey. Following this evidence the judge dismissed an arrest warrant and contempt charges filed against him.

The following night in London, a dozen or more peers and peeresses attended a private showing of Andy Warhol's controversial film *Flesh* to see what the police had objected to.

The following Monday, February 23, President Pompidou and his wife arrived in Washington amidst protests about the sale of French jets to Libya. At a welcoming dinner at the White House that night, fresh salmon blanketed with a light and creamy Lafayette sauce was served.

The following night in London, there was a party at 10 Downing Street for the Yugoslav Prime Minister, Mr Ribičič. Guests included comedians Morecambe and Wise, artist David Hockney who wore black-rimmed specs, *Private Eye* editor Richard Ingrams, and actress Julie Christie who wore thigh-high boots and a shiny mini-dress and carried a fringed leather shoulder bag.

The following day, Wednesday February 25, a controversial new portrait of the Queen by Pietro Annigoni went on show at the National Portrait Gallery. 'Personally, I like it,' said the Gallery's director pint-sized Dr Roy Strong, who wore a pink pyjama shirt and tie at the unveiling ceremony. *Time* Magazine said the portrait made the Queen look 'like a heroine of the Bolshevik revolution'.

On Thursday February 26, the Pompidous left the White House for Chicago where they were booed by 10,000 demonstrators as they arrived at a dinner party.

On Saturday February 28, the wedding took place of the Crown Prince of Nepal. Among those present was Col Algernon Asprey, managing director of the Bond Street firm which had recently decorated the king's throne room with a fifty foot high chandelier and a specially made gold and turquoise carpet.

On Monday March 2, the health of Herr Rudolf Hess, who had recently undergone a serious operation in a hospital in Berlin, was discussed in the House of Commons. Liberal leader Jeremy Thorpe asked that Hess should not be sent back to Spandau gaol, where he was now the sole inmate, and pleaded for 'a more humane method of visiting by his family'.

That night pop artist David Hockney, made his second appearance in less than a fortnight at 10 Downing Street where a party was given in honour of West German Chancellor Willy Brandt.

Meanwhile, President Nixon had flown to New York to apologize to President Pompidou for the rough treatment he had been getting in America. On Tuesday March 3, the Pompidous left for Paris with the controversy still raging.

On Monday March 9, 68-year-old romantic novelist Barbara Cartland, dressed in shocking pink, furs and jewellery, gave a luncheon in London to launch a new love elixir – 'the secret of youth and vitality'. Guests were served ugli fruit and passion fruit salad, chicken with honeyed sauce and bread rolls with poly-unsaturated margarine.

Back in Washington, on Friday March 13, President Nixon paid an impromptu visit to the city's Technological Institute. His motorcade lost its way en route and was forced to make a nine automobile U-turn.

Meanwhile, the Queen had arrived in New Zealand. On Sunday March 15, the royal party was crossing the Tasman Sea on board the royal yacht *Britannia* when they ran into 'very severe weather indeed'. The vessel pitched and rolled and was assailed by forty foot waves and a seaman on an escorting frigate was swept to his death.

The same day, aircraft were prevented from taking off at Los Angeles airport by the presence of teenagers using the runway for 'jogging': a new keep-fit craze which had swept America.

Back in New Zealand, on Thursday March 19, crowds waiting to see the Queen at Lake Wakatipu clashed with reporters. Journalists were kicked, punched and assailed with stones and there were cries of 'Get out of the way, you parasites!'

That weekend, John Lennon revealed in a long interview in the French weekly magazine *L'Express* that the Beatles had smoked pot at Buckingham Palace when they had received their MBEs five years earlier. On Sunday March 22 a Buckingham Palace spokesman refused to comment on this statement but admitted, 'Obviously when people come along to an investiture toilet facilities are available.'

The following day, the Postmaster General John Stonehouse said that it was intended to increase Post Office revenue by £65 million a year. 'Post office tele-communications is a profitable and rapidly expanding business,' he told the House of Commons.

On Tuesday March 24, attention turned to the new safari park at Woburn Abbey where a herd of white rhinoceroses were being unpacked after a long journey from Africa. The 52-year-old Duke of Bedford watched the event wearing a short fur collared suede overcoat.

On Saturday March 28, Scotland Yard appealed to the public to keep watch for escaped train robber Ronnie Biggs, last seen in Australia three months earlier, who was thought to have chartered a private yacht and landed at a small harbour on the south coast of England.

On Monday March 30, the Queen arrived in Sydney, Australia. A young man dashed forward and placed his sports coat in a puddle. The Queen discreetly avoided the coat and walked round the puddle.

Back in London, on Wednesday April 1, a new exhibition of paintings by David Hockney featuring California's biscuit-thin buildings, sparkling swimming pools and carpet-like green lawns opened at the Whitechapel Art Gallery.

On Saturday April 4, it was disclosed that 28-year-old baronet and former royal pageboy Sir Mark Palmer was settling down at last after spending the previous three years travelling round Britain in a horse-drawn caravan. 'Mark tells me he wants to buy a farm in Wales,' said his mother, Lady Abel Smith.

That night in Washington, the Duke and Duchess of Windsor dined at the White House. Among the 106 others present was President Nixon's new adviser on national security, Dr Henry Kissinger, who leaned wearily on the mantelpiece.

On Monday April 6 in New South Wales, Prince Charles went swimming at Elwood Beach and complained afterwards that the water was 'like diluted sewage'. The local Mayor protested that this was 'a most unroyal-like remark'.

Back in Britain the following day, a pair of binoculars belonging to the Queen Mother were pinched from the stewards box where she had left them on a seat when she went to make a presentation in the members enclosure.

On Friday April 10, Paul McCartney issued his first solo record and announced that the Beatles had ceased to exist as a group and he might never work with his old colleagues again. 'My own plan at the moment is to grow up,' he said.

Meanwhile, the share price of Bernie Cornfeld's IOS had suddenly collapsed and on Saturday April 11, an emergency meeting of the company's executives took place, while the façade of the company remained intact.

On Sunday April 12, Henry Ford arrived in Moscow for talks with Soviet officials as a guest of the State Committee for Science and Technology. He was accompanied by his wife Cristina who said later: 'Of course they treated us like heads of state.'

Back in London, on Tuesday April 14, the 50-year-old the Marquess of Milford

The frail but still socially active Duke and Duchess of Windsor arrive at a show business function in Paris

Haven, who had acted as best man at the marriage of the Queen and Prince Philip twenty-two years earlier, collapsed on Liverpool Street Station and died afterwards in St Bartholomew's Hospital.

The same day in France, a court rejected a plea by 22-year-old Claude Picasso to be declared a legal heir to his 88-year-old father's enormous fortune. Claude's sister Paloma, twenty, said, 'This is heart-breaking. Until three years ago I was closer than anyone to my father. I loved him very much and still do.'

Meanwhile Mrs Rose Kennedy had arrived in Paris and installed herself at the Ritz Hotel. On Wednesday April 15 she was taken out to dinner by her former daughter-in-law Mrs Jackie Onassis and her husband at Maxim's. After dropping Rose off at the Ritz afterwards Mr and Mrs Onassis went on to a new Paris nightclub, Open One, where they sprawled together on multi-coloured cushions.

On Saturday April 18, the Royal Family gathered in bitter weather for the Badminton Horse Trials. Princess Margaret wore a scarf and two cardigans while her 5-year-old daughter Lady Sarah Armstrong-Jones cuddled a long haired dachshund.

On Sunday April 19, President and Mrs Nixon flew to Hawaii to greet the Apollo 13 astronauts whose spacecraft had limped back to earth after the occurrence of a perilous series of technical problems. An airforce band played 'God Bless America' as the President and the astronauts shook hands.

The same day in England, 31-year-old Australian lecturer Germaine Greer spoke of her forthcoming book *The Female Eunuch*. 'It's a sort of hymn to womankind, or at least what womankind might have been if she'd got a fair deal from the start', she said.

On Monday April 20, Princess Anne admitted at Townsville, Australia, that it was 'quite likely' she had used the swear-word 'bloody' in public a few weeks earlier. 'There are always people around waiting for me to put my foot in it, just like my father.'

Meanwhile the eccentric Earl of Longford had been appointed chairman of the publishers Sidgwick and Jackson by the firm's new owner Charles Forte. 'We hope to expand rapidly,' said Lord Longford on Wednesday April 22. 'We want all the best books by all the best authors.'

On Sunday April 26, it was announced that police were checking on the movements of members of an East End gang following a strong underworld tip that there was a plot to kidnap 8-year-old Lord Linley, son of Princess Margaret and Lord Snowdon, and hold him captive to secure the release of two well known criminals. Parents of the notorious Kray twins, gaoled thirteen months earlier, strongly denied that their children had anything to do with the matter. 'They have great respect for Princess Margaret and Lord Snowdon. Ronnie and Reggie would have nothing to do with anything that would harm them. They are patriots,' said Charles Kray Snr.

Lady Churchill at a dinner party in London

On Tuesday April 28, Lord Linley was driven to Ashdown House preparatory school in Sussex by his father Lord Snowdon in a Mark 10 Jaguar. Two specially trained detectives moved into the school the same day to protect him.

Meanwhile, the Duke and Duchess of Windsor had moved from Washington to New York. On Thursday April 30, the 73-year-old Duchess, dressed in a Dior lilac coat, lunched at Restaurant Z with her old friend Elsie Woodward. At the same restaurant that day were Frank Sinatra and his elderly mother, Mrs Dolly Sinatra.

Later that day President Nixon went on television to announce his decision to invade Cambodia to clean out the Vietcong 'sanctuaries'.

On Sunday May 3, a panic stricken meeting of the board of IOS whose shares now became virtually unsaleable, began at the Villa Bella Vista beside Lake Geneva.

The same weekend found a crowd of international celebrities gathered in southern Spain for a 'skigolfswimbang' organized by Prince Alfonso Hohenlohe to promote his Marbella Beach Club. Among those present were Baron Heinrich Von Thyssen, the Vicomtesse de Ribes and 23-year-old Georgiana Russell, daughter of Britain's ambassador to Spain, who wore a see-through dress made of two strategically placed horizontal bars.

Further along the Mediterranean in the early hours of Monday May 4, Mrs Eugenie Niarchos was found dead on her husband's private island Spetsopoula, fifty-six miles south west of Athens. The circumstances of her death puzzled the local authorities and, as a material witness, Mr Niarchos was asked not to leave the country until preliminary enquiries had been carried out.

The same day in America at Kent State University, Ohio, the National Guard opened fire killing four students who had been demonstrating about the Vietnam War.

On Wednesday May 6, Liberal MP Peter Bessell urged the President of the Board of Trade to ground all airliners fitted with engine fan blades made of carbon fibre. 'Unless and until he does, thousands of air passengers will be in an agony of doubt', he said.

On Friday May 8, thirty young people marched into the luxury Fauchon grocery store in Paris and grabbed caviare, pâté de fois gras and other delicacies which they planned to distribute to the poor. Scuffles took place with shop assistants.

Meanwhile in America, student unrest over Vietnam had reached a new peak and early on Saturday May 9, President Nixon left the secret service 'petrified' when he boldly emerged from the White House, accompanied only by his valet M. Sanchez to chat with demonstrators gathered at the Lincoln Memorial. 'I know you probably think I am a S.O.B.,' he said, 'but I want you to know that I understand just how you feel.'

The same weekend the long drawn out meeting of the IOS board ended with dramatic scenes. On Friday the company's chairman Bernie Cornfeld had signed a complex comprehensive letter of resignation and then tore it up. The following day he was deposed as chief executive.

Back in London, on Sunday May 10, Frank Sinatra was guest of honour at a dinner hosted by film producer Cubby Broccoli at Tiberio's Restaurant. Among those who tucked into Scampi Calamari alla Sinatra and other delicacies were the Duke and Duchess of Bedford, Rex Harrison and newly knighted publisher Sir George Weidenfeld.

The following day, Sinatra lunched quietly at White's Club in St James's Street as a guest of 34-year-old Michael Bowater, son of a former Lord Mayor of London. Among those present was Douglas Fairbanks Jnr, who said afterwards, 'I don't think the members were particularly surprised to see him there. Not many noticed.'

On Tuesday May 11, Mr Niarchos was questioned at length by the public prosecutor of Piraeus about the circumstances of his wife's death eight days earlier.

Over in New York on Thursday May 14, a six foot high painting of a Campbell's soup tin by leading underground figure Andy Warhol was sold at the Parke Bernet gallery for $60,000 and became the most expensive painting by a living artist ever sold at auction.

Back in Paris, on Tuesday May 19, one of the students who had raided the Fauchon grocery store earlier in the month was sentenced to thirty months' imprisonment. 'It is not just a few tins of preserves that are at stake here,' said the prosecutor. 'It is disorder, anarchy and violence that we have to condemn.'

On Thursday May 21, Maria Callas and her old friend Aristotle Onassis dined together at Maxim's in a blaze of publicity. Onassis was said to have been humiliated by the publication of letters written by his wife Jackie to Mr Roswell Gilpatric and was seeing his old girl-friend in revenge.

A few hours later, Mrs Jackie Onassis flew into Paris from New York and on Monday May 25 she dined with her husband at the same table at Maxim's where he had sat with Maria Callas four days earlier. After dinner Mr and Mrs Onassis went on to Regine's club and stayed there till 2.30 a.m.

The following morning, Radio Luxembourg falsely announced that Maria Callas had attempted to commit suicide.

Meanwhile, preparations for a General Election had begun in Britain. On Thursday May 28, Liberal leader Jeremy Thorpe's plan to use a helicopter to tour the West Country was thwarted when the machine was grounded by fog after only one flight.

On Monday June 1, a young man, who claimed to be protesting at the cancellation of the South African cricket tour, threw a fresh egg at Prime Minister Harold Wilson, hitting him over the right eye. Wilson took the incident in good heart and said, 'With a throw like that he would have made a good shot at a wicket.'

On Wednesday June 3, the Derby was won by Nijinsky, ridden by Lester Piggott. The winning owner, eighteen stone Charles Engelhard Jnr, said to be 'one of the world's ten richest men' and the model for Ian Fleming's Goldfinger, was later introduced to the Queen. Among those present at Epsom that day were the 88-year-old Earl of Rosebery, bearded property magnate Harry Hyams, and the Earl of Carnarvon, who was to be struck down by a slipped disc while at the racecourse.

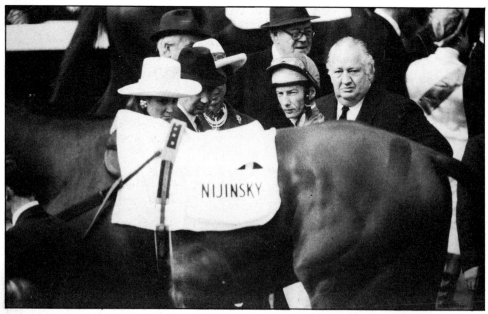

Charles Engelhard Jnr., Lester Piggott, Vincent O'Brien and other sporting figures gather round the world's most celebrated racehorse. Mr Engelhard was said by some to be the model for the character 'Goldfinger' in the James Bond books

On Thursday June 4 a bag of flour was thrown at Mrs Harold Wilson outside an election meeting in Battersea.

Over in Washington on Friday June 5, President Nixon called a meeting in the Oval Office at the White House attended by Edgar Hoover of the FBI and three colleagues at which he spoke of his plans for strengthening domestic intelligence.

Meanwhile the tax-exiled Duke of Argyll had returned to England for a few days. On Saturday June 6 he paused at Claridge's Hotel on his way to Scotland, 'I am looking forward very much to seeing Inverary Castle again,' he said, 'but my visit will be marred slightly by having to count every day in case I outstay my welcome.'

On Monday June 8, the election campaign took a sour turn when Mr Harold Wilson declared that the Conservatives did not want England to win the World Cup in Mexico. Relaxing over a beer at a pub in Bristol, Mr Heath responded, 'Is there no triviality to which this man won't descend?'

The following Sunday, June 14, Britain was defeated by West Germany in the World Cup quarter-finals after a gruelling match in punishing conditions 6,000 feet above sea level.

Back in Britain, on Tuesday June 16, the Queen Mother and other members of the Royal Family attended the opening day of Royal Ascot. Others present included fashion designer Michael Fish, who wore a grey wild silk morning dress coat, and hairdresser Teazy Weazy Raymond, who wore an electric blue tail coat and trousers and a blue carnation.

On Wednesday June 17, Mrs Harold Wilson was trodden on by a police horse at an election meeting at Trafford Park, Manchester. 'It wasn't the horse's fault,' she said afterwards, 'the crowd surged forward.'

The following day, the country went to the polls and voted a Conservative government to power.

On Friday June 19, the new Prime Minister, 53-year-old bachelor Edward Heath, moved into 10 Downing Street while his predecessor Harold Wilson left by the back exit where his sons Giles and Robin were found thrusting blankets and suitcases into the back of two blue mini estate cars. Temporarily homeless, after his unexpected defeat, Wilson was to move into the Piccadilly flat of his old friend Colonel Brayley, chairman of the Canning Town Glass Works.

That night there was a ball at Windsor Castle to celebrate the seventieth birthdays of the Queen Mother, the Duke of Beaufort and Lord Mountbatten of Burma. A cheer went up when the new Prime Minister arrived and he blushed to the collar.

The following day, red paint was hurled at Mr Heath outside his new residence.

On Sunday June 21, 60-year-old international architect John Poulson returned from Beirut in high spirits after securing contracts to design two new hospitals in the Lebanon.

The same day in Djakarta, former Indonesian President Achmed Sukarno died in an army hospital. His beautiful wife Dewi, who had flown in from Paris the previous day, was at his bedside and was present when her husband's body was placed in a plain teak coffin.

On Tuesday June 23, it was announced that Mr and Mrs Wilson had taken a short lease, at 80 guineas a week, of a house in Vincent Square, Westminster, belonging to film producer Jerome Epstein.

Over in New York that night, Mae West's arrival at the première of her new film *Myra Breckinridge*, caused bedlam. Police used their truncheons, co-star Raquel

Baron Guy de Rothschild and his controversial second wife Marie-Hélène talking with British Ambassador Christopher Soames at Chantilly race-course

Welch was stuck in a traffic jam in her black cadillac and the 31-year-old Earl of Lichfield was innocently involved in a scuffle.

Back in Britain on Wednesday June 24, the popular Maharajah of Jaipur, one of the best polo players of his generation, collapsed and died between chukkas at Cirencester.

Meanwhile, the relationship between Mick Jagger and Marianne Faithfull had ended. It was said that Marianne had now transferred her affections to shy Irish peer Lord Rossmore, known to his friends as Paddy.

On Wednesday July 1, Bernie Cornfeld was voted off the board of his tottering company IOS.

The same day, a BAC One-Eleven jet ordered by the 43-year-old tycoon the previous autumn was to be found in a hangar at Wisley, Surrey. The £1,800,000 plane had a full-size bar and brown suede upholstery throughout.

The next morning the state opening of the new British parliament took place with the usual pageantry. Earl Mountbatten appeared to falter under the weight of the Sword of State but brushed aside two attendants who offered assistance.

On Friday July 3, the new Prime Minister was to be found sandwiched between Princess Anne and Princess Alexandra in the Royal Box at Wimbledon, where the big event of the day was Australian Margaret Court beating Billie Jean King in the women's finals.

On Sunday July 5, the Queen arrived in the Canadian Arctic, stepping off an Air Canada DC-8 into thirty degrees of cold dressed in a chilly, semi-lightweight turquoise coat and matching hat.

Meanwhile, Prime Minister Edward Heath had been entertaining his old friend concert pianist Moura Lympany at his country home Chequers. 'Now that Mr Heath is Prime Minister I think it would be wrong to discuss our friendship,' she said.

On Monday July 6, it was revealed that the Duke of Bedford's family were taking steps to avoid their wealth falling into the hands of the Chancellor of the Exchequer. 'My solicitors and the solicitors to the Bedford Settled Estate are looking at the possibility of making everything over to my eldest son,' said the Duke's heir, 30-year-old Lord Tavistock.

On Wednesday July 8, in the North West Territories of Canada, Prince Charles ate a piece of buffalo meat daubed in red barbecue sauce.

The next day, at a barbecue for young people at the same place, Princess Anne tackled a corn-on-the-cob.

The following morning, Friday July 10, at the Club del'Aretusa in Swinging Chelsea, Londoners gathered at a breakfast fashion show. Among those present were the Duke and Duchess of Bedford, the young Maharajah of Jodhpur, Orson Welles's daughter Beatrice, jewellery designer Ken Lane and Lady Sarah Courage, whose motor racing husband Piers had been killed in the Dutch Grand Prix a few weeks earlier.

Later that day at Hyannis Port, Massachusetts, 16-year-old Robert Kennedy, son of the late Bobby Kennedy, broke his wrist when he fell from a tree trying to retrieve a pet falcon.

On Monday July 13, an international scandal erupted over a letter written by the aged Field-Marshal Montgomery to his friend American industrialist Mr Cyrus Eaton, in which Monty had said that President Nixon was 'totally unfit to be Commander-in-Chief of the Armed Forces of the US. His knowledge of the conduct of war is nil.' 82-year-old Montgomery commented later, 'It was a private letter and should never have been published.'

The same day, Mr Niarchos was at last permitted to leave Greece where he had stayed since his wife's death on May 4. He quickly boarded his private jet for London, where he kept a permanent penthouse suite at Claridge's Hotel.

On Thursday July 16, Prince Charles and Princess Anne arrived in Washington as guests of President Nixon who greeted them on the South Lawn of the White House with his daughters Tricia and Julie. A few hours later, the Nixon daughters and the Prince and Princess flew to Camp David where hamburger steaks, corn-on-the-cob and baked beans were cooked on an outdoor barbecue.

Back in Washington, the following day, Princess Anne found the attentions of American journalists a strain and when asked how she was enjoying the city snapped, 'I do not grant interviews.'

Back in London, on Monday July 20, the new Chancellor of the Exchequer 56-year-old Iain Macleod died suddenly of heart failure at his official residence, 11 Downing Street.

On Wednesday July 22, Prime Minister Edward Heath, Mr Harold Wilson and scores of other prominent politicians were present at a memorial service for Mrs Jeremy Thorpe who had died in a car crash the previous month.

The following day, the Kirov ballet began a season at the Royal Festival Hall. On the opening night 22-year-old Mikhail Baryshnikov astounded the audience with his soaring double cabrioles, grand pirouette and range of jetés en tournant.

On Sunday July 26, the elderly and autocratic Sultan of Oman was admitted to the Harley Street Clinic, suffering from bullet wounds after a palace coup, organised by his own son, had got out of hand. The same day in Oman, the new Sultan, Oxford and Sandhurst educated Qabus Bin Said, explained, 'I have watched with growing dismay and increasing anger the inability of my father to use the new wealth of this country for the needs of the people. That is why I have taken control.'

On Monday July 27, it was revealed that photographer Lord Lichfield and Britt Ekland had parted after a nine month romance. As Britt flew off to film commitments in California, Lord Lichfield explained, 'Both having incredibly busy professional lives did not help matters, but I am sure we will remain the best of friends. It is always sad when things don't work out.'

That night the controversial show *Oh Calcutta*, which had been running in America for over a year and included nude and sexual scenes, opened in London. Impresario Michael White said, 'There are tremendous changes afoot in the theatre and we have to get sex out of the way and put it in its proper place.'

On Friday July 31, the show got the 'all clear' from Attorney-General Sir Peter Rawlinson. Michael White hailed this as a 'commonsense decision' though Greater London councillor Frank Smith said it had 'set back the cause of civilisation and a decent way of life in Britain'.

The following Sunday, Bernie Cornfeld, ousted chief of IOS, threw a party at his villa beside Lake Geneva at which he tried to explain how the company could be saved by investing in a new cinema city built in the desert between Los Angeles and Las Vegas. 'I want my company back,' he said.

Over in America on Monday August 3, President Nixon blundered by stating that Charles Manson, now on trial in California accused of causing the death of Sharon Tate and seven others the previous year, was 'guilty, directly or indirectly, of seven murders without reason'. Manson's defence lawyer said he was bewildered by the President's remarks and would make a motion that the case against his client and three co-defendants should be dismissed.

Back in London, on Wednesday August 5, there was much excitement over the Kirov ballet's performance of *Giselle*, starring Natalia Makarova, whose dancing was said to have 'a certain fugitive grace to it'.

The Aga Khan enjoys a joke with Prince Rainier of Monaco while the beautiful Princess Grace looks on

The following day, the Dissolution Honours were announced. These included a knighthood for Mr Joseph Kagan, manufacturer of the former Prime Minister's distinctive tartan-lined raincoats and a CBE for his personal secretary, Mrs Marcia Williams. Mrs Williams was to refuse to go to Buckingham Palace to receive her honour on the grounds that the Queen 'is a Tory', but later complained when the medal was sent to her 'in a brown paper parcel'.

On Saturday August 8, the Shah of Iran and his family were found holidaying at the royal villa on the shores of the Caspian Sea, just 100 miles from the Russian border; the 50-year-old Shah played in the surf with his 9-year-old son, Prince Reza.

On Monday August 10, the 'beautiful people' of Los Angeles motored down the coast to a party at La Jolla, the jewel city hugging the southernmost tip of California, to a party where peaches soaked in champagne were served.

On Friday August 14, it was reported that President Nixon had lost a pair of cuff-links when friendly crowds grabbed his hands as his motorcade passed through New Orleans.

The following day, Aristotle Onassis flew by helicopter to the Greek island of Tragonisi where his old friend Maria Callas was staying with the island's owner, bachelor Perry Embiricos. He presented his old friend with a pair of antique earrings and kissed her poodle.

On Sunday August 16, Baron Marcel Bich threw a ball at the Miramar estate at Newport overlooking the ocean. Among the 800 guests were Princess Lee Radziwill and her mother and step-father Mr and Mrs Hugh Auchincloss, Mrs Thomas Cushing and the David Rockefellers. As the party wore on, barefooted guests performed the Mexican Hat Dance.

The following Wednesday, August 19, film star Zsa Zsa Gabor was attacked in the lift of New York's Waldorf Towers and robbed of gems worth £250,000. She later described her ordeal, dressed in a lavender silk dress and ostrich feathers and cuddling a fluffy white dog called Zig Zag.

Meanwhile, the peace of the Marbella Club on the Costa del Sol had been disturbed by a visit from a party of Michael Pearson's friends on board his £250,000 yacht *The Hedonist*. 'We all feel that they are letting down the Union Jack badly,' said one of the British residents after the party had moved on. 'It wasn't so much their long hair and scruffy appearance but their attitude. I think everyone was happy to see the last of them.'

On Thursday August 21, the magistrate investigating the death of Mrs Niarchos formally recommended the institution of proceedings against Stavros Niarchos, currently cruising on board the *Creole*. This recommendation was immediately referred to the Piraeus High Court who, after studying the evidence ruled that Eugenie Niarchos had committed suicide and accordingly the case was closed.

On Monday August 24, the marriage took place between 23-year-old Miranda Quarry, step-daughter of Lord Mancroft, and 44-year-old Peter Sellers. At the ceremony in London's Caxton Hall, Sellers wore a conventional pin-striped suit and his bride wore a gypsy style maxi dress. The comedian's valet, Bert Mortimer, acted as best man.

The following day, at Woburn Abbey, a lioness in the Duke of Bedford's newly opened Safari Park attempted to maul a 5-year-old child, making a hooking movement with its paw. 'We have people watching all the time and have taken every precaution with fences and many notices,' said the Duke later, 'it is absolutely safe if you follow the precautions.'

On Wednesday August 26, a barefooted and suntanned Paul McCartney spoke of his future plans at his remote Scottish hideaway. 'The Beatles have stopped playing together. The Beatles will not get together again for financial or any other reasons. The reasons should be perfectly plain to everyone.' Speaking of his new Scottish retreat he said, 'This life and place could do us for the rest of our lives.'

On Monday August 31, Italian high society was shaken by the deaths of the wealthy Marquis Camillo Casati and his wife and her lover. The bodies of all three were discovered in the Marquis's Via Veneto apartment and it was revealed that the Marquis, owner of several estates, castles, and racing stables, had killed his wife and her lover and then committed suicide. The Vatican newspaper *Osservatore Romano* said these revelations shed 'a sinister light on the increasing relaxation of morals in our time'.

On Friday September 4, Russian ballerina Natalia Makarova escaped from the Kirov ballet as the company was about to leave for Holland, and was granted asylum in Britain. 'Natalia is recognized by many people as the best dancer in the world,' said an admirer.

That weekend, four jets bound for New York were hijacked over Europe. Three of the flights were diverted to the Middle East by members of an Arab guerrilla movement. The fourth did an emergency landing at Heathrow Airport and its 24-year-old hijacker Leila Khaled was arrested and taken to West Drayton Police Station.

In the midst of this confusion, Mrs Imelda Marcos, beautiful wife of the President of the Philippines, flew into London with her 12-year-old son, Ferdinand Marcos Jnr, who was to attend a preparatory school in Sussex. In a press handout issued on this occasion, Madame Marcos was described as 'an overwhelmingly active person who goes about her duties with fixity of purpose and sincerity of heart'.

The following Tuesday, TV personality David Frost had his luggage examined at Heathrow Airport, where stringent new security procedures had now been introduced.

On Thursday September 10, the marriage took place in a church in Hampstead between conductor André Previn and Frank Sinatra's former wife, Mia Farrow, who had already presented Mr Previn with twin sons. At the ceremony, the bride wore a long nineteenth-century style brocaded gown with large puff sleeves.

On Saturday September 12, British race-goers watched wonder horse Nijinsky, ridden by Lester Piggott, win the St Leger, romping past the winning post to a roar of applause with his ears pricked.

The following day, Mrs Jackie Onassis arrived in New York. Asked the purpose of her visit, she replied, 'What d'you mean? I live here!'

Back in Britain, on Tuesday September 15, authoress Agatha Christie celebrated her eightieth birthday. 'I know nothing about pistols and revolvers,' she said in a birthday interview at her Devonshire home, 'which is why I usually kill my characters off with blunt instruments or better still poisons. Poisons are neat and clever and really exciting.'

The following day in Berlin, hundreds of youths tried to gatecrash a concert given by the Rolling Stones and were driven back by police using tear gas, clubs and water cannon.

In Chicago, the next day, President Nixon's limousine was stuck in a traffic jam. The President made use of the delay by nipping into the nearby Marshall Field department store and purchasing eight new neck-ties.

Back in Britain on Saturday September 18, the grammar school educated Prime Minister Edward Heath arrived at Balmoral Castle to spend the weekend with the Queen.

The new Prime Minister Edward Heath leaves 10 Downing Street for a private luncheon with friends

In London, on Monday September 21, the former Prime Minister's wife Mrs Mary Wilson signed copies of a slim book of poems at an Oxford Street store. Dressed in a pale green suit, discreet pearls and sporting a new hair-do, she said, 'I think everyone likes to see their stuff in print. It's a personal ambition I have long cherished.' Mr Wilson puffed his pipe in the background and a few hours later it was disclosed that a further print run of 10,000 copies had been ordered.

The next day, in Washington, a luncheon at the White House in honour of 'Dresden Doll' Madame Marcos, was enlivened by the presence of Mrs Joan Kennedy in a pale blue see-through blouse and metallic leather longuette.

On Wednesday September 23, California's Governor, 59-year-old ex-actor Ronald Reagan, now campaigning for re-election, toured the Sacramento district in a Lincoln Continental escorted by half-a-dozen security men.

The same day, Onassis's 21-year-old son Alexander arrived in London where he was greeted by his old friend Fiona Baroness Thyssen. 'There has never been any question of marriage,' the young man said later at his suite at Claridge's. 'Can't people be friends?'

Meanwhile, the British public had been diverted by the presence at Barnwell Manor in Northamptonshire of Hungarian-born divorcée Zsuki Starkloff, close friend of Prince William of Gloucester. On Thursday September 24, she flew off alone to New York telling reporters at Heathrow Airport, 'We are just good friends.'

On Monday September 28, President Nasser died suddenly of a massive heart attack at his Cairo home. His body was quickly removed to the Kubbeh Palace, a former residence of the late King Farouk, where he was laid in state.

The following day, it was revealed that King Hassan of Morocco was to construct four championship standard golf courses near his palace, calling in Robert Trent Jones, the world's top golf course architect, to give advice. It was noted that the King was already getting golfing tuition from US Masters title-holder Claude Hammon.

On Wednesday September 30, hijacker Leila Khaled was released from custody in England and flown in an RAF plane to Egypt where she was to be given a hero's welcome.

The same day, President Nixon arrived in Belgrade on the start of an eight-day hustle through Europe.

Back in Britain on Thursday October 1, it was disclosed that Jim Callaghan had purchased a £273 prize bull for his new Sussex farm. 'He may not have been in farming long but he certainly seems to be learning fast,' said a local farmer, praising the former Labour Home Secretary's choice of animal.

Meanwhile, Prince Charles was enjoying a holiday in France with the British Ambassador Sir Christopher Soames. On Saturday October 3, after a day's shooting near Paris, the 21-year-old Prince paid an impromptu call on his great-uncle the Duke of Windsor at the latter's home in the Bois de Boulogne. The two, who had only met once before, spent an hour together in a corner of a crowded drawing-room. The Prince addressed the Duchess of Windsor as 'Aunt Wallis'.

The next day at Longchamps, Nijinsky was beaten in the Prix de l'Arc de Triomphe, in spite of frantic riding by jockey Lester Piggott. 'He just didn't show the fire that he has in the past,' said the unsmiling jockey afterwards.

Back in England that day, Prime Minister Heath was entertaining President Nixon and Dr Henry Kissinger to lunch at Chequers. The Queen had flown down from Balmoral for the occasion and lunch was served round a heavy oak oval table. Heath recalled afterwards that a special supply of water had been flown in for the President's use but this had been overlooked by the Chequers' kitchen staff and he had been served ordinary tap water instead.

The same day in Boston, Senator Edward Kennedy declared that he would not be running in the race for the US Presidency, explaining: 'The uncertainty of higher office would place a great burden on my family.'

On Monday October 5, 27-year-old rock star Janis Joplin, who had recently declared, 'Kids who touch drugs are crazy', died of a drug overdose in a Hollywood motel with her left arm full of hypodermic syringe marks.

Meanwhile, the New York scene had been enriched by the presence of Sophia Loren, who on Wednesday October 7 was found shopping at Bergdorf Goodman with her two-year-old baby Carlo. She was to purchase $300 worth of baby clothes, mostly corduroy and crinkle vinyl.

The same day, President and Madame Pompidou had arrived in Moscow on an eight-day visit. After meeting Soviet leader Brezhnev for the first time Madame Pompidou had declared that she found him 'very charming and polite, especially to the ladies'. Madame Pompidou later appeared at a tea party at the Kremlin dressed in a chicly unobtrusive dress designed by Coco Chanel.

During their visit a rumpus blew up over the award of the Nobel Prize for Literature to writer Alexander Solzhenitsyn, who had last been seen at the villa near Moscow of Soviet cellist Rostropovitch and whose current whereabouts were unknown. On Sunday October 11, Solzhenitsyn issued a statement that he would go to Stockholm to collect the award from 87-year-old King Gustaf of Sweden.

The same day in New York, Sophia Loren was robbed of £200,000 worth of jewellery from her hotel suite overlooking Central Park. Armed men burst into her suite and, fearing for the safety of her baby son Carlo, the 36-year-old film star had handed over her jewels. She was later comforted by a friend, film producer Joseph Levine.

Back in Britain, on Friday, October 16, it was disclosed that the memoirs of the former head gardener at Sandringham, 66-year-old Mr Horace Parsons, had been withdrawn by the publishers after talks with Buckingham Palace officials.

On Sunday October 18, thieves broke into Britain's largest stately home, the 365-room Wentworth Woodhouse in Yorkshire, and made off with the cream of the 66-year-old Earl Fitzwilliam's Rockingham china. 'These were no ordinary burglars,' said the Earl. 'They selected only the best pieces. I am amazed that they managed to wrap and pack all that delicate china in the dark.'

The following day in New York, society leader Mrs Brooke Astor lunched at Restaurant X and nestled into the huge fox collar of her tweed coat.

On Tuesday October 20, Prime Minister Edward Heath arrived in Manhattan for a five-day visit during which he was to take time off to pay a late night visit on his friend Leonard Bernstein in the Dakota building to gossip about music.

On Wednesday October 21, representatives of Dr Armand Hammer, President of Occidental Petroleum, paid record prices at Parke Bernet for a collection of drawings by French eighteenth-century masters being sold by Mrs Jesse Straus, widow of the President of Macy's.

The following day, Dr Hammer flew from California to New York in his private jet to inspect his purchases.

A great big beaming smile from Mrs Jacqueline Onassis as she arrives at Claridge's Hotel on a surprise visit

Back in London, on Saturday October 24, Sir John Betjeman revealed that he was now receiving fifty letters a day asking for his help in saving threatened buildings and redundant churches from demolition. 'I was made to be a writer,' he protested, 'and I'm being turned into a Post Office. Mind you, I wouldn't do it if I didn't think it was worthwhile.'

On Sunday October 25, security guards were on duty at the London Coliseum when ballerina Natalia Makarova danced for the first time since her defection from Russia earlier in the year. 'She is an absolutely exquisite dancer,' said fellow defector Rudolf Nureyev who partnered her in an extract from *Swan Lake*.

Meanwhile, Soviet Foreign Minister Mr Gromyko had arrived in London. On Tuesday October 27, he was found lunching with his British counterpart, Sir Alec Douglas-Home, at the Carlton Club in St James's Street. The Soviet minister appeared undaunted by this ultra-capitalist setting and talks were said to be 'forthcoming and friendly'.

On Thursday October 29, it was revealed that Dick Gangel, director of the crumbling IOS empire, had placed his London home on the market for £400,000, the highest price ever asked for a London house, and was moving to Switzerland. The six storey Knightsbridge house contained a heated indoor swimming pool, a cinema and twin gothic-style toilets for the children.

On Tuesday November 3, jet set TV personality David Frost presented himself at Buckingham Palace to receive the OBE. 'How unusual to see you in London in the middle of the week,' said the Queen. Frost gave a luncheon afterwards at Quaglino's restaurant and later the same day flew back to America.

Meanwhile, in the American elections held that day, former actor Ronald Reagan had been re-elected Governor of California and 46-year-old peanut farmer Jimmy Carter had become the new Governor of Georgia.

On Wednesday November 4, 21-year-old Prince Charles took delivery of a £6,000 Aston Martin DB6 Volante with wire wheels and stereo record player and radio. The Prince had given his old car, an MGC, to the Queen's head chauffeur, 50-year-old Mr Harry Purvey.

On Saturday November 7, Mr Nikita Krushchev was said to be seriously ill in Moscow suffering from cardiac insufficiency.

The following day, Mrs Krushchev denied that the memoirs of her husband now being published by *Time Life* were authentic.

On Monday November 9 in France, 79-year-old General de Gaulle collapsed with a massive heart attack at his home while leafing through a TV journal to see if there was a programme he wanted to watch. He died thirty minutes later but the event was kept secret for several hours and President Pompidou was not informed until 5 o'clock the next morning.

Later that day, Elizabeth Taylor appeared at Buckingham Palace wearing her new £437,000 diamond ring to see her husband Richard Burton, immaculate in grey morning dress, invested with the CBE, which took place to strains of 'Men of Harlech'.

The same afternoon, Sir Noël Coward arrived in Britain and was pushed through Heathrow Airport in a wheelchair. 'I've done it for years,' he explained. 'I see no reason to traipse three-quarters of a mile after paying all that money. I can assure you I feel very spry.'

The following day, Sir Noël was admitted to St Thomas's Hospital in London suffering from pleurisy.

Back in France, on November 12, there was a spectacular gathering of world leaders at a service at Notre Dame in honour of the late General de Gaulle. Among those present were Prince Charles, the Shah of Iran, President Nixon and Mr Harold Macmillan, who wore a black top hat. Six wreaths came from Peking alone, including one from Chairman Mao.

Meanwhile, the Hon. Michael Pearson had been driving around London in a 1941 vintage Daimler 'Dingo' bump-proof armoured car. 'I can't think of a better vehicle for avoiding being eternally cut out by taxis and London Transport buses,' he said on November 13. 'It weighs nearly three tons and looks so fearsome I expect a wide berth from anything on the road.'

On Sunday November 15, Earl Mountbatten of Burma called on Sir Noël Coward in St Thomas's Hospital bearing a box of chocolates for his old friend.

The following morning, Margaret Duchess of Argyll announced that she was adopting two young boys, 9-year-old Richard Gardner and his 7-year-old brother Jamie. 'I am taking over all responsibility for their upbringing,' she explained. Asked if the boys would become heirs to her fortune, she replied, 'I am not here to be quizzed. I am saying what I am saying and that is that I am adopting them.'

That evening, Princess Grace of Monaco stood in for Sir Noël Coward at a charity show at London's Festival Hall, over which he was to have presided. Also on stage was Frank Sinatra, now sporting a rejuvenating £3,000 hair transplant.

Later that night, Sinatra dropped in at Clarence House for a nightcap with the Queen Mother.

On Wednesday November 18, the wealthy Vicomtesse de Ribes was attacked in her suite at Claridge's Hotel, overcome with a chloroform pad and robbed of £200,000 worth of jewels which she had been planning to wear that night at a party given by American Ambassador Walter Annenberg. Later that evening the party, described as 'a purely private affair', went on without her and the beautiful Vicomtesse flew back to Paris in a state of shock.

International statesman Averell Harriman and American Ambassador to Britain Walter Annenberg share an arm-chair

On Friday November 20, the Miss World Contest at London's Albert Hall was disrupted by Women's Lib protestors, who hurled stink and smoke bombs onto the stage, declaring that the competition was 'a symptom of a sick society and an affront to the dignity of women'.

On Tuesday November 24, an anti-pollution campaign was launched in Tokyo where there was now a new hazard: photochemical smog caused by noxious sulphur gases borne on southerly winds from the coastal industrial zones of Kawasaki and Yokohama.

The following day, Japanese novelist Yukio Mishima entered an army head-quarters in the same city, castigated his fellow citizens for having lost their national spirit and then committed hara-kiri.

Early the following morning, multi-millionaire recluse Howard Hughes fled from the Desert Inn Hotel in Las Vegas in his pyjamas and bath robe.

Back in the Far East, on November 27, there was another violent scene when a man dressed as a priest and armed with a twelve-inch knife lashed out at the Pope at Manila Airport. The Archbishop of Djakarta was wounded in the affray and the Pope's sleeve was splashed with blood. 'I wanted to eliminate the Pope to enlighten the Filipinos because he is the symbol of superstition and hypocrisy', said the attacker Benjamin Mendoza, a Bolivian artist.

The same day in London, polo playing art dealer Daniel Wildenstein paid a record £2,310,000 for Velasquez's portrait of Juan de Paraja which was being sold by the Earl of Radnor to help pay estate duty. Following this sale, the Duke of Westminster complained, 'Taxation and inflation have now reached such a pitch that owners of such pictures can afford neither to live or die.'

The following day, 77-year-old General Franco, dictator of Spain for the past thirty-one years, went out hunting wild pig at his El Pardo estate near Madrid and suffered a mild stroke.

Back in Britain, on Monday November 30, the 73-year-old Duchess of Beaufort, cousin of the Queen, announced that she was giving up fox-hunting. 'I have had a good innings,' she said. 'After all I have been riding since I was four. I hunt for pleasure but because of arthritis, my wrists hurt so much when I ride that I have decided to give it up.'

On Tuesday December 1 in London, 20-year-old American actress Vicky Prin-cipal obtained a court order preventing Bernie Cornfeld, ousted chief of the IOS empire, from seeing her. She claimed that the tycoon, whose personal wealth was said still to run into many millions, had attacked her more than once, kicking her and half-throttling her on one occasion.

That night in New York, celebrities gathered for the Imperial Ball at the Plaza Hotel. Among those present were Margaret Duchess of Argyll, Mrs Lyttle Hull, the Duke and Duchess d'Orleans, Colonel Serge Obolensky, Mr Spyros Skouras and Walter Annenberg's sister Mrs Joseph Neff, who wore a Japanese dress and danced every waltz and foxtrot.

Five days later, in New York, Muhammad Ali beat Oscar Bonavena, delivering a thunderous left hook to the chin sending his opponent to the canvas in the last round.

Meanwhile, rubbish and debris had begun to fill the streets of London and on Wednesday December 9 the Conservative-controlled council of the Royal Borough of Kensington and Chelsea was said to be considering the idea of dismissing the 200 striking dustmen and hiring private contractors instead.

On Thursday December 10, the Nobel Prize ceremony went ahead in Stockholm, without Russian prize winner Alexander Solzhenitsyn who spent the day in seclusion at a village near Moscow because he was afraid he would not be allowed back into Russia if he left.

Meanwhile, Aristotle Onassis was engulfed in attempts to buy the Belfast shipyard Harland and Wolff where he already had two super-tankers in the process of construction. On the night of Sunday December 13, seven union leaders were flown to London in Mr Onassis's private jet and were put up for the night at Claridge's Hotel. One of the union men complained afterwards that the bed was too soft for his liking and the talks were inconclusive.

John Lennon and his wife Yoko Ono playing in the snow at North Jutland, Denmark. Lennon announced 'The dream is over it's time we got down to so-called reality'

On Monday December 14, the Earl of Snowdon entered the London Clinic for a haemorrhoids operation. During his brief stay in the hospital he was to receive a number of visits from his friend Lady Jackie Rufus Isaacs, 24-year-old daughter of the Marquess of Reading.

The next day in the House of Commons, handlebar moustached Conservative MP Sir Gerald Nabarro presented a bill ordering tobacco manufacturers to print 'graphic and lurid health warnings' on all their products.

The following Friday December 18, in Washington, David Frost gave a cabaret at the White House which was said by the *Washington Post* to have upset some of those present, especially evangelist Billy Graham. Frost later dismissed these suggestions as 'absolute rubbish' and declared, 'The enthusiasm of the President, First Lady and their guests made it the most exciting night I can remember.'

On Monday December 21, Lord Bernstein's butler was found murdered in a house in Wilton Crescent, Belgravia. TV chief Lord Bernstein was in the West Indies at the time but staff at the next door house said that the dead man, who always wore regulation black jacket and striped trousers, was 'a typical below stairs man. We only saw him when he was going about his duties'.

Christmas Day found elusive multi-millionaire Howard Hughes settled in a hotel suite on Paradise Island, a few hundred yards across the water from Nassau, Bahamas.

The following day, young athletics champion Lillian Board died of cancer at the Munich University clinic. Dr Josef Issels, who had been treating Miss Board at his Ringberg clinic in Bavaria and had been besieged by phone calls from across the world, said he would think carefully before admitting another famous person for treatment.

Meanwhile, Britain was shivering under widespread sleet and snow and on Tuesday December 29, Heathrow Airport was closed while snow-ploughs were brought in to clear the runways.

Late the following night, Sir Malby Crofton, leader of the Kensington and Chelsea council, was observed giving instructions as an official garbage truck took away rubbish from in front of his Kensington home. Sir Malby later explained that he was only using the emergency night refuse collection service available to all citizens.

On December 31, Paul McCartney began an action in the Chancery Division of the High Court to dissolve all his remaining connections with his three fellow Beatles and for the affairs of the partnership to be wound up.

Meanwhile, in America, John Lennon had given a 24,000 word interview with *Rolling Stone* magazine during which he had confessed that he had always needed a drug to survive. 'The dream is over,' he said, 'I'm not just talking about the Beatles. I'm talking about the generation thing. It's over and we gotta – I have to personally – get down to so called reality.'

That night, New Year's Eve, President Nixon invited newsmen into his office at the White House to taste a 'secret' new martini formula, prepared by himself.

1971

Though the year that follows finds Flesh star Joe Dallesandro being shown round the House of Lords, the youth culture as a whole now suffers a set-back. In America, Manson and his followers are sentenced to die and anti-war protestors are arrested in a gigantic dragnet operation. Nearer home, the Earl of Longford attempts to start a swing against the Permissive Society: he visits strip clubs in Denmark and describes what he finds there as 'pure evil', while his colleague Mrs Mary Whitehouse, undeterred by a hail of stink-bombs, brings a much publicised prosecution against Oz magazine accusing its long-haired editors of attempting to corrupt the morals of the young. The ultra-establishment Princess Anne meanwhile declares that she is no friend of the Women's Lib movement and, along with the elderly Duke of Norfolk, says she draws the line at hot pants. There is a grim new note of violence in the air. Across the world, urban guerrillas flourish: the monstrous General Idi Amin seizes power in Uganda and the Queen is soon obliged to entertain him at Buckingham Palace; in New York the mafia godfathers fight it out; in Northern Ireland, tarring and feathering becomes a national sport, forty-three British soldiers die and internment only makes matters worse. In this new climate, few socialites share Lord Longford's love of publicity and several people take active steps to preserve what little privacy is left to them. Lord Snowdon at last comes to blows with nosy Raymond Bellisario. Jackie Onassis obtains a legal ruling preventing photographer Ron Galella coming within fifty yards of her and Howard Hughes's fear of publicity is such that young author Clifford Irving is able to perpetuate the publishing hoax of the century. Meanwhile, British Prime Minister Edward Heath drips with sweat as he tries to manoeuvre his country into the Common Market, Prince Philip gives up polo and the international gang of partygoers welcomes into its midst Mick Jagger's beautiful bride.

On New Year's day, it was announced that the Queen Mother had given a Royal Warrant to Emmetts Stores in the village of Peasenhall, Suffolk, makers of her favourite delicacy: sweet pickled ham. 'We have a very old recipe for curing and pickling,' said Mr Emmett.

On Saturday January 2, British television viewers were shown photographs of the dental chart of escaped train robber Ronnie Biggs, whom underworld informants now insisted was living in the Norwood area of South London.

Meanwhile, arctic weather had been complicated by freezing fog. On Monday January 4, shipping was stopped on the Thames estuary, while at Heathrow Airport 10,000 passengers faced delayed flights. Undismayed by these circumstances were David Frost and his current constant companion, Diahann Carroll, who flew off to New York the same day in an exuberant mood.

That night in London, the hallucination generation turned out for the première of the film *Performance*, starring Mick Jagger and James Fox, which was later hailed as a minor masterpiece.

On Friday January 8, the British Ambassador in Uruguay, Mr Geoffrey Jackson, was kidnapped by urban guerrillas as he drove to his embassy in a chauffeur-driven Daimler. It was stated that an event of this sort had long been expected and Mr Jackson, a youthful fifty-five, was 'unlikely to flap'.

On Sunday January 10, 87-year-old Coco Chanel died in her suite at the Ritz Hotel in Paris where she had lived for the past thirty-five years. 'I saw her about three weeks ago: incredibly frail but still galvanizing everyone,' said her old friend Cecil Beaton. At her funeral held three days later at the Church of the Madeleine, floral tributes included a wreath of camellias in the shape of a pair of scissors, inscribed 'To Mademoiselle from her mannequins'.

Meanwhile, Paris society had been adorned by the presence of Madame Dewi Sukarno, widow of the former President of Indonesia, who was now keeping herself in trim with judo lessons. 'These days a woman is so likely to be attacked she ought to know how to defend herself,' she explained.

Back in Britain, on Tuesday January 12, two bombs planted by the Angry Brigade exploded at the Hertfordshire home of Employment Minister Robert Carr. Among those to quickly condemn this outrage was Mr Carr's old adversary Vic Feather, General Secretary of the TUC. 'Anyone who could even attempt this sort of thing is nothing short of a stupid lunatic.'

Over in America on Thursday January 14, President Nixon visited the University of Nebraska. After exchanging snowballs with students, he declared, 'There can be no generation gap in America.'

The following day, British post office workers went on strike. During the stoppage that followed Lord Montagu of Beaulieu and the Earl of Lichfield were to provide their own private postal services, and multi-millionaire Paul Getty was to welcome the strike as 'a blessed relief from begging letters'.

On Saturday January 16, a brief statement went out from the headquarters of IOS in Geneva that ousted chairman Bernie Cornfeld had severed all connections with the company. While this announcement was being flashed around the world, Cornfeld was flying to his new base in Acapulco in a private plane.

On Sunday January 17, Edward Heath took time off from the Commonwealth Conference in Singapore to go sailing with slim bikini-clad Miss Annie Hughes, daughter of Sir Rochford, air adviser to the Singapore government. Meanwhile, in Britain, the Prime Minister had been branded by Opposition leader Harold Wilson as irresponsible, reckless, mulishly stubborn, arrogant and lacking in courage.

Over in Los Angeles two days later, the jury at the Sharon Tate murder trial withdrew to listen to several Beatles' records which, it was suggested, could have influenced Charles Manson and his followers to go on their killing spree fourteen months earlier.

On Sunday January 24, attention turned to Tehran when the Shah of Iran gave his first press conference for twelve years to warn Western oil companies of the terrible consequences if they did not accept the demands of the world's main oil producing countries for higher royalties and taxes.

On Monday January 25, a former heavyweight boxer and British army sergeant, the powerfully built Major-General Idi Amin, emerged as head of the new military government in Uganda after a military coup that had taken place in the absence of the country's leader Mr Obote at the Commonwealth Conference.

Back in London, on Tuesday January 26, Princess Margaret attended the christening of the twin daughters of Colin and Lady Anne Tennant at the chapel of the Royal Hospital in Chelsea. Two days later, the 40-year-old Princess flew off to Barbados to join her husband on a winter holiday at the home of his uncle Oliver Messel. The Princess flew economy class from London and was publicly welcomed at Barbados by her husband to try and disprove rumours that the marriage was in difficulties. It was noted that Lord Snowdon wore a snakeskin-patterned silk shirt and a brass buckled leather belt.

Women's lib champion Germaine Greer whose pioneering book *The Female Eunuch* sold many copies

The same day in London, Prince Charles was attacked in the *Tailor and Cutter* magazine for his 'sheer lack of style', out of date trousers and the 'boxy' cut of his jackets. The magazine's fashion consultant Karl Dallas suggested that the 22-year-old Prince might be 'trying to adjust to the age of the common man' and accused him of deliberately disarranging his pocket flaps.

At the end of the month, Roman Polanski was found at Bamburgh Castle in Northumberland shooting outdoor scenes for his new version of *Macbeth*. 'These epic scenes bore me to death,' said Polanski. 'The real stuff is in the studio where you can get into the characters.' It was noted that the cast were being fortified against the weather by daily rations of vitamin C.

Polish film director Roman Polanski; his actors were fortified with daily rations of vitamin C

Back in London on Tuesday February 2, the publication of Miss Barbara Cartland's autobiography *We Danced All Night* was celebrated with a Foyle's Literary Luncheon at the Dorchester Hotel attended by among others Miss Cartland's daughter, the Countess of Dartmouth.

On February 3, Prince Charles responded to the attack on his clothing by arriving at a dinner in aid of the Master Tailors' Benevolent Fund wearing an old shooting jacket which he soon whisked off to reveal impeccable evening dress. 'I am often asked whether it is because of some generic trait that I stand with my hands behind my back, like my father,' he joked later. 'The answer is that we both have the same tailor. He makes our sleeves so tight that we can't get our hands in front.'

The following day, public morale in Britain was shaken by the announcement that the Rolls-Royce company had collapsed. In a grave statement to the House of Commons, the Minister of Aviation Supply, Mr Frederick Corfield, announced that the company would be nationalised and its motor-car division sold off to private enterprise.

On Friday February 5, thieves broke into the Venetian palace of Miss Peggy Guggenheim and stole a dozen modern paintings. Miss Guggenheim flew from London to help the police identify which pictures had gone.

The following day in Northern Ireland, a soldier was shot dead, the first British soldier to be killed since the army had moved into the troubled province eighteen months earlier.

On Tuesday February 9, it was disclosed that Mr Heath had had his quarters at Chequers done up. The Prime Minister's television room had been re-papered with a jungle design of tree trunks and vines, his bathroom covered in a new floral fabric and Sir Winston Churchill's old four-poster had been re-lined. 'The people at Chequers were very fussy,' said interior decorator James Montague.

Meanwhile, Opposition leader Harold Wilson had purchased a country retreat in the stockbroker belt in Buckinghamshire. Set in one acre, the house had once belonged to a prominent Tory.

The following Sunday February 14 in Kenya, Prince Charles made world-wide headlines when he took part in a polo match at the Nairobi Polo Club mounted on a horse named Christine Keeler.

Back in London on Monday February 15, an exhibition of paintings by Andy Warhol, Brillo boxes and soup cans and portraits of Elizabeth Taylor and Jackie Onassis opened at the Tate Gallery. Asked if his paintings would be looked at in fifty years time, Mr Warhol said, 'I used cheap paint. I think it will have fallen off by then.'

On Friday February 19, Paul McCartney applied in the High Court for the appointment of a receiver to take over the Beatles' assets, pending the full trial of his action to have the group's partnership dissolved. In a deposition opposing this move, Ringo Starr called McCartney 'a spoiled child'.

On Wednesday February 24, Princess Anne was at the wheel of her new Reliant Scimitar sportscar when it crashed into a mini-cab in Brompton Road. 'I've been in a lot of crashes with women drivers,' said the cab driver Patrick Ling, 'but this one takes the prize.'

The same day, there was a press showing of Andy Warhol's film *Flesh* which had now been released with an X certificate by film censor John Trevelyan. Among those present were Irish novelist Edna O'Brien and veteran journalist Godfrey Winn. After the screening, Mr Warhol and the film's star Joe Dallesandro, who had his hair tied in a pony-tail, were escorted round the House of Lords by Conservative MP, Norman St John-Stevas, who said later, 'They are charming and terribly nice but rather bizarre.'

On Monday March 1, international financier Robert Vesco was appointed chairman of the troubled IOS empire.

The same day in New York, Mrs Jackie Onassis went shopping at the Cordoba shop on Madison Avenue and purchased a pair of faded denim glove suede hot pants priced at $45.

On Thursday March 4, the marriage took place in a remote area of North Vancouver between Canadian Prime Minister Pierre Trudeau and an ex-hippy Margaret Sinclair, noted for her taste for brown rice. As they left for their honeymoon in the mountains, the happy couple were pelted with more buckets of rice.

On Saturday March 6, millionaire Clive Raphael died in a plane crash near Poitiers in France, apparently leaving a will in which his attractive model wife Penny Brahms was left a shilling and four nude photographs of herself.

The same day, eight inches of snow at Rome Airport caused Mr and Mrs Aristotle Onassis to abandon their executive jet. They spent the rest of the weekend night-clubbing in the city and eventually flew on to Athens late on Sunday night.

The following day, Monday March 8, Prince Charles began a five-month jet flying course with the RAF. The Prince already had a pilot's licence and flew himself that morning to Cranwell in a twin-engined Basset.

Later that day in New York, 28-year-old Muhammad Ali lost his World Championship title to Joe Frazier. Among the audience was Frank Sinatra, who took twenty-eight photographs of the fight which were later sold for charity for $10,400. Ali took his defeat in good heart, declaring afterwards, 'I feel no depression, no sadness. I'm just another person who lost a fight. I still eat. I still sleep. I still see my wife and children.'

Meanwhile, in Northern Ireland the situation was continuing to deteriorate and on Wednesday March 10 three young soldiers in civilian clothes were lured into a Belfast public house and murdered in cold blood.

Two days later it was disclosed that 37-year-old playboy Tommy Sopwith had ordered a £250,000 luxury motor yacht, complete with helicopter pad, internal telephone system and push-button electric lavatories.

On Monday March 15, a strike at the Ford factories in England entered its sixth week and Mr Henry Ford lunched that day at 10 Downing Street with Mr Heath and his colleagues. 'Things have to be cleared up,' he said afterwards. 'There is no stability in Britain. Companies like Ford are at the mercy of the situation.' Union leader Moss Evans had meanwhile urged workers not to give up their struggle.

American tycoon Henry Ford arrives at 10 Downing Street for an informal lunch with Mr Heath. He discussed the current industrial scene and the Ford Motor Company's future in Britain

On Saturday March 20, the 47-year-old Earl of Dalkeith, Conservative MP for Edinburgh North, had a serious riding accident. 'I realized quite clearly that I was paralysed from the chest down and that I would have to adjust to a completely new way of life,' he said later. By the time he was rescued he had 'weighed up the situation and was ready to start the process of recovery'.

On Monday March 29, actor David Niven revealed that he was writing his autobiography for British publisher Hamish Hamilton. 'Jamie Hamilton urged me to write for an hour a day,' he explained at Château d'Oex where he was currently enjoying a ski-ing holiday.

The same day in Los Angeles, Charles Manson and three women followers were sentenced to die in the gas chamber after being found guilty of the brutal murder of actress Sharon Tate and six others two years earlier. 'You don't have no authority over me. You're not as good as me,' Manson shouted at the judge before being escorted, chained and manacled, to Death Row in San Quentin Gaol.

Back in London, on Tuesday March 30, 24-year-old Lady Jacqueline Rufus Isaacs, whose name had been romantically linked with that of Lord Snowdon, was found canoodling with 25-year-old Dai Llewellyn, son of Olympic show jumping gold medallist Colonel Harry Llewellyn, at a midnight party at a Fulham Road art gallery. 'We're just good friends,' she said.

The previous day, the young Prince Sayajirao of Baroda had been seized near his Mayfair flat and robbed of two gold and diamond bracelets, three rings and a necklace worth a total of £20,000. 'These were normal ornaments which I wear day by day,' he said.

On Sunday April 11, a lengthy television interview with Princess Anne was broadcast during which she declared, 'Hot pants are the limit. People complain you are not with it but there are certain things I will not do.'

On Monday April 12, 48-year-old reputed Mafia leader Joe Colombo and 5,000 of his 'family' attended a special service in St Patrick's Cathedral in New York. Afterwards Colombo said, 'I am an honest businessman of Italian origin who is being crucified for no good reason,' and dismissed the idea of a 'mafia' or 'cosa nostra' as 'myths created by the FBI and the newspapers'.

On Wednesday April 14, attention turned to the South of France where Mick Jagger refused to discuss reports that he was planning to marry 21-year-old South American beauty Bianca de Macias, who was currently sharing his exile.

The same day in Peking, a new chapter in American–Chinese relations began when 72-year-old Chinese premier Chou En-lai told the visiting American table tennis team, 'Take back to the United States the regards of the Chinese people.'

Back in Britain, on Friday April 16, Lord Longford, Mrs Whitehouse and others were present at a special preview of a film *Growing Up* by genetics lecturer Dr Martin Cole. After sitting through scenes of full frontal nudity and male and female masturbation Lord Longford stormed out saying, 'Balderdash!'

The following day, the marriage took place in the thirteenth-century chapel of Merton College, Oxford, between master spy Kim Philby's daughter Miranda and barrister James Badenoch. The spy's son John took the wedding photographs and said afterwards that his father had sent a greetings telegram from Moscow.

On Sunday April 18, there was a further denial from Mick Jagger, now staying at the Byblos Hotel in St Tropez with his constant companion Bianca de Macias, that he had any marriage plans.

On Tuesday April 20, it was announced in Paris that the 42-year-old Marchioness of Blandford, former wife of Aristotle Onassis, had begun divorce proceedings against her husband, heir to the Duke of Marlborough. At his home at Charlbury in Oxfordshire, Lord Blandford said, 'No comment.'

Later that day in Moscow, Kim Philby popped up in the star-studded audience at the Bolshoi Hall, where the London Symphony Orchestra was making its debut, conducted by Benjamin Britten 'It was an exciting evening and a great triumph for the orchestra and Britten,' said impresario Victor Hochhauser.

The same night in London, the Earl of Longford paid a visit to a striptease club in a Soho cellar. 'I find it neither pleasant nor unpleasant. I certainly do not find it obscene,' said the bald-headed peer who was due to open a debate in the House of Lords on the problem and incipient menace of pornography a few hours later.

On Thursday April 22, it was announced that the Earl of Longford was to become a Knight of the Garter. 'Such an imaginative appointment,' murmured Lord Mountbatten when he heard the news.

In Washington the following day, American Attorney-General John Mitchell insisted on the government's right to wire-tap in special circumstances. 'The FBI has not tapped the telephone of any member of the House or Senate – now or in the past,' he said and went on to state that Representative Hale Boggs of Louisiana who had accused the FBI of tapping his home telephone was a victim of 'a new type of paranoia – called Tappanoia'.

Meanwhile, the Queen and other members of the Royal Family were attending the Badminton Horse Trials, in which Princess Anne was a competitor. On Sunday April 25 the contest was won by 22-year-old Mark Phillips, a lieutenant in the 1st Queen's Dragoon Guards, on his horse Great Ovation. Princess Anne, on Doublet, came fifth.

On Tuesday April 27, the Queen's representative at Ascot, the 62-year-old Duke of Norfolk, made it clear that hot pants would not be acceptable in the Royal Enclosure at this year's Royal Ascot. 'The only form of lady's trousers permitted will be suits with long trousers,' he insisted.

On Monday May 3, a gigantic dragnet operation began in America. Over 13,000 anti-war protestors who had tried to paralyse Washington were arrested. Radical leader Abbie Hoffman had his nose broken and Dr Spock, apostle of child care, was among those apprehended.

Back in the South of France, on Thursday May 6, Mick Jagger and Bianca de Macias applied for a marriage licence.

Meanwhile, the Queen and Prince Philip had begun a tour of Canada. On Sunday May 9, the royal couple burst out laughing when a bucking and snorting one ton bull leapt into the press enclosure at a cattle ranch in British Columbia causing terror among attendant journalists.

Two days later in Washington, President Nixon called for an all out attack on cancer. 'If a hundred million dollars this year is not enough, we will provide more money; to the extent money is needed it will be provided.'

The same day, Mr and Mrs Joe Jagger arrived in the South of France for their son's wedding. 'We can never understand all this fuss about him,' said Joe Jagger. 'He is basically a very serious boy.' Said Mrs Jagger: 'Bianca is a very nice girl, very easy to get on with.'

On Wednesday May 12, cameramen from all over the world squeezed into the St Tropez council chamber to witness the marriage. The civil service was followed by a ceremony in a nearby fisherman's chapel at which the bride wore a white midi length suit made by Yves St Laurent and was escorted up the aisle by the Earl of Lichfield, in a white suit. After the ceremony the couple disappeared in a white Bentley.

Two days later, 82-year-old Charlie Chaplin was found staying at a hotel at Cap D'Antibes on the same coast. 'I find all this sex stuff very dull,' he told a reporter. 'Well, you expect that at my age. Let's say, sex *in films* doesn't interest me.'

The following weekend in Britain, Edward Heath was found relaxing on board his new ocean-going racing yacht *Morning Cloud*. 'I come back fresh,' said the deeply tanned Prime Minister, whose passion for yachting had developed rather suddenly.

Back on dry land, on Monday May 17, gossip writer Nigel Dempster, shortly to have his own column in the *Daily Mail*, embarked on a brief marriage to Miss Emma de Bendern, granddaughter of the late Marquess of Queensberry.

The following day in Washington, Women's Lib campaigner Germaine Greer became the first woman to address the all male National Press Club, causing a sensation by accusing pharmaceutical firms of degrading the female image by producing 'all sorts of things to squirt on women to stop them being so offensive'.

Back in Britain, on Wednesday May 19, 20-year-old Arianna Stassinopoulos, an undergraduate dubbed 'the Greek Goddess', was adopted as president of the Cambridge Union.

On Thursday May 20, Princess Margaret was spotted producing a non-fattening sweetener from her handbag at a reception at the headquarters of St John Ambulance in Belgravia.

Meanwhile, Mr Heath had flown to Paris for final talks with President Pompidou about Britain's entry into the Common Market. On Friday May 21, there was excited chattering when the two leaders took their seats on gilt armchairs on the platform in the Grand Salon of the Elysée Palace to announce that they had reached complete agreement on Britain's entry into the Common Market.

Back in Britain, on Monday May 31, at Handcross in Sussex, there was a collision between Lord Snowdon's red Vauxhall estate car and a vehicle driven by freelance photographer Raymond Bellisario, who immediately announced that he was going to take out a private summons against the Queen's brother-in-law.

On Wednesday June 2, the Derby was won by Mill Reef owned by 63-year-old Mr Paul Mellon, who after the race was invited to the Royal Box to receive the Gold Derby Trophy from the Queen. 'I've owned horses since 1930,' he said, 'but winning the Derby is my happiest moment.' Of the £61,625 prize money, Mr Mellon said, 'I need every penny of it. I have a big tax problem in America.'

The same day, celebrated oil millionaire Nubar Gulbenkian celebrated his seventy-fifth birthday at a hospital in Cannes, where he was receiving treatment for a heart attack. 'I shall be taking him one of his favourite dishes for lunch: chicken in cream and tarragon,' said his devoted wife Marie.

Further along the same coast two days later, David Niven protested at plans to build a new yacht marina near his home at St Jean Cap Ferrat. 'These ports are ruining this lovely bit of coastline. I'm going to look at Fiji soon and if I like it I might even stay there.'

Back in London, on June 5, it was announced that the Slater Walker company had purchased a substantial share holding in Haw Par Brothers, the Singapore company mainly known for purveying a popular panacea known as Tiger Balm.

On Tuesday June 8, journalist Bernard Levin published a scathing attack on the former Lord Chief Justice Goddard who had died a few days earlier aged ninety-four.

The following day, Mr Levin's application to join the 141-year-old Garrick Club where Lord Goddard had been a popular figure ran into difficulties. One member of the club scrawled across Levin's entry in the Candidates' Book in black ink 'Over My Dead Body'.

On Saturday June 12, in Washington, much excitement surrounded the wedding of President Nixon's daughter Tricia and lawyer Ed Cox, which took place in the Rose Garden at the White House. At a reception afterwards, a band played 'Thank Heaven for Little Girls' and guests nibbled miniature brioches stuffed with chicken and mushrooms and munched jumbo shrimps fried in coconut. Some controversy surrounded the seven-foot-high wedding cake which was described in the press as 'mush on the outside, soup on the inside'.

The following day, the *New York Times* began publishing the Pentagon Papers, the most serious leak of classified material in the history of America, describing America's secret involvement in Vietnam under the previous two presidents.

Back in England, on Monday June 14, Education Minister Margaret Thatcher moved the second reading of her bill to end free milk for schoolchildren between the ages of seven and eleven.

That night, the Queen's Ascot house party assembled at Windsor Castle. Among the twenty-eight guests was Sir Winston Churchill's vivacious 21-year-old grand-daughter Emma Soames who was now working as a journalist. One of those who braved bitter winds and torrential rains to attend the races the following day was the Chinese Chargé d'Affaires, Tseng Pei Chang.

On Wednesday June 16, an encounter took place in the Royal Enclosure between the Earl of Snowdon and his old friend Lady Jackie Rufus Isaacs who was now being escorted by 25-year-old man about town Dai Llewellyn.

Over in New York the same day, two gun-men interrupted Walter Annenberg's sister Mrs Janet Neff, while she was lunching at her apartment at 1, Sutton Place, handcuffed her to her cook and liftman, and seized $200,000 worth of jewellery. Twenty pieces of the missing jewellery were later found in a city garbage can.

Meanwhile, the Duke and Duchess of Windsor had settled into New York's Waldorf Astoria Hotel. On Saturday June 19, they emerged to celebrate the Duchess's seventy-fifth birthday with a party of American friends.

The same night in Paris, the Hon Michael Pearson threw a party to celebrate his twenty-seventh birthday, at the flat of photographer Baron Arnaud de Rosnay, flying in many of his friends and billeting them at the best hotels. Asked how much this celebration had cost, he replied, 'I've no idea. When you have to ask questions like that, there is no point in doing the thing.'

Back in Britain, on Monday June 21, a select committee appointed by the House of Commons began a thorough investigation of the royal finances. The committee was to discover that the annual royal wine cellar bill had increased by over £8,000 and was now £12,000 a year and the royal laundry bill now stood at £7,267 a year.

The following day, the trial of the editors of *Oz* magazine opened at the Old Bailey in a carnival atmosphere. The three long-haired young men were accused of publishing obscene, lewd, indecent and sexually perverted articles and illustrations with intent to debauch and corrupt the morals of children and other young persons.

Meanwhile, Elizabeth Taylor and her husband Richard Burton had arrived in London, both deeply sun-tanned after a holiday in Mexico. On Wednesday June 23 the charismatic couple attended a party at Kensington Palace given by Princess Margaret. At this floodlit event, Miss Taylor wore the Krupp diamond which her husband had given her three years earlier.

Two days later the Burtons left London for Geneva and were said to be on their way to a holiday cruise in the Caribbean.

Over in America, on Sunday June 27, Mrs Rose Kennedy told David Frost that she had forgiven the killers of her two sons. 'We all have our crosses to bear,' said the elderly matriarch. 'It's up to us to rise above them. God wants us to enjoy and laugh and love and have fun.'

In Boston, Dr Daniel Ellsberg admitted to the theft of the controversial Pentagon Papers and, looking calm and confident, surrendered himself to the police.

A few hours later, in New York, mafia leader Joseph Colombo Snr. was shot and critically wounded at a big Italian-American civil rights rally. His attacker was himself shot dead immediately afterwards. From a secret hideout, rival gangland boss Joe Gallo sent word that accusations that he had something to do with the killing were 'a lot of dirty lies'.

Back in London the following night, art historian Sir Anthony Blunt gave a reception and dance at 20 Portman Square for the Friends of the Courtauld Institute. The event was attended by Lord and Lady Harlech, the Hon Patrick Lindsay, art dealer Geoffrey Agnew and other members of the establishment. Sir Anthony had recently made headlines by stating that the government had got itself into 'an absolutely unholy muddle' over its plans to introduce admission charges to the eighteen national museums and galleries.

On Thursday July 1 in Moscow, Russian leader Mr Brezhnev wept openly as he paid tribute to the three astronauts who had died as a result of a mechanical failure in their spacecraft.

Back in Britain that weekend, Colonel Gerard Leigh made news when he threw himself in the path of a polo ball which was whizzing towards the Queen during a match in Windsor Great Park. 'I just did what any gentleman sitting next to any lady would have done,' said the Colonel afterwards.

On Wednesday July 7, Mr Jack Heinz's birthday party at his Mayfair mews home was disrupted when Lord Snowdon threw a glass of red wine at the Queen Mother's racehorse trainer Peter Cazalet who was dancing with Lady Westmorland.

Meanwhile, a heat-wave had hit England and on Friday July 9 a temperature of 84 °F was recorded in London. That night, singer Frank Sinatra was found dining with American Ambassador Walter Annenberg at Tiberio's restaurant in Mayfair.

Two days later in Rome, Talitha Getty, 30-year-old daughter-in-law of Paul Getty, was discovered in her apartment suffering from an overdose of a heroin-based substance and was taken to a clinic where she died a few hours later. Her husband, Paul Getty II, explained afterwards that he had begun divorce proceedings a few weeks earlier.

Back in London, the heat-wave had continued and on Monday July 12, Prime Minister Heath was dripping with sweat at a reception in the gilt and gold Music Room at Lancaster House when he told the world's press he was completely confident of carrying Britain into the European Economic Community.

That night, Mr Heath gave a dinner at 10 Downing Street for the new President of Uganda, General Idi Amin.

On Wednesday July 14, President Amin lunched with the Queen at Buckingham Palace.

The same day, the marriage of the young Earl Alexander of Tunis and banana heiress Hilary van Geest took place at St Margaret's Westminster. Among the 600 guests at the ceremony was the bridegroom's cousin, 36-year-old Lord Lucan. Uninvited was the bride's aunt, fishmonger's wife Hilda Harriss, who nevertheless put in an appearance outside the church. 'We live in totally different worlds now,' she said, 'but it has been a lovely day and I wouldn't have missed it for anything.'

The following day in Washington, President Nixon announced on television that he had accepted an invitation to visit China the following year. The purpose of the trip, organized by Dr Henry Kissinger during a secret visit to Peking the previous weekend, would be 'to seek normalization of relations between the two countries'.

Meanwhile, American Attorney-General John Mitchell and his wife Martha had arrived in London. At 4 p.m. on Friday July 16, Mrs Mitchell gave a press conference on the twenty-seventh floor of the Hilton Hotel, dressed in an emerald green satin cocktail dress and matching shoes. 'I'm the most liberated woman in the world,' she said. 'Any woman can be liberated if she wants to be.' An aide explained that while in London Mrs Mitchell had a party schedule which ran from breakfast to 3 a.m. each day.

Three days later, on Monday July 19, comedian Marty Feldman gave evidence at the Old Bailey in favour of the three defendants in the *Oz* trial. 'There is more obscenity contained in the Bible than there is in this issue of *Oz*,' he said. As he left the witness box, Feldman declared that the Judge hearing the case was 'a boring old fart'.

A week later, on Monday July 26, publisher Sir George Weidenfeld gave a party at his London home to launch Opposition leader Harold Wilson's 790-page book on his years in office. Pro and anti Common Marketeers kept to separate sides of the room and Mrs Mary Wilson, who wore a full length floral gown, tactfully avoided controversy by admiring her host's tapestry.

On Wednesday July 28, Prince Charles made his first parachute jump, leaping from a plane 1200 feet above Studland Bay in Dorset. Due to an unexpectedly strong slip-stream the prince's feet were caught for a while in the parachute rigging and he described the ordeal afterwards as 'a rather hairy experience'.

The following day in Las Vegas, the marriage took place between 20-year-old Christina Onassis and 47-year-old Californian real estate dealer Joseph Bolker, whom she met earlier in the year beside the swimming pool at the Hotel Metropole in Monte Carlo. Christina's father was informed of this event on the island of Skorpios where he was celebrating his wife's forty-second birthday. According to one of those present, he 'did not try to hide his anger'.

Greek ship owner Aristotle Onassis embraces his 20-year-old daughter Christina

That weekend, Mick Jagger and his wife Bianca passed briefly through Heathrow Airport on their way to Ireland. 'Yes, she's pregnant, man, that's all I'm going to say,' said the 26-year-old pop star.

On Monday August 2, Princess Anne gave a party for 120 friends on board the royal yacht *Britannia*, moored beside a railway jetty at Portsmouth Harbour. The event, to celebrate the Princess's forthcoming twenty-first birthday, was described by a royal spokesman as 'a strictly private function'.

The following day, four dog-handlers were used to arrest two men and a girl who were found in the gardens of Buckingham Palace.

Meanwhile, the trial of the three editors of *Oz*, the longest obscenity trial in history, had reached its climax at the Old Bailey. On Thursday August 5, Richard Neville, Felix Dennis and Jim Anderson were sentenced to various terms of imprisonment. Outside the Old Bailey, the effigy of Judge Argyle was burnt, while in

Ireland pop star Mick Jagger commented, 'If there has been a moral crime committed it is by the police and the judge.'

On Monday August 9, it was announced that the British government would introduce internment without trial in Northern Ireland. The same day in Belfast twelve people were killed as British troops tried to separate warring Catholics and Protestants in the burning streets.

The same day in London, the three *Oz* editors were released from Wormwood Scrubs pending the hearing of their appeals against conviction and sentence. All three had had their hair cut and had shared a cell 'the size of a match box'.

On Tuesday August 10, the Aga Khan's private Grumman Gulf Stream jet collected Princess Margaret and Lord Snowdon and their two children at Heathrow Airport and whisked them away to his Sardinian 'Costa Smeralda' development, where the 40-year-old Princess was soon found relaxing in a kaftan embroidered with an enormous heart.

Two days later there was more excitement in Sardinia when banker Dino Daponte threw an all night party at the new resort of Punta Sardegna. Among the 600 guests was the vivacious Countess of Normanton, Prince Egon von Furstenberg and 64-year-old Maureen, Marchioness of Dufferin and Ava, whose newly built vast pink-roofed villa, Casa Maureeno, dominated the bay.

On Sunday August 15 in Moscow, Nobel prize winner Alexander Solzhenitsyn protested at the way ten KGB men had beaten up his friend, scientist Alexander Gorlov, who had been bound and gagged, and dragged into the woods. 'I have been spied upon, had my letters opened, my telephone tapped, my friends intimidated,' he added.

Meanwhile, in Britain a row had erupted over a controversial two fingered gesture made by champion show jumper Harvey Smith at Hickstead racecourse. 'The man made a gesture at me,' said Hickstead's owner Mr Douglas Bunn. 'It is more than odd. It is disgusting.' An official stewards' enquiry later studied a film of the incident and ruled that no insult had been intended. 'All is now forgiven and forgotten,' said Mr Bunn.

On Thursday August 19, there was excitement in business circles over the acquisition of the Bovril company by 38-year-old Old Etonian tycoon Jimmy Goldsmith. A former playboy and intrepid gambler, Mr Goldsmith was known as the constant companion of Lady Annabel Birley, estranged wife of Mark Birley, proprietor of Annabel's nightclub.

On Friday August 20, Prime Minister Heath took part in the Ramsgate Regatta on board his yacht *Morning Cloud*. That evening he was first across the line in the first leg of the Round-the-Goodwins race.

The following Monday, August 23, the deeply sun-tanned Prime Minister gave a dinner party at 10 Downing Street attended by, among others, André Previn and Mia Farrow, Bryan Forbes and Nanette Newman and Hollywood's Olivia de Havilland. After dinner Miss de Havilland, who wore a multi-coloured chiffon Grecian-style Dior dress, told Mr Heath's fortune over a glass of champagne. 'Both Mr Heath and I were born under the dragon. I told him that this was a favoured sign.'

On Tuesday August 24, the Earl of Longford and members of his newly formed pornography study group flew to Copenhagen. During the flight, the 65-year-old peer read his bible. That night he visited a nightclub where a tall nude female coiled a whip round his head and 'vibrated' him.

The following day, Lord Longford stormed out of a live sex show pursued by a protesting manager. 'But sir – you haven't seen any intercourse yet!' Longford said afterwards: 'I was disgusted, but it is our duty to see such things. They were pure evil. Much worse than I expected.'

Meanwhile, Mrs Mary Whitehouse had arrived in Rome to try and drum up support for her 'anti-smut' campaign at the Vatican. On Wednesday August 25, she was granted an audience with Pope Paul. 'I didn't give the Pope any dirty magazines,' she said afterwards.

On Monday August 30, Mrs Jackie Onassis and her sister and brother-in-law and two children were found in Warsaw, where her sight-seeing tour was disrupted by over-attentive crowds and she was obliged to board a bus to escape.

Two days later, Mr Joe Cahill, a leading member of the Provisional wing of the IRA, arrived at New York's Kennedy Airport to launch a propaganda and money raising campaign. He was refused entry and put in a detention centre. 'We will not sleep in our efforts to have this injustice rectified,' said a member of his committee. 'It is very definitely the work of the British government.'

On Sunday September 5, Princess Anne and her eight-year-old chestnut horse Doublet won the European Championships at Burghley. At a champagne celebration afterwards the Duke of Edinburgh said, 'Don't look at me, I'm only here for the beer.'

On Wednesday September 8, a new art centre opened in Washington in honour of the late President Kennedy. Missing from the opening ceremony was Mrs Jackie Onassis who was now said to be 'crowd shy' after her unpleasant experiences in Warsaw the previous weekend.

Early that day, IRA leader Joe Cahill left America. 'It has been a big inconvenience,' he grumbled. 'I came here hoping to put the lie to British propaganda and also raise money.' On his return flight to Ireland Mr Cahill tucked into a steak but ignored the in-flight movie *The Private Life of Sherlock Holmes.* He told reporters travelling with him, 'We have the manpower and the means to achieve our aims. I believe that the campaign of bombing and disorder should continue.'

Meanwhile, in Northern Ireland Mr Cahill's wife had lodged a claim for Supplementary Benefit of £14 a week.

On Thursday September 9, the Earl of Snowdon was fined £20 for driving without due care and attention following his collision with free-lance photographer Ray Bellisario. 'There is no vendetta between Lord Snowdon and me,' said Mr Bellisario, who had brought a private prosecution against the Queen's brother-in-law, 'but I think he went too far on this occasion.'

The following day, the marriage took place quietly in Warwickshire between 36-year-old social lion Dr Roy Strong, director of the National Portrait Gallery, and theatre designer Miss Julia Trevelyan Oman.

On Saturday September 11, the kidnapped ambassador to Uruguay, Mr Geoffrey Jackson, arrived back in London looking frail and tired after eight months in the hands of the Tupamaros guerrillas. He was taken from Gatwick Airport to his family home, 63 Cadogan Square, where a 'slap up' celebration awaited him.

On Wednesday September 14, the marriage took place at Chelsea Old Church between admiral's son, Tom Troubridge and the beautiful young Baroness Marie-Christine von Reibnitz.

Back in New York, on Monday September 20, the New Metropolitan Opera Season opened with tempestuous singer Maria Callas in the audience. 'I'm so used to being on stage I don't like to be seated for a long time,' she said.

Two days later, celebrities gathered at New York's Whitney Museum to celebrate a new film by Norman Mailer called *Maidstone*. The thrice married author turned up at the party without his ageing poodle, Tibo, and left later for Elaine's restaurant, growling, 'I want everyone in America to see this film.'

On Friday September 24, Bobby Kennedy's son Joseph celebrated his nineteenth birthday at his family home in Massachusetts. 'I think it is my destiny to follow my father and his brothers into politics. I learned from them that all people should be treated with fairness and dignity. I think that I have a special obligation to contribute to that life-style.'

Back in Britain, on Saturday September 25, naturalist Peter Scott suggested that the army should be called in to fell and dispose of trees affected by the dreaded Dutch Elm disease now raging across the country.

The same weekend, there was much excitement over a Foreign Office announcement that 105 Russian diplomats had been accused of espionage and been ordered out of the country in a purge of unprecedented proportions. Former Prime Minister Harold Wilson described this move as 'a bit of a phoney'.

Back in New York, on Monday September 27, the marriage took place of Mrs Pamela Hayward, former wife of the late Randolph Churchill, and 79-year-old statesman Averell Harriman. The ceremony was followed by a party attended by the bride's son, Winston Churchill MP, the Jock Whitneys, Clay Felker, Mrs Ethel Kennedy and other notabilities.

Later that day, for the first time in 2,000 years, a reigning Japanese monarch set foot on foreign soil when Emperor Hirohito arrived at Anchorage on the start of a world tour. The 70-year-old Emperor stumbled on the steps of his aircraft and was steadied by President Nixon's firm handclasp. During their brief meeting, Nixon gave his illustrious visitor a photo of his daughter Tricia's recent wedding. 'I shall treasure it,' said the Emperor.

A few hours later, the Japanese monarch flew on to the fun city of Copenhagen.

On Thursday September 30, it was disclosed that the ruler of Abu Dhabi, Sheik Zayid bin Sultan al-Nahyan had purchased for £250,000 the Buxted Park health hydro in Sussex, famous haunt of recovering statesmen and starlets.

On Friday October 1, master spy Kim Philby popped up in Moscow to accuse British diplomats of spying in Russia and elsewhere. 'These acts are calculated to slow down progress in European detente,' he declared.

On Sunday October 3, over a hundred offending Russian diplomats and their families left on board the Russian cruise ship, *Baltika*. Many of them were well-dressed in British made clothes and carried toys and souvenirs. As the ship sailed off into the mist, its loudspeakers suddenly began to play the hit song 'If I were a rich man'.

The same day in France, race-goers gathered at Longchamps for the Prix de l'Arc de Triomphe, which was won this year by Mill Reef ridden by Geoff Lewis and owned by Mr Paul Mellon. 'Wonderful!' said the delighted owner as he was whisked off to receive congratulations from President Pompidou.

Also in France at this time was Emperor Hirohito of Japan who, on Monday October 4, took time off from his official schedule to visit the Duke and Duchess of Windsor at their mansion overlooking the Bois de Boulogne.

The following day, the Japanese monarch crossed the Channel and was met at Victoria Station by the Queen and taken in an open carriage to Buckingham Palace, where that night there was a banquet in his honour. Absent from this event was the Queen's uncle Earl Mountbatten of Burma who stated that he was 'previously engaged in the country'. He was to meet the Emperor later in informal

Empress Nagako of Japan and the Duke of Edinburgh drive to Buckingham Palace in an open carriage

circumstances at Buckingham Palace.

On Wednesday October 6, Emperor Hirohito visited London's Kew Gardens and planted a *cryptomeria japonica* and received a round of applause from fellow naturalists. A few hours later, the tree was found cut down and acid poured into its roots. A man was arrested but police decided to press no charges against him.

The following Tuesday, October 12, in Geneva, the beautiful Begum Aga Khan presented her husband with a son and heir.

Later that day in London, a fashion exhibition organized by Mr Cecil Beaton opened at the Victoria and Albert Museum. Among those who attended the preview that night were Baroness Spencer-Churchill, 38-year-old Lady Antonia Fraser, Sir John Gielgud and Prince and Princess Stanislaus Radziwill, Lady Abdy, Mrs Gilbert Miller, Mrs Ian Fleming and Lady Diana Cooper.

Meanwhile, celebrations had begun in Iran for the 2,500th anniversary of the founding of the Persian Empire. The climax came on Thursday October 14, with a banquet in a desert pavilion at Persepolis forty miles south of Tehran at which items on the menu included quails eggs stuffed with golden imperial caviare, mousse of crayfish tails, stuffed roast lamb with truffles, champagne water ice, and roasted peacocks presented with their tail fans and served with a nut and truffle salad. This incredible event was attended by eight kings, five queens, three prime ministers and a cardinal. Other miscellaneous figures present included Princess Anne, Liberal leader Jeremy Thorpe, Mrs Henry Ford, Madame Imelda Marcos and the vivacious Mrs Vere Harmsworth.

On Wednesday October 20 it was announced that Princess Anne had caught a cold during these celebrations and was obliged suddenly to retire from an official

The Shah and Empress of Iran arrive at a function in their honour at the Paris Opera

reception held on board the royal yacht *Britannia* which was anchored off Izmir.

The same day, Senator Edward Kennedy made a controversial speech in the U.S. Senate in which he demanded the recall of all British troops from Northern Ireland, accusing the government of Ulster of ruling 'by bayonet and bloodshed'.

On Thursday October 21, at a nursing home in Paris, Bianca Jagger gave birth to a baby girl. The pop star Mick Jagger said both mother and child, later to be named Jade, were doing 'marvellously'.

The following day in Paris, Mr Stavros Niarchos was secretly married to the Marchioness of Blandford, former wife of Mr Niarchos's arch-rival Aristotle Onassis and mother of his two children Alexander and Christina, who were informed of the marriage by registered mail.

On Monday October 25, Pablo Picasso celebrated his ninetieth birthday with his wife Jacqueline at his vine-covered house near Cannes. It was noted that Picasso – one of the world's richest men – had recently acquired a white Lincoln Continental which would occasionally rumble out to the airport, to pick up or drop off a visiting friend.

Over in London the following day, the Earl of Dalkeith, who had been crippled in a hunting accident earlier in the year, was given a hero's welcome when he returned to the House of Commons in a wheelchair. 'What a crazy place this is!' he remarked. 'You make speeches to an empty chamber for eleven years. Then you fall off a horse and everybody says what a great fellow you are.'

Back in Paris that night, serious traffic jams were caused by the opening of a retrospective exhibition of paintings by Francis Bacon at the Grand Palais. The event was marred by the death of the painter's friend, George Dyer, who collapsed on the lavatory at his Paris hotel on the eve of the opening.

The following day, October 26, an interview with chain smoking Russian leader Mr Brezhnev was published in the French communist daily paper *L'Humanité* during which the Russian leader praised his new cigarette case with a built in timing device. 'With this system I manage to smoke only seventeen cigarettes a day,' he explained.

The same day in Buenos Aires, American chess champion Bobby Fischer defeated Russian master Tigran Petrosian in forty-six moves and entered the world chess final to be held the following year.

Back in London, on Thursday October 28, American millionaire Ralph Stolkin began a remarkable action in the High Court to reclaim jewellery and property valued at £224,000 which he had given to his former girl-friend Mrs Patricia Wolfson. The beautiful Mrs Wolfson, the subject of a famous painting by Annigoni, claimed that these gifts had been given to her outright.

The beautiful Mrs Patricia Wolfson in Eaton Square during the famous Love Gifts law case which fascinated transatlantic society during the autumn of 1971. Note the car's fashionable 'blacked out' windows

That night, there was further excitement in the House of Commons when MPs voted by a majority of 112 in favour of Britain entering the Common Market. At Dover this decision was celebrated by 77-year-old former Prime Minister Harold Macmillan lighting a huge bonfire, a gesture which was seen and reciprocated in Calais.

The following day, 82-year-old veteran Common Market statesman Jean Monnet arrived in London to visit his Savile Row tailor. 'I admire the English cut,' he said. 'I've been getting my suits made here for forty years.'

On Wednesday November 3, Polish film director Roman Polanski was found at the basement Tandoori Indian restaurant in London's Fulham Road surrounded by a bevy of beautiful young girls.

On Thursday November 4, headlines blazed the news that 50-year-old Prince

Philip was to give up playing polo, due to recurring attacks of synovitis in his right wrist, which made wielding a polo stick extremely painful. It was predicted that Prince Charles would find a home for his father's fine stable of polo ponies.

On Friday November 5, the High Court Love Gifts case, which had enthralled the world's press for the last week, was settled out of court. It was announced that the jewels would be sold and the proceeds split between the two contestants. Mr Stolkin's attorney said afterwards 'He is pleased with the terms and I understand Mrs Wolfson is pleased also. My client holds no rancour or bitter feelings against her.'

The same day, the three Oz editors had their conviction and sentences quashed by the Court of Appeal when three learned judges ruled that the trial judge had misdirected the jury on the definition of obscenity. 'It is a disaster,' said Mrs Mary Whitehouse who had initiated the prosecution. 'I do not have anything personal against these three young men, but I think it is an unmitigated disaster for the children of our country.'

The following Wednesday, November 10, 43-year-old Richard Gangel, former chief executive of IOS in Britain, appeared in the London Bankruptcy Court facing debts of £836,567. Mr Gangel's personal fortune had once been assessed at £3 million and his house in Rutland Gate was soon to be sold for £291,000 to Dubai-based businessman Mr al-Tajir.

Later that day, a 19-year-old Londonderry girl had her head shaved and was tarred and feathered and left tied to a lamppost as punishment for going out with a British soldier. The girl in question was undeterred by her ordeal and was to marry the soldier soon afterwards.

A few days earlier, IRA leader Joe Cahill had been seen lunching at the Royal Hibernian Hotel in Dublin off a T-bone steak and specially ordered fresh salmon.

On Sunday November 14, the Earl of Longford took part in a soccer match in East London dressed in short trousers and brown suede shoes after being warned by the referee 'Now, we don't want any dirty play.' After the match, during which he had touched the ball only twice, the publicity-mad Earl explained, 'I'm sixty-five, so my games-playing days are really over. But I did captain the winning house football team at Eton.'

The following weekend, Foreign Secretary Sir Alec Douglas-Home flew to Rhodesia in an RAF VC10 to begin difficult and tense consultations with the Prime Minister Ian Smith. He was accompanied by 58-year-old solicitor Lord Goodman, who had already conducted some preliminary negotiations with the illegal regime.

Back in East London, on Thursday November 18, the Queen opened a new centre for social projects in East London and shook hands with Mr John Profumo, who had been engaged in charity work in the area since his sensational resignation as Secretary of State for War eight years earlier.

On Tuesday November 23, it was announced that the Queen was suffering from chicken-pox and had been confined to her room in Buckingham Palace. Among those doctors in attendance was her faithful homeopathist, Dr Margery Blackie.

The following day, Lord Goodman arrived back from Rhodesia where Sir Alec Douglas-Home and Mr Ian Smith had reached some sort of settlement. 'I now plan to go back to private life,' said Lord Goodman. 'I have more important things to do in London now.'

On Tuesday November 30, in London, an appeal was launched to raise the £231,000 needed to save Titian's *Death of Actaeon* for the nation. 'I hope we will be home and dry in six months,' said Sir John Witt, Chairman of the Trustees of the National Gallery. 'Comfortable desks will be installed in the boardroom where the exhibition is mounted for people to sit down at and write what we hope will be generous cheques.'

On Thursday December 2, the British government announced plans to raise the Queen's income to £980,000 a year. In the House of Commons, Labour MP Willie Hamilton protested that this was 'the most insensitive and brash pay claim made in the last two hundred years'.

That night, at his château near Paris, Baron Guy de Rothschild gave a fancy dress party, said to have cost £50,000, in honour of the centenary of Proust. Among the many celebrities present were Richard Burton, in white tie and tails, and Elizabeth Taylor, who wore black plumes and over £1 million worth of jewellery including her latest bauble the Peregrina Pearl.

The following day in New York, Mrs Jackie Onassis protested that she had become a virtual prisoner in her Fifth Avenue apartment due to persecution by a free-lance photographer, Ronald Galella. In a legal affidavit that day Mrs Onassis described a recent incident in a Broadway theatre and restaurant when she had been repeatedly 'humiliated' by the photographer. A judge ordered that Galella was not to appear nearer than fifty yards of Mrs Onassis and her children.

Meanwhile, Christina Onassis had already left her Californian husband Joseph Bolker and fled to London. 'Since our marriage Christina and I have been subjected to extraordinary parental pressures which are now severely affecting her health,' said Mr Bolker. 'At my suggestion she has gone to London to see her doctor.'

On Sunday December 5, vegetarians gathered in London to protest at the opening of the Royal Smithfield Show and the consumption of Christmas turkeys. 'We shall take note of what you say,' said the Show's organizer, Mr Kunz, 'but personally I prefer my roast beef and Yorkshire. Still, each to his own and I wish you success.'

On Monday December 6, it was disclosed that the Duke of Windsor was undergoing X-ray treatment as an out-patient at the American Hospital in Paris. 'Right now, he is just a day patient,' said a hospital spokesman.

Meanwhile, surgeons had won a battle to save the Duchess of Kent's finger, which had been crushed in a car door when she collected her daughter, Lady Helen Windsor, from school. 'The Duchess was in great pain when she was admitted,' said a spokesman for Slough's Wexham Park hospital. On Tuesday December 7, the Duchess's arm was in a sling when she went to Gatwick Airport to welcome the King of Afghanistan to Britain.

Later that day, there was great excitement in New York over an announcement by the McGraw Hill publishing company that it had acquired the autobiography of billionaire Howard Hughes. In a press release, it was stated that the 65-year-old recluse had had almost a hundred sessions with young author Clifford Irving 'in various motel rooms and parked cars throughout the Western Hemisphere'.

A few hours later, there came a vigorous denial from the Hughes Tool company that such a book existed and for the next few weeks unheard of confusion was to reign in American publishing circles.

Later that week, Christina Onassis was reunited with her husband in California and on Saturday December 11 a party to celebrate her twenty-first birthday, held in a French restaurant in Beverly Hills, was said to be a gloomy occasion.

Back in England, on Monday December 13, the Jockey Club decided to permit women riders. 'Details will be discussed by the stewards in the near future,' said Major-General Sir Randle Feilden, 'but the principle of ladies' races has now been accepted.' Said Mrs Judy Goodhew, who had applied for a jockey's licence two months earlier, 'It's marvellous to get a foot in the door.'

Meanwhile, Richard Burton and Elizabeth Taylor had left Paris on the Lausanne Express to spend Christmas at their chalet at Gstaad. On board the train, Miss Taylor cradled a new pet, a Siamese kitten called Trujillo, on her lap. The Burtons had decided to travel by train on the advice of their chauffeur, Gaston, who had decided that the roads were too slippery for their Rolls-Royce.

On Tuesday December 14, the Queen's finances were the subject of a lively debate in the House of Commons. In his bitterest attack ever on the Royal Family, Mr Willie Hamilton described Princess Margaret as 'an expensive kept woman' and spoke slightingly of the Queen Mother's smile: 'We say she always has a pleasant smile on her face. My God, if my wife had that pay she would never stop laughing.' Following these insulting remarks, Mr Hamilton was challenged to a duel by a boxing teacher, Mr Winston Hughes.

The following morning, December 15, in Upper Phillimore Gardens, bullets smashed through the rear window and coachwork of a Daimler car carrying Jordan's Ambassador Mr Zaud al-Rifai. The Queen later wrote to King Hussein to express her shock at this 'dastardly attack'.

That night in Paris, the Duke and Duchess of Windsor attended a gala evening at the Lido nightclub. The Duke, who wore dark glasses and a carnation in the buttonhole of his dinner jacket, sat next to Madame Edmond Bory, wife of the chain store owner.

The following day, in Venice, thieves arrived by gondola or barge at the palazzo of art collector Peggy Guggenheim, broke in through a window and left with seventeen paintings, valued at $500,000.

Back in London, on Saturday December 18, celebrities gathered in London for a memorial service for Gladys Cooper at St Martin-in-the-Fields. Among those present was the aged Dame Sybil Thorndike who shouted as she drove away, 'I hope my service will be as gay as this one. It won't be long now: You know I'm nearly ninety!'

On Sunday December 19, gales swept Britain. Trees were blown down or ripped from the ground and homes were damaged. Ten miles off Land's End, the 700 ton coaster *Tralee Trawler*, bound from Rotterdam to Cork, sank in mountainous seas.

The following day, Prime Minister Heath met President Nixon in Bermuda with Ambassador Walter Annenberg dancing attendance. The two leaders were to agree on the need for 'the closest possible degree of understanding and unity of purpose'.

The following day, President Nixon slipped on a gang plank after attending a state dinner on board the British destroyer *Glamorgan* and was grabbed by Mr Heath under the arm.

Back in London earlier that day, Home Secretary Reggie Maudling had sampled sixteen wines at a wine tasting competition at the Savoy Hotel. 'Of course I like to drink expensive wine when I can,' he said, 'but usually I drink everyday plonk, the cheapest I can find.' The contest was won by a garage-owner from Basingstoke.

Meanwhile in New York, confusion over the autobiography of millionaire Howard Hughes knew no bounds. On Thursday December 23, author Mr Clifford Irving, submitted to a lie detector test. A few hours later he flew to the Mediterranean island of Ibiza to spend Christmas with his family.

The same day, the Queen left London for Windsor Castle to spend Christmas with her family.

Meanwhile, Mrs Jackie Onassis arrived in England to stay with her sister Princess Lee Radziwill at her hill top Berkshire home.

Jackie Onassis's sister, Princess Lee Radziwill, who was later to establish herself as an interior decorator

On Christmas Day, there was much excitement at Blenheim Palace over the announcement that the 74-year-old Duke of Marlborough was to marry his friend Mrs Laura Canfield, to whom he had already given the famous Marlborough pearls said to have once belonged to Catherine the Great.

Meanwhile in Paris, there was concern about the health of 83-year-old Maurice Chevalier, who was gravely ill in hospital. On Monday December 27, *France Dimanche* jumped the gun and published a six page article on the death of the famous entertainer, including a vivid description of the 'death rattle which escaped from his mouth' although he was not in fact to die till five days later.

On Tuesday December 28, President Nixon was found sailing in 79°F in Florida with his old friend Bebe Robozo on board the latter's forty foot ocean-going houseboat. Later that day, Nixon welcomed Herr Willy Brandt to his Presidential villa at Key Biscayne and assured him that he would not remove any American troops from Western Europe.

Back in Britain, on December 29, where the temperature was 36°F, the Duke of Beaufort's hounds pursued a fox onto the new M4 motorway, disrupting traffic and causing hunt servants to dismount in order to collect them together. The fox had scaled, or squeezed through, a six foot fence.

1972

During the year that follows there are further signs of the death of
Swinging London. Industrial troubles soon lead to restaurants being lit
by hurricane lamps and Mr Fish is obliged to close his famous male
boutique. The pop aristocracy of the Sixties go their separate ways. John
Lennon and Yoko Ono try to settle in New York, Mick Jagger says he
wishes to live permanently in England and former Oz editor Richard
Neville says he is 'dropping out of dropping out' and returning to his
native Australia. Meanwhile, fellow Australian and high priest of
Women's Lib Germaine Greer appears in couture clothes and is said to be
'no fun any more'. The horrible atrocities that take place in Northern
Ireland, Munich and elsewhere cast a grim shadow over the social events
of the year. The revelations at the Poulson bankruptcy hearing encourage
a growing public reaction against the activities of financial operators,
though things are still going well for whizz kid Jim Slater, who
optimistically buys a grouse moor and thousands of acres in Sussex,
telling his agents, 'Go on buying till you reach the sea.' In America the
excitements of the Howard Hughes caper are followed by the first
rumbles of the Watergate Affair and the strange phone calls of Mrs
Martha Mitchell: it's hardly surprising that Mr Nixon greets his
landslide re-election victory with a tight-lipped smile.

On Sunday January 2, a band of well-dressed gun-men arrived by limousine at the Hotel Pierre on Park Avenue, handcuffed nineteen hotel employees and guests and then looted forty-seven safe deposit boxes containing jewellery and cash valued at over $5 million. One of the gun-men was thought to be wearing a false nose.

On Tuesday January 4, London's post-Christmas social vacuum was filled with another fancy dress ball at Christie's on the theme 'all the world's a stage'. The Marquess of Blandford appeared as an archbishop, 22-year-old Nicholas Soames was dressed as Al Capone and the suave 33-year-old Marquess of Dufferin and Ava was one of several Hamlets.

Meanwhile in America, the battle over the authenticity of the Howard Hughes autobiography was still raging and on Friday January 7, a telephone link was established between Mr Hughes's ninth floor suite at the Britannia Beach Hotel in Nassau and a group of journalists at the Sheraton Hotel in Los Angeles to enable the eccentric multi-millionaire to dismiss the book as a work of 'totally fantastic fiction' and explain that he had never met Clifford Irving. He went on to describe how he cut his fingernails and unfairly to brand his former employee Robert Maheu as 'a no good dishonest son of a bitch who stole me blind'.

The following day, Clifford Irving flew into Kennedy airport from his home on Ibiza and announced that the voice on the telephone from Nassau was not that of Howard Hughes. 'In my opinion it was a damn good imitation of his voice as it may have been three or four years ago,' he said.

Back in Britain, on Sunday January 9, all coal production ceased as 280,000 miners went on strike.

The following night, businessman Jimmy Goldsmith gave a private dinner party for 130 friends at the Café Royal, with his friend 37-year-old Lady Annabel Birley at his side.

Back in New York, on Wednesday January 12, television personality David Frost donned a strawberry coloured suit and flew sixty friends to Bermuda on board a BOAC jumbo jet. Included in this junket were author Arthur Schlesinger, Senator Jacob Javits, John Lennon and Yoko Ono and Frost's long-term girl friend Diahann Carroll, who wore a diamond brooch spelling the word 'Love'. 'No, we are not getting married today,' said Frost, 'we are just flying down to Bermuda for a New Year lunch.'

Back in London on Monday January 17, Lord Snowdon was found lunching at Scott's, wearing a green battledress tunic over a brown polo-neck sweater.

That night, Prince Charles dined at the same restaurant, wearing a sober lounge suit.

The following day, investigations began at the Swiss Credit Bank in Zurich into the account in the name of H. R. Hughes into which McGraw Hill had paid nearly $1 million. On Thursday January 20, it was disclosed that the cheques had been cashed by a mysterious blonde calling herself Helga R. Hughes and that the money had all gone. In New York, McGraw Hill responded to this development by announcing that the publication of the Hughes autobiography would be suspended while these latest revelations were 'cleared up'.

Meanwhile, in the Caribbean property developer Harry Hyams' yacht *Shemara*, purchased from Sir Bernard and Lady Docker three years earlier, had struck a coral reef and been taken to dry dock in Trinidad for repairs.

On Saturday January 22, Mr Edward Heath arrived in Brussels to sign the agreement taking Great Britain into the Common Market. The ceremony was somewhat disrupted when a bottle of ink was hurled at him. 'We chose ink because it was non-toxic; said a colleague of the assailant, 'We didn't want to harm him in any way.'

Meanwhile, Clifford Irving had briefly returned to his home on Ibiza where, on Tuesday January 25, he and his wife Edith were quizzed about the latest development in the Howard Hughes caper. 'There are lots of fishy things and this looks like a trumped up case. Boy, oh boy, is this a scaring affair,' said Irving. Said Mrs Irving, 'All I can say is that I am not the woman in question.'

The following day, the marriage took place in London between the elderly Duke of Marlborough and the already thrice-married Mrs Laura Canfield. The ceremony at Caxton Hall was followed by a luncheon in a private room at the Connaught Hotel, prepared by a chef who had once worked for the Duke at Blenheim Palace.

74-year-old 'Bert' Marlborough and his bride Mrs Laura Canfield. The ceremony at Caxton Hall was followed by luncheon in a private room at the Connaught Hotel prepared by a chef who had worked at Blenheim Palace

On Friday January 28, Irving publicly admitted that his wife Edith was the mysterious blonde who had opened the bank account in the name of H. R. Hughes. A spokesman for the McGraw Hill company said, 'We are stunned by today's development,' and a few hours later Irving's lawyer Martin Ackerman issued a terse statement that he was resigning. 'Basically I am not a criminal lawyer and I think Clifford Irving needs a criminal lawyer in a case like this.'

Meanwhile in London, experts at the British Museum were unpacking the gold funeral mask of the 3,300-year-old boy king Tutankhamen which was to go on show with other priceless pieces from the same tomb later in the spring. 'My responsibility ends here,' said Mr Ian Pearson, managing director of the packing firm which had flown the mask from Egypt. 'This job has had its headaches.'

On Sunday January 30, thirteen civilians were killed by British troops in Northern Ireland.

The following day in the House of Commons, Irish MP Bernadette Devlin called the Home Secretary Mr. Maudling a 'murdering hypocrite' and then ran across the chamber and seized him by the hair. She was restrained by officials and escorted from the chamber but later permitted to return without making any apology.

Meanwhile in Paris, Yuri Brezhnev, 40-year-old son of the Russian leader, had made news by paying a visit to the Crazy Horse Saloon, the city's most expensive strip-tease club, and allegedly tipping the head waiter $100.

On Tuesday February 1, it was learnt that businessman Jim Slater whose standing in the City of London was now at a new peak, had purchased a thousand acres in Sussex. In a statement he said he planned to enjoy 'farming' the land and had apparently told his representatives to 'go on buying till you reach the sea'.

The following morning in the Bahamas, folk singer Baroness Nina Van Pallandt revealed that she had accompanied Clifford Irving on a trip to Mexico the previous year and that he had hardly ever been out of her sight. It was therefore deduced that Irving could not possibly have had the long meetings with Howard Hughes which he had claimed.

Later that day in Dublin, a mob of 20,000 besieged the British Embassy and, using litter bins to ferry petrol, set the building on fire.

Back in London, on Thursday February 3, Princess Anne met Twiggy at the royal première of *The Boyfriend* at the Empire Cinema Leicester Square. 'She was lovely,' said Twiggy afterwards. 'She has a beautiful skin and is so gracious.'

The following day in Miami, the shape of the Princess's nose won high praise at a conference of plastic surgeons.

On Monday February 7, former *Oz* editor Richard Neville appeared at Bow Street Magistrates' Court and was fined £25 after admitting possessing cannabis. 'I am dropping out of dropping out,' he said later. 'I am deporting myself, I expect to go abroad and write a book.'

Later that day in New York, Clifford and Edith Irving appeared before a grand jury and replied to questions and requests for handwriting samples by pleading the Fifth Amendment. The couple's troubles were complicated by a demand from the Internal Revenue Service for nearly $500,000. 'We wanted to be sure we were not left out of it,' said an IRS spokesman. 'We wanted to be first in line for their money.'

The following day in Greece, freelance photographer Nikos Koulouris was sentenced to six months' imprisonment on four charges relating to his attempts to take photographs on the island of Skorpios. 'Mr Onassis is thinking of giving up Skorpios because of Koulouris,' said a witness. 'Mrs Jackie Onassis is very upset with the defendant who has made her life unliveable.' Koulouris had apparently interfered with the landing of the Onassis amphibious plane.

Meanwhile in Britain, the miners' strike had entered its fifth week and, on Wednesday February 9, a State of Emergency was declared.

On Friday February 11, the government ordered a massive shut down of industry. In London, the Mirabelle, Scott's and other restaurants coped with the power cuts that followed by installing hurricane lamps, while the Savoy Grill, which was heated and lit by electricity powered by its own oil-powered generators, remained aloof from the crisis.

The following Monday February 14, it was announced that Prince Richard of Gloucester was to marry 25-year-old Birgitte van Deurs who had been working as a secretary at the Danish Embassy and was said to design and make many of her own clothes.

On Wednesday February 16, Mr Howard Hughes slipped out of the Britannia Beach Hotel in Nassau, which had been his home for the past fifteen months, boarded a yacht anchored 200 yards away, and sailed for Miami. He was followed by an odd assortment of belongings, including a blood plasma carrier, six television sets, mattresses, an old electric stove, pots and pans and a hospital bed. 'It was not rich man's stuff,' said an onlooker.

The following day, President Nixon left Washington on the first step of his historic journey to China.

On Friday February 18, it was revealed that Howard Hughes had found a new home in Managua, Nicaragua, where he had taken over the whole of the eighth floor of the Intercontinental Hotel. 'This will really put us on the map,' said a local radio commentator. 'This is as important as Nixon's trip to China.'

Three days later, President Nixon arrived in Peking. His first day in the Chinese capital ended with a banquet hosted by Premier Chou at which the President used chopsticks to tackle steamed chicken with coconut, fried and stewed prawns, sharks' fins and almond junket washed down by Mao Tai and Chinese red wine.

On Tuesday February 22, a bomb exploded at the Parachute Brigade's head-quarters at Aldershot, killing a Roman Catholic padre and five women cleaners. The IRA described the incident as 'a successful retaliatory operation'.

The following day, senior Conservative peer Lord Salisbury died at his Hertford-shire stately home, Hatfield House. A patrician figure said to have impregnable social assurance, 'Bobbety' Salisbury had first made news as a train bearer at the coronation of King George V in 1911.

On Friday February 25, another link was forged between the aristocracy and the pop music world when former Lancashire weaver Georgie Fame married the Marchioness of Londonderry. After the ceremony at Marylebone Registry Office, at which he wore a green velvet suit and open necked shirt, the bridegroom left for Elstree to work on a television spectacular.

On Saturday February 26, it was announced in California that the seven month old marriage between Californian businessman Joseph Bolker and 21-year-old Christina Onassis was to be amicably dissolved. 'He may soon be my ex-husband but he will always be my best friend,' said Christina. 'I am too Greek and he is too Beverly Hills. That's really the trouble.'

On Sunday February 27, the world's attention turned to Budapest where Richard Burton was giving a party to celebrate Elizabeth Taylor's fortieth birthday. The event, which was attended by several dozen of Mr Burton's Welsh relations, turned slightly sour when one of the guests turned on Miss Taylor and accused her of ignoring the Hungarian Revolution. Miss Taylor who was wearing a grecian style white dress and both her famous diamonds, immediately burst into tears.

The following morning in Britain, the miners went back to work after receiving a pay settlement which undermined the government's attempt to curb wage in-flation.

Later that day, Princess Margaret and 200 others dined off watercress soup, lobster and sucking pig at a ceremonial dinner at Lincoln's Inn. The party came to an abrupt halt at 9 p.m. when there was a power cut.

Meanwhile, Italian police had recovered the seventeen paintings stolen from Miss Peggy Guggenheim's Venetian palace a few months earlier, when three men were spotted unloading five bulky packages from a motor-boat. 'I'm sick and tired of being robbed' said 72-year-old Miss Guggenheim. 'All my pictures are going to be wired electrically which will make a noise if any of them are touched. I'm particularly glad to have this latest lot back because they were not insured.'

On Thursday March 9, Clifford Irving's 'autobiography' of Howard Hughes was at last officially discredited when he appeared with his wife Edith, and researcher Richard Suskind, before a grand jury in New York and was charged with grand larceny, forgery, mail fraud and other offences. After the ceremony, the Irvings, who were now living at the Chelsea Hotel on 23rd Street, were released on bail.

The following day, the eighth birthday of Prince Edward, now a pupil at Gibbs School in Kensington, was celebrated with a tea party at Buckingham Palace.

Earlier that week, flamboyant Irish chef Peter Langan had opened a new restaurant in Devonshire Street, Marylebone, and stated that he had moved one step nearer to achieving his ambition of owning a restaurant 'like the Café Royal of a hundred years ago.'

On Saturday March 11, the 74-year-old Duke of Marlborough died in a London hospital. His body was laid to rest in the chapel at Blenheim Palace and his widow, Laura, whom he had married only six weeks earlier, was obliged to return the famous Marlborough pearls.

That weekend in Australia, Women's Lib crusader Germaine Greer was pelted with eggs by a young man wearing a swastika armband. Miss Greer gave chase but was outpaced by her assailant.

Back in New York, on Monday March 13, Clifford and Edith Irving appeared before Federal Judge John Cannella and pleaded guilty to conspiring to defraud the McGraw Hill company. After a date had been fixed for sentencing, the famous couple stepped out of the panelled court room to be jostled by cameramen and dazzled by television lights.

Author Clifford Irving faces the press during the final stages of the Howard Hughes autobiography hoax. Irving declares: 'This isn't really my cup of tea'

Three days later, on Thursday March 16, John Lennon and Yoko Ono began a battle with the American immigration authorities to become American citizens. It was stated that their visas had run out and they faced deportation on account of Lennon's conviction in Britain four years earlier for possessing marijuana. 'New York is the centre of the earth,' said Lennon. 'That's where we want to be.'

On Monday March 20, Mrs Nancy Reagan, wife of the Governor of California, disclosed that she took frequent long baths to alleviate the tensions of political life.

Back in Britain, on Friday March 24, Mr Heath went on television to announce the end of home rule in Northern Ireland by the appointment of Mr William Whitelaw as 'supremo' in the troubled province. 'The army will stay in Northern Ireland as long as any faction seeks to terrorize or intimidate ordinary people,' he said.

The following night, Princess Anne attended Crookham Horse Trials Dance near Aldershot and was found dancing with the previous year's Badminton winner, 23-year-old Lieutenant Mark Phillips.

On Wednesday March 29, the Queen opened the Tutankhamen Exhibition at the British Museum. Among the 800 people who attended the opening ceremony was 70-year-old Lady Evelyn Beauchamp whose father, the Earl of Carnarvon, had discovered the boy king's tomb in 1922. Lady Evelyn stated that she was 'utterly thrilled' by the exhibition and declared that the treasures looked 'so much more beautiful than they did down the tomb'.

Meanwhile the Mr Fish shop, which had opened in the late sixties and provided clothes for Lord Snowdon, Mick Jagger, David Niven and other trend setting males, yet failed to make a profit, had closed its doors. 'All I own are these clothes, two cats and some rather nice pictures by Patrick Procktor,' said 31-year-old Michael Fish sadly.

On Saturday April 1, Muhammad Ali, now describing himself as 'the fat young man with the fast left hand', entered a boxing ring in Tokyo dressed in an exotic oriental dressing-gown to fight Mac Foster. Ali won this non-title fight but gave a sloppy performance, using his right hand, according to one commentator 'like an outraged woman swinging her handbag'.

Over in New York, on Monday April 3, new star Baroness Nina Van Pallandt, began a highly successful cabaret engagement at the plush St Regis Hotel. She quickly acknowledged that she owed her success to her involvement in the Howard Hughes affair. 'God bless his soul,' she said. Her manager later stated that the publicity Nina had received from the Hughes scandal had been 'worth five hit records and an Academy Award'.

In the early hours of the following morning, shots were fired at mafia leader Joe Gallo as he sat in Umberto's Clam House in Little Italy. The 43-year-old gangster staggered from the restaurant and collapsed in the street near his black Cadillac. His pin striped suit was removed and he was placed on a cardiac resuscitation cart but died a few minutes later. 'This is a gangland operation,' said senior detective Albert Seedman. 'Speculation is wide open at this time.'

Later that day, a young hijacker who had seized a Boeing 727 bound for Los Angeles from Denver, Colorado, parachuted out of the plane over the Utah desert clasping $500,000 in ransom. Helicopters and jeeps headed for the area and began a search for the swarthy, bespectacled man.

Back in Britain, on Sunday April 9, Prince Charles took 24-year-old beauty, Georgiana Russell, daughter of the British Ambassador to Madrid, to watch polo at Windsor. Said to be able to speak seven different languages, Miss Russell wore black slacks and a cream tail-out shirt. The couple had travelled to the ground in the Prince's two year old dark blue Aston Martin DB6 Volante.

Meanwhile, at his stately home in Surrey, 79-year-old Paul Getty had plunged into a depression following the death of his loyal Alsatian, Rex.

On Monday April 10, it was disclosed that 22-year-old Christina Onassis was seeing her old friend Mick Flick, heir to the Mercedes Benz fortune and a suitor approved of by her father.

The following day, it was disclosed that Dubai businessman Mohamed al-Tajir, had purchased Dropmore, a thirty-two bedroom stately home in Buckingham-shire once the home of newspaper magnate Lord Kemsley. 'I shall be moving in with my wife and three children in a few months,' he said. 'I'm changing the decor but doing nothing to alter the façade. I'm very proud to own such an historic house.'

Meanwhile, enormous queues formed outside the Tutankhamen exhibition at the British Museum and loudhailers were being used to give hourly reports to those waiting on the prospects of getting into the exhibition before nightfall. On Friday April 14, Sir John Wolfenden, director of the museum, praised attendants for their patience, and an exhibition official said, 'We are satisfied that the present queuing system is the most democratic way.'

The following day in Paris, the Soviet Ambassador's wife turned up at a Cardin fashion show upstaging Twiggy, Justin de Villeneuve and other celebrities present.

Photographer Justin de Villeneuve and his featherweight friend Twiggy at the Pierre Cardin fashion show in Paris. Others present on this occasion included the Soviet Ambassador's wife

Ten days later on Tuesday April 25, film star George Sanders was found dead in his hotel room near Barcelona. The 65-year-old actor, celebrated for his cruel mocking eyes and curling lip, had left a note saying he had 'lived enough' and signing off with the words 'Goodbye world.'

On April 27 in Geneva, a 17 carat diamond ring and other jewels which had been at the centre of the Love Gifts court case in London the previous autumn came up for sale but fetched only £117,000.

On Tuesday May 2, John Lennon and Yoko Ono won the first round in their battle to obtain American citizenship when the US immigration services authorities ruled that the couple were 'outstanding artists'.

That night in London, the deb season kicked off with Queen Charlotte's birthday ball at Grosvenor House. The evening took an odd turn when deb's mother Mrs Andrew Hughes-Onslow was hit by a glass that had fallen off a balcony. She was wheeled out of the ballroom, her head swathed in ice-packed tablecloths and taken to St George's Hospital. 'It's damn funny when it happens in films,' said a deb's father who watched the drama from a nearby table.

Three days later in Rome, there was a drama at the Osteria del Orso when the restaurant was invaded by twenty-seven local paparazzi anxious to photograph Elizabeth Taylor dining with Aristotle Onassis. Miss Taylor, who had arrived in the city in her husband's private jet, ducked under a table while Mr Onassis hurled champagne at the intruders.

Meanwhile, artist Marc Chagall was said to be hard at work in his studio at Vence on a series of paintings to adorn Mr Onassis's 17-year-old yacht, *Christina*.

Back in Britain, on Monday May 8, Princess Margaret, the Earl of Snowdon, the Duke of Kent and Prince William of Gloucester had their first taste of supersonic travel when they took a ninety minute trip on Concorde, flying from Fairford in Gloucestershire over the Bay of Biscay and back. 'It was a fascinating sensation to sit in Concorde and watch the clouds go by like a speeded up film,' said Princess Margaret.

On Wednesday May 10, six-month-old Jade Jagger got her first peep at England when she arrived with her parents, after an extraordinary world trip taking in the

Mick and Bianca Jagger both carry canes as they drift through Heathrow Airport

French Riviera, New York, Los Angeles, Tahiti and the Middle East. Mick Jagger told reporters he hoped to live permanently in England again.

Over in New York, on Friday May 12, John Lennon reiterated his desire to become an American citizen. 'This city is the centre of the artistic world,' he said. 'Just the way Paris used to be.'

That weekend, it was revealed in American *Good Housekeeping* magazine that Mrs Joan Kennedy was receiving psychiatric treatment for feeling inferior to the other Kennedy women. 'I have lost my self-confidence,' she said. 'It's very easy to feel insecure when you marry into a very famous, intelligent, exciting family.'

On Monday May 15, Governor George Wallace, champion of white racialism, was shot and gravely wounded campaigning in the suburbs of Washington. With a bullet lodged in his spine he was rushed by ambulance and helicopter to the city's Holy Cross Hospital to face a series of emergency operations.

Earlier that day, the Queen and Prince Philip had begun a state visit to France, being met at Orly airport by President Pompidou and driven into Paris in a new bullet-proof Citroen SM sports coupé. Their first evening in France began with a state banquet at the Grand Trianon, at which the menu included Perigord foie gras, lobster pie, leg of lamb St Florentin, ice cake and strawberries, accompanied by Dom Perignon 1962, Château Margaux 1959 and Château d'Yquem 1949. In a speech on this occasion, the Queen, who wore an orchid mauve satin dress and many jewels, declared, 'We drive on different sides of the road but we are both going the same way.'

Meanwhile, a drama was being played out in the mid-Atlantic following an anonymous call to the New York office of the Cunard company saying that there were six bombs on board the QE2. On Wednesday May 17, four explosive experts were parachuted into the sea near the liner but after an exhaustive search found no sign of any bomb. Cunard chairman Mr Victor Matthews commented 'I think it was a very clever confidence trick but with all those people on board we dare not take a chance.'

Back in France, on Thursday May 18, the Queen joined Marisa Berenson, Mrs Rita Lachman and other celebrities for racing at Longchamps. Later that afternoon, the Queen, Prince Philip and Prince Charles paused at the Bois de Boulogne to visit the Duke of Windsor now seriously ill with throat cancer. The Queen first took tea with the Duchess of Windsor, who wore a Dior afternoon dress of dark blue crêpe and served finely cut sandwiches and cakes and china tea from a white and gold service, and then spent fifteen minutes with her uncle, who was said to be delighted to see her.

On Sunday May 21 in Rome, a mentally disturbed man entered St Peter's and attacked Michelangelo's priceless white sculpture, the *Pietà*, with a hammer, breaking off the virgin's left arm and damaging the face. He declared, 'I am Christ. If you kill me it will be better because I shall go to Heaven.' Pope Paul later inspected the damage and was said to be 'ill with grief'.

On Monday May 22, Mr Nixon became the first American President to set foot in Russia. That night there was a banquet in his honour in the Kremlin at which over a hundred guests sat down to fish soup, roast pheasant, gammon baked with fruit and cucumbers and strawberry ice-cream. Massive brass chandeliers shone overhead and a diamond pin gleamed on Mr Brezhnev's tie.

The following day, the two leaders got down to talks, during which they were to re-affirm the principle of peaceful co-existence.

On Friday May 26, physician Dr Arthur Antonucci flew from New York to Paris to attend the ailing Duke of Windsor. The Duke's faithful secretary John Utter confirmed that his master was 'not in very good shape'.

Two days later, the Duke of Windsor was dead. In London, the news was marked by the chiming of the Great Bell of St Paul's Cathedral, while in Moscow, President Nixon put out a statement that the Duke was 'a man of noble spirits and high ideals, for whom millions of Americans felt a deep respect and affection'.

The following day, Nixon left Russia after presenting Mr Brezhnev with a Cadillac to add to his already impressive collection of foreign motor-cars which included a Rolls-Royce, a Renault and a Maserati-Citroen. The President then flew on to Tehran where he was greeted by the Shah of Iran at the airport.

On Wednesday May 31, the body of the Duke of Windsor was flown home to England on board a VC10 jet. Among officials meeting the plane at the airfield at Benson in Oxfordshire were government ministers Earl Jellicoe and Lord Lambton.

At 7 a.m. the following morning, the coffin was taken by road to St George's Chapel, Windsor, where it was to lie in state for two days.

Later that day in London, the committee of the Garrick Club decided not to elect journalist Bernard Levin a member. 'I am exceedingly sorry Bernard has not been elected,' said Mr William Rees-Mogg, Editor of *The Times* and a long-standing member of the club.

Meanwhile in Tehran, Dr Henry Kissinger had been found relaxing in a night-club. Photographers had been hustled away by the police before a belly dancer had plopped onto Dr Kissinger's lap.

On Friday June 2, the 75-year-old Duchess of Windsor arrived in England on board an aircraft of the Queen's Flight. She was met at Heathrow by her husband's old friend, Earl Mountbatten of Burma, and driven to Buckingham Palace. After lunch with the Queen and Princess Anne, she retired to a State Suite on the first floor overlooking the Mall.

The following afternoon, the Duchess was wearing an enormous string of pearls when she peered from a window as the Queen rode out to take part in the Trooping of the Colour ceremony.

Over in New York, on Sunday June 4, a spray of bullets was fired at a white cadillac carrying the two sons of mafia leader Joseph Colombo when the car drew up at their Brooklyn home. Neither man was hurt.

Back in England, on Monday June 5, the funeral of the Duke of Windsor took place at St George's Chapel, Windsor, and was attended by many of the former

Ageless beauty Lady Diana Cooper and her old friend photograper Cecil Beaton stand together at the funeral of the Duke of Windsor

King's old friends, including the newly knighted Sir Cecil Beaton and Lady Alexandra Metcalfe, who had both been present at the Duke's wedding thirty-five years earlier. Late arrivals at the ceremony included the staff at the late Duke's French home, whose plane from Paris had been delayed.

A few hours later, the Duchess of Windsor climbed aboard the aircraft that was to take her back to her home in France without a backwards glance. A Buckingham Palace spokesman said later, 'The last few days have been a massive strain for her,' while in the House of Commons Willie Hamilton criticized the treatment meted out to the Duke and Duchess of Windsor over the years. 'This all shows,' he said, 'the worthlessness of the claim that the Royal Family is the supreme example of family life and affection in Britain.'

The following day, it was revealed that the Duke of Kent had sold his Buckinghamshire home, Coppins, to 48-year-old property millionaire Commander Eli Gottlieb.

Meanwhile, Mrs Bianca Jagger, whose husband was now touring North America, had appeared on her own at the Tramp discothèque in Jermyn Street dressed in top hat and tails and carrying a cane.

Four days later, it was disclosed that White's Club in St James's Street had dispensed with the services of its barman, Henry. 'I was working the evening shift and was – er – a little inebriated. I don't blame them for sacking me. I deserved it,' said the man in question, who had already obtained another job at the Royal Thames Yacht Club in Knightsbridge.

On Monday June 12, the Pied Piper Ball was held at London's Dorchester Hotel, organized by the Hon Mrs Vere Harmsworth and 22-year-old Emma Soames and attended by Miss Estée Lauder, the new Duke and Duchess of Marlborough and the American Ambassador Walter Annenberg. In the tombola, the young Duchess of Marlborough won a pair of brown jeans. 'I can't think when I'm going to wear them,' she said.

The following night, the former Foreign Secretary Lord George-Brown was arrested in North London and breathalised after his 4.2 litre Jaguar had ploughed into a brick wall. 'I'm perfectly sober,' he shouted before being taken away from the scene in a white police car.

Back in New York, on Friday June 16, Mr and Mrs Clifford Irving appeared before Judge John Cannella to receive their sentences. 41-year-old Mr Irving was sentenced to two and a half years imprisonment for masterminding the conspiracy. His wife Edith, who was described by her attorney as 'a tired, beaten, emotionally drained human being', was given two months. In a compassionate gesture, the judge arranged that the couple should serve their sentences at separate times so that their children, Ned and Barnaby, could be looked after. The McGraw Hill company declined to comment on the proceedings.

The same day, a dum-dum bullet was fired at the elderly Mrs William Randolph Hearst as she drove to the airport from the Biltmore Hotel, missing her by inches.

Meanwhile, Mrs Hearst's 18-year-old grand-daughter Patty had left for a cultural tour of Europe with a party of seven male students, chaperoned by art historian Professor Patrick Tobin.

At 2.30 a.m. the following morning in Washington, five men were arrested at the headquarters of the Democratic National Committee in the city's Watergate complex. They wore Playtex rubber surgical gloves and carried pen-size tear-gas guns and a wide range of photographic, electronic and bugging devices.

A few hours later at the *Washington Post*, reporters Bob Woodward and Carl Bernstein were given the job of investigating this incident.

On Monday June 19, Presidential press secretary Ronald Ziegler described the recent Watergate break in as 'a third rate burglary attempt not worthy of further White House comment'.

Meanwhile, Dr Henry Kissinger had set off to Peking for secret talks with Chinese premier Chou En-lai exciting world-wide speculation that a new Vietnam peace initiative was under way.

On Tuesday June 20, Royal Ascot began, giving the Queen the opportunity to wear some of the same clothes she had worn during her state visit to France the previous month. On the opening day, the Queen drove up the course in an open carriage drawn by the famous Windsor Greys and accompanied by the Emperor Haile Selassie of Ethiopia who had been staying at Windsor Castle for the last few days.

On Wednesday June 21, the Queen shared her open carriage with the Shah of Iran.

British racehorse enthusiasts keep a stiff upper lip during a tense moment at Royal Ascot

On Thursday June 22, President Nixon made his first public comment on the Watergate break-in. 'The White House has had no involvement in this particular incident,' he said during a routine press conference in Washington.

The same day, Mrs Martha Mitchell telephoned United Press International and said she was 'sick of the whole operation' and had threatened to leave her husband, the former Attorney-General, who was now the President's campaign manager.

The following weekend, the Emperor of Ethiopia began a four day private visit to Paris. His arrival at Orly Airport was complicated by the presence of his two chihuahuas, which were not permitted to walk on the red carpet provided.

On Monday June 26, Mrs Martha Mitchell telephoned United Press International again and declared that she had been beaten up by government security agents. 'Five men threw me down on a bed and stuck a needle in my behind. I've never been treated like this before. If you could see me, you wouldn't believe it. I'm black and blue.'

Meanwhile, tension was mounting in Reykjavik, Iceland, as to whether chess champion Bobby Fischer would arrive for the world chess championship due to start the following Sunday. On Thursday June 29, Fischer was seen at Kennedy Airport but ran off when approached by press men and the plane for Iceland left without him.

The same day in Reykjavik, Russian world chess champion Boris Spassky waited calmly, looking relaxed and sharing jokes with his colleagues. Asked what he thought Fischer was doing, he said, 'I think he is in his bath in New York, gazing at the ceiling and thinking of me waiting here.'

Back in London, on Friday June 30, American Ambassador Walter Annenberg, who was said to be spending £100,000 a year on entertaining, threw a spectacular dance at his official residence, Winfield House. Meyer Davis and his band had been flown over from America for the evening and the ballroom was decorated with looped garlands of freshly cut roses. Among the 600 guests were Prince Charles, Princess Margaret, Lord Goodman, Mr Paul Getty, Mr and Mrs Henry Ford, Frank Sinatra, Dr and Mrs Roy Strong and the vivacious Mrs Vere Harmsworth.

Late the following day in Washington, John Mitchell resigned as President Nixon's campaign manager, explaining that his wife Martha had insisted he quit.

Meanwhile in London, 79-year-old Lady Diana Cooper had crashed her white mini in Hyde Park. 'I shall be driving again as soon as I get my car back from the garage,' she said.

On Monday July 3, the public examination of bankrupt international architect John Poulson excited great interest when Mr Poulson disclosed that his firm had paid £22,000 to the Adeline Genée Theatre, East Grinstead, a favourite cause of Mrs Maudling, wife of the Home Secretary. In the House of Commons, Liberal leader Jeremy Thorpe immediately demanded a government enquiry into 'allegations of financial corruption in public life'.

Early the following morning, temperamental chess champion Bobby Fischer set off at last for Iceland, following an offer by businessman Jim Slater to raise the prize money by £50,000. 'I am a keen chess player myself,' Mr Slater explained, 'and would be very disappointed, along with a lot of other people, if the match did not take place.' Fischer eventually arrived at Reykjavik at 6.55 a.m. on Tuesday July 4, rushed to a waiting Mercedes and was given a police escort to his villa.

Back in Washington that night, police skilled in crowd control were on duty at a concert given by the Rolling Stones at the Robert F. Kennedy Stadium. Mick Jagger began his act by yelling at the 47,000 people present 'Hello campers!'

The following Friday, July 7, Governor Wallace left hospital at Silver Springs, Maryland, and speaking from a wheelchair behind a bullet-proof screen, stated that he still wanted to be President of the United States.

The following day, the marriage took place at Barnwell in Northamptonshire between Prince Richard of Gloucester and Miss Birgitte van Deurs. Among the guests at the ceremony were Princess Margaret and the Queen Mother, both of whom carried transparent plastic umbrellas. Missing from the ceremony was the bridegroom's father, the 72-year-old Duke of Gloucester, who had been immobilized by a severe stroke two years earlier.

The Queen Mother steps into the rain following the marriage of her nephew Prince Richard of Gloucester. Her grandson Charles struggles with his umbrella in the background

Meanwhile, the start of the chess championship in Iceland had been delayed by more tantrums by American challenger Bobby Fischer. On Sunday July 9 he objected to the marble Italian chess board saying that the squares were too big. He also demanded the same chair that he had sat on when he had defeated Tigran Petrosian in Buenos Aires the previous year.

On Tuesday July 11, the contest began at last. In the first game, Fischer surprised his aides by employing the Nimzowitsch defence and then making an amateurish move. The game ended when he complained about the press photographers present and stormed out of the hall.

The following day in Hanoi, actress Jane Fonda spoke of the 'fake propaganda' on the American bombing of North Vietnam and said that the Americans who attacked North Vietnam were 'fatly paid, conditioned killers who have been told that when they bomb Vietnamese they are in fact only bombing monkeys'.

On Monday July 17, black bearded property tycoon Harry Hyams, whose empty Centrepoint office block was causing some controversy, appeared at the annual general meeting of his company Oldham Estates. Looking tanned and healthy, he quipped his way through the meeting with courtesy and aplomb.

Meanwhile in Iceland, Bobby Fischer had had his first victory over Boris Spassky.

His breakthrough came when Spassky was unable to find a strategy to cope with Fischer's all-important eleventh move: knight to rook four.

Back in Britain, on Tuesday July 18, Mr Reginald Maudling resigned as Home Secretary to clear the way for a thorough police investigation into accusations of corruption arising from the Poulson affair.

The following day, it was announced that Occidental Petroleum had signed a $3,000 million scientific and technical co-operation contract with the Soviet Union. The deal, which included the building of a 400-room Holiday Inn in the heart of Moscow, was a personal triumph for the company's 74-year-old owner Dr Armand Hammer, who had been wheeling and dealing with Russia since the 1920s.

On Thursday July 20, the death occurred of Herr Friedrich Flick, an 89-year-old industrialist and supposedly the richest man in West Germany, whose interests included a forty per cent holding in the Daimler Benz company. His fortune passed into the hands of his grandsons, 'Mick' and 'Muck' Flick, both of whom were in their twenties.

Early in the morning of Saturday July 22, the death occurred in the London Zoo of Chi-Chi, the giant panda. It was announced that her body would be preserved in the Natural History Museum in South Kensington.

The following Tuesday, playboy Lance Reventlow, only son of Barbara Hutton, died when his plane crashed in the Colorado Rockies. Chief mourners at his funeral were his step-father Cary Grant, his widow Cherry and former wife actress Jill St John. His invalid mother remained at her palace in Tangiers.

Back in London, on Friday July 28, Mr Maurice O'Regan, former butler to property magnate Sir Francis Peek, appeared in the dock at the Old Bailey accused of stealing cheques from his employer's wife for nearly £15,000. He successfully pleaded not guilty to the charge and claimed that he was having an affair with Lady Peek and that the money was for 'services rendered'.

On Saturday July 29, Prince Charles attended the Royal Tournament at Earls Court, appearing for the first time in public with a new companion, Lady Jane Wellesley, 21-year-old daughter of the Duke of Wellington. Meanwhile the Prince's young brother Edward had been confined to his quarters on board the royal yacht *Britannia* suffering from chicken-pox.

The following day in Reykjavik, world chess champion Boris Spassky, now trailing two points to five in his battle with the temperamental Bobby Fischer, tried to relax by playing tennis.

Meanwhile, at a clinic in Casablanca, celebrated travel writer James Morris had undergone sex change surgery. Returning to London after the operation he had begun his new life as a woman by disposing of his dinner jacket and resigning from the men only Travellers' Club in Pall Mall.

Back at the Old Bailey, on Monday July 31, butler Maurice O'Regan was found not guilty of stealing cheques from Lady Peek and was released from custody. 'If this is British aristocracy I don't want anything more to do with them. I never intend to become a butler again,' he said as he left the Old Bailey. 'I'm not answering any more questions. I've had enough.'

The following day, the public examination of bankrupt architect John Poulson, who had once employed 750 people, resumed at Wakefield in Yorkshire with further comments from Mr Poulson about Reginald Maudling. 'I must make it quite clear that what Mr Poulson is saying does not correspond with the truth,' said the former Home Secretary, who said he was 'hopping mad' at the allegations that had been flying about.

On Friday August 4, show-jumper Harvey Smith was hit in the stomach by a heavy pole at Hull Show.

The same day in Uganda, President Idi Amin stated that there was 'no room' in his country for 40,000 British Asians, whom he accused of sabotaging the economy. 'I want the economy to be in the hands of Ugandan citizens, especially black Ugandans,' he explained.

On Monday August 7, Jackie Onassis arrived in London from Sardinia where she had been staying on the Aga Khan's Costa Smeralda development. During her brief stay in the capital, Mrs Onassis was found at Fortnum and Mason, sampling chocolates with her children, 15-year-old Caroline and 11-year-old John John.

The following day in America, Jackie's brother-in-law Teddy Kennedy hit out at stories of a romance between him and a young New Yorker. 'People write this sort of thing about me all the time. It's unfortunate that this time someone else is being hurt by it.'

Back in London, on Thursday August 10, Sir Winston Churchill's granddaughter Arabella married 23-year-old schoolteacher James Barton. Guests at the ceremony included sex change model April Ashley, fashion designer Michael Fish and the bride's grandmother Baroness Spencer-Churchill, who arrived at the church on the arm of her grandson, Winston Churchill MP. The couple announced that they were planning to develop their own organic farm. 'We will be growing our own fruit and vegetables,' said Arabella. 'As we become established we will sell any excess.'

Fashion designer Michael Fish arrives at the wedding of Sir Winston Churchill's 22-year-old granddaughter Arabella

On Thursday August 17, it was revealed that Mick and Bianca Jagger and their daughter Jade were moving into Lord Gowrie's house in Eire for a few days' rest.

On Monday August 21, it was revealed that City whizz-kid Jim Slater had paid £1.1 million for a 20,000 acre Scottish estate belonging to the late Countess of Seafield. A Slater Walker spokesman said the estate, which included four fishing beats on the river Spey, had been bought 'as an investment'.

The following day, it was revealed that the Duchess of Windsor was now advertising her late husband's country estate, the Moulin de la Tuilerie, in the *Wall Street Journal* after unsuccessful attempts to sell the property earlier in the summer in the European newspapers. It was said that the Duchess was now getting back to normal life and had recently spent a three week holiday at Biarritz with her old friend, Lady Dudley.

Meanwhile, 39-year-old Jimmy Goldsmith, whose personal wealth was now assessed at £5 million, had been on holiday at Deauville, where he had won the modest sum of £210 during a visit to the Casino.

Back in London, on Wednesday August 23, celebrities who gathered for a charity preview of *The Godfather* included Margaret Duchess of Argyll and Paul Getty. Among those who had already seen the film at a private preview was city tycoon Jim Slater, now at the height of his powers.

On Saturday August 26, Sir Francis Chichester died at the Royal Naval Hospital in Plymouth. 'He has contributed immensely to our national life and his death is a great loss,' said fellow yachtsman Mr Heath.

On Monday August 28, Prince William of Gloucester was killed when his Piper Cherokee aircraft crashed at an airshow in Warwickshire. It was revealed later that the Queen was watching TV at the time and saw the tragedy as it happened.

On Tuesday August 29, President Nixon invited reporters to his oceanside home at San Clemente, California, and informed them that his counsel, John Dean, had now conducted an investigation into the Watergate break-in. 'I can say categorically that no one on the White House staff, no one in this administration presently employed was involved in this very bizarre incident.'

The following day, it was revealed in New York that Yoko Ono had purchased a tennis outfit and racket. 'I like the dress as a costume and the racket discourages muggers,' she explained.

Back in Britain, on Thursday August 31, it was revealed that the Earl of Longford was now guiding convicted child murderers Ian Brady and Myra Hindley towards 'Christian understanding'. 'Hindley has regained her Catholic faith and I believe has recovered from the corruption under which she suffered,' said Longford. 'Brady is not yet a Christian but . . . is moving in that direction.'

Later that day, a revival of *Private Lives* opened in London and ended with a great ovation for Sir Noël Coward who had watched the play from a box with Lady Diana Cooper and others.

On Friday September 1, Bobby Fischer became the new World Chess Champion when his opponent Boris Spassky telephoned the referee and said that his position was hopeless. Among those to offer congratulations to Fischer was President Nixon, who praised him for his 'complete mastery of the world's most difficult and challenging game'.

On Saturday September 2, Shell oil heiress Olga Deterding and her boyfriend TV personality Jonathan Routh were found lunching at the Meridiana restaurant in London's Fulham Road both dressed in faded battledress in the style of Vietnam war veterans.

On Sunday September 3, Liberal leader Jeremy Thorpe offered his Devonshire cottage for the use of one of the British Asian families now being ejected from Uganda by President Amin. 'I would be delighted to have an Asian family come and take shelter under my roof,' he said. He was later obliged to limit his offer to a couple with only two children on the grounds that there was 'only one bathroom and one small living-room'.

The following morning, 27-year-old Lucia Santa Cruz, glamorous daughter of the former Chilean Ambassador to London, returned to London on an overnight train from Balmoral where she had spent the weekend with Prince Charles. 'There is no romantic attachment between us,' she insisted.

On Tuesday September 5, a band of hooded Arab commandos armed with automatic weapons entered the Olympic village at Munich and killed two Israeli athletes and took another nine hostage. Twenty-three hours later there was a shoot-out at a nearby military airport in which the hostages and four of the Arab terrorists were killed.

Meanwhile, Sir Noël Coward had returned to his home in Switzerland where later that week he received his old friend Sir Cecil Beaton dressed in a scarlet jacket. 'It's awful I'm so old,' he remarked.

On Monday September 11, the English Country Cheese Council held a press reception to promote British cheeses against foreign ones from the Common Market. Among journalists apparently already won over to the cause was 32-year-old Auberon Waugh who wrote later, 'Give me scrumptious, mumptious *cheesy* Cheddar every day!'

Later that day, President Amin sent a lengthy telegram to the Secretary General of the United Nations praising the Arab terrorists for the Munich murders. Foreign Office officials in London decided to maintain 'a dignified silence' about this latest behaviour by Uganda's leader and the state of his mental health.

On Tuesday September 12, in Moscow, master spy Kim Philby was found lunching with an attractive, fashionably dressed, red-haired female companion at the city's swish Metropole Hotel.

Earlier that day in London, the Governor of Holloway Prison, Mrs Dorothy Wing, caused an outcry by taking murderess Myra Hindley for a stroll in a park. 'I suppose I shall get a rocket for this,' said Mrs Wing, 'but I am prepared to take it on my broad back because I think it is the right thing.' Much of the fury that this incident aroused was directed at the Earl of Longford who had visited Miss Hindley in prison and had stated that she was full of 'very deep remorse' for her crimes.

The following Friday September 15, Mr Heath set off for Japan. He arrived at Tokyo on Saturday September 16 and became the first British Prime Minister to set foot on Japanese soil. A torrential downpour of rain and high gusts of wind prevented the welcoming party from making their way to the steps of the aircraft.

That night, a typhoon rocked the city of Tokyo while Mr Heath slept soundly in his bed at the British Embassy.

Back in London on Wednesday September 20, a party to launch Lord Longford's 520 page report on pornography was held at the Waldorf Hotel. Among those present was 29-year-old Xaviera Hollander, a self-confessed former prostitute and author of the best-selling *Happy Hooker* who questioned the 66-year-old peer closely about his views on prostitutes. When Lord Longford replied, 'I am too old for all that', Miss Hollander retorted, 'I once had a client of seventy-three'.

The following day in America, it was reported that proceedings to evict Jackie Onassis's aunt Mrs Beale and her daughter from their mansion on Long Island had been dropped after Mrs Onassis and her sister Princess Radziwill had spent $4,000 cleaning up the dilapidated twenty-eight room mansion.

On Friday September 22, Mrs Martha Mitchell was interviewed by *Washington Post* reporter Bob Woodward at her apartment on Central Park South. She said she was much happier having made her family 'a non-political entity' and predicted that President Nixon would win the forthcoming election by 'the biggest landslide in the history of this country'.

On Wednesday September 27, the American public were informed that Mrs Onassis had dismissed her chef, Karle Jerome, who was said to be the nineteenth chef to pass through her employment in the past four years. Following his dismissal, 23-year-old Mr Jerome revealed that he had to mix skim milk with cottage cheese and prepare cucumber sandwiches for tea at Jackie's Fifth Avenue apartment.

Later that day, the controversial film *Deep Throat* opened at a cinema at Princeton in New Jersey. The distributor said that the presentation in such a fashionable area showed the new wave of sexual liberation and public acceptance of such a film.

On Thursday September 28, it was reported that the Duchess of Windsor had turned down an offer to appear on the Bob Hope Show.

Later that day, *Washington Post* reporter Carl Bernstein telephoned John Mitchell and informed him that the newspaper would be printing a story the following day to the effect that while Attorney-General he had controlled secret funds to finance widespread intelligence gathering activities against the Democrats. Mitchell responded to this news by threatening the newspaper's proprietor, Mrs Graham. 'Katie Graham's gonna get her tit caught in a big fat wringer if that's published,' he said.

The following morning, the offending story and Mitchell's comments were published in full in the *Washington Post*.

Washington Post proprietor Katharine Graham addresses a staff meeting

Back in Europe on Wednesday October 4, British Prime Minister Edward Heath had a forty minute audience with Pope Paul at the Vatican during which they discussed the problems of Northern Ireland. Earlier, when one of the papal courtiers remarked on the fine weather, Mr Heath replied, 'Glorious!'

On Monday October 9, the Women of the Year luncheon at London's Savoy Hotel was attended by Princess Anne, Mrs Mary Whitehouse, the recently widowed Lady Chichester, journalist Jill Tweedie, tennis star Virginia Wade and many more. Princess Anne avoided controversy by chatting about fashion with actress Glenda Jackson.

The following morning, it was announced that Sir John Betjeman was to be the new Poet Laureate. 'My first reaction when invited was "Good Lord, how extraordinary",' said the 66-year-old poet.

Later that day in America, the *Washington Post* reported that the recent break-in at the Watergate complex was linked to an extensive campaign of political sabotage conducted by high ranking aides of President Nixon. These claims were quickly dismissed by a White House official as 'a collection of absurdities' and 'a senseless pack of lies'.

Meanwhile, 18-year-old newspaper heiress Patty Hearst had returned from a cultural tour of Europe with seven male students and moved into a five room duplex apartment at Berkeley University in California, setting up house with her live-in boyfriend, Stephen Weed.

Back in London, on Thursday October 12, it was reported that the once grubby Women's Lib campaigner Germaine Greer had undergone a transformation and was now appearing in expensive couture clothes with her long hair pampered by a hairdresser. 'She's no fun anymore,' said an old friend.

On Friday October 13, Princess Alexandra arrived for an official visit to Afghanistan, accompanied by her hairdresser, 32-year-old Michael, from the Michael-John outfit in Mayfair.

The same day, some 10,000 feet up in the Andes, a chartered Fairchild F-227 aircraft carrying members of an amateur rugby team crashed in deep snow. A fruitless search for the missing plane was immediately mounted.

Back in Britain, on Sunday October 15, Princess Anne was among spectators at the Cirencester Park Horse Trials where competitors included the young Lieutenant Mark Phillips. Also present at this event was the beautiful 15-year-old Princess Caroline of Monaco, who wore brown suede trousers and dark red lace-up boots.

The same weekend in Boston Mrs Joan Kennedy commented on recent rumours about her husband's sex life. 'I am bored to tears with gossip about Ted and his so-called illicit romances but they do not affect the relationship between him and me.'

At 4 a.m. on Monday October 16, New York police began a series of lightning raids throughout the eight counties of New York State. Brooklyn District Attorney Mr Eugene Gold said later that almost every well known underground figure had been arrested, with the noted exception of 73-year-old Carlo Gambino, universally regarded as 'the Godfather'.

On Tuesday October 17, the Queen and Prince Philip began a state visit to Yugoslavia. At a luncheon that day at the Dedinje Palace near Belgrade the Queen presented 80-year-old President Tito, famous for his big appetite, with an English bone china dinner service.

The same day in Belgrade, the death occurred of 85-year-old Prince George of

Yugoslavia, who had remained in the city after the Communist take-over and was a familiar customer at a café near the British Embassy, where he dressed in old clothes and a Basque beret and sipped Turkish coffee and brandy.

The following Monday in Leningrad, an exhibition of paintings belonging to American multi-millionaire Dr Armand Hammer opened at the Hermitage Museum. The 74-year-old tycoon chose this occasion to present the museum with a Goya painting worth about $1 million which he had acquired earlier in the year.

Later that day in Uganda, President Amin was taken to hospital in Kampala amidst speculation that he was suffering from hypomania, an abnormal mental state in which the thought processes are speeded up.

Back in Britain, on Tuesday October 24, Dame Sybil Thorndike celebrated her ninetieth birthday with a party attended by Edith Evans, Peggy Ashcroft and other members of her profession. Accepting a knife to cut her birthday cake, Dame Sybil asked in ringing tones, 'Is this a dagger that I see before me?'

The following day in Washington, President Nixon's chief press officer Ronald Ziegler denounced the *Washington Post* for a full thirty minutes, accusing the paper of practising 'shabby journalism'.

Back in Britain on Friday October 27, Cyril Smith's victory in the Rochdale by-election was described by his party leader Jeremy Thorpe as 'a dose of salts for all Liberals'. Later that day the new twenty-seven stone MP went shopping in his constituency for tripe, pigs trotters and a bag of toffees. Between mouthfuls of pork pie, he declared, 'I feel so tired I could sleep for a week.'

On Sunday October 29, Sir Alec Douglas-Home arrived in Peking after a gruelling twenty-seven hour flight over the North Pole and got down to talks in the city's Great Hall of the People, the elegance of which was said to be marred by the presence of white enamel spittoons. Said Lady Douglas-Home, 'I haven't quite known where I've been since I woke up somewhere or other last night or this morning or whenever it was.' It was noted that the Douglas-Homes had brought with them forty pounds of Scottish pork sausages for the consumption of British Embassy staff.

On Monday October 30, President Amin left hospital in Kampala, driving himself back to his headquarters in a jeep, where he announced later that day that European farms in Western Uganda would now be subject to compulsory purchase.

Back in Britain on Wednesday November 1, 33-year-old David Frost attended a macrobiotic luncheon at London's Café Royal and was said to be looking ashen-faced and jet-lagged.

On Thursday November 2, forty-one hours of argument at 10 Downing Street ended when union leaders walked out declaring that Mr Heath's elaborate package of proposals to contain inflation was 'not a basis for negotiation'. Mr Heath spoke of his 'bitter disappointment' at this outcome.

On Sunday November 5, David Frost was in better form when he welcomed pressmen into his suite in a Manhattan hotel to inform them of his forthcoming marriage to black actress Diahann Carroll, daughter of a New York subway conductor. 'Thank you all for coming,' said Mr Frost. 'This is the most exciting thing that has ever happened to me. Super, simply super,' adding that they would probably be setting up home 'on a BOAC jet'.

Two days later, Richard Nixon was re-elected President of the United States in one of the greatest landslide victories in the history of the country. On learning of his extraordinary victory, the President gave a tight-lipped smile.

Back in Britain, on Saturday November 11, Princess Anne had her first day's hunting when she went out with the Zetland Hunt. 'We were delighted to see her,' said the president of the hunt. 'She spoke to farmers and rode ninety per cent of the hunt.'

Later that day, the 22-year-old Princess was flagged down while allegedly speeding on the M1 motorway near Bletchley. 'A report has gone to the senior officer concerned, in this case the Chief Constable,' said a spokesman for the Thames Valley Police, who were later to send her a cautionary letter.

That night in Westminster Hospital an emergency operation was performed on 87-year-old Baroness Spencer-Churchill, who had had a fall in her Kensington flat. 'In view of her age, her general condition must inevitably cause some anxiety,' said a spokesman.

On Monday November 13, it was reported that George Harrison was sinking a test bore hole on his new Oxfordshire estate, Friar Park, to find water to fill his ornamental lakes, which were said to require 3,000 gallons a day. Other adornments at the ex-Beatle's home included light switches designed as friars' noses.

On Tuesday November 14, an Old Bailey jury decided that the will of property tycoon Clive Raphael, in which he had left his wife a shilling and four nude photographs of herself, had been faked and the following day members of the gang responsible were given gaol sentences. Mastermind behind the plot, Ronald Schulman, had escaped and fled abroad some time before and was believed to be in Rio.

On Thursday November 16, the Queen's uncle Earl Mountbatten and his grandson Mr Norton Knatchbull were each fined £20, after pleading guilty to possessing watered milk for sale at their farm at Broadlands. The defending counsel stated that Lord Mountbatten and his grandson were 'most concerned that they are unable to find a logical explanation after an exhaustive enquiry'. It was noted that there were no previous convictions.

The same day, at Wells Street Magistrates' Court in London the Queen's cousin, 33-year-old Lord Lichfield, was fined £50 and disqualified from driving for twelve months after pleading guilty to driving with an excess of alcohol in his blood.

On Friday November 17, Labour MP John Stonehouse, now devoting much of his time to business activities, announced the formation of the British Bangladesh Trust to provide banking facilities for the Bengali community in Britain. 'Nobody must think it is a charity or a speculation,' said Mr Stonehouse, a former Minister for Posts and Telecommunications.

On Saturday November 18, Princess Anne went out again with the Zetland Hunt, causing considerable distress in certain quarters. 'I think it is a great shame that the Princess has taken up such a barbaric sport,' said Mr Iain McNay of the Hunt Saboteurs Association. 'It will be a matter of regret that this has taken place,' said Lord Soper, President of the League Against Cruel Sports.

On Monday November 20, the Queen and Prince Philip attended a service of thanksgiving for their Silver Wedding at Westminster Abbey, after which the royal couple went on their first ever 'walkabout'.

That night, there was a party at Buckingham Palace. Among the 200 guests present were Prime Minister Edward Heath, Prince Rainier and Princess Grace of Monaco and Princess Anne's new friend Olympic Gold Medallist Lieutenant Mark Phillips.

Meanwhile, in the House of Commons Labour MP Willie Hamilton had criticized the sale of silver spoons and other objects commemorating the Silver Wedding and spoken of 'the sordid, greedy commercialism of the event'.

Over in France the following day, Dr Henry Kissinger took time off from secret Vietnam peace talks to lunch with an old girlfriend, Mrs Jan Rose Cushing, at the Chez Tante Louise restaurant at Gif-sur-Yvette near Paris.

On Friday November 24, nine pages of full frontal nude photographs of Mrs Jackie Onassis – some of which showed her in inelegant poses – taken on the island of Skorpios were published in an Italian magazine. Mr Onassis later acknowledged that it was possible for the photographs to have been taken. 'I have to take off my pants to put on my bathing suit,' he explained.

On Saturday November 25, the Marquess of Bristol and his 18-year-old son Lord Jermyn gave a shoot at Ickworth in Suffolk. Those participating included David and Lady Pamela Hicks, Sir Michael Havers QC and King Simeon of the Bulgarians.

Back in London, on Wednesday November 29, a car carrying Prime Minister Edward Heath got stuck in traffic between 10 Downing Street and the House of Commons. To the consternation of his bodyguards, Mr Heath chose to abandon the vehicle and walk the rest of the way in the rain. Later that day, the Prime Minister placed a personal call to Sir Desmond Plummer, leader of the Greater London Council, to complain about the traffic chaos currently prevailing in the capital.

On Friday December 1, thieves broke into a car parked in Park Lane belonging to Princess Alexandra and Mr Angus Ogilvy and stole Christmas presents, jewellery and Mr Ogilvy's business diary.

The following day, Princess Anne and her friend Lieutenant Mark Phillips attended the Bedale Hunt Ball in Yorkshire exciting the anger of Mr Brian Seager, leader of the reform group within the RSPCA. 'This latest episode just proves that Princess Anne is riding roughshod over the wishes and feelings of many, many people.'

Meanwhile in Paris, the Duchess of Windsor's social life was in full swing again. On Tuesday December 5, she appeared at a party at Maxim's also attended by 22-year-old Christina Onassis. It was noted that Christina had now dyed her hair blonde, had lost at least twenty pounds and was being escorted by her old friend Mick Flick.

On Wednesday December 6, publisher Sir George Weidenfeld gave a party at his Hyde Park home in honour of Mrs Marcia Williams, personal and political secretary to Mr Harold Wilson. Among those present were Mr Wilson himself, the Earl of Longford and his daughter Lady Antonia Fraser, and Mr Richard Crossman.

The following day, there was a violent scene at Manila in the Philippines when Madame Marcos, wife of the president, was attacked by a man armed with a machete as she was handing out awards to civic leaders. Her assailant was shot dead by security guards and Madame Marcos was rushed to hospital by helicopter where she was later reported to be making a good recovery after seventy-five stitches in her arms and face.

Back in Britain, on Monday December 11, it was revealed that the Queen had taken delivery of a £300 video cassette recorder, already in wide use in Japan and America, in order to enable her to record her favourite TV programmes and watch them later at her leisure.

The following day, at Marlborough Street Magistrates Court, a Saudi Arabian princess collapsed in the dock when she was fined £30 for shop-lifting. She had admitted stealing seven pairs of briefs from an Oxford Street store.

On Wednesday December 13, the League Against Cruel Sports claimed that their battle to stop Princess Anne's hunting activities was hotting up. 'We have spies everywhere, which includes Windsor Castle,' said secretary Mark Davies.

On Thursday December 14, Margaret Duchess of Argyll threw a party at the Dorchester Hotel to celebrate the eightieth birthday of her old friend Paul Getty. Among those present were Sir George Weidenfeld, the Duke of Bedford, banker Sir Kenneth Keith, American Ambassador Walter Annenberg, novelist Barbara Cartland, the vivacious Mrs Vere Harmsworth and President Nixon's daughter, Mrs Edward Cox. Absent from the event was Mr Getty's butler Bullimore, who felt obliged to remain in charge at Mr Getty's country home, Sutton Place.

American multi-millionaire Paul Getty gets a helping hand from his friend Margaret Duchess of Argyll as he cuts his eightieth birthday cake. President Nixon's daughter Mrs Patricia Cox is on the left

On Sunday December 17, Walter Annenberg was greeted with cries of 'Hypocrite' and 'Stop bombing in Vietnam' when he arrived at the Grand Ballroom in Broadstairs to see Mr Heath conduct the annual carol concert.

The following Tuesday December 19, 22-year-old fashion model Merilyn Lamb whose right arm had been mauled by one of John Aspinall's tigers two years earlier was awarded £10,600 in damages. A High Court judge ruled that Mr Aspinall himself was in no way to blame and gave judgement instead against his half-brother James Osborne who had invited Miss Lamb to stay at Mr Aspinall's house in Kent, where the tiger had lived in a private zoo.

On Thursday December 21, the twenty-first birthday of Earl Grosvenor, son and heir to the Duke of Westminster, was celebrated at Eaton Hall in Cheshire. Two giant marquees had been erected in the garden and there was a mammoth birthday cake, weighing 220 pounds, to cut into. Among those present were Earl Grosvenor's two sisters, Lady Jane and Lady Leonora Grosvenor, both of whom wore white.

The following day, some 10,000 feet up in the Andes, sixteen people were found alive where their plane had crashed ten weeks earlier. It was later revealed that they had survived only by eating the flesh of their dead comrades.

On Saturday December 23, an earthquake devastated the town of Managua in Nicaragua and disrupted the life of Mr Howard Hughes, who had occupied a floor of the Intercontinental Hotel for the past ten months. The billionaire recluse was carried from his suite and spent the next night in a limousine outside the battered hotel.

On Wednesday December 27, Princess Anne and her friend Lieutenant Mark Phillips went hunting in Gloucestershire. 'We killed a brace of foxes,' said the joint master of the Beaufort Hunt, Major Gerald Gundry. 'Princess Anne was not in at either kill. Then the weather deteriorated, the scent disappeared and it became very cold, damp and miserable.'

The same day, Mr Howard Hughes left earthquake-stricken Nicaragua in a private Jetstar aircraft.

Early on Thursday December 28, the eccentric multi-millionaire arrived at Gatwick airport near London where his plane taxied to a private part of the tarmac to deter intrusion. Hughes was then transferred to a curtained Rolls-Royce and driven into London where he was to find sanctuary in two penthouse suites at the Inn on the Park Hotel.

Later that day, various members of the Royal Family left London for Sandringham on board the royal train, accompanied by seven corgis.

Back in London the following day, a fellow guest of Mr Howard Hughes at the Inn on the Park Hotel, found that two pheasants he had shot had disappeared from the balcony of his suite. Enquiries revealed that aides of Mr Hughes had taken the birds, suspecting that they might contain bombs.

On Sunday December 31, a crowd of over 3,000 watched Princess Anne and her friend Lieutenant Mark Phillips arrive at church at Sandringham. The Lieutenant had already dismissed rumours that they were to marry as 'absolute nonsense'.

1973

During the next twelve months, things turn increasingly weird. In London, the Rocky Horror Show plays to packed houses, Andrew Logan launches his 'Alternative Miss World' contest and Angie Bowie and Bianca Jagger dance together at a party. The release of a four foot python at Queen Charlotte's Birthday Ball seems to signal the death rattle of the old-fashioned deb season. Meanwhile, ex-deb Jayne Harries appears at the Old Bailey on drug charges and another heiress Rose Dugdale faces the first of far more serious charges. Disaster also hits the international 'children of the night' when 16-year-old Paul Getty III disappears in Italy and is mutilated by his kidnappers. At the White House, President Nixon has an eerie summer as he becomes more and more isolated and incapacitated by the Watergate Affair and the resignation of his vice-president Spiro Agnew in scandalous circumstances is the least of his problems. International businessmen also come unstuck. Bernie Cornfeld begins a long spell on remand in Geneva's St Antoine prison, things begin to turn sour for Jim Slater, and the new Biba department store is doomed to disaster. In the autumn, the Arab oil embargo has massive repercussions causing petrol stations to close throughout the Western world. In America, there is indignation at being held to ransom by 'six sheiks and a shah', while in England the oil shortage is interlocked with a coal crisis and by the end of the year, the three-day week has been announced. Against this grim background the young Earl of Lucan leaves his wife, John and Martha Mitchell go their separate ways, Princess Margaret takes up with Roddy Llewellyn and the Burtons split up in a blaze of publicity. Throughout the year the press becomes more threatening. Messrs Woodward and Bernstein continue their dogged investigations in Washington while in England the News of the World is castigated for its unethical intrusion into the private life of Lord Lambton.

On New Year's day, thick fog prevented Mr Heath landing at Heathrow on his return from Canada. His RAF VC10 was diverted to Gatwick, where a car was waiting to drive him to Chequers.

On Wednesday January 3, Britain's entry into the Common Market was celebrated with a gala at the Royal Opera House, attended by the Queen, the Archbishop of Canterbury, the Prime Minister, Lord Goodman and hundreds of other illustrious figures.

The following night, a further celebration at Christie's auction rooms was thrown into confusion when a middle-aged woman accused Mr Heath of being a traitor and attempted to effect a citizen's arrest. After being bundled out of the building by security guards she explained, 'I am adamantly anti-Common Market and I felt this was the only way to put my views.'

Meanwhile, Lieutenant Mark Phillips, who had seen in the New Year at Sandringham, had been flown to Germany with his regiment, the 1st Queen's Dragoon Guards.

Over in Washington, on Monday January 8, the trial began of the seven men accused of breaking into the Democratic headquarters in the Watergate building the previous year. One of the defendants, Gordon Liddy, arrived at the court smoking a large cigar and smiling and waving confidently. The proceedings which followed were to be carefully scrutinized by Carl Bernstein and Bob Woodward.

Back in London, on Wednesday January 10, businessman Jimmy Goldsmith gave an all night party at the Ritz Hotel for his 18-year-old daughter Isabel. 250 guests danced to the music of the New Orleans Jazz orchestra which had been specially flown in from Louisiana. During the course of the night, a romance blossomed between Isabel Goldsmith and photographer Arnaud de Rosnay, whose eyes were said to have the greenish colour of fresh continental oysters.

On Sunday January 14, Dr Henry Kissinger left Paris after drafting terms for the ending of the Vietnam War. A few hours later he landed on a heavily guarded helicopter pad at Key Biscayne, and reported at once to President Nixon at his Florida villa.

The following morning in Washington, four of the defendants in the Watergate break-in case pleaded guilty to conspiracy and were led off to gaol.

A few hours later, reporter Bob Woodward lunched with Mrs Katharine Graham, proprietor of the *Washington Post*, in her private dining-room. Over eggs benedict, he was closely questioned about the sources of his Watergate stories. 'You've reassured me. You really have,' said Mrs Graham finally.

Back in London, on Tuesday January 16, in the High Court, author Ross McWhirter got a temporary ban on the showing of a TV documentary on Andy Warhol which he claimed contained obscene episodes. Warhol was informed of this decision in New York and remarked, 'How quaint and old-fashioned the English must be.'

The following Friday January 19, 24-year-old Prince Charles was on his way to visit the Hampshire home of his friend Tommy Sopwith when his new 160mph Aston Martin collided with a Triumph Herald saloon. 'The road is narrow, full of twists and turns and there was a hell of a fog around,' explained the licensee of the nearby Malthouse Inn.

Meanwhile, 28-year-old millionaire playboy Michael Pearson had discarded his famous yacht *The Hedonist* and ordered a new £600,000 vessel, complete with Westland Gazelle helicopter and landing pad.

On Monday January 22, a plane carrying Aristotle Onassis's 24-year-old son, Alexander, crashed on take off from Athens airport. He was taken from the wreckage severely injured and, after a three-hour operation, was placed on a life support system. Neurosurgeons were flown in from across the world in a vain attempt to save his life.

The following day, this family tragedy took away attention from the announcement in Washington that the Vietnam War, in which 56,000 American soldiers had died, was at an end.

Back in London the following weekend, the new Poet Laureate Sir John Betjeman was found wandering along King's Road, Chelsea, dressed in an old trilby, flapping overcoat and bright purple tie. 'Oh what fun it all is. Oh what fun. Gosh,' he was heard to remark.

On Monday January 29, the long drawn out examination of bankrupt architect John Poulson was enlivened when it was revealed that he had given former Labour Minister Anthony Crosland a silver coffee pot. 'I don't care tuppence about that damned pot,' said Crosland. 'It's of no interest to me. All I want to do is to get rid of the bloody thing.'

Back in Washington, on Tuesday January 30, Watergate burglars Gordon Liddy and James McCord were found guilty of wire-tapping, burglary and other offences. Judge Sirica commented afterwards, 'I have not been satisfied that all the pertinent facts that might be available have been produced.'

On Saturday February 3, Princess Anne and Lieutenant Mark Phillips, who had now been spotted kissing in public, spent the day at Mrs Alison Oliver's stables in Berkshire. 'There was a young man here with the Princess,' said Mrs Oliver, 'but it's so easy to confuse one with the other. I can't confirm anything.'

On Monday February 5, the ban on the TV documentary on Andy Warhol was lifted by the Court of Appeal. 'Viewing it as a whole, the film struck me as dull and dreary,' said 74-year-old draper's son Lord Denning. Sir Lew Grade, chief executive of ATV, which had originally commissioned the film said later, 'We will definitely transmit it.'

Back in Washington, on Wednesday February 7, the Senate passed a resolution to establish a select committee to investigate the planning and circumstances of the recent Watergate break-in.

Two days later, in New York, it was announced that the marriage arranged between David Frost and black actress Diahann Carroll would not take place. 'We can confirm that while remaining the best of friends after three glorious years together, we recently decided not to go ahead with our plans to get married,' ran the couple's statement.

On Saturday February 10, Princess Anne set off for an official visit to Ethiopia and the Sudan. En route to Addis Ababa she paused to be welcomed on board a Soviet warship in the Red Sea. 'I thought her very vivacious,' said her host Admiral Krugalov. 'She has got a brilliant future.'

Earlier that week in the House of Commons, Conservative MP Sir Gerald Nabarro had turned his attention to the Opposition leader's pipe smoking activities. 'I particularly deplore the sight of Mr Wilson going through the lobby with a large curved briar stuck in his mouth, puffing out fumes, noxious in character, which hang about the lobby.'

On Monday February 12, the first lot of American prisoners of war to be released in Hanoi arrived at the Clark Air Base in the Philippines. They wore tired, timid smiles and carried their own belongings out of the aircraft in plastic bags along with home-made banners reading 'God Bless America and Nixon.'

On Wednesday February 14, Princess Margaret arrived in Mustique for a month's private stay at her newly built four bedroom, three bathroom holiday home, Les Jolies Eaux. It was stated that Lord Snowdon had been prevented from joining her owing to pressures of work.

Meanwhile, a controversy over the film *Last Tango in Paris* was raging in Britain. On Friday February 16, the anti-pornography campaigner Raymond Blackburn said he was taking legal action against the film censor following the granting of an X certificate to the film, which was said to feature anal sex. Lord Harlech, President of the British Board of Film Censors, attempted to calm the storm by declaring, 'In the final analysis it is *I* who decide policy and *I* am the final arbiter of what is good taste and what is not.'

On Sunday February 18, tummy trouble forced Princess Anne to cut back on her tour of Ethiopia and the Sudan. 'We do not plan to fly out a British doctor for Princess Anne this time,' said a Buckingham Palace spokesman. 'She is only suffering from what any traveller can have and there are pills for that condition.'

The following day, the Princess watched thousands of pink flamingos, pelicans and storks land on Lake Abiata and was said to have completely recovered.

Three days later in Las Vegas, David Frost's former fiancée Diahann Carroll was married to boutique tycoon Fredde Glusman. 'Life is full of surprises,' said Frost, 'but if Diahann is happy then I am happy too. I wish them both all the happiness in the world.'

Back in Britain, on Sunday February 25, Liberal leader Jeremy Thorpe announced his engagement to the 46-year-old Countess of Harewood, to whom he had proposed a few days earlier over lunch at the Ritz. 'I have not been in the political world at all,' said Lady Harewood, former wife of the Queen's first cousin, at a champagne party at Mr Thorpe's Westminster flat. 'I shall have to learn my way.'

The same day, Princess Anne returned from the Sudan and climbed into her royal blue Reliant Scimitar sportscar and drove straight to the Wiltshire home of Lieutenant Mark Phillips. 'We have no knowledge of Princess Anne's movements since she arrived in Britain,' a Buckingham Palace spokesman said later.

The following Tuesday, there was an unpleasant encounter between the Princess and the press at Mrs Oliver's stables at Warfield in Berkshire. Lieutenant Phillips said 'Hello, chaps' to waiting reporters but Princess Anne said angrily, 'You're getting on my goat. Horses are very sensitive. They don't understand what all the fuss is about. Now you've upset him!'

On Thursday March 8, Paul McCartney was fined £100 by a court at Campbeltown, Argyllshire, for growing five cannabis plants in his Scottish greenhouse. 'I don't plan to come back to Campbeltown for some time,' he said after the hearing, throughout which his wife Linda had worn their lawyer's bowler hat.

The same day in Zurich, Mrs Edith Irving faced further charges in connection with the Howard Hughes affair and had been sentenced to two years' imprisonment. 'One must not joke with Swiss banks,' she had remarked earlier.

On Saturday March 10, the new Governor of Bermuda Sir Richard Sharples, his aide-de-camp Captain Hugh Sayers and his Great Dane, Horsa, were shot dead at close range as they strolled through the grounds of Government House after dinner.

The same night, a few hundred miles away on the island of Mustique, Princess Margaret gave an impromptu performance of the Bert Bacharach song 'Walk on by' at a private party given by Colin Tennant, accompanied by black barman Basil Charles.

On Wednesday March 14, Liberal leader Jeremy Thorpe and his new bride arrived in the South of France on their honeymoon. At Nice Airport, the Liberal leader, dressed in black homburg and velvet-collared overcoat, was spotted pushing his luggage to a hired car.

Earlier that week in London, Women's Lib campaigner Germaine Greer had lunched with Hollywood gossip columnist Sheilah Graham and had compared fur coats. 'She was wearing lynx, I think,' said Miss Graham. 'Mine was mink.'

On Thursday March 15, *Last Tango in Paris* opened in London. One of the first people to see the film was 92-year-old Mrs Emily Tippett from Midhurst in Sussex, who was helped up the cinema steps by a doorman. 'I have come because I want to see the muckiest film advertised. If it sounds mucky then it's for me. What I am interested in is a bit of fun. You're never too old. I like variety.'

Later that day in Washington, President Nixon's historic announcement that veteran diplomat David Bruce was to become America's first *de facto* ambassador to China was ignored by journalists, whose only interest was the continuing Watergate Scandal.

The following day, high cheek boned Mrs Pat Nixon celebrated her sixty-first birthday. 'I look forward very much to spending the next five years in the White House,' she said.

Back in Britain that night, Lieutenant Mark Phillips denied that there was any romance between him and Princess Anne. 'I hope now that all this interest in Princess Anne and myself will stop,' he said at his Wiltshire home. 'Princess Anne and I are just good friends with a common interest and a great love for horses. There is nothing more to it than that.'

The elderly Duchess of Windsor potters about outside her house in the Bois de Boulogne, accompanied by her pug dogs

Two days later at Nashville, Tennessee, there was an illustrious gathering of members of the wealthy and widespread Vanderbilt family. Among those present was the new Duke of Marlborough, whose grandfather had married Miss Consuelo Vanderbilt in 1895.

On Wednesday March 21 a crucial meeting took place in the Oval Office at the White House between President Nixon and his aide John Dean who told him, 'There is a cancer growing on the Presidency.'

The following day, it was revealed that Senator Proxmire had put down his $2,758 hair transplant as a medical expense on the previous year's tax form.

On Friday March 23, former Beatle John Lennon was told that he must leave the United States within sixty days on account of his conviction in London five years earlier for possessing marijuana. His wife, Yoko Ono, was permitted to stay in the country. Announcing that he would appeal against the ruling, Lennon said, 'Having just celebrated our fourth anniversary, we're not prepared to sleep in separate beds.'

On Saturday March 24, writer Christopher Isherwood, who had been resident in America for many years, made a public statement about his homosexuality but claimed that he had now achieved 'senior citizen respectability'.

Two days later, fellow bachelor Sir Noël Coward died at his hilltop retreat in Jamaica. He had gone to bed the previous night in high spirits, telling his guests Cole Lesley and Graham Payn, 'Goodnight my darlings, I'll see you tomorrow.'

On Tuesday March 27, Mrs Martha Mitchell telephoned the *New York Times* and said that someone was trying to make a 'goat' of her husband. 'They are not going to pin anything on him,' she declared. 'I won't let them, and I don't give a damn who gets hurt; I can name names.'

That night in Britain, the controversial documentary on Andy Warhol was shown on TV generating about a hundred telephone calls of complaint. 'Most people thought it was a load of old rubbish,' said a spokesman.

The same day, in the High Court a judge had ruled that model Penny Brahms was entitled to the fortune left by her husband Clive Raphael, whose will had been shown to be a fake. 'It may sound corny,' said Miss Brahms from her Dorset manorhouse, 'but my life won't change. I lead a very quiet life these days and don't get up to London often.'

Meanwhile, the four times married Duke of Argyll, a tax exile in Paris for the past four years, had been struck down by a stroke and flown home to Scotland for emergency treatment at a National Health hospital. This move incensed Labour MP Willie Hamilton who, on Friday April 6, challenged the Duke's right to National Health facilities and said he should be 'sent packing back to France'.

On Saturday April 7, the 73-year-old Duke died in a private nursing home in Edinburgh.

The following day, 95-year-old Pablo Picasso died at his barbed wire barricaded villa in the South of France. His demise was followed by worldwide speculation about his huge fortune and the whereabouts of his enormous collection of paintings. 'No one knows just how many of his works he kept,' said his old friend Sir Roland Penrose. 'They are scattered around all over the place.' At his house at Mougins, near Nice, wads of notes and uncashed cheques were found.

Back in London, on Tuesday April 10, the Earl of Longford and Mrs Mary Whitehouse lunched together at the Gay Hussar restaurant in Soho. After lunch, the two anti-pornography campaigners embraced warmly before departing in separate taxis.

Early the following morning, Picasso's embalmed remains were taken in a black Citroen DS across the snow covered Provençal countryside for burial at his forty-room castle in Vauvenargues.

The following day, the painter's grandson, Pablito, who had been working as a telegraphist and had been refused permission to pay his last respects to his grandfather, killed himself by drinking concentrated bleach.

Back in London, on Friday April 13, the marriage took place at the Chapel Royal, St James's Palace, between the Hon Anthony Tryon, only son of Lord Tryon, and Miss Dale Harper, daughter of popular Melbourne publisher, Mr Barry Harper. Among those present was Princess Margaret, who had lent the happy couple her new house on Mustique for their honeymoon.

The same day, it was revealed that Bernie Cornfeld was selling his luxurious Swiss home. 'It's probably the nicest property in Geneva,' said an aide. 'Bernie's spending so little time in Europe now that he doesn't need the house any more.'

On Saturday April 14, Lieutenant Mark Phillips was thrown by his horse Columbus and totally immersed in a lake at the Badminton Horse Trials.

That night in Washington, the White House Correspondents Association held its annual dinner at the Hilton Hotel. Among those present were *Washington Post* reporters Carl Bernstein and Bob Woodward and White House aides H. R. Haldeman and John Ehrlichman. President Nixon looked in on the event after dinner, flanked by a retinue of Vietnam prisoners of war.

On Tuesday April 17, President Nixon's hands were shaking when he told a press conference at the White House that there had been 'major developments' in the Watergate case and White House executives must now answer all proper questions and none should be given immunity. His press officer, Ron Ziegler, then informed those present that all previous statements on the Watergate matter were 'inoperative'.

Back in Britain that night, the Queen gave a dinner party at Windsor Castle which was attended by the Soviet Ambassador, Mikhail Smirnovsky and his wife Lyudmila, Prime Minister Edward Heath and the new Poet Laureate Sir John Betjeman.

Earlier that day, a nationwide Petition for Public Decency had come to its climax when Mrs Mary Whitehouse and seventeen young supporters called at 10 Downing Street carrying bundles of petitions bearing 1,350,000 signatures. 'Young people are waking up to the fact they've been conned,' she declared.

On Wednesday April 18, the boardroom drama of the decade began when self-made millionaire 'Tiny' Rowland obtained an injunction in the High Court to prevent his dismissal as chief executive of the Lonrho company.

On Easter Saturday April 21, the Queen gave another dinner party at Windsor Castle, at which the guests of honour were the Prime Minister of Australia and Mrs Gough Whitlam. The menu on this occasion included fresh salmon, boiled potatoes, cucumber in sour cream and a pineapple bombe.

On Thursday April 26, there was further excitement in business circles when it was announced that Slater Walker was to merge with Britain's biggest merchant bank, Hill Samuel. Grammar school educated Jim Slater and Norfolk squire Sir Kenneth Keith explained the deal to financial journalists with expressive hand gestures by Mr Slater, whom an admirer described as 'a man with an instinct for the clever deal, something you can't analyse or copy'.

The following Monday, April 30, President Nixon went on television to announce the resignation of White House executives Bob Haldeman and John Ehrlichman, the dismissal of John Dean and to praise the 'vigorous free press' which had brought about about their downfall. 'There can be no whitewash at the White House,' he said. 'Two wrongs do not make a right.'

The following day, White House Press Secretary Ronald Ziegler, publicly apologized to the *Washington Post* and its two reporters, Woodward and Bernstein, for his earlier criticism of their investigative reporting. 'I was over-enthusiastic in my comments,' he confessed, 'particularly if you look at them in the context of the developments that have taken place.'

Later, Bob Woodward telephoned Mr Ziegler at the White House and thanked him for his statement.

On Thursday May 3 in New York, a warrant was issued for the arrest of tycoon Robert Vesco after he failed to appear before a grand jury to answer accusations of illegally contributing $200,000 to President Nixon's re-election campaign. Vesco had last been seen in Nassau, Bahamas, and his present whereabouts were unknown.

The same day in Washington, former White House officials Haldeman and Ehrlichman appeared before a grand jury accused of conspiring with former Attorney-General John Mitchell to effect the Watergate cover-up. Both men said they could clear themselves of all accusations against them.

Later that night, President Nixon suddenly left the White House in a deep depression to spend a long weekend at his home in Florida.

Back in London, on Monday May 7, 22-year-old ex-debutante Jayne Harries, who had run away to marry a hairdresser five years earlier, pleaded guilty to possessing cannabis and was remanded in custody for the night in Holloway gaol.

The following morning, she reappeared in the dock at the Old Bailey to be fined £350 and be told by Judge Gwyn Morris, 'You appear to be a useless member of the community enjoying a large income which you do not earn.' She said afterwards, 'I am going to prove the judge wrong. I am going to do some good in the world.'

That night, debutantes at Queen Charlotte's birthday ball at Grosvenor House were sent scurrying when a four foot python was released in the ball-room. The organizer of this practical joke was identified as 21-year-old Stephen Evans-Freke, whose mother Lady Carbery said later, 'These things don't amuse me very much but I'm not surprised. Stephen has always been fond of animals. He once trained a pig to follow him round the house like a dog.'

On Thursday May 10, the indictment of former American Attorney-General John Mitchell on charges of conspiring to obtain a secret contribution of $200,000 from Mr Robert Vesco to President Nixon's re-election campaign fund made headline news throughout the world. 'There has been no wrong-doing on my part,' he insisted.

The following day in Los Angeles, the trial of Dr Daniel Ellsberg ended in chaos with the dismissal of all charges against him. 'I am planning to file a suit against the President,' said Ellsberg afterwards. 'We will bring a suit against all the conspirators – of which the President appears to be the ring-leader.'

On Monday May 14, Bernie Cornfeld was arrested in Geneva, given ten minutes to pack and bundled off to the city's St Antoine Gaol to face charges of defrauding IOS investors. The financier had spent the previous weekend at his château in France and had come to Geneva confident that he would not be 'personally inconvenienced'.

The same day in Paris, talks began between King Faisal of Saudi Arabia and

President Pompidou, who was anxious to sell his royal guest Mirage jet fighter bombers. During the King's speech at the Elysée Palace that night, the President appeared unwell and repeatedly mopped his neck.

The following day in London, Prime Minister Heath condemned some of the business practices being revealed by the currently running Lonrho affair as 'the unpleasant and unacceptable face of capitalism'.

Back in Washington, on Thursday May 17, the Senate Watergate Committee began its public hearings in the great marble caucus room of the Old Senate Building. Many VIPs were present and the proceedings were dominated by 76-year-old constitutional scholar Senator Sam Ervin of North Carolina. Millions were to watch the dramas that followed on colour TV.

Over in Windsor Great Park, on Friday May 18, the Queen was found sprinting after a disobedient corgi. The offending pet was quickly snatched up, scolded and bundled into a Land-Rover.

Earlier that day, Russian leader Mr Brezhnev had arrived in Bonn in an extremely friendly mood. On meeting the Norwegian-born Mrs Rut Brandt, he first kissed her hand and then showered her with compliments. 'You are the first person I am going to invite to Moscow.' Later that day after a formal banquet, he settled down on a sofa beside Mrs Brandt and said, 'All Moscow will lie at your feet.' During his day visit the Russian leader was frequently seen fumbling for his cigarette case and then borrowing cigarettes from whichever aide was closest to him.

Soviet Leader Leonid Brezhnev poses with Chancellor Willy Brandt and his wife Rut. Mr Brezhnev later tells Mrs Brandt, 'All Moscow will lie at your feet'

Back in London on Monday May 21, the Queen and many members of the royal family were present at a belated ninetieth birthday party for Princess Alice, Countess of Athlone, only surviving grandchild of Queen Victoria. Princess Alice wore a tiara and a white mink stole and Queen Juliana of the Netherlands arrived at the party in Carlton House Terrace carrying a gift-wrapped present.

On Tuesday May 22, junior minister Lord Lambton announced that he was retiring as both minister and MP 'for personal and health reasons'.

Later that day in Washington, President Nixon issued a 4,000 word statement denying any knowledge of the Watergate burglary and subsequent cover-up and stating his firm resolve to stay in office and 'do the job he was elected to do'.

Back in London, on Wednesday May 23, Lord Lambton issued a full statement admitting to 'a casual acquaintance with a call girl and one or two of her friends' but emphasizing that there had been 'no high life vice ring, no security leak and no blackmail'. The statement ended with a plea that criticism for his wrong-doings should be 'instantaneous and not prolonged'.

On Thursday May 24, there was further excitement when Earl Jellicoe resigned as Lord Privy Seal after admitting to some casual affairs with call girls.

The following day, former minister John Profumo, who had been at the centre of another major sex scandal ten years earlier, was present with his wife Valerie at a memorial service for the late Sir Noël Coward at St Martin-in-the-Fields. Also present were Mr Charles Chaplin, Earl Mountbatten of Burma, Margaret Duchess of Argyll, Sir Cecil Beaton, Mr and Mrs Jeremy Thorpe and Lady Diana Cooper. In an address to the congregation, Sir John Betjeman stated, 'Noël not only possessed all the Christian virtues. He practised them.'

Later that day, Lord Lambton explained his recent sexual behaviour in a very frank TV interview with Robin Day. Sipping a drink with a slice of lemon in it, Lord Lambton said, 'I think people sometimes like variety. I think it's as simple as that and I think this impulse is understood by almost everybody.' Meanwhile Lady Lambton had stated that it was 'utterly ridiculous' to suggest that her husband's recent confessions would break up their marriage.

On Monday May 28, the police announced that they were anxious to interview Mrs Norma Levy, the call girl in the Lambton affair, and her husband Colin 'in

'Sloane Ranger' Princess Anne and her fiancé Lieutenant Mark Phillips arrive in London on the royal train after spending the spring holiday at Balmoral Castle. Note the Princess's headscarf tied to her handbag

connection with criminal offences'. The couple had last been seen at the Moham-media Hotel in Casablanca, Morocco, a former haunt of the late Sir Winston Churchill.

On Tuesday May 29, Buckingham Palace announced that Princess Anne was to marry Lieutenant Mark Phillips, Olympic equestrian and son of a director of the Walls pork pie and ice-cream firm. Among those to express their delight at the match was the 76-year-old Duchess of Windsor, who said at her Paris home, 'I have never met the young man but of course I know Princess Anne very well. I wish them all the happiness in the world.'

The following day, the happy couple posed for photographs with their respective parents on the lawn at Buckingham Palace. Later, Lieutenant Phillips's blue BMW failed to start and its flat battery was quickly fixed by palace staff.

Meanwhile, down at the Phillipses' sixteenth-century home at Great Somerford in Wiltshire, Mark's grandmother, Mrs Tiarks, had declared, 'I'm just Old Gran. I had nothing to do with it.'

Mr 'Tiny' Rowland, who successfully withstood an attempt to dismiss him as chief executive and managing director of the giant mining and trading company, Lonrho

On Thursday May 31, the boardroom battle at Lonrho ended with a wild meeting at the Central Hall, Westminster, at which one portly shareholder gave an imper-sonation of Sir Winston Churchill. Mr 'Tiny' Rowland was finally reaffirmed as chief executive of the company and left the hall stating, 'I am an extremely happy man.'

On Sunday June 3, an admission by the *News of the World* that compromising photographs of Lord Lambton had been taken by one of its photographers was followed by demands for a full Press Council enquiry into this unethical behaviour.

The same day, an ancient scandal was revived when 76-year-old Lord Ampthill died leaving two putative sons and heirs: 52-year-old Geoffrey Russell, whose legitimacy had been the subject of lengthy court cases fifty years earlier, and his 24-year-old half-brother John. Both men were to make applications to the House of Lords to succeed to the title.

On Monday June 4, Princess Anne and her fiancé arrived at Wolfsgarten Castle near Frankfurt in a borrowed Mercedes 350 SL to dine with Princess Margaret of Hesse and fifteen other German relatives of Princess Anne.

Meanwhile, in St Antoine prison in Geneva, 45-year-old Bernie Cornfeld was passing the time playing backgammon with fellow inmates. 'Don't forget that he didn't always live in luxury,' said his lawyer, Raymond Nicolet. 'He tells me it has not been difficult to accept a simple life.' The famous financier's trial date had still not been fixed.

Back in London, on Tuesday June 5, Jim Slater appeared at his company's annual general meeting looking bronzed and fit. 'I will go on in this business until I die or until I retire,' he stated, adding that he was unperturbed by recent press reports about the state of the company. 'It was an attempt to get at us by innuendo. All the facts I have checked so far were wrong.'

On Wednesday June 6, 80-year-old Paul Getty was dining with his friend Margaret Duchess of Argyll at her house in Upper Grosvenor Street, Mayfair, when he learnt that his 48-year-old son George had died in Los Angeles after an overdose of barbiturates and alcohol. 'A great sadness has descended on this place,' a lodge keeper said later at the multi-millionaire's 1,000-acre Surrey estate.

The following day, the United States government requested the extradition of financier Robert Vesco from Costa Rica. It was soon discovered that he had already left the country and was now thought to be in the Bahamas.

On Monday June 11 in London, Princess Margaret joined financier Sir Charles Clore, Baron Heinrich Thyssen, David Frost and other celebrities at the Pied Piper Ball at the Dorchester Hotel organized by the fun-loving Mrs Vere Harmsworth, now known in certain circles by the nickname 'Bubbles'.

Two days later, Lord Lambton appeared at Marylebone Magistrates Court in his usual dark glasses and pleaded guilty to possessing cannabis and amphetamines. He made no statement during the thirty-minute hearing and was fined £300.

On Monday June 18, Opposition leader Harold Wilson made some scathing remarks about the new price levels and said his wife Mary had recently returned from shopping almost in tears. 'She had seen a little old lady clutching a pathetic little plastic package of two slices of meat loaf,' he said.

On Tuesday June 19, it was announced that Slater Walker Company and the Hill Samuel Bank were severing their engagement following the disclosure of 'fundamental differences in work-style and personalities'. The announcement was followed by a terse 'No comment' from 44-year-old Mr Slater.

Later that day, Mick and Bianca Jagger and their 20-month-old daughter Jade left London for Rome, unconcerned about claims by American singer Marsha Hunt that Jagger was the father of her two-year-old baby girl. 'I don't give a damn,' said Bianca at Heathrow Airport. 'People can say what they like. Mick and I are very happy.'

That night, a weird new musical *The Rocky Horror Show* opened in London. The production, staged by impresario Michael White, was said to combine elements of science fiction, rock music, bondage, rubber wear, high camp and the Dracula myth.

On Thursday June 21, 32-year-old Rose Dugdale, an ex-debutante and doctor of philosophy, appeared in court at Axminster in Devon accused of stealing £100,000 worth of paintings, jewellery and silver from the home of her father, Colonel James Dugdale. Applying for bail, Dr Dugdale said, 'I am in this court accused of the heinous crime of stealing from my parents and there is absolutely no question that I shall answer bail and clear myself of that charge.'

The following morning, a warrant under the Sexual Offences Act was issued for the arrest of Mrs Norma Levy, the prostitute at the centre of the Lambton Affair, and her husband Colin. The couple had last been seen in San Tropez and were thought to be staying in a rented villa somewhere on the Spanish coast.

Later that day, architect John Poulson and Scottish civil servant William George Pottinger were arrested by officers of the Fraud Squad and charged with conspiracy to corrupt. Mr Poulson was watching a TV programme *Money at Work* when the police arrived and Mr Pottinger was apprehended after being called from a golf club dinner.

Meanwhile, Soviet leader Mr Brezhnev was on an extended visit to the United States. On Sunday June 24, he and President Nixon signed a joint communiqué at San Clemente, California which was followed by a Hollywood-style party attended by Dr Henry Kissinger and actress Jill St John at which the Soviet leader was lifted off the ground by cowboy actor Chuck Connors.

The following morning, sacked White House executive John Dean finally appeared before the Watergate Committee. For the next three days, he was to accuse President Nixon of lying about the affair and volunteered to take the lie detector test if any detail of his testimony was questioned. 'I think that when the facts come out the President will be forgiven,' he said.

On the night of Wednesday June 27, the White House broke its silence and unleashed its counter-offensive naming Mr Dean as 'the chief actor in the Watergate cover-up'.

Back in Britain on Thursday June 28, squealing teenage admirers of 17-year-old Swedish tennis player Bjorn Borg turned out in force to watch their hero make his Wimbledon debut and beat Germany's Karl Meiler in the third round of the tennis championships.

Female fans of Bjorn Borg reach out to touch their hero as he enters the court at the start of the Wimbledon lawn tennis championship

That night in Paris, the marriage of Jimmy Goldsmith's 19-year-old d[...]
Isabel and dashingly handsome jet-set photographer Baron Arnaud de[...]
was celebrated at a banquet at the Restaurant Laurent in the Champs[...]
Among the 200 guests were Lady Annabel Birley, Michael Pearson, John [...]
Dominic Elwes, Nicholas Soames and the 38-year-old Earl of Lucan.

Two days later, on Saturday June 30, novelist Nancy Mitford died of can[...]
her home in Versailles.

Jimmy Goldsmith's daughter Isabel and photographer Baron Arnaud de Rosnay after their marriage in Paris. The bridegroom's eyes were said to have 'the greenish colour of fresh continental oysters'

On Tuesday July 3, headlines blazed the news that the nine-year marriage between Richard Burton and Elizabeth Taylor was on the rocks. 'I am convinced it would be a good and constructive idea if Richard and I separated for a while,' said Miss Taylor in a statement from the Regency Hotel on New York's Park Avenue. 'Wish us well please during this difficult time.' At his cottage on Long Island, her husband declared, 'There is no question of our love and devotion for each other.'

On Wednesday July 4, the marriage took place in the Guards Chapel in London between amateur rider Major Andrew Parker-Bowles and Miss Camilla Shand, great-grandaughter of the late Mrs Keppel, mistress of King Edward VII. At the ceremony, which was attended by Princess Margaret and the Queen Mother, the bride wore a gown of wild silk organdie and a tulle veil held in place by a diamond tiara.

That night, the 'beautiful people' of the pop music world gathered at the Café Royal to celebrate singer David Bowie's retirement from concert life. Among those present, some of whom arrived in white Rolls-Royces with smoked glass windows, were Mick and Bianca Jagger, fashion designer Ossie Clark, Ringo Starr, Barbra

Streisand and Britt Ekland. At the party David Bowie, who wore a satin suit and had his hair dyed a fluorescent red, looked on while his wife Angie danced with Bianca Jagger.

The following day, the new Soviet Ambassador Mr Nikolai Lunkov was taken in a horse drawn carriage to present his credentials to the Queen at Buckingham Palace. As his coach passed through Hyde Park, a woman demonstrating on behalf of Soviet Jewry attempted to throw a bundle of 300 letters into his lap.

Meanwhile, the Duke and Duchess of Windsor's former country home at Gif-sur-Yvette near Paris, had at last found a purchaser. The new owner, Swiss millionaire Edmond Antar, said he would be preserving the property's walled English garden and keeping on the Windsors' old gardeners, Henri and René.

Back in Britain, on Monday July 9, Princess Anne made headlines when she refused to show her engagement ring to unruly children at a playschool near Edinburgh and told some of those present that they were 'twits'.

On Tuesday July 10, Prince Charles was attending Independence Day celebrations in Nassau when a heavy steel cable snapped and a yellow and aquamarine canopy collapsed on top of dignatories. The Prince reacted to this catastrophe with a hearty laugh.

The same day in Beverly Hills, Elizabeth Taylor had stated that she was still in love with Richard Burton. 'There is no other man in my life and there is no other woman in his life,' she said. Her friend Edith Head added, 'No two people could love each other more.'

That night, Miss Taylor went round to some friends to watch the former Attorney-General John Mitchell appear on television before Senator Sam Ervin and, with his hands trembling, admit his own complicity in the Watergate plot but claim that he had kept the President totally in the dark.

Meanwhile in Italy, a nationwide search had begun following the disappearance of Paul Getty's 16-year-old grandson, Paul Getty III. It was noted that the long haired youth, one of Rome's 'children of the night', had stayed the previous weekend with film director Roman Polanski and had last been seen in Rome's Piazza Navona.

On Wednesday July 11, the 77-year-old Duchess of Windsor paid a secret visit to England to visit her husband's grave in the royal burial ground at Frogmore and lunch at Windsor Castle with Lord Mountbatten and the Duke of Kent.

On Thursday July 12, President Nixon was admitted to Bethesda Naval Hospital in Washington suffering from viral pneumonia. 'We have a sick man on our hands,' said his physician Dr Walter Tkach.

The following day, the Watergate proceedings took a dramatic turn when a junior White House executive, Alexander Butterfield, revealed that the President had secretly tape-recorded his conversations with every visitor to the White House. This awe-inspiring statement was greeted with a stunned silence.

On Saturday July 14, competitors in the British Grand Prix included young racing motorist James Hunt, whose sporting activities were now being financed by the refreshingly flamboyant 22-year-old Lord Hesketh, noted for his mono-grammed and coronetted shirts and diamond-encrusted Rolex watch hewn from solid gold.

On Sunday July 15, Mrs Norma Levy arrived at Heathrow Airport and was immediately arrested by special branch police and accused of attempting to procure a girl for prostitution. 'I want to face up to everything,' she said. 'The only worries I have are the creases in my skirt. I hate to look scruffy.' Twelve hours

Dishy 25-year-old stockbroker's son James Hunt, a member of Lord Hesketh's motor racing team

later she was to appear in court and be released on £10,000 bail.

On Tuesday July 17, the death occurred in London's Dorchester Hotel of millionaire shipping recluse Sir John Ellerman who had successfully avoided personal publicity all his life. His funeral took place in private and it was later disclosed that he had left a fortune of over £57 million.

Meanwhile, further down Park Lane, fellow millionaire recluse Howard Hughes had emerged from his ninth floor suite at the Inn on the Park and made several excursions, heavily disguised with the help of wig-maker Leonard Pountney.

On Wednesday July 18, attention turned to Italy where a four-page letter from the missing Paul Getty III had revealed that he was being held by unscrupulous men though no specific ransom was mentioned.

Two days later, a reunion between Elizabeth Taylor and Richard Burton took place at Rome Airport. Miss Taylor had flown in from California in a private jet dressed in faded denim jeans and accompanied by her two shih-tzu dogs and black cat, Cassius. Burton cradled his wife's head in his arms as they were driven off in a bottle green Rolls-Royce to the home of film producer Carlo Ponti.

The same day in Washington, President Nixon was released from hospital declaring, 'Let others wallow it in Watergate. We are going to get on with the job we were elected to do.' That weekend, he was to drive seventy miles to Camp David to think over his reply to Senator Ervin's demand for immediate access to the White House tapes.

Back in London, on Sunday July 22, Mr and Mrs Jeremy Thorpe celebrated their recent marriage with a party at the Royal Opera House attended by over 900 guests. Among them were new Liberal MP Cyril Smith and his mother, actress Honor Blackman, violinist Yehudi Menuhin and Mr and Mrs Reggie Maudling, who arrived in a five-year-old Triumph Herald.

On Monday July 23, President Nixon's flat refusal to hand over the White House tapes was met with a unanimous vote by the Senate Watergate Committee to serve a subpoena on him.

The following night, the President welcomed the Shah of Iran to a state dinner at the White House.

On Wednesday July 25, financier Robert Vesco, for whose arrest a warrant had been issued months earlier, was found relaxing on his tennis court on the Island of Grand Bahama, 100 miles off the Florida coast. 'I'm staying put until I think the time is right to answer all the charges,' he said.

Back in Britain the following day, multi-millionaire Paul Getty explained why he had refused to meet any ransom demand for his kidnapped grandson. 'I have fourteen other grandchildren,' he said. 'If I paid out a brass farthing for one I would have fourteen kidnapped grandchildren.'

On Friday July 27, bearded television personality and cookery expert Clement Freud, grandson of the founder of psychoanalysis, was elected Liberal MP for Ely.

Meanwhile, on his Mediterranean island of Skorpios, 67-year-old Aristotle Onassis had had a glass fibre slide attached to his yacht *Christina* specially 'water-ized' so that he could glide into the sea.

On Monday July 30, Elizabeth Taylor swept out of the Italian home of film producer Carlo Ponti and Sophia Loren where she had been staying with her husband Richard Burton, and moved into Rome's Grand Hotel. An announcement followed that steps were being taken to 'legally conclude' the Burtons' nine-year-old marriage.

Back in Britain, on Tuesday July 31, Princess Anne's fiancé Lieutenant Mark Phillips appeared before Salisbury magistrates to answer a charge of dangerous driving in his BMW sports saloon. The 24-year-old Lieutenant told the court that 'a car just popped up from nowhere on the right-hand side of the road' and the case against him was dismissed.

The same day in London, 26-year-old Norma Levy appeared before Marylebone magistrates in a neat brown and white check suit and pleaded guilty to three charges of influencing prostitutes for gain. She was fined £75 on each charge and told by the magistrate, 'It is not an offence to be a prostitute but activities connected with prostitution are regarded as serious offences by the law.'

Back in Italy, on Thursday August 2, it was announced that the kidnappers of Paul Getty III had demanded 10,000 million lire ransom. The Getty family's lawyer replied that they must make their demands 'more realistic'.

On Monday August 6, it was revealed that Princess Anne disliked marzipan and her wedding cake, currently being made by the Army Catering Corps, would contain only the minimum of this substance.

On Tuesday August 7, the Watergate Committee adjourned for the summer recess. It was noted that the official transcript of the proceedings so far already ran to three times the length of the Bible. Meanwhile, President Nixon had declared, 'Let others spend their time dealing with murky, small, unimportant things. We have spent our time, and will spend our time, building a better world.'

On Wednesday August 8, Vice-President Spiro Agnew dismissed allegations that he had received $1,000 a week in pay-offs for contracts as 'damned lies'. At a press conference, he stated, 'I have no intention of being skewered in this fashion.' This firm denial brought him a flood of praise and telegrams and letters.

Back in Europe, on Thursday August 9, the elderly Duchess of Windsor arrived in Biarritz for a holiday at the Hôtel de Palais with her old friends Grace, Countess of Dudley and the Countess of Sefton, known to her friends as 'Foxy'.

The following day, Harold Wilson and his labrador Paddy were hauled out of the sea by holiday-makers off the Scilly Isles. It was explained that the small rubber dinghy carrying him to a friend's boat had capsized and the Opposition leader, who was wearing a high buoyancy jacket, had spent half an hour in the water. 'It was that bloody dog's fault,' he said later.

The same day, Prime Minister Heath flew home from the Commonwealth Prime Ministers' conference in Canada and drove straight from Heathrow to take part in the 605-mile Fastnet Race on board his £40,000 yacht *Morning Cloud*. It was noted that fast patrol boats and a long range Sea King helicopter would be monitoring the race in order to take the Prime Minister back to land in the event of urgent affairs of state.

On Tuesday August 14, Elizabeth Taylor was found on holiday at film producer Franco Zeffirelli's seaside home at Positano. She was accompanied by a new friend, Californian businessman Henry Wynberg.

Back in London, on Thursday August 16, where the temperature had now hit 88°F, the wife of a middle-eastern banker was gaoled for thirty days for stealing a pair of mittens, a hat and a sweater from a Mothercare shop. Refusing bail, magistrate Mr St John Harmsworth said, 'This is a typical case of a wealthy woman shop-lifting.'

Two days later, a Saudi Arabian princess and her maid, currently staying at the Dorchester Hotel, were arrested at another Mothercare shop and charged with shoplifting. 'There is no need for me to steal from your shop. I don't take £30 or £40 when I go shopping. I take millions,' said the princess, who later successfully claimed diplomatic immunity.

On Tuesday August 21, a spate of IRA fire and letter bombs hit London. Deputy Assistant Commissioner Ernest Bond of New Scotland Yard urged the public to be wary when opening mail. 'These bombs are lethal and could blow a man in half,' he said.

Three days later, a book bomb exploded on the twenty-second floor of the Stock Exchange building, injuring Mr George Brind, who had worked for the institution since 1928, and blowing a hole through his desk.

On Sunday August 26, it was announced that artist David Hockney had become disenchanted with the London scene and was leaving for Paris. He had asked his dealer, Kasmin, to rent a flat for him in Montparnasse or Saint-Germain. It was noted that he could only speak a few words of French.

On Monday August 27, terrorist violence spread to Washington when a letter bomb exploded at the British Embassy, blowing the hand off a woman secretary.

The following day in Moscow, Nobel Prize winning novelist Alexander Solzhenitsyn told Western correspondents that his life had been threatened. 'If I am suddenly declared dead or suddenly mysteriously killed the world could conclude that I have been killed with the approval of the KGB, or by it,' he said.

Five days later, on Sunday September 2, Moscow society was enlivened by the presence of the Duke of Edinburgh, who had arrived in the capital piloting his own plane. That night, the Duke dined with the retiring British Ambassador Sir John Killick, whose Trinidadian butler Grafton was said to be one of the leading 'personalities' in the capital.

Back in London, on Tuesday September 4, Mr Heath claimed that the IRA terror campaign had already failed because of the determination of the government and the British people not to give in to 'the wicked men who have conspired to commit these crimes'.

On Wednesday September 5, Colin Tennant gave a lunch party at the Café Royal in Edinburgh at which Princess Margaret was introduced to 25-year-old

Roddy Llewellyn, handsome younger son of Olympic equestrian Harry Llewellyn. After lunch the Princess took Mr Llewellyn shopping in the city and helped him purchase a pair of swimming trunks emblazoned with the Union Jack.

The following day, there was a reception at Blenheim Palace to launch a new tour of England by the Rolling Stones. During this party, the Duke of Marlborough's butler Mr Wadman told Mick Jagger, 'I always thought you were detestable. I now know that you are a very nice man.'

Back in Moscow that day, author Alexander Solzhenitsyn told Western correspondents that the police had seized the manuscript of his unpublished book about the Stalinist labour camps.

The following day in Kiev, Princess Anne and Captain Mark Phillips were driven away at high speed in official Soviet cars to avoid the attentions of Western reporters attending the Kiev horse trials.

On Saturday September 8, the Princess fell at the second jump during the cross-country phase of this event, breaking her collar-bone. She was attended by the British Embassy doctor Dr David Woodhead and later described her mishap as 'like landing on tarmac'.

Back in London that night, Mick Jagger wriggled and pranced in front of 10,000 people at a concert at Wembley stadium wearing a motorcycle jacket on top of a skin-tight one piece leather garment designed by Ossie Clark. Twenty feet away from the platform were his wife Bianca and 23-month-old daughter Jade. Bianca had a long cigarette-holder in her mouth and according to one observer looked 'like a Sunday school teacher.'

On Monday September 10 the new Thirties-style Biba department store opened in London complete with art deco cash registers and seven miles of specially woven carpet.

On Wednesday September 12, Lord George-Brown was banned from driving for twelve months and fined £75 after the incident the previous year when he had crashed his Jaguar into a brick wall and was found to have an excess of alcohol in his blood. 'Since the accident, I've only driven two or three times. I've found you can get around very successfully by public transport,' he said.

On Friday September 14 in New York, a Court of Appeal permitted freelance photographer Ron Galella, who specialized in photographs of Jackie Onassis and her two children, to come within twenty-five feet of his subjects. An earlier court ruling had forbidden Galella to go within 150 feet of Mrs Onassis and her children and he had claimed that he was unable to earn a living.

On Saturday September 15, the world's oldest reigning monarch 90-year-old King Gustaf of Sweden died in hospital and the throne passed to his 27-year-old grandson Carl Gustaf who was described as a 'disco-dancing playboy'.

On Tuesday September 18, the Watergate Committee said it was focusing its investigations on 'the President's own possible criminality'.

The same day, the confirmation of President Nixon's security adviser Dr Kissinger as new Secretary of State prompted a journalist to ask, 'Can Kissinger wear two hats and still keep his head?'

Back in Britain, on Sunday September 23, 22-year-old Lady Jane Wellesley said she was 'absolutely horrified' by rumours of an engagement between herself and Prince Charles. Her father, the Duke of Wellington, added, 'There is no question of any romance. It's complete fabrication.'

On Monday September 24, Lord Rothschild, head of the Think Tank, made a grim speech warning Britain to stop acting as if it were a wealthy nation. 'Unless we take a very strong pull at ourselves and give up the idea that we are one of the wealthiest, most influential and important countries in the world we are likely to find ourselves in increasingly serious trouble,' said the outspoken peer, who was later summoned to 10 Downing Street and privately rebuked for his remarks by Prime Minister Heath.

73-year-old Earl Mountbatten of Burma leaves Westminster Abbey after representing the Queen at a memorial service for King Gustaf of Sweden

The following day in Savile Row, tailor Ben Ramasawmy of J. Dege and Sons was found working on the pair of trousers which Captain Mark Phillips was to wear on his wedding day. 'Because they are such a tight fit I have to be very, very careful,' he said. The trousers were being made of fine woollen cloth known as barathea, with a two inch wide stripe down each leg.

Over in Washington, on Thursday September 27, the gloom at the White House was temporarily lifted by a dinner-dance in honour of New Zealand's premier Mr Kirk. There was a fanfare when the controversial Vice-President Agnew entered the room and the 110 guests applauded.

On Sunday September 30, the Japanese Prime Minister Mr Tanaka took time off during an official visit to England to play golf at the Royal St George's Golf Club at Sandwich with Mr Willie Whitelaw, Secretary of State for Northern Ireland. They were joined for lunch in the club house by Mr Heath, who wore a check beige suit, yellow socks and pullover, and flew to the golf course in an RAF helicopter.

The following day, at the opening of the Labour Party conference at Blackpool shadow chancellor Denis Healey promised increased income tax and the introduction of a wealth tax if his party won the next general election. 'I warn you there are going to be howls of anguish from the 80,000 rich people,' he said menacingly.

Three days later, on Thursday October 4, the death occurred of the 78-year-old

Duke of Buccleuch, who had saved his family millions of pounds in tax by skilfully transferring his 300,000 acre estate to trustees retaining only a nominal shareholding for himself. The title passed to his 50-year-old son, the Earl of Dalkeith, who had been paralysed in a riding accident two years earlier.

The following day, the trial began in Exeter Crown Court of ex-debutante Dr Rose Dugdale who was accused of stealing valuables from her father's home. Dr Dugdale had chosen to defend herself and on the opening day addressed her father in court. 'I love you,' she said. 'If your life was in danger I would want to stand between you and that danger but at the same time I hate everything you stand for and you know it.'

On Saturday October 6, Egypt and Syria launched massive co-ordinated attacks across the cease-fire lines of the Suez Canal and the Golan Heights.

The following day in Watkins Glen, British racing motorist James Hunt came second in the American Grand Prix. 'Watching James come within a couple of yards of winning was the most exciting thing that has ever happened to me,' said his new sponsor the portly Lord Hesketh.

Meanwhile, King Faisal of Saudi Arabia had sent a terse message to Washington promising to put all his potential and capabilities behind President Sadat if America continued to support Israel in the war now raging in the Middle East.

King Faisal of Saudi Arabia in audience. He could speak English and French but preferred to converse with foreigners through an interpreter

On Tuesday October 9, Elizabeth Taylor and Richard Burton tried to patch up their marital difficulties over a candle-lit dinner at Rome's Grand Hotel.

On Wednesday October 10, Vice-President Agnew did not contest charges of tax dodging, entering a plea of *nolo contendere* explaining that a trial 'would consume several years'. After being fined $10,000 and placed on probation, he announced that it was in the best interests of the nation that he should relinquish the Vice-Presidency.

Two days later, President Nixon selected 60-year-old Gerald Ford to replace him. At a press conference, the athletic new Vice-President declared, 'I'm deeply honoured. I'm extremely grateful and I'm terribly humble.'

The same day, the Appeals Court ordered the President to release the White House tapes to Judge Sirica, explaining, 'Even the Chief Executive is subject to the law when he has no valid claim to privilege.'

Back in London, on Saturday October 13, the new 'in' crowd gathered at the

East End home of sculptor Andrew Logan to participate in a mock 'Miss World' contest. Judges of this weird event included photographer David Bailey, fashion designers Zandra Rhodes and Ossie Clark and Miss Barbara Hulanicki, proprietor of the new Biba department store.

Artist Andrew Logan during his mock 'Miss World' contest in which many transvestites took part

The following Monday, it was announced that Britain's largest booksellers, the high-minded W. H. Smith, had refused to handle the autobiography of former call girl Norma Levy. 'The same thing happened over *The Carpetbaggers*,' said the book's publisher Old Etonian Anthony Blond. 'When the book starts selling out, I trust that Smith's will be sensible enough to take it.'

The same day in Haiti, said to be one of the world's poorest countries, a new hotel opened to be known as the Habitation Leclerc and described by its promoter Olivier Coquelin as 'the most extraordinary, lascivious and decadent place on earth', consisting of thirty-eight chalets with gold plated toilet fittings and private swimming pools.

On Wednesday October 17 in Kuwait, Arab oil ministers resolved that all oil-exporting countries should cut production by five per cent per month until Israeli forces made a full withdrawal from Arab territories.

Back in London, on Thursday October 18, it was disclosed that the ten-year-old marriage of the Earl and Countess of Lucan was on the rocks. It was stated that the 38-year-old Earl, a familiar figure at the Clermont Club in Berkeley Square, had moved out of their Belgravia home. 'I think he did it on the spur of the moment,' said Lady Lucan. 'He simply decided he would like to live apart from me.'

The following Sunday, twenty fans awaiting the arrival of the Osmond Brothers at Heathrow airport, were injured when an over-crowded balcony collapsed. A British Airports Authority spokesman said, 'We just cannot cope with this again. We are holding top level meetings this week to discuss what to do about future pop arrivals.'

On Monday October 22, 32-year-old Dr Rose Dugdale was found guilty of stealing £82,000 worth of valuables from her father's home. Before being remanded for medical reports, the prisoner told the judge, 'I am not going to ask you for mercy. You will give me the longest possible sentence because of fear of the united strength of people of no property, brave men and true.'

The same afternoon, Egypt and Israel agreed to accept a cease-fire call from the Security Council of the United Nations.

Over in Washington the following day, twenty-two bills were introduced in Congress calling for an impeachment investigation. The White House responded by immediately promising to surrender all the tape-recordings to Judge Sirica.

That night in New York, the sombre world background did not dampen the spirits of the Scotsmen who gathered for the annual Scottish Ball at the Plaza Hotel. Among those present were the Earl of Elgin, the Earl and Countess of Lindsay, the bachelor Duke of Atholl and the new Duke of Argyll, whose father had died in the midst of a controversy earlier in the year. It was noted that haggis had been flown in specially for the occasion.

Meanwhile, 68-year-old former war criminal Albert Speer, released from Spandau Gaol seven years earlier, had been permitted to enter Britain after being held for eight hours at Heathrow Airport. On Wednesday October 24, the former Nazi armaments minister was found lunching at the RAF Club in Piccadilly as a guest of Group Captain Dudley Saward. 'It was a great honour,' he said afterwards. 'I'm not proud of my past. It is very difficult to explain how one got involved.'

The same day, it was disclosed that the Sheikh of Kuwait had ordered a 600-piece dinner service in gold and silver designed by English silversmith Christopher Lawrence. The service was to include ice buckets, cocktail shaker, tongs, ash-trays and cigarette boxes.

Back at Exeter Crown Court, on Friday October 26, Mr Justice Park told Rose Dugdale, 'I think the risk that you will ever again commit burglary or any dis-honesty is extremely remote', and ordered her to be released from custody. 'Class justice if I may so,' she replied. 'If there was any justice in sentencing I should have received ten years.' She said later that she was returning to London to continue her work as a 'freedom fighter for the under-privileged'.

The same day, Sir Roger Hollis, former director general of the Security Services, died at his Somerset home where he had lived quietly since his retirement eight years earlier.

On Tuesday October 30, London's traffic was fouled up for several hours when the Queen drove in the Irish State Coach, drawn by four grey horses, to open parliament.

The same day, Heathrow Airport was engulfed by thick fog. Forty-five departing flights were cancelled and incoming flights were diverted to Manchester or Frank-furt.

That night, Prime Minister Edward Heath dined at Wilton's restaurant in Bury Street, St James's, where he was attended by the head waiter Mr Thomas and octogenarian manager Mr Marks.

On Thursday November 1, four generations of the Churchill family were present in Parliament Square at the unveiling of a twelve-foot bronze statue of Sir Winston Churchill by his 88-year-old widow Baroness Spencer-Churchill. Handing Lady Churchill the gold lanyard attached to the Union Jack covering the statue, the Queen said quietly, 'Just pull it.'

The following Tuesday, November 6, fugitive financier Robert Vesco was at last arrested in the Bahamas in connection with illegal payments to President Nixon's re-election campaign fund and other offences. After appearing before a magistrate, he was released on $75,000 bail.

On Wednesday November 7, Elizabeth Taylor flew into London from Hamburg accompanied by her new boyfriend Henry Wynberg and eleven pieces of luggage. That night, they dined with actor Laurence Harvey and his wife Paulene Stone. The latter said afterwards, 'Mr Wynberg was perfectly charming. Laurence hasn't been feeling very well recently and I think the visit bucked him up.'

Back in Washington, on Thursday November 8, Mrs Rose Mary Woods, personal secretary to Mr Nixon for the past twenty-three years, gave evidence to Judge Sirica's court wearing a red dress. She explained that there were no more missing tapes and she was in the process of transcribing the existing ones when her other duties permitted.

On Saturday November 10, a tuft of hair and a human ear belonging to 16-year-old Paul Getty III were sent to the offices of the Italian newspaper *Il Messagerio*. The kidnappers of the missing boy threatened to send a foot if their demands were not met within five days.

Back in London, on Monday November 12, there was a dance at Buckingham Palace to celebrate Princess Anne's wedding, due to take place two days later. Among those present in the crimson and gold ballroom were lady equestrians Mary Gordon-Watson and Lucinda Prior-Palmer, broadcaster Dorian Williams, motor-racing driver Jackie Stewart and various members of the Beaufort Hunt, who wore evening dress coats of dark blue with buff facings. It was noted that chauffeurs taking guests to this event were provided with tickets enabling them to obtain refreshment in another part of the palace.

The following day in Paris, the death occurred of 83-year-old Elsa Schiaparelli, the celebrated couturier who was said to have introduced the zip-fastener and man-made fibres into dress-making.

That night in London, Captain Mark Phillips and his best man Captain Eric Grounds celebrated together at Julie's restaurant in Holland Park, both managing to drink a whole bottle of champagne in one gulp.

On Wednesday November 14, the wedding of the year took place in Westminster Abbey and was watched by 50 million television viewers across the world. The ceremony was followed by stories that the kilt worn by Prince Edward was upside down. A tartan expert explained later that the kilt might have been made 'sideways' in order to be more economical of the cloth.

Meanwhile in Paris, the elderly Duchess of Windsor, who had not been invited to the wedding, had given a long interview to a woman's magazine. 'It's a bomb-shell world full of violence and horror. I no longer understand or like it too much,' she said, adding, 'I don't dance any more. Nor do my friends. We've suddenly become old.'

On Thursday November 15, Princess Anne and her husband left for the Caribbean where they were to spend part of their honeymoon on the island of Mustique now a popular resort where fellow holidaymakers included composer Lionel Bart and Harrods owner Sir Hugh Fraser.

On Friday November 16, President Pompidou arrived in Britain to spend a working weekend with Mr Heath. The following day, in the Great Hall at Chequers the two leaders signed the Channel Tunnel treaty.

On Saturday November 17, the death occurred of Sir Gerald Nabarro, who had had a major stroke after watching the royal wedding on television. 'He was one of the last real personalities in the House of Commons,' said his old friend, Lord Boothby.

On November 19, the trial began in Leeds Crown Court of former architect John Poulson and Scottish civil servant George Pottinger. In their opening remarks, the prosecution stated that both men had been 'thirsty for fame and fortune' and spoke of the 'ceaseless cascade of gifts' that Poulson had showered on Pottinger over a six-year period, including Savile Row suits, bottles of brandy and Mediterranean holidays.

The same day in the House of Commons, Edward Heath had an icy expression on his face when he announced that the oil squeeze would continue until 1980.

The following day, Princess Margaret left London on a chartered flight to Barbados, from which she was to fly on to the island of Mustique to join up with royal honeymooners Anne and Mark.

The same day, Prince Charles took a scheduled British Airways flight to Malaga, for another holiday on the Spanish estate of the Duke of Wellington. Among those who welcomed him to the 3,000 acre property was the Duke's daughter, 22-year-old Lady Jane Wellesley.

On Thursday November 22, Mrs Gail Harris, mother of the kidnapped Paul Getty III, broadcast an appeal to her son's captors. 'I promise you we will never seek who you are, never search for you or follow you, if you just give him to me.' It was said that Mrs Harris had also appealed to President Nixon to persuade the boy's multi-millionaire grandfather to do a deal with the kidnappers.

On Friday November 23, a court in Paris ordered the seizure of copies of the new issue of the *Ladies Home Journal* containing an article on alleged romantic affairs of the Duchess of Windsor. In a public statement, the 77-year-old Duchess said, 'If some readers are naive enough to believe what is printed about me, I can only feel sorry for them.'

On Sunday November 25, Prince Charles and Lady Jane Wellesley flew home together from Spain on a scheduled flight. 'I can only repeat what was said two months ago,' said Lady Jane, 'there is no romance. We are just very great friends.'

The following day in Washington, seven Watergate tapes were at last handed over to Judge Sirica. A White House spokesman explained that a controversial conversation between the President and John Dean had not been recorded due to 'a basic inadequacy of the system' and the President's personal secretary, Mrs Rose Mary Woods, testified that an eighteen and a half minute gap on one of the seven tapes was caused by her accidentally pressing the wrong button on the tape recorder.

That night, the tempestuous Maria Callas returned to the London stage after an absence of eight years and gave a faultless performance at the Royal Festival Hall.

The following night in Paris, the Duchess of Windsor was in happier mood when she dined out at Maxim's alongside film star Marisa Berenson, granddaughter of the late Elsa Schiaparelli, Mrs Loel Guinness and other celebrities as a guest of the Norton Simon conglomerate.

On Wednesday November 28, the Saudi Arabian oil minister Sheikh Yamani flew into London. At Heathrow Airport, he stepped from the first class exit of a BEA Trident into a Cadillac Fleetwood, which was waiting on the tarmac to take him to the Grosvenor House Hotel, Park Lane. He told reporters he would 'see what can be done' to lift the Arab oil embargo.

Back in Paris that night, there was a floodlit party in the royal apartments at Versailles to raise money for the upkeep of the palace, at which it was estimated that the 700 guests, who included Princess Grace of Monaco and the Vicomtesse de Ribes, wore jewellery worth over £10 million. At 3 a.m. icy winds swept the palace as tiara-clad guests waited for their cars.

The following morning in London, the Harvard-educated Sheikh Yamani was driven to the Department of Trade and Industry in a vast blue Buick Electra convertible flying the green and gold Saudi flag. He later lunched off fried scampi and crown of lamb with Foreign Secretary Sir Alec Douglas-Home in the State dining-room at Lancaster House and then spent half an hour at 10 Downing Street with Premier Heath.

Saudi Arabia's Harvard-educated oil minister Sheikh Yamani. His cars in London included a Cadillac Fleetwood and Buick Electra

The same day, 22-year-old Christina Onassis arrived in London from Nice. It was noticed at the airport that she had got her tights in a twist.

Meanwhile in Los Angeles, 41-year-old Elizabeth Taylor had been rushed to hospital suffering from a severe stomach pain. On Friday November 30, doctors at the UCLA Medical Center successfully removed an ovarian cyst and corrected an intestinal disorder. A statement was issued to say that the actress was 'looking great and doing very well'.

Back in Britain that weekend, it was announced that flamboyant bachelor Norman St John-Stevas had been appointed Minister of Arts. He responded to this honour by identifying Mr Heath as 'the most civilized Prime Minister of the century'.

On Thursday December 6, Prince Charles was involved in a three car pile up when his new Aston Martin collided with an Austin A40 and a Ford Granada police car in the wilds of Dorset. 'Prince Charles was most charming and polite,' said school-teacher Mrs Cleghorn, who was driving the Austin.

On Friday December 7, film star Richard Burton flew into London from Sicily in a chartered Mystere executive jet. At Heathrow, he boarded a jumbo jet for Los Angeles where his estranged wife, Elizabeth Taylor, was still recovering in hospital. 'I understand my wife is pretty sick,' said Burton. 'I shall be going to see her in hospital as soon as I get off the plane.'

Two days later, the famous couple flew back to Europe together on board a Pan Am jumbo jet. 'I am happier than I have ever been in my life,' said Miss Taylor, who wore a new diamond necklace in the shape of a heart. 'I don't need to tell you how happy I am,' said Burton.

Meanwhile, in Bogota, Colombia, Captain Mark Phillips had spent part of the weekend confined to bed suffering from acute gastro-enteritis.

On Monday December 10, Mr Heath's friend Lord Aldington left London for Saudi Arabia to explain to King Faisal the damaging effects the oil cuts were having on the British economy.

Over in Paris on Wednesday December 12, the Duchess of Windsor attended the Duc de Rochefoucauld's birthday party, which was described as a cosy, sit down affair for 110 close friends, at the Rochefoucauld house on the Avenue Montaigne. During dinner, the Duchess waved her arms in the air and demonstrated flamenco to General Franco's nephew Serrano Suñer. 'I remember dancing flamenco in Madrid. What a fabulous dance,' she said.

Later that night, nightclub entrepeneur Regine opened new premises just off the Champs Elysées featuring a see-through glass ceiling. Regine stated that membership of the club had already closed.

Meanwhile, financier Robert Vesco, currently free on bail in the Bahamas, had been offered asylum in Argentina. On Thursday December 13, it was announced that his visa had been cancelled and the official who granted him asylum dismissed from his post.

On Saturday December 15, kidnap victim 17-year-old Paul Getty III was found on a snow covered motorway in a mountainous part of Southern Italy. He was taken to a clinic in Rome amidst rumours that his family had paid £1½ million to secure his release. Back at his stately home near London, the boy's multi-millionaire grandfather said, 'I am so happy the boy is alive. I am anxious to know how much harm has come to him. He is very welcome to come here for Christmas.'

The same day in Uganda, President Amin had set up a 'Save Britain Fund' to help the British survive their current economic crisis. It was announced that the General had contributed nearly £600 of his own savings to set the ball rolling.

On the morning of Monday December 17, Princess Anne and Captain Mark Phillips returned from their honeymoon and made their way to their new home, Oak Grove House, near Sandhurst, which had been re-decorated at a cost of £22,000 with miles of thick wall-to-wall green carpet.

Later that day, Liberal leader Jeremy Thorpe won widespread respect when he resigned all his City directorships. He explained that he wanted to devote all his time to the party leadership at a time of 'grave national crisis' and in preparation for the lead up to a general election.

On Wednesday December 19, Mr Howard Hughes and his entourage left London after almost a year's sojourn at the Inn on the Park Hotel. They flew to Freeport on the island of Grand Bahama, where they took over the top two floors of the Xanadu Princess Hotel for $2,000 a day.

The following day in Madrid, the Spanish premier Luis Carrero Blanco died when a terrorist bomb hurled his car 100 feet into the air. The mangled remains of the vehicle landed on the second floor of a block of flats.

On Friday December 21, Mr Heath told the British nation to prepare for a three-day week as a final attempt to conserve fuel and ration scarce supplies.

The following day, the Prime Minister went shopping at Marks and Spencers in Aylesbury and purchased two lambswool sweaters for £3.50 each. He then visited the nearby Woolworth's store and bought three packets of tinsel. Asked by an ignorant passer-by who he was, he replied, 'I am me.'

On Sunday December 23, Britain's troubles were increased by a proud announcement by the Shah of Iran that the oil price would be doubled to $11.65 a barrel. The Shah admitted that this move would 'create chaos in the industrial world and create a burden for the poorer countries,' and explained, 'Everyone will have to tighten their belts.'

Meanwhile, the young Paul Getty III had partly recovered from his long kidnap ordeal and had been found skiing at a resort near Innsbruck with his mother, Mrs Gail Harris.

Back in Britain, miners' leader Joe Gormley prepared to spend the festive season at his centrally-heated four bedroom house at East Molesey in Surrey with his two married children and six grandchildren. 'We're having turkey with all the trimmings and wine – but no champagne,' said his wife Nellie.

On Thursday December 27 in America, President Nixon tried to save precious fuel by taking a scheduled flight to his Californian home, accompanied by assorted staff, including his personal secretary Rose Mary Woods and valet Manolo Sanchez. During the flight, the President moved about the plane chatting with other passengers.

Back in Britain, on Friday December 28, Lady Jane Wellesley arrived at Sandringham to spend the weekend with the Royal Family. It was noted that 'structural deficiency' had recently been discovered at the house and a repair programme costing £250,000 had been commissioned.

The following day, Prince Charles led a team of seven guns and bagged more than 200 pheasants. The shoot was briefly interrupted for a lunch attended by the Queen and Lady Jane Wellesley.

On the night of Sunday December 30, a masked Arab gunman entered the London home of Marks and Spencer chief Edward Sieff, one of Britain's wealthiest Jews, and opened fire. Mr Sieff was seriously wounded but his strong teeth absorbed much of the impact of the bullet. His wife's quick action in turning him over prevented him inhaling too much blood.

1974

Early in the new year unemployment figures in Britain reach Great
Depression proportions and the Governor of the Bank of England is soon
forecasting years of economic austerity. In the twelve months that
follow, the quadrupling of oil prices causes the West to strain all its
sinews. In March, the British General Election is held in the midst of an
acute economic, political and social crisis. Mr Heath steps down and is
soon found eating chips in the street, while Mr Wilson's new term of
office is immediately dogged by scandal and the Slag Heap Affair makes
the soft, half-frightened face of his secretary Marcia Williams famous
overnight. In America, 'the long national nightmare' of Watergate ends
with the departure from the White House of the ailing President Nixon,
who is to spend much of the rest of the year in hospital. In the summer,
London becomes the Mecca of the North as the new oil-rich Arabs
descend on the capital and buy up stately homes and make Belgravia and
Mayfair their new playground to the delight of interior decorator Colonel
Algie Asprey and other shopkeepers. Meanwhile, the Duke of Bedford
has quit the country declaring that owning a stately home is 'a very
mixed blessing and frequently a nightmare' and multi-millionaire Paul
Getty threatens to do likewise if Mr Healey's proposed programme of
taxation is activated. More dramatic exits are made by former minister
John Stonehouse and the gambling Earl of Lucan. Throughout the year a
hurricane blows through the financial world unabated – but not everyone
keeps their heads down. Deep Throat star Linda Lovelace was flaunted
at Royal Ascot, Mrs Vere Harmsworth and others continue their breath-
taking social round, and in Boston senior Congressman Wilbur Mills
appears on stage at a strip joint and asks 'What's all the fuss about?'

On New Year's Day, 22-year-old Lady Jane Wellesley left Sandringham, where she had seen in the New Year with the Royal Family, and returned to her modest home in Fulham, West London, where she was spotted putting a bag of rubbish in the dustbin.

On Wednesday January 2, Lady Jane was back at work at Colnaghi's Art Dealers in Bond Street.

On Thursday January 3, Clifford Irving was unexpectedly released from the Federal prison at Danbury, Connecticut, after serving sixteen months of his two and a half year sentence for engineering the Howard Hughes biography hoax. Later that day, he lunched in the back room at P.J. Clarke's on New York's 3rd Avenue and said he felt 'totally disorientated'. It was noted that he had his prison belongings with him, which filled two cartons and an airline flight bag.

Two days later, on Sunday January 6, there was a party at the Rainbow Grill in New York following Liza Minnelli's debut at the Winter Garden Theatre. Liza wore spidery eyelashes, a man's white suit and a brown Borsolino hat and was spotted grabbing a puff of someone else's cigarette.

Meanwhile in Washington, arch-conservative Senator Strom Thurmond was having 200 strands of hair removed from the sides of his head and replanted on the receding areas on top.

Back in Britain, on Wednesday January 9, the Duke of Wellington said he was fed up with rumours about his daughter Lady Jane Wellesley and Prince Charles. 'Our lives have been disrupted by all this speculation,' he said. 'I am getting so fed up, I hesitate to answer the telephone.'

On Thursday January 10, the three day week appeared to have no effect on London's restaurant trade. Lunching that day at Claridge's Causerie were Lord Chesham, champion of the safety belt, playwright William Douglas-Home and Lady Honor Svejdar, former wife of 'Chips' Channon, who was soon to leave for her new home on the island of Mustique.

On Monday January 14, Trade Union leaders spent five and a half hours with the Prime Minister Edward Heath at 10 Downing Street but failed to agree on any formula for ending the miners' dispute. 'We are deeply disappointed,' said TUC General Secretary Len Murray.

On Tuesday January 15, Marks and Spencer chief, Edward Sieff, who had escaped death by centimeters two weeks earlier, was back at his office, ready to 'catch up on a big back-log of work', accompanied by an armed detective.

Later that day, the Governor of the Bank of England, Mr Gordon Richardson, spoke of the vast balance of payments deficit and forecast years of economic austerity for Britain, 'perhaps until 1984'.

The same day, the pound slumped to its lowest ever level against the dollar.

The following day in California, several hundred specially invited guests inspected the new Roman Villa style art gallery built by Mr Paul Getty to house his vast art collection. 'He did all this with oil at the old price,' said one guest.

Meanwhile in Calabria, Southern Italy, three men had been arrested and charged with kidnapping and mutilating the multi-millionaire's grandson.

Back in Britain on Monday January 21, it was disclosed that Prime Minister Edward Heath had been missing at the Grosvenor House gym for his usual keep fit sessions. 'I haven't seen the poor devil now for months, not since last May,' said his insructor Len Hine. 'When I see him on TV I can see he's dying for a work-out. He does not even have time for a dip in the hotel pool like he used to.'

Two days later, Mr Heath's colleagues, Chancellor of the Exchequer Mr Barber and Peter Walker, arrived in St Moritz for urgent talks with the Shah of Iran. During their stay the British politicians were put up at the Suvretta House, one of Switzerland's finest hotels, with open log fires, indoor swimming pool, massage parlours and skating rink.

Lady Jane Wellesley and her brother John set off for lunch in Bond Street where she was working for the art dealers, Colnaghi's

The same day, the Earl of Snowdon was apprehended while taking photographs in Detroit on the suspicion that he might be the accomplice of an unlicensed hawker. The police soon realized their mistake and acknowledged that Lord Snowdon had 'a perfect right to take pictures'.

On Friday January 25 in London, grocery tycoon Sir Jack Cohen announced that he was cancelling the Golden Wedding party he was to have given at the Dorchester Hotel the following week. 'There's so much trouble in this country at this time that we didn't think it right to hold such a large celebration. I feel very deeply about Britain's troubles and they come first as far as I am concerned.'

Over in New York three days later, serious traffic jams were caused on Broadway as 20,000 people made their way to Madison Square Gardens to watch Muhammad Ali get his revenge on Joe Frazier.

On Tuesday January 29, a Los Angeles judge ordered President Nixon to testify as a material witness at the trial of his disgraced former lieutenant John Ehrlichman. A White House official indicated that this subpoena would be 'respectfully declined'.

The following day, in Washington, the President delivered his annual State of the Union message to a joint session of the House and Senate. 'One year of Watergate is enough,' he declared, imploring the country to turn to more urgent matters. 'I want you to know that I have no intention whatsoever of walking away from the job the American people elected me to do for the people of the United States.'

Back in London, on Thursday January 31, Lady Diana Cooper, Lady Antonia Fraser, Sir Cecil Beaton, Cyril Connolly and other leading personalities attended a requiem Mass for royal biographer James Pope-Hennessy who had been murdered at his home a few days earlier.

The following day in Rio de Janeiro, escaped train robber Ronnie Biggs was arrested after eight years on the run. It was reported that he was about to leave for the beach wearing red bathing briefs when Detective Chief Inspector John Slipper of Scotland Yard entered his ninth floor hotel room and said 'Nice to see you again Ronnie.'

During the next few days, the world's press descended on Rio while Inspector Slipper tried to arrange extradition proceedings. Brazilian detectives were said to be furious that they had been up-staged by Scotland Yard.

On Monday February 4, 20-year-old newspaper heiress Patty Hearst was abducted from her home at Berkeley, California, and bundled into a white Chevrolet convertible. Her live-in boyfriend Steve Weed was knocked to the ground and badly beaten. News of the abduction was kept secret from Patty's grandmother who was over ninety and living in New York.

On Tuesday February 5, Chief Inspector Slipper returned to London from Rio de Janeiro empty-handed. On arrival at Gatwick Airport, he said, 'We are all disappointed that we have not brought him back, but I have every reason to believe I will be bringing him back within a few weeks. Now I want to get a good night's sleep.'

Meanwhile, Mick and Bianca Jagger and their two-year-old daughter Jade were enjoying a holiday on Mustique, where they had rented Princess Margaret's four bedroom, three bathroom house designed by Oliver Messel for £400 a week.

On Wednesday February 6, Edward Heath announced that the country would go to the polls at the end of the month. Later that day, Mr Heath attended a party at the Soviet Embassy where vodka flowed and he came face to face with miner's leader Joe Gormley.

On Saturday February 9, Britain's troubles worsened when the miners ignored the advice of their leader Joe Gormley and the appeals of the Prime Minister and went on strike.

On Sunday February 10, there came an announcement from Lord Weymouth, eccentric son and heir to the Marquess of Bath, that he would be standing in the forthcoming election as candidate for the Wessex Regionalist Party which believed in a world government centred on the Sinai peninsula. 'Don't treat me as a joke, please,' he said.

On Monday February 11, former international architect John Poulson and Scottish civil servant George Pottinger were both sentenced to five years' imprisonment for conspiring to corrupt. 'To offer corrupt gifts strikes at the very foundations of our government,' said the judge. 'To accept them is betrayal of trust.' A controversy followed over whether Mr Pottinger would be permitted to keep his pension.

The following day in Moscow, writer Alexander Solzhenitsyn was arrested by eight policemen, stripped of his Soviet citizenship and flown out of the country in the first class compartment of a Soviet airliner.

On Wednesday February 13, Solzhenitsyn arrived in Zurich by train where it was said that his large fortune was banked. Over 1,500 people crowded into the railway station to watch him arrive. 'Too much, too much,' he muttered.

The same weekend, Richard Burton and his wife Elizabeth Taylor were found established at the Palace Hotel, Gstaad, looking radiantly healthy and happy.

Meanwhile, in California, kidnappers of 20-year-old Patty Hearst had demanded that her family give $70 worth of food to each of tens of thousands of poor people in San Francisco and Los Angeles. On Sunday February 17, Patty's father, Randolph Hearst said, 'I'll move as fast as I can and let them know what I can do.'

That night, in New York, the tempestuous Maria Callas cancelled a concert at the Carnegie Hall one and a half hours before she was to sing. Her doctor explained that she was suffering from 'an acute inflamation of the upper respiratory tract, bordering on influenza'. One of her disappointed fans said, 'She did the same thing in Hamburg. She did the same thing in London. I could have gone away for the weekend.'

Back in Britain the following day, Opposition leader Harold Wilson's voice began to fail him after a gruelling weekend during which he had given four major speeches. 'This is a young man's game and I'm getting too old for it,' said Mr Wilson, who had been travelling around the country in a Jet Ranger helicopter personally loaned to him by a new friend, Eric Miller, who was at that time Chief Executive of the Peachey Property Corporation.

On Thursday February 21, attention turned to California where it was reported that Mr Randolph Hearst's agreement to distribute $2 million worth of food to the poor had resulted in chaos. 'It's turned out to be a crazy mess,' said a social worker. 'We'd rather do without all this food than have all this violence.'

Meanwhile in Uganda, President Amin had appointed the beautiful and rangy ex-fashion model Princess Elizabeth of Toro to be his new foreign minister.

Back in Britain on Saturday February 23, Enoch Powell dealt a severe blow to Conservative hopes when he said he would not be fighting the election as a Tory candidate and accused Mr Heath of 'hijacking' the country into the Common Market.

On Sunday February 24, a new hunt began for 32-year-old Rose Dugdale, who had now been accused of hijacking a helicopter in Ireland. Though her passport was still in the custody of the English police, it was thought that she could easily have slipped across the Irish Sea because of 'her expert knowledge of small sailing craft'. A police spokesman added that the ex-debutante 'could have purchased a wig'.

On Monday February 25, the London and County Securities banking group of which Liberal leader Jeremy Thorpe had been a director, collapsed with losses of over £16 million.

Later that day, Mr Thorpe said that the Liberal Party was 'back in business' and a Liberal majority was 'on the cards'. He told an election meeting at Barnstaple, 'I want to make it clear once again that the Liberal Party is in this election, first and foremost, to form a government.'

The same day in Washington, President Nixon held his first press conference for four months. 'I do not expect to be impeached and I will not resign,' he said.

On Tuesday February 26, it was announced that a romance had blossomed between 20-year-old Tina Brown, whose first play had already been produced, and was now in her third year at St Anne's College, Oxford, and 23-year-old novelist Martin Amis. 'We've been seeing each other regularly for the past three months,' said Tina.

That night, former Conservative MP Enoch Powell went on television and urged the electorate to vote Labour.

Meanwhile, 77-year-old Sir Oswald Mosley had returned from exile to watch the election. On Wednesday February 27, the former fascist leader declared that he did not know Mr Wilson or Mr Heath – 'only Jeremy and he's charming'.

On Thursday February 28, no clear winner emerged when the country went to the polls.

The following day, Mr Heath went to Buckingham Palace and reported on the political deadlock to the Queen, who had flown home overnight from the Far East.

On Saturday March 2, Mr Heath summoned Liberal leader Jeremy Thorpe to 10 Downing Street and promised him a cabinet post if the Liberals would form a coalition with the Conservatives. 'It is not the first time I have been there and one day I hope to be there in my own right,' said Mr Thorpe afterwards, before consulting his colleagues about Mr Heath's offer.

In the midst of this confusion, the Café Royal restaurant was fined £50 at Bow Street court for falsely describing a battery hen on their menu as a free range chicken.

On Monday afternoon, Mr Thorpe, who had increased his own majority by a massive 11,000 votes, returned to 10 Downing Street and informed Mr Heath that influential Liberals were opposed to a pact with the Conservatives.

Early that evening, Mr Heath went to Buckingham Palace to offer his resignation as Prime Minister.

Seven minutes later, Mr Harold Wilson went to the Palace and was invited to form a government. Two hours later he waved to the TV cameras outside Downing Street and said, 'We have a job to do. I'm going right in to start that job now.' Said his secretary Marcia Williams, who had earlier accompanied him to the Palace, 'It's nice to be back. And so sudden.'

Two days later, on Wednesday March 6, it was announced that the new Prime Minister had come to terms with the miners: pit leaders had accepted a £103 million pay settlement.

The same day, Mr Heath's grand piano was removed from 10 Downing Street by the front door.

On Thursday March 7, it was announced that Mr Wilson would be using 10 Downing Street as a place of work only and would continue to sleep at his home in Lord North Street, five minutes walk away. 'He does not want to live above the shop,' said his press officer, Joe Haines.

The same day, the Earl of Snowdon celebrated his forty-fourth birthday in London lunching at Scott's oyster bar with Derek Hart, Quentin Crewe, Billy Hamilton and other male friends while Princess Margaret and her new friend Roddy Llewellyn were frolicking together in Mustique.

On Friday March 8, in Mexico, the world's leading socialites gathered for a fiesta organized by 76-year-old multi-millionaire Antenor Patino. Among those present were the Earl of Lichfield, actor Michael York, Georgiana Russell, Baron Heinrich von Thyssen and his new Brazilian wife, and the host's granddaughter Isabel Goldsmith and her husband Arnaud de Rosnay. During the extended festivities, over 1,600 lobsters were eaten.

Back in Britain, on Monday March 11, the Archbishop of Canterbury, Dr Ramsey, announced his resignation. Before retiring to a small house in the country, 69-year-old Dr Ramsey was to auction off his surplus linen, silver, deck-chairs and tea-sets and give the proceeds to charity.

On Tuesday March 12, at Grasse in the South of France, Picasso's children Claude and Paloma won their fight to obtain legal recognition as his heirs. Experts were meanwhile still hard at work cataloguing and assessing all the painter's considerable property.

The following morning, art historian Sir Anthony Blunt described plans to build an international airport close to the Medici villa of Poggio a Cajano near Florence as a 'catastrophic development'.

The same day, it was reported that the tap water at Balmoral Castle was dangerous because of its high lead content. 'I have twice tried to warn the Royal Family but I have not even had a reply to my letters,' said pollution expert Professor Derek Bryce-Smith who had analysed a glass of water he had taken from the Castle's public tea rooms the previous summer.

On Friday March 15, Prince Charles's ship HMS *Jupiter* berthed at San Diego, California, and the 25-year-old Prince began a weekend of fun. At Walter Annenberg's estate he met the Governor of California Ronald Reagan and at the San Diego Yacht Club he met Admiral's daughter 20-year-old Laura-Jo Watkins, who described him afterwards as 'super'. Later, in Hollywood, he took tea with film star Barbra Streisand.

Back in Northern Ireland, on Wednesday March 20, two British soldiers were accidentally shot dead by members of the Royal Ulster Constabulary.

That evening in London, Princess Anne and her husband Captain Mark Phillips were driving home after a charity function in the City, when a gun-man in a Ford Escort overtook their limousine in the Mall and attempted to kidnap the Princess. Journalist Brian McConnell jumped out of a nearby taxi and ran up to the gunman saying, 'Look, old man, these people are friends of mine. Don't be silly, just give me the gun.' The gun-man was soon over-powered and the Princess and her husband reached Buckingham Palace 'very thankful to be in one piece'.

The same night, outside a house in Cheyne Row, royal photographer Sir Cecil Beaton was involved in a scuffle with Berkshire landowner Robert Heber-Percy, which sent Sir Cecil's wide brimmed velvet hat rolling in the gutter. 'I don't want to make any comment,' said Sir Cecil afterwards at his home in Pelham Place.

The following day in Java, a few hours after learning of the attack on her daughter, the Queen inspected a display of handicrafts looking calm and relaxed.

Later that day in Paris, doctors were called to the Elysée Palace to see President Pompidou who had been taken ill with haemorrhoids and was unable to host a diplomatic dinner.

Back in Britain, on Saturday March 23, Princess Anne and Mark Phillips braved a cold drizzle to take part in the Amberley Horse Trials watched by a huge press corps. 'Go away please,' said the Princess to a photographer with a movie camera. 'Novice horse. Never seen you before.'

The following Monday, Jim Slater told Slater-Walker shareholders, 'There's a hurricane blowing in the financial world. You must put your heads down and wait for the hurricane to finish blowing.'

The same day, disaster befell the Duke of Edinburgh when a wagonette he was driving in the grounds of Windsor Castle overturned and he was thrown out and kicked by one of the horses. He was taken back by car to the castle, from which a statement was issued later saying 'Nothing was broken but he was badly bruised and shaken'.

On Wednesday March 27, strict security was in force when Princess Margaret arrived at Heathrow after a long holiday on Mustique with her new friend 26-year-old Roddy Llewellyn. She was met at the airport by her husband Lord Snowdon, who had thoughtfully brought her mink coat.

Two days later at Zurich Airport, writer Alexander Solzhenitsyn bounded up the steps of a Swiss DC10 which had just arrived from Moscow bearing his wife and family.

On Saturday March 30, the marriage took place at Arlington, Virginia, between sex symbol Dr Henry Kissinger and the beautiful political researcher Nancy

Maginnes, who wore a fur-trimmed outer garment and was seen to be several inches taller than her new husband.

Secretary of State Dr Henry Kissinger and his new wife Nancy return to Washington after their honeymoon in Acapulco

On Monday April 1, the 63-year-old Governor of California, Ronald Reagan, declared that he did not wear make-up or dye his hair, despite what the press corps might say.

The following night in Paris, President Pompidou died suddenly at his apartment on the Ile St Louis.

On Wednesday April 3, the British newspapers were full of stories linking the Prime Minister with land deals by Tony Field, brother of his personal secretary Marcia Williams, and a letter on House of Commons paper bearing Mr Wilson's forged signature now in the possession of a Wolverhampton businessman Ronald Milhench.

Late that day, kidnapped newspaper heiress Patty Hearst announced in a tape recorded message delivered to a radio station in San Francisco that she had decided to stay with her captors. 'I have decided to stay and fight for oppressed people,' she said, and went on to make a sharp attack on her father, who had already spent more than $2 million trying to obtain her release.

Meanwhile in Britain, Prime Minister Harold Wilson and his secretary Marcia Williams had issued writs for libel against a number of newspapers which had printed stories about them earlier in the week. On Thursday April 4, Mr Wilson hit out at 'Tory smear tactics' and claimed that there was a difference between 'land speculation' and the 'land reclamation' practised by his friends.

On Friday April 5, the former head of IOS, Bernie Cornfeld, was released from St Antoine prison in Geneva, where he had spent the last eleven months, after being granted bail of 5 million Swiss francs. He immediately flew to London in a private plane and that night put in an appearance at the Tramp discothèque in Jermyn Street, dressed in a jungle jacket. He was presented with a bottle of vintage champagne by the management.

The following day in Paris, 33-year-old Madame Dewi Sukarno could be found lunching at Maxim's off asparagus and scrambled eggs, alongside Baron Heinrich von Thyssen, the Duc d'Orléans and Jimmy Goldsmith's daughter Isabel de Rosnay.

Meanwhile, the 57-year-old Duke of Bedford had suddenly handed over control of Woburn Abbey to his son the Marquess of Tavistock and taken up residence in Switzerland. The 34-year-old Marquess arrived at Woburn Abbey that weekend in a green Bentley and said, 'I could not believe him at first.'

On Monday April 8, Prime Minister Harold Wilson made a full statement to the House of Commons about the Land Deals affair. 'There is no reason why any of my staff should forfeit the trust I place in them,' he said and went on to attack the press for harassing his personal secretary, Marcia Williams, on her doorstep.

The following day, the Duchess of Windsor arrived in New York on board the Italian liner *Rafaello* and was driven to the Waldorf Astoria Hotel.

On Wednesday April 10, the Earl of Snowdon made his maiden speech in the House of Lords. Watched by Princess Margaret and 12-year-old Viscount Linley in a gallery, he called for new efforts to discover the needs of the disabled and described existing invalid chairs as 'intrinsically lethal'.

That night, Mrs Marcia Williams declared that her conscience was clear in the Land Deals affair. She said she was 'a back room girl, a private person with no redress of any kind,' and added, 'Neither I nor my family are involved with Mr Wilson for glamour, for power or for influence.'

Over in California, on Monday April 15, kidnapped newspaper heiress Patty Hearst was photographed holding a semi-automatic carbine gun during a robbery of the Hibernia Bank in San Francisco's Sunset district. The American Attorney-General, William Saxbe, said later that he believed Miss Hearst was 'not a reluctant participant' in the crime and was now 'a fugitive'.

Back in Britain, on Thursday April 18, the Harold Wilson letter scandal took another turn when it was announced that Wolverhampton businessman Ronald Milhench was helping police with enquiries 'regarding alleged forgeries and other offences'.

Four days later, on Monday April 22, Mr Milhench at last appeared in court, dressed in a claret-coloured corduroy suit, and was accused of criminal deception.

Back in California, on Thursday April 25, a further tape-recorded message was received from kidnapped heiress Patty Hearst, in which she stated that she was now a willing member of the radical group which had abducted her and dismissed the suggestion that she had been brainwashed as 'ridiculous to the point of being beyond belief'.

The following night in Ireland, a gang of thieves, said to be controlled by a woman with a French accent, raided the home of 71-year-old Sir Alfred Beit near Dublin and made off with £8 million worth of paintings. 'No amount of money can compensate for the loss of objects which we have had in the family for eighty years. We do not think of them in money terms,' said Sir Alfred, who had been listening to records in his library when the gang burst in.

On Sunday April 28, Captain Mark Phillips's victory in the Badminton Horse Trials was followed by an announcement that proceedings were being brought against him under the Protection of Animals Act 1911. 'I can't understand what is being said,' said Mark later. 'The horse's ears were pointing forward at all the fences which is a sign that he is enjoying himself.'

The same day in New York, former Attorney General John Mitchell was acquitted on all charges of accepting a $200,000 contribution from international swindler, Robert Vesco, in order to influence the Security and Exchange Commission. 'We got to the Jury System and that always works,' said Mitchell afterwards.

On Monday April 29, President Nixon, elated by this news, went on television to announce that he was going to make public a 1,200 page transcript of the Watergate tapes. 'In giving you these records, blemishes and all, I am placing my trust in the fairness of the American people,' he said.

The following day, the heavy official volume, purged of swear words, was an instant best-seller at $12.50 a copy and the City of Washington ground to a temporary standstill as everyone settled down to read it.

On Thursday May 2, the affair took another twist when White House Chief of Staff, General Haig, acting on the President's orders, flatly refused to give evidence to the Senate Committee. He had no reply to more than a hundred questions about a $100,000 contribution that eccentric billionaire Howard Hughes was supposed to have made to Mr Nixon's campaign fund.

Three days later, intensive checking on holiday accommodation in Ireland led to the recovery of the nineteen paintings stolen from Sir Alfred Beit the previous month, and the apprehension of 33-year-old Rose Dugdale, who was thought to have masterminded the raid.

On Monday May 6, pandemonium broke out in West Germany following the resignation of Herr Willy Brandt as German Chancellor after one of his closest aides, Gunter Guillaume, had admitted to being a spy. The resignation was particularly regretted on Bonn's social circuit, where Willy and Rut Brandt were very popular figures.

Back in London, on May 7, in the House of Commons, Labour MP John Stonehouse asked the Home Secretary if he would review arrangements for preventing drowning accidents.

Later that day in New York, Princess Margaret and Lord Snowdon called in on the 77-year-old Duchess of Windsor in her opulently furnished suite in the Waldorf Astoria Hotel, on their way to a performance of the Royal Ballet. The Princess and her husband were in full evening dress while the Duchess wore a blue cocktail frock.

Two days later in Brazil, 44-year-old escaped train robber Ronnie Biggs, still fighting to avoid extradition to Britain, was mobbed by reporters when his car ran out of petrol on a coastal road near Rio de Janeiro. 'I am not in financial trouble,' said Biggs, 'but the money from the train robbery ran out eight years ago.'

On Sunday May 12, Mr Nixon told an audience in Oklahoma that he would face trial rather than quit the Presidency.

On Tuesday May 14, it was announced in London that Dr Donald Coggan would be the next Archbishop of Canterbury. It was later revealed that Dr Coggan had spent four days thinking over the matter and had also undergone a complete medical check up before accepting this high office. 'The Prime Minister wanted the answer earlier, but I wanted time to say my prayers and talk to my wife,' he said.

That night in New York, Andy Warhol's new film *Frankenstein* opened at Translux East with a great fanfare, attended by Princess Yasmin Aga Khan, Bobo Rockefeller, Rudolf Nureyev, Maxine de la Falaise and other leading luminaries.

On Wednesday May 15, at the Hotel Palacio at Sintra in Portugal, the exiled Duke of Bedford criticized the new proposed Wealth Tax and stated that owning a stately home was 'a very mixed blessing and frequently a nightmare'.

The following Monday May 20, one of France's most distinguised theologians, 69-year-old Cardinal Danielou, was found dead in the apartment of a Paris cabaret girl.

Later that day in Los Angeles, the FBI announced that they were now hunting Miss Patricia Hearst as 'an armed and dangerous fugitive' following an incident at a sporting goods shop in the city. 'If she opens fire on FBI agents or police, the fire will be returned,' said a spokesman.

Back in Britain, on Wednesday May 21, 26-year-old Ian Ball, who had attempted to kidnap Princess Anne earlier in the year, was sentenced to indefinite detention in Rampton mental hospital. The court had been informed that Ball had made elaborate arrangements for Princess Anne's comfort while in his custody and had planned to demand a £3 million ransom from the Queen, and get her to give a specimen signature to prove her identity.

On Friday May 24, it was announced that Harold Wilson's secretary, Mrs Marcia Williams, was to become a peeress. Conservative MP Kenneth Lewis described the announcement as 'the most exciting news since Caligula made his horse a consul', and Labour MP Willie Hamilton said, 'This just confirms my view that the sooner we get rid of the bloody nonsense of the honours list, the better.' Mrs Williams herself, who was to take the title Lady Falkender, issued a statement that her ennoblement had come as 'a complete surprise'.

Meanwhile, Opposition leader Edward Heath had left for an official visit to China, travelling on a scheduled flight of Air France. On Saturday May 25, Mr Heath was welcomed to Peking by enormous crowds but there were no porters on call and his staff, Sir Timothy and Lady Kitson, Mr William Waldegrave and his doctor Sir Brian Warren, were obliged to carry their own luggage round the square.

Back in Britain the following day, Prince Philip's dog-cart overturned after crashing into several obstacles at the Lowther Horse Driving Trials and he was eliminated for taking the wrong route.

That night, a drunken van-driver crashed his vehicle into the gates of Buckingham Palace.

On Wednesday May 29, Miss Linda Lovelace, star of the banned pornographic movie *Deep Throat* arrived in London and moved into the Ritz Hotel. 'I'm going to show Linda around,' said her sponsor Jimmy Vaughan. 'I'm going to take her to the Stock Exchange and lunch with the stockbrokers. She has a lot of fans in the City.'

On Thursday May 30, 45-year-old former whizz kid Jim Slater told his shareholders that he had turned his company's assets mainly into cash. 'The world economy is in a critical condition. Everyone seems to agree there is a risk of hyperinflation,' he said.

That night at the Hyde Park Hotel, the Countess of Ancaster, wealthy daughter of the late Nancy Lady Astor, gave a dance attended by 80-year-old Harold Macmillan, Lord Weymouth, who had won 521 votes in the recent General Election, Somerset Maugham's grandson Jonathan Hope in a velvet suit, the Bishop of Lincoln, Simon Phipps, and Mme Pol Roger, whose family's champagne flowed throughout the evening.

The same evening, the 92-year-old Earl of Rosebery died at Mentmore, his famous stately home in Buckinghamshire. The celebrated sporting peer, who had been noted for his snort of contempt or disbelief, died leaving his heirs to find over £4 million in estate duty.

On Friday May 31, the Director of Public Prosecutions announced that he did not have enough evidence to prosecute Captain Mark Phillips for ill-treating his mount, Columbus, during the recent Badminton Horse Trials.

That night in France, banker David de Rothschild gave a party to celebrate his engagement to his childhood sweetheart Olympia Aldobrandini. Among those present were Mrs Jackie Onassis and her sister Princess Lee Radziwill, Yves St Laurent and Madame Dewi Sukarno, who arrived on the arm of her new friend, 34-year-old tycoon John Bentley.

Elegant young banker David de Rothschild and his fiancée Olympia Aldobrandini, 18-year-old daughter of an Italian aristocrat

Meanwhile, financier Bernie Cornfeld had flown to Los Angeles and re-established his court of international lotus-eaters at his neo-Gothic mansion in Beverly Hills. On Saturday June 1, the grey-bearded tycoon was found beside his pool wearing Gucci swimming trunks and surrounded by beautiful women. 'Women give life a sparkle,' he said. 'I gained a stone in weight from lack of exercise in prison.'

Back in London, on Tuesday June 4, 24-year-old Martin Amis was presented with the Somerset Maugham award for his first novel, *The Rachel Papers*, published the previous winter, describing a young man mulling over his first love affair.

The same night in Ireland, the Earl and Countess of Donoughmore were seized by kidnappers on returning to their Tipperary mansion after a dinner engagement. After a struggle in the forecourt of the house, they were bundled into a light green Ford Cortina. It was noted that the 72-year-old Earl was wearing a dinner jacket at the time.

The following day, other members of the aristocracy gathered at Epsom for the Derby which was won this year by a 50–1 outsider, Snow Knight, owned by a Canadian tax lawyer Mr Neil Phillips and his wife who were later invited into the Royal Box by the Queen's racing manager, Lord Porchester.

That night, Mr and Mrs Phillips dined with Princess Margaret and Lord Snowdon at Kensington Palace, taking along a gold replica of the Derby Cup in a leather case.

On Friday June 7, it was revealed that multi-millionaire Paul Getty had written to the new Chancellor of the Exchequer, Denis Healey, threatening to leave the country if his proposed wealth tax became law.

Back in Ireland, in the early hours of Sunday June 9, Lord and Lady Donough-

International playboy Bernie Cornfeld, still said to be worth 70 million dollars, mixes business with pleasure at his Beverly Hills home

more were found in Phoenix Park, Dublin, after being released by their captors. They were taken to a hotel for a rest, a change of clothes and some champagne and later explained that they had been held captive in the converted sitting-room of a modern bungalow and had been given fried breakfasts and chops and steaks for their dinner. 'We were treated with the greatest possible courtesy,' said 67-year-old Lady Donoughmore.

Early the following morning, the elderly Duke of Gloucester, missing from public life for the past six years after suffering a severe stroke, died peacefully in his sleep.

On Wednesday June 12, President Nixon was given a hero's welcome when he arrived in Cairo on a peace-making mission. Three thousand American flags fluttered as he drove from the airport in an open Cadillac. During the talks with President Sadat that followed, Mr Nixon stated that it might turn out to be 'one of the great turning points in history'.

Back in London, on Thursday June 13, Prince Charles made his maiden speech in the House of Lords, calling for better co-ordination of leisure facilities to meet the challenge of 'removing the dead hand of boredom and frustration from mankind'. Among those who watched his debut was his new American friend Laura-Jo Watkins who sat with Mrs Walter Annenberg in a gallery.

The following afternoon, the Prince attended the funeral of the Duke of Gloucester which took place in St George's Chapel, Windsor. Among others present was the Duke's old valet, Mr Amos, whom he had inherited from the Duke of Windsor after the abdication.

Later that day, President Nixon arrived in Saudi Arabia and was welcomed with a banquet in his honour presided over by King Faisal who pledged Mr Nixon full support in his Watergate struggle.

Back in Britain, on Saturday June 15, it was discovered that Rubens's *Adoration of the Magi* in King's College Chapel, Cambridge, had been scratched with the initials 'I.R.A.' The Dean of the College said later that he would be taking 'unusual care' of the £1 million painting in the future.

On Sunday June 16, the Queen flew over to France for the day to watch her filly, Highclere, win the Prix de Diane at Chantilly in brilliant sunshine. Dressed in a green turban and blue and green printed silk summer dress, the Queen led in the winning horse to a round of applause.

The same day, Mr Nixon was warmly welcomed when he arrived in Israel and the King David Hotel in Jerusalem was almost entirely cleared of guests to make room for the Presidential party.

Back in London the following morning, a twenty pound gelignite bomb exploded in the Houses of Parliament, injuring eleven people and blowing a hole in the roof of the historic Westminster Hall. 'It was a moment which many of us had been expecting and dreading for some time,' said Liberal MP David Steel.

On Tuesday June 18, 23-year-old film star Miss Linda Lovelace attended the opening day of Royal Ascot, dressed in a startling see-through black chiffon outfit and feather boa wrap. Other showbiz personalities present included TV personality John Wells who attempted to get into the Royal Enclosure with the wrong badge and was shooed away to another entrance.

The following day, Miss Lovelace turned up at the races in a black bow tie, grey topper, tail coat and pinstriped trousers and described the decision by customs officers not to allow her film *Deep Throat* into the country as 'ridiculous, terrible'. During the afternoon an encounter took place between Miss Lovelace and Fleet Street columnist Jean Rook who asked her, 'Who are you, luv, and where do you come from?'

On Thursday June 20, Madame Dewi Sukarno appeared in the High Court in her Ascot finery to bring a successful libel action against Mrs Norma Levy, the call girl in the Lambton affair, who had claimed in her autobiography that she had slept with Madame Sukarno's late husband, the former President of Indonesia. Norma apologised for the false allegation and her publishers, Blond and Briggs, promised to pulp all the copies of the book unsold.

Over in Dublin, on Tuesday June 25, Dr Rose Dugdale appeared before the Special Criminal Court and surprised court officials by pleading 'proudly and in-corruptibly guilty' to charges of receiving nineteen Old Masters from the home of Sir Alfred Beit. She was sentenced to nine years' imprisonment.

The following day in Switzerland, the marriage between Richard Burton and Elizabeth Taylor was finally terminated on the grounds of their 'irreconcilable differences'. Miss Taylor was present at the forty-five minute hearing but Mr Burton sent a medical certificate from New York saying he was too ill to attend. It was stated that the couple had come to 'an amicable agreement'.

Meanwhile in Brussels, there had been a brief encounter between Prime Minister Harold Wilson and President Nixon. The two men were thought to have discussed energy problems and balance of payment questions as well as East-West re-lations, while journalists noted the crumpled condition of Mr Wilson's suit, with bursting 'pipe pocket'.

On Thursday June 27, there was a warm welcome waiting for Mr Nixon when he flew into Moscow. Soviet leader Mr Brezhnev strode across the tarmac, with his grey hair blowing in the breeze, to pump the President's hand.

On Saturday June 29 at Oxford, star undergraduate Tina Brown threw a 'going down' party attended by gossip columnist Nigel Dempster, author Auberon Waugh, *Private Eye* editor Richard Ingrams, and Martin Amis. Guests helped themselves to Moroccan chicken and mixed fruit salad and brie from the buffet.

Early the following morning on the Black Sea, President Nixon and Mr Brezhnev strolled through the heavily wooded grounds of the Russian leader's country estate. 'We have agreed on everything, now we can take a rest,' Brezhnev joked to reporters. The stroll was followed by four hours of talks and then a cruise on the Black Sea and a late lunch. Asked about the progress of the talks, Dr Kissinger replied, 'Nobody tells me anything. I just follow ten paces behind.'

Back in France that night, the wedding of David de Rothschild and 18-year-old Olympia Aldobrandini was celebrated with a party at the Château de Reux at which guests were offered cold lobster, cold chicken, foie gras and wedding cake accompanied by Château Lafite Rothschild '64 and Lodoucette '72. Among those present were the glamorous Mrs Loel Guinness, Yves St Laurent, and the bridegroom's cousin, Philippe de Rothschild, who wore his familiar custom-made smock.

Meanwhile in Canada, 26-year-old ballet dancer Mikhail Baryshnikov, currently on tour with the Bolshoi Company, had defected and gone into hiding in Toronto with Miss Christina Berlin, daughter of a senior Hearst executive. Canadian police and government officials declined to comment on the incident.

On Monday July 1, in Washington, the special Watergate prosecutor Leon Jaworski said that he now had 'substantial evidence' that President Nixon was involved in the Watergate cover-up and had conspired to obstruct the course of justice.

Meanwhile in Moscow, Mr Nixon and Mr Brezhnev had agreed to limit their nuclear bombardment missiles. On Tuesday July 2, the Soviet leader toasted the President in Californian wine at a banquet at the American Embassy.

Back at Wimbledon, on Wednesday July 3, five times women's champion Billie Jean King was beaten in the Wimbledon quarter-finals by Mrs Morozova. It was said that Mrs King had served badly, could not volley sharply enough and had found the wind wickedly deceptive. Mrs Morozova's hair was tied in be-ribboned bunches which tossed about during the game.

On Thursday July 4, President Nixon arrived back in Florida after his extended tour of Europe and the Middle East. A few hours after his return his chief physician, Dr Walter Tkach, disclosed that the President was suffering from a pain and swelling in his left leg and had run the risk of fatal thrombosis while abroad.

The following morning in Paris, Dr Henry Kissinger breakfasted with the new French President, M. Giscard d'Estaing on the terrace of his private apartments at the Elysée Palace. Croissants, fruit juice and coffee were served by a tail-coated, white gloved footman.

On Saturday July 6, the Baden-Baden Ball was attended by the usual glittering group of international celebrities including Madame Dewi Sukarno now being escorted by peripatetic Chilean playboy Guy Burgos, Prince Alix Napoleon and Prince Johannes Erbprinz von Thum und Taxis, a millionaire bachelor said to own seven châteaux.

The following day, 81-year-old General Franco entered a Madrid hospital suffering from arteriosclerosis and Parkinson's disease. 'All the Chief of State needs is some rest,' said his doctor.

Meanwhile, Frank Sinatra's tour of Australia had got off to a bad start with the singer refusing to give interviews at the airport and his security men got into a scuffle with reporters. On Tuesday July 9, matters worsened when Sinatra described the Australian press as 'bums, parasites and whores worth a dollar fifty'. Members of other unions immediately retaliated by refusing to re-fuel the entertainer's jet and threatening to strand him in Australia if he did not apologise.

On Wednesday July 10, 76-year-old Pope Paul cancelled his general audience at the Vatican because of a recurrence of arthritis in his right knee.

The same day, at her penthouse apartment in Rome's Via Veneto, the beautiful Princess Ira von Furstenberg dismissed rumours that she had multiple plastic surgery on her face, bosom, eyelids and bottom. 'It's all a story. Other women are bitches,' she said, explaining that she had only had plastic surgery on her cheeks and one eyelid.

Baron Heinrich von Thyssen meets the beautiful Princess Ira von Furstenberg. Architect Roberto Federici is in the middle

Back in Australia, on Thursday July 11, Frank Sinatra issued a double-edged apology expressing his regret for 'any physical injury suffered as a result of attempts to ensure his personal safety'.

On the night of Monday July 15, American singer 'Mama' Cass Elliott began a short season at the London Palladium. On her opening night, she created a sensation by confessing that on a visit to London seven years earlier she had stolen two blankets from a Kensington hotel, though she had been found not guilty in court at the time.

The following day, the engagement of racing motorist James Hunt and Miss Suzie Miller was celebrated. 'I know motor-racing is dangerous,' said Miss Miller, 'but I feel I can bring something to James's private life which will help him. A racing driver needs the stability of a home.' Said Hunt, 'Some sort of intuition told me that this was the girl with whom I wanted to spend the rest of my life.'

Meanwhile, 60-year-old Archbishop Makarios had been rescued from Cyprus after a coup and flown to London on board an RAF comet. On Wednesday July 17, the Archbishop arrived at Claridge's Hotel with only the robes he was wearing and addressed 2,000 supporters from the balcony of his suite.

Later that night, there was a Royal Gala at Covent Garden Opera House in honour of the Earl of Drogheda, who was retiring as its chairman. The Queen was in turquoise and gold, the Queen Mother was in pleated white organza and silver lamé, Lady Diana Cooper wore green and gold harem pants and Mr Edward Heath wore his favourite white dinner jacket.

On Friday July 19, 81-year-old General Franco, still seriously ill in Madrid, signed papers provisionally transferring power to Prince Juan Carlos, 36-year-old grandson of the last King of Spain, who had been groomed to succeed him since boyhood.

The following Monday, it was revealed that Sir Cecil Beaton was slowly recovering in a fourth floor room at the London Clinic after suffering a severe stroke three weeks earlier. The royal photographer was still too tired to see visitors.

The same day, Jackie Onassis's younger sister, 41-year-old Princess Lee Radziwill, was granted a divorce on the grounds that she and her husband had lived apart for more than two years.

On Tuesday July 23, the newly ennobled Lady Falkender entered the House of Lords, dressed in the traditional red mantle with white fur collar, black tricorn hat and white satin shoes. Prime Minister Harold Wilson watched the event with interest from the steps of the throne.

The same day, a man in the Strangers Gallery threw two cannisters of CS gas into the chamber of the House of Commons. 'How do you like that, you bastards?' he shouted. 'Now you know what it's like in Belfast!'

On Friday July 26, there was fresh speculation about an engagement between Prince Charles and Lady Jane Wellesley when the Queen and Prince Philip visited the Game Fair at Stratfield Saye, home of Lady Jane's parents, the Duke and Duchess of Wellington. 'I can't say anything,' said Lady Jane, 'I'm rather busy.'

That evening saw the retirement of Mr Jock Macleod, head carriage attendant at the Ritz Hotel in London for the past forty years. 'Before the war you needed a banker's reference to come here as a guest,' he said. 'Now people arrive for tea in jeans and T-shirts.'

On Saturday July 27, popstar Mick Jagger celebrated his thirty-second birthday party in the Chelsea studio of interior designer David Mlinaric. Among those present were Angie Bowie, whose husband was in New York, Britt Ekland, Debbie Reynolds, Rod Stewart and 'Mama' Cass Elliott, who came after a triumphant final appearance at the London Palladium.

The following day, General Sir Walter Walker, who had retired two years earlier as Commander-in-Chief of the Allied Forces in Northern Europe, advocated the setting up of regional volunteer forces to provide essential services 'in the event of a collapse of law and order'.

The following evening, 'Mama' Cass Elliott was found dead in her rented Mayfair flat. 'It looks like a most tragic accident,' said her physician Dr Tony Greenburgh. 'There is no question of any drugs being involved.' An inquest later resolved that the sixteen stone singer had suffered a heart attack on account of her obesity.

On Tuesday July 30, it was revealed that plans were underway to introduce capital transfer tax to prevent rich people avoiding estate duty by making gifts.

Over in Washington that same day, the House Judiciary Committee passed its third and final article of impeachment amidst speculation that the President would resign rather than defend himself which would reduce him to bankruptcy or land him in prison.

That night, the Iranian Ambassador Ardeshir Zahedi, who had emerged as

Washington's most generous host, gave a lavish dinner at his embassy, after which guests adjourned to a yellow and white tented garden to listen to Persian music.

Back in London, on Thursday August 1, a diamond Cartier bracelet and a pair of diamond drop ear-rings belonging to 67-year-old Lady Docker, whose activities had filled the gossip columns twenty years earlier, were sold at Sotheby's for £11,000. 'Of course we don't need the money,' said Lady Docker at her home on the island of Jersey, 'but the bracelet had been lying in the bank and who wears long droopy ear-rings now? Anyway, I'm not really a jewellery person.'

Meanwhile, members of the Royal Family were to be found on board the royal yacht *Britannia*, which was anchored at Cowes and had recently been re-fitted at a cost of £1,800,000. On Monday August 5, there was much excitement when a 27-year-old man on a neighbouring yacht appeared stark naked in front of Princess Alexandra and the Duke of Edinburgh. 'I had no idea royalty was there,' said the man afterwards, adding that he would like to apologise personally to the Princess.

Over in New York, on Wednesday August 7, 24-year-old French acrobat Philippe Petit crossed back and forth on a tightrope strung between the tops of the twin towers of the World Trade Center. Charges of trespass were later dropped by the police and the stunt man was discharged after a psychiatric examination. 'Anyone who does this 110 storeys up can't be entirely right,' said a doctor.

The following morning in Washington, 61-year-old Richard Nixon breakfasted off cold cereal, orange juice and milk, had his hair cut by the White House barber, Milton Pitts, and then went on television to announce his resignation as President of the United States.

The next day, Friday August 9, Mr and Mrs Nixon said goodbye to the butlers, maids, chefs and other household staff who had served them for the past five and a half years. 'There is only one White House and I will never forget,' said Mr Nixon.

Less than an hour later, Mr and Mrs Nixon walked down to the South Portico of the White House to board a waiting helicopter. Vice-President Ford waved them farewell, then grasped his wife's arm with both hands and walked back into the White House to be sworn in as the new President. 'Our long national nightmare is over,' he said.

Back in Britain, on Sunday August 11, the former Prime Minister Sir Alec Douglas-Home was pessimistic about the forthcoming grouse season. 'Everything looked marvellous until a week ago when suddenly heather beetle was discovered,' he said at his Lanarkshire estate. 'If too much heather has been destroyed it will have driven the birds away.'

On Monday August 12 the start of the season was also spoilt by howling winds and torrential rain.

The same day, the Chancellor of the Exchequer, Denis Healey, who had recently announced two new taxes aimed at great redistribution of wealth, flew off with his wife, Edna, to Corsica, which they were to explore in a rented green Simca 1100.

Back in Washington, on Tuesday August 13, it was announced that the new President and his wife would be sleeping in the same bed. 'We've been sleeping this way for twenty-five years and we're not going to stop now,' said Mrs Ford, a former dancer with the Martha Graham company.

Meanwhile in London, mice had been found in Fortnum and Mason's grocery store in Piccadilly.

On Friday August 16, in Rio de Janeiro, the girl-friend of escaped train robber

Ronnie Biggs gave birth to a baby boy. Under Brazilian law, Biggs was now permitted to stay in Brazil indefinitely to care for his son and no longer needed to fear being extradited.

Back in Britain that weekend, shy TV rental millionaire David Robinson announced that he was selling his home, Mereworth Castle in Kent, and going to live abroad. 'I have nowhere to go. I shall just travel wherever the whim takes me,' he said. 'I'm certainly not coming back to Britain. It's much too depressing here with tax on unearned income as high as 98 per cent and inflation and so on.'

Meanwhile, 47-year-old Mohamed Mahdi al-Tajir, United Arab Emirates Ambassador to Britain, had transformed his country home, Dropmore House, into an oriental palace by installing solid silver arm-chairs, a sixty-seven foot glass domed swimming pool and oil fired central heating. The operation was said to have cost £750,000.

Muhamed Mahdi al-Tajir whose personal fortune was said to be in excess of £2,000 million. He had a liking for Savile Row suits and acquired a number of homes in and around London. 'You must not be jealous of us and our money', he said

On Tuesday August 20, Prime Minister Harold Wilson, his wife Mary and his personal secretary Lady Falkender were found on holiday together in the Scilly Isles. Lady Falkender wore a headscarf and fawn slacks and was accompanied by her two children, Tim and Dan, whose existence had only recently been revealed to the public.

The following day, Opposition leader Edward Heath popped into a fish and chip shop at Bexley in Kent and purchased five penn'orth of chips, with lashings of salt and vinegar, which he then proceeded to eat in the street.

Meanwhile in Washington, the nomination of 66-year-old Nelson Rockefeller as Vice-President had been followed by calls for him to reveal the details of his vast family fortune, which some estimates placed at $5,000 million.

On Sunday August 25, Prince Charles drove from Balmoral Castle to attend morning service at Crathie Church, accompanied by a new girl-friend, 23-year-old Davina Sheffield, who was described by friends as 'full of fun with a serious side to her'.

Later that day, at the Osberton Horse trials in Nottinghamshire, Princess Anne was dismounted by her favourite chestnut Goodwill. Within seconds she was back in the saddle and galloping away. Her husband, Captain Mark Phillips, came to grief thirty minutes later.

Meanwhile, on the French Riviera, the oil sheikhs had been enjoying considerable gambling successes. 'It just isn't fair,' said a croupier at the Palm Beach Casino at Cannes. 'These Arabs just keep on betting right through their bad spells until their fortunes change.'

Back in Britain, on Thursday August 29, fifty-one people were injured when police broke up an illegal pop festival in Windsor Great Park. Among those hurt was 33-year-old old Etonian playwright Heathcote Williams who announced that he would be suing the Chief Constable of the Thames Valley Police for £35 in compensation for shock, bruising and loss of a sleeping bag.

President Gerald Ford announces that his choice for Vice-President is the former Governor of New York, multi-millionaire Nelson Rockefeller (left)

The following day, the hovercraft being used by Liberal leader Jeremy Thorpe to harangue holiday-makers on West Country beaches was badly damaged by heavy seas; its 'skirt' was torn and luggage belonging to Mr and Mrs Thorpe floated out of the cabin. Mr Thorpe took charge of the rescue operation with a brown trilby on his head.

Three days later, on Monday September 2, the same savage seas destroyed Mr Heath's yacht *Morning Cloud* and took the lives of two of those on board. 'I am tremendously distressed,' said Mr Heath. 'What seems to have happened is that they were hit by a very large, possibly freak, wave.'

The following day in Spain, it was announced that General Franco had been 'clinically cured' and he had once again taken over the running of the country.

Over in New York, on Thursday September 5, a new skyscraper, the fifty-two storey Olympic Tower, was formerly dedicated. A joint development by Aristotle Onassis and the Arlon Realty Corporation, the building included 250 condominium apartments and was proclaimed as 'one of the most secure residential buildings in the world' with a foolproof computerised security system.

The same day in California, a spokesman for film star Elizabeth Taylor denied that she had married her friend Henry Wynberg the previous week.

The following day at San Clemente, it was said that ex-President Nixon was 'terribly depressed' and was passing the time playing the piano in a desolate way. It was said that his servants still addressed him as 'Mr President'.

On Sunday September 8, David Frost and other members of the world's press gathered in Idaho to witness stunt man Eval Knievel's attempt to leap over the 600 foot deep Snake Canyon in a 13 foot rocket. The attempt failed but the stunt man bailed out and parachuted down onto a narrow ledge.

The same day in Washington, President Ford announced that Mr Nixon would be given 'full, free and absolute pardon' for any offences he might have committed in office. In San Clemente, the ex-President immediately accepted the pardon amidst furious reactions in other quarters. 'This is appalling,' said Mrs Martha Mitchell. 'I still don't believe it.'

The following day in New York, elderly literary agent Irving 'Swifty' Lazar announced that Mr Nixon had authorized him to negotiate the sale of his memoirs.

On Thursday September 12, in Ethiopia, the 44-year-old reign of Emperor Haile Selassie ended when he was formally deposed by the armed forces and driven away from his palace in a Volkswagen car.

That night in London, former Vice-President Agnew was found wandering alone through the West End in a blue trench-coat and studying the menu outside the Café Royal. 'I'm just looking, not eating,' he said. 'I'm in London for a break. I want time to think. I have a lot to think about.'

The following day in Italy, the marriage took place between Paul Getty III, who wore a Mao suit, and his girl-friend 25-year-old Martine Zucher, who was said to be five months pregnant.

On Friday September 13, Princess Margaret arrived at Llanvair Grange, near Abergavenny, to spend the weekend with Colonel Harry Llewellyn, father of her friend Roddy, accompanied by her 10-year-old daughter Lady Sarah Armstrong-Jones. The Princess was given a twin-bedded room with its own bathroom.

Back in California, on Sunday September 15, the marriage took place between actress Liza Minelli and film producer Jack Haley Jnr. The ceremony in a small church in a coastal village was followed by a party at Cyro's Club in Hollywood which was attended by Elizabeth Taylor, Fred Astaire, Jack Benny, Johnny Carson and other 'legendary all time greats'. Miss Minelli wore a yellow cardigan pant suit and yellow chiffon blouse and scarf.

Back in Britain, on Monday September 16, it was disclosed that animal lover Jean Pyke had accused Captain Mark Phillips of cruelty to animals following his appearance in the Burghley horse championships. 'It was obvious from the way Captain Phillips was looking at the horse's hind legs that something was wrong,' she said. 'Cruelty to horses is something I cannot stand.'

The same day, pop star Elton John denied that he was moving to America. 'Everyone who is a major star in this country has been told to get out by their accountants and lawyers. I think everyone is panicking,' he said at his Virginia Water home. 'There are other considerations apart from the money that make me want to stay here.'

On Tuesday September 17, creditors of a company owned by former Liberal MP Peter Bessell, who had gone missing some nine months earlier, met in London. The Assistant Official Receiver stated that his enquiries had been 'hampered by the fact that Mr Bessell had not been traced and is believed to be living in the United States'.

On Thursday September 19, the London scene was enriched by the presence of Mrs Martha Mitchell. 'Stress was hardly the word for what I have been under,' she said at Heathrow Airport. 'But I am over the hump now.'

That night, thieves broke into the Sussex home of former Prime Minister Harold Macmillan and stole thirteen items including two clocks, a Dutch painting, a Meissen porcelain figure and a pair of damask curtains. The 80-year-old former Prime Minister slept through the burglary undisturbed.

On Sunday September 22, Mrs Mitchell left London and made a difficult scene at Heathrow Airport when she refused to be searched by the security staff. 'You can't do that to me,' she cried. She later agreed to be examined by an electronic device.

On Monday September 23, Mr Nixon received much publicity when he entered Long Beach Memorial Hospital, California, to receive treatment for two painful blood clots in his left leg. A nineteen-room wing had been placed under a tight guard by his Secret Service 'detail' and it was noted that it was possible to see the *Queen Mary* at her permanent birth from his bed.

Meanwhile, Britain was in the throes of another general election. Among Conservative candidates this time was Lord Douro, brother of Lady Jane Wellesley, who was fighting the North Islington seat and said of his famous sister, 'Someday soon she'll be referred to as *my* sister.'

On Wednesday September 25, Army Minister Lord Brayley, whose company the Canning Town Glass Works had suddenly been engulfed by scandal, resigned from the government after a meeting with his friend, Harold Wilson, at 10 Downing Street. 'The poor chap has had a tough day,' said his solicitor.

On Friday September 27, the Opposition spokesman for the Environment, Mrs Margaret Thatcher, announced 'absolutely unshakable' plans by the Conservatives to reduce mortgage rates to $9\frac{1}{2}\%$ if they won the election. Mr Wilson responded to this statement by praising Mrs Thatcher's 'pretty hats' and dismissing her promise as an 'electoral bribe'.

Later that day in Washington, it was revealed that Dr Henry Kissinger was gravely concerned about the oil crisis and had told visitors that failure to solve the world's economic problems could lead to a break-up of the political fabric of the West.

Meanwhile, the President's wife Mrs Betty Ford had entered Bethesda Naval Hospital for surgery to determine whether a lump in her right breast was benign or malignant. On Saturday September 28, her right breast was removed and doctors said they were 'optimistic for a prolonged survival'. President Ford flew to the hospital from an economic summit and after seeing his wife declared, 'Our faith will sustain us.'

On Tuesday October 1, the Watergate cover-up trial opened in Washington. John Mitchell, Ehrlichman, Haldeman and other defendants were jeered at, hustled and spat on as they arrived at court.

On Monday October 7, scandal erupted around Mr Wilbur Mills, one of the most powerful members of the Congress, when late that night a go-go dancer named Fanne Foxe jumped out of his car and plunged into the Potomac tidal basin.

Back in Britain, on Thursday October 10, the second general election of the year took place and was won by Labour with a striking majority. This second defeat for the Conservative leader Mr Heath was followed by immediate demands from within his own party that he should step down in favour of 'a more sensitive grass roots politician'.

The following day in Paris, 47-year-old Mrs Tina Niarchos was found dead in her apartment in the Hotel de Chanaleilles. She had apparently suffered an oedema of the lung or a heart attack. On hearing of the tragedy, her daughter, 23-year-old

Christina Onassis flew in from America and immediately ordered an autopsy.

Back in London that night, an IRA bomb exploded at the Army and Navy Club in Pall Mall and burning armchairs were thrown across the pavement. Seventy members of the Royal West African Frontier Force, who were having a reunion dinner in an upper room, escaped unhurt.

Meanwhile, the Conservative Party had plunged into a leadership crisis and there was mounting pressure for Mr Heath to resign. On Monday October 14, the 1922 Committee met at Edward du Cann's house to discuss the matter, while the right wing Monday Club put out a demand for his resignation so that the party could return to 'true Conservative principles'.

The same day at Canterbury Crown Court, 24-year-old Saudi Arabian Prince Sultan bin Nazir Abdul Azis al-Feuad was fined £200 after crashing his Lamborghini sports car against a tree while trying to overtake. 'He must learn that he cannot react to a challenger as his ancestors would have done in the desert,' said the judge.

On Wednesday October 16, the funeral of Mrs Tina Niarchos took place in Lausanne, Switzerland, and was attended by her husband Stavros Niarchos, her former husband the Duke of Marlborough, her daughter Christina Onassis, and her mother Mrs Arietta Livanos. The only notable absent figure was her first husband, Aristotle Onassis, who avoided graveside acrimony with his arch-rival Mr Niarchos by staying in Greece.

Back in London, on Thursday October 17, it was announced that actor Richard Burton was to marry 37-year-old Princess Elizabeth of Yugoslavia 'as soon as is practically possible'. At his rented Hampstead home, the famous actor declared, 'I suppose it appears staggering. We've known each other casually for years. Suddenly we're in love.'

On Saturday October 19, car racing ace James Hunt donned a tail coat for his marriage to Suzy Miller. After the ceremony in Brompton Oratory, the happy couple drove off in a 1932 Rolls-Royce.

That night socialites gathered at the Hampshire home of Lord Montagu of Beaulieu for a Great Gatsby ball. Among those present were oil heiress Olga Deterding, Lord Mountbatten of Burma, the Marquess of Bath, journalist Quentin Crewe, actress Diana Dors and tailor Tommy Nutter who had designed the host and hostess's three-piece white worsted suits with white satin facings. A Charleston competition was won by vivacious Irish-born Mrs Carolyn Zervudachi.

Back in London, on Tuesday October 22, Mrs Vere Harmsworth gave a spectacular party at her Eaton Square home in honour of Mr Walter Annenberg who was retiring after five years as American Ambassador to London. Princess Margaret attended with her husband Lord Snowdon and at the end of the evening accompanied singer Sammy Cahn at the piano in a sing-a-long of all her favourite songs.

During the same night, an IRA bomb exploded in Brooks's Club, St James's Street, disturbing a dinner party attended by trade union leader Len Murray. He explained afterwards, 'I've never been to the club before and I had been invited to meet this group of City men who I thought needed educating in the ways of finance.'

On Saturday October 26, four bombs blasted the Rockefeller Center in New York. Puerto Rican militants demanding 'liberation' from the United States claimed responsibility.

On Monday October 28, attention turned to south-western France where the trial had begun in the crowded assizes of the Gironde of eighteen wine-dealers, including two members of the very highly respected Cruse family, accused of fraudulently transforming ordinary table wines of the Languedoc area and elsewhere into noble Pomerols and Médocs by means of subtle doctoring.

Back in London the following day, one of the horses pulling Princess Anne's coach to the opening of the new parliament kicked out and caught the bar of the coach with its fetlock. The Princess and her husband were obliged to transfer to a Rolls-Royce. At the ceremony that followed there was further aggravation when the voice of a radio commentator, broadcasting from a supposedly sound-proof box in the gallery, could clearly be heard throughout the chamber of the House of Lords.

That night in California, it was said that the life of ex-President Nixon hung in the balance as a result of severe shock and internal bleeding caused by an operation to remove a large blood clot from his leg.

Early the following day in Kinshasa, Zaire, Muhammad Ali regained the Heavyweight title from George Foreman, knocking him out with a barrage of punches in the eighth round. The fight, which Ali described later as 'a rumble in the jungle', was staged in the early hours of the morning in order to coincide with late night television viewing in the United States. Among those who watched the fight in person were David Frost and his new girl friend 33-year-old Mrs Caroline Cushing.

Back in California, on Friday November 1, President Ford visited ex-President Nixon in hospital and spent fifteen minutes beside his bed. 'He is very alert and very interested but it was very obvious to me that he's been very, very ill,' he said.

On Monday November 4, Aristotle Onassis entered a New York hospital suffering from an incurable facial muscle affliction known as myasthenia gravis.

Three days later, on Thursday November 7, London society was stunned by the sudden disappearance of the 40-year-old Earl of Lucan after an upheaval at his Belgravia home during which his wife had been attacked and his children's nanny murdered. Later that night, Lord Lucan wrote a letter to his wife's brother-in-law Bill Shand Kydd saying that he would 'lie doggo for a bit'.

The 7th Earl of Lucan who disappeared from the social scene following the murder of his children's nursemaid

The following day, gambler John Aspinall gave a lunch party at which friends of Lord Lucan discussed what they could do to help him. Aspinall stated that the missing Earl should 'die on his sword'.

Later that day, Mrs Rose Kennedy arrived in London to promote her auto-biography. 'I would certainly advise any of my twenty-eight grandchildren to go into politics,' she told a press conference. 'I regard it as the noblest of ambitions.'

Meanwhile, at Stafford Crown Court, businessman Ronald Milhench had pleaded guilty to forging Harold Wilson's signature and other offences and had been sentenced to three years' imprisonment. It was noted that his house with sauna cabin and £350 waterbed was now up for sale.

On Saturday November 9, it was stated that the missing Earl of Lucan had been seen driving around London in a black or blue car, wearing a polo-neck shirt or jersey and a sleeveless brown pullover.

On Sunday November 10, the missing peer's blood-stained Ford Corsair was found abandoned at Newhaven on the Sussex coast.

The following night, the re-elected Prime Minister Harold Wilson appeared in white tie and tails at the Lord Mayor's Banquet at the Guildhall. In a speech to the assembled dignatories, Mr Wilson said that the quadrupling of oil prices was 'going to strain all our national sinews'.

The same night at Sapporo in Northern Japan, opera singer Maria Callas, who was now suffering from internal bleeding due to a hernia, gave a last performance before returning to her home in Paris in a state of collapse.

Back in London, on Tuesday November 12, a warrant was issued for the arrest of Lord Lucan on a charge of murdering his nursemaid and the attempted murder of his wife. 'We have a number of addresses in the South of France and the United States being checked for us through Interpol,' said Detective Chief Inspector Roy Ransom who was leading the hunt for the missing Earl. 'We are also considering the possibility that someone may be harbouring him in this country.'

Over in California, on Thursday November 14, ex-President Nixon left hospital in pyjamas, dressing gown and slippers and was helped into a limousine for the fifty mile drive back to his home at San Clemente. His doctor, John Lungren, said that his patient's erratic blood pressure would make his return to Washington to give evidence at the trial of his former aides extremely dangerous.

Back in Britain, police had begun to comb the country estates of fourteen wealthy friends of the missing Earl of Lucan. Detectives were also said to be considering the possibility that the Earl had committed suicide a few hours after the murder of his children's nanny the previous week. At Newhaven in Sussex, police divers had begun to search the coves for signs of his body.

On Friday November 15, Lady Lucan returned to the four storey Belgravia house where the murder had taken place. She was accompanied by two private nurses and a close friend, Miss Mary-Geraldine O'Donnell, who said 'she seems to be getting over this terrible matter'.

Over in Los Angeles on Tuesday November 19, Bernie Cornfeld announced that he was returning to business as chairman of a real estate company selling recreational and retirement land in southern Arizona. 'I will be glad to get back to work. I have missed the excitement of corporate living,' said Cornfeld, who still faced charges in Switzerland arising from the collapse of the IOS empire.

The same day, President Ford arrived in Tokyo on the start of a five day visit, during which his ill-fitting trousers, wing collar and tail-coat caused much amusement among the world's press. 'The President does not emphasise sartorial splendour,' said a member of his entourage.

The following day in Miami, 49-year-old Labour MP John Stonehouse disappeared from the Fontainbleau Hotel where he had been staying on a business trip. His clothes were found in a bathing hut near the hotel and it was feared that he had drowned. In London, his attractive secretary, Mrs Sheila Buckley said, 'He is a very strong swimmer and one who swam whenever he had the opportunity. It is the only recreation he has.'

On Tuesday November 26, the Japanese Prime Minister, Mr Tanaka, who had played host to President Ford the previous week, suddenly resigned as a result of scandals surrounding his extensive private business interests.

Back in England that day, the new Miss World, Helen Morgan, resigned after the disclosure that she was an unmarried mother and had been allegedly cited in a divorce case. 'She is very distressed about it,' said Mrs Morley, wife of the contest's organiser. 'She telephoned today to say that in the circumstances she felt she had to relinquish the title.'

The following day in London, 102 pieces of Georgian family silver belonging to the missing Earl of Lucan came up for sale at Christie's and fetched £17,410. Most of the collection, including a set of forty-eight George III dinner plates, was bought by mystery buyers believed to be close friends of the missing peer.

Meanwhile, Tory economics spokesman Mrs Margaret Thatcher had started hoarding tinned ham, tongue, fish and fruit, pots of jam and canisters of coffee. 'I am a grocer's daughter so one knows a little bit about this,' she said.

On Thursday November 28, the engagement was announced of 35-year-old eligible bachelor Lord Lichfield and 24-year-old Lady Leonora Grosvenor, daughter of the Duke of Westminster. 'We are all delighted' said Lady Leonora's brother 22-year-old Earl Grosvenor. 'Leonora has always played her cards close to her chest.'

Later that day in Uganda, President Amin suddenly sacked his newly appointed Foreign Minister, Princess Elizabeth of Toro, falsely accusing her of making love in a lavatory at Orly Airport. 'The allegation is totally absurd,' said the Princess, who later won handsome libel damages from newspapers who had published the story.

Over in Washington, on Friday November 29, a panel of three approved doctors who had examined the former President Nixon stated that he was not well enough to testify in the Watergate cover-up trial, now in its eighth week.

On Saturday November 30, it was reported that the Earl of Lucan had been seen in South Africa. Photographs and a full description of the missing peer were immediately telegraphed from London to the South African police.

That night in Boston, Massachusetts, 65-year-old senior congressman Wilbur Mills appeared on the stage of a local strip joint and introduced his friend dancer Fanne Foxe, who had created headline news the previous month when she had fallen into the Potomac tidal basin near Washington, as 'The Washington Tidal Basin Bombshell'. It was noted that Miss Foxe had previously been known as 'The Argentinian Firecracker'.

Back in Britain that weekend, it was suggested that missing MP John Stone-house, who had disappeared in Florida twelve days earlier, might have been murdered. 'Terrible though it is,' said the MP's former Parliamentary Private Secretary, Mr William Molloy, 'I believe it is on the cards that he has been destroyed by the mafia.'

On Monday December 2, dancer Fanne Foxe arrived in New York and spoke of her friendship with Congressman Wilbur Mills. 'I love him and he loves me. But we are not lovers. We're just friends – very close friends,' she said. 'What's all the fuss about?' asked Mr Mills. 'Fanne's act is not vulgar. She does not tell dirty jokes. She is very talented.'

Two days later, the New York Supreme Court ordered billionaire recluse Howard Hughes to pay his former aide Robert Maheu $2,823,333 in libel damages following his famous telephone interview in January 1972 when he had described Maheu as a 'no good son of a bitch who stole me blind'.

Earlier that day, British Prime Minister Harold Wilson flew home from France with tummy trouble after eating oysters with President Giscard at the Elysée Palace.

On Thursday December 5, 14-year-old Prince Andrew was taken from Gordonstoun School to hospital at Elgin, Morayshire, suffering from the after effects of a blow to the head. 'There was a sort of rag in the dormitory involving three or four boys,' said housemaster Mr Larkman. 'These things happen, one cannot stop young schoolboys from larking about.'

On Friday December 6, it was revealed that the Earl and Countess of Dartmouth were selling their handsome house in Hill Street, Mayfair. Lady Dartmouth explained that the fourteen bedroom, six bathroom house was too large for her current needs.

Back in Paris that weekend, a banquet attended by Russian leaders Brezhnev and Gromyko was disturbed when the French Foreign Minister M. Jean Sauvagnargues was carried out on a stretcher said to be suffering from an unfortunate combination of wine and amphetamines.

Meanwhile, the seventeen-month-old marriage between photographer Baron Arnaud de Rosnay and Jimmy Goldsmith's daughter Isabel had run into difficulty. 'Our relationship is going through a lot of troubles because of my work,' said Arnaud on Monday December 9. 'I spend four days a week in Mexico and one day in New York on my way through to home.'

The following day in Stockholm, author Alexander Solzhenitsyn appeared in white tie and tails before an audience of scholars, scientists and royalty to receive his Nobel Prize from the young King Carl Gustaf of Sweden.

On Wednesday December 11, Prime Minister Harold Wilson returned from another visit to Paris, suffering from a more severe stomach upset which obliged him to cancel all his engagements for three days and retire to his bed.

Over in Ireland, on Thursday December 12, Rose Dugdale, now serving a nine year sentence in Limerick Gaol, gave birth to a 7 pound 8 ounce baby boy in her cell. 'Both mother and baby are in fine form,' said Dr Ivor Holloway who had assisted at the birth.

The following Monday December 16, Employment Minister Michael Foot was fined £40 for careless driving when he had reversed from the courtyard of a public house onto a main road at Kingswood in Buckinghamshire, causing a three car collision.

On Tuesday December 17, Prime Minister Harold Wilson re-emerged from his sickroom to inform the House of Commons that there was no truth whatsoever in rumours that missing MP John Stonehouse had been spying for either Czechoslovakia or the United States 'and was being kept under investigation or surveillance at the time of his disappearance. I have no information about the disappearance,' he said. 'I only wish I had.'

The following day in the Gironde, the Bordeaux wine fraud case ended with eight of the eighteen defendants being found guilty of doctoring and mislabelling vin ordinaire. One of them received a prison sentence and two others suspended sentences. The public prosecutor spoke of the need 'to prune ruthlessly a few diseased branches to show that the Bordeaux vine plant is healthy'.

Back in London, on Friday December 20, many members of the literary scene attended a memorial service at the church of St Mary-Le-Strand for the critic Cyril Connolly. Among those present were the Earl of Longford, publisher Sir George Weidenfeld, jazz musician George Melly, author Jonathan Gathorne-Hardy, and 29-year-old journalist James Fox to whom Connolly had bequeathed all his notes on the 1941 Erroll murder case.

The following Sunday evening, a bomb was lobbed onto the balcony of Opposition leader Edward Heath's new Belgravia home. Mr Heath returned to the house a few minutes later after conducting a carol concert at Broadstairs and inspected the damage. 'The windows have gone and there has been some damage to furniture and in particular to a painting of the South of France by Sir Winston Churchill,' he said. 'My piano, which is at the back of the living room on the first floor, was fortunately not damaged.'

Meanwhile, in Saudi Arabia, London antique dealer Colonel Algernon Asprey had completed the refurbishment of King Faisal's palace at Riyadh. 23,000 yards of carpet, 134 beds and 200 tables had been flown out in eleven specially chartered Boeing 707s.

On Monday December 23, Aristotle Onassis rose from his sick bed to offer a reward of £220,000 for anyone who could provide evidence that the death of his son Alexander in a plane crash the previous year had been caused by an act of sabotage.

The following morning in Paris, President Giscard d'Estaing invited four garbage collectors into the Elysée Palace for breakfast and gave them each a bottle of champagne and a turkey.

Later that day in Melbourne, Australia, missing Labour MP John Stonehouse was found living under another name and carrying a large quantity of cash. He was taken to a barbed wire detention centre as a suspected illegal immigrant. In a telegram to the Prime Minister, he apologized for the trouble he had caused and explained, 'My wish was to release myself from the incredible pressures being put on me particularly in my business activities and various attempts at blackmail.'

On Thursday December 26, Mrs Stonehouse arrived in Australia and was reunited with her husband. 'What worries me is that I still cannot find out why he did it at all ,' she said later. 'He needs to see a psychiatrist as soon as possible.'

Back in London the following day, Stonehouse's attractive secretary, Mrs Sheila Buckley said at her parents' home, 'I will do anything I can to help.'

Over in New York on Friday December 28, 66-year-old Amy Vanderbilt, whose books on etiquette had sold in millions, fell to her death from her apartment on the Upper East Side.

Meanwhile, friends of the missing Earl of Lucan were rallying their forces and, on Sunday December 29, it was revealed that private detectives had been hired to clear the peer's name. Forty-year-old Ian Maxwell-Scott, gambling companion of the missing peer, said he was convinced of his friend's innocence.

Over in Washington, on Monday December 30, 65-year-old Congressman Wilbur Mills admitted that he was an alcoholic and swore total abstinence in future and refused to resign his seat in the House of Representatives. He blamed recent colourful events in which he had been involved on 'the fatigue and pressures built up by years of dedicated work'.

1975

During the next twelve months, the world recession shows no sign of abating. While self-pitying pronouncements issue from fallen businessman John Stonehouse on the other side of the globe, multi-millionaire oil sheikhs continue to buy spectacular town and country properties in England and throw their weight about in the various international resorts. On the death of Aristotle Onassis, Saudi Arabia based arms dealer Adnan Khashoggi emerges in the popular imagination as 'the world's richest man'. In the City of London and elsewhere, other changes are afoot. Recession-victim Jim Slater is replaced by his friend Jimmy Goldsmith as chief executive of the troubled Slater Walker company. Iron Maiden Margaret Thatcher takes over the Conservative leadership from Mr Heath, who retires hurt to begin writing a series of coffee-table books for the Earl of Longford's publishing concern. As IRA bombs crash through the windows of fashionable restaurants, quarrels break out between friends of the missing Earl of Lucan, Lady Antonia Fraser leaves her husband for Cockney playwright Harold Pinter, the Earl of Lichfield finally makes a very suitable marriage to the daughter of the Duke of Westminster while his ex girl-friend Britt Ekland goes off with pop star Rod Stewart. Meanwhile, Princess Margaret and Lord Snowdon spend most of the year apart, and the Queen's sister sees more and more of her young friend Roddy Llewellyn. On return from the Commonwealth Prime Ministers' conference in Jamaica, Mr Wilson denies there is a crisis and accuses journalists and aristocrats of crashing around like 'wet hens'. While he bows low to Crown Prince Fahd of Saudi Arabia and asks for a rise in the Queen's pay, his secretary, Lady Falkender, begins an endless social round with her mainly show business acquaintances. On the international scene, the accident-prone President Ford fêtes the Shah of Iran and former President Nixon is signed up by David Frost. In this confusing new world, the gossip columnists flourish and by the end of the year Nigel Dempster has been described as more famous than most of the people he writes about.

New Year's Day found the Royal Family squeezed into a modest six bedroom farmhouse on the Sandringham estate while the big house was being modernized and reconstructed at a cost of £250,000.

On Thursday January 2, Detective Chief Superintendent Kenneth Etheridge of Scotland Yard's fraud squad left for Australia to question former Labour minister John Stonehouse about alleged passport irregularities and aspects of his business affairs.

Meanwhile, at a secret address in London, Stonehouse's 28-year-old secretary Mrs Buckley said she was willing to join her former employer in Australia 'if he needs me'.

Monday January 6 saw the retirement of 63-year-old Ronald Reagan as California's Governor. It was announced that he was to keep in the public eye by writing a weekly column on current affairs to be syndicated to 1,500 newspapers across America. He would also be giving a five-minute radio commentary each day.

Three days later in Switzerland, Mr Andreas Badrutt, owner of the Palace Hotel, St Moritz, complained that certain Arab playboys were booking his best suites and then not showing up. 'It is becoming a daily occurrence,' he said. 'The Arabs insist on nothing but the best. Then they cancel at the last moment with absurd excuses. Either their grandmother has died or they've fallen off a camel.'

Meanwhile at Gstaad, actor Jack Nicholson was receiving skiing instruction from his friend film director Roman Polanski, who described the actor's style as 'like a guy who scratches his left ear with his right hand'.

Back in Britain, on Friday January 10, there was jubilation among aircraft officials over the Shah of Iran's promise to purchase two or three Concordes. 'We are confident that a contract will be signed in the very near future,' said a spokesman.

The following Monday, in Chicago, scandal engulfed the Playboy empire when 34-year-old Bobbie Arnstein, secretary to Playboy boss Hugh Hefner for the past eleven years, killed herself in a local motel after being charged with carrying cocaine.

On Tuesday January 14, it was announced in London that in view of the economic crisis Opposition leader Edward Heath was cutting back on his sailing activities. A representative of the firm now working on the politician's new yacht said, 'He will probably leave the yacht for a large part of the year under a sailing master.'

That night, Mr Heath visited the gym at Grosvenor House and chatted with the popular 67-year-old instructor Mr Len Hine beside the swimming pool.

The following day, Mr Hine suddenly collapsed and died in the street.

The same day, the French Catholic Church was engulfed in another scandal when Monsignor Roger Tort, Bishop of Montauban, was found dead in the corridor of a small Paris brothel.

On Thursday January 16, Mrs Barbara Stonehouse returned from Australia where her husband was now seeking to become a permanent citizen.

On Friday January 17, Mr Stonehouse was in high spirits when he dined out at the Hilton Hotel, Melbourne, wearing a dark grey suit and carrying a miniature chess set. He ate lobster soup, steak Diane with french beans and sauté potatoes, washed down with Australian wine and crème de menthe.

Back in London, on Sunday January 19, an unidentified terrorist group fired fifteen bullets through the plate-glass windows of the Rib Room restaurant in

Knightsbridge. 'There was a terrible series of bangs,' said Mrs Doreen Cohen who was dining at the restaurant with her family. 'Everybody crashed to the floor. The bullets came waist high.'

The following day, the government announced that it was abandoning the Channel Tunnel project. 'It is bitterly disappointing that this decision has come now,' said one of the project managers. 'We were just ready to start up the tunnelling machine.'

On Wednesday January 22, an announcement came from President Amin of Uganda that he was planning to visit Britain later in the year. 'I hope there will be, at least during my stay, a steady and reliable supply of essential commodities,' he said. Buckingham Palace said that they had no official notice of the visit.

On Thursday January 23, it was revealed that Sheikh Sayed Mohamed Mahdi al-Tajir, Dubai's multi-millionaire ambassador to London, had purchased Mereworth Castle in Kent. 'You must not be jealous of us and our money,' he said. 'We want to preserve Britain. We like your beautiful houses. After all, we can afford them. I saw this castle, I liked it and I bought it. Just like that.' It was understood that the ambassador had paid well over the £550,000 asked by the vendor, shy millionaire David Robinson.

Mereworth Castle, former home of shy millionaire David Robinson, which was purchased by Dubai-based businessman Mr al-Tajir for over £550,000

On Thursday January 23, strict security attended the enthronement of Dr Donald Coggan as Archbishop of Canterbury. As she entered Canterbury Cathedral, the Archbishop's wife Mrs Jean Coggan had her handbag searched.

Two days later in Washington, President Ford took delivery of a pair of contact lenses.

Meanwhile in Los Angeles, the wife of former kidnap victim Paul Getty III had given birth to a baby boy, to be named Paul Balthazar. At his stately home near London that weekend 82-year-old oil billionaire J. Paul Getty said, 'He's my first great-grandson and it all seems rather strange. It feels only a short while ago that *I* was the youngest member of our family.'

Back in London, on Monday January 27, an IRA bomb exploded at the Bond Street premises of the military tailors, Gieves. Glass and debris were scattered about 100 yards down the exclusive shopping street.

The following day, the House of Commons set up a special committee to consider the position of MP John Stonehouse, now seeking to become an Australian citizen. In a debate on the subject, Liberal leader Jeremy Thorpe described the case as 'a rare and unhappy episode' and said he hoped the committee would proceed 'with extreme caution'.

On Friday January 31, film star Elizabeth Taylor arrived in London from Los Angeles and was helped off the jumbo jet by the pilot. The film star, whose relationship with Californian businessman Henry Wynberg now hung by a thread, was on her way to Moscow to start work on a new film *Bluebird of Happiness*.

The same day, 44-year-old Princess Margaret boarded a plane for Barbados, from where she was to fly on to the Caribbean island of Mustique for another holiday with her friend, Roddy Llewellyn.

On Monday February 3, 44-year-old Lord Snowdon left for Australia to make a film called *The Explorers* and was accompanied by attractive production assistant, 33-year-old Mrs Lucy Lindsay-Hogg.

The same day, more than a hundred passengers on board a Japanese Airlines flight from Tokyo to Paris were taken ill with acute food poisoning and were given emergency treatment at Copenhagen Airport. The cause of infection was later traced to a ham omelette served for breakfast during a stop-over in Alaska and prepared by a cook with boils on his fingers. A Japanese director of the catering company involved later committed suicide.

Later that day in New York, banana tycoon Eli Black jumped to his death from his forty-fourth floor office in the Pan Am building. It was understood that Mr Black's business had been adversely affected by poor weather two years earlier and he had tried to 'erase' the difficulties by unsuccessfully attempting to bribe the President of the Republic of Honduras.

Back in Britain, on Tuesday February 4, 49-year-old Mrs Margaret Thatcher won the first ballot in the contest for the Conservative Party leadership. Meeting colleague Nigel Fisher in a corridor after her victory, she kissed him on both cheeks and said, 'Isn't it exciting, Nigel? Isn't it exciting?' The following morning, in Marjorie Proops's column in the *Daily Mirror*, Mrs Thatcher was dubbed 'The Iron Maiden' for the first time.

Meanwhile, defeated leader Mr Heath announced that he would not be standing in the second ballot and it was thought in some quarters that he might quit politics, and possibly even Britain too.

On Wednesday February 5, Mr William Whitelaw, who had now decided it was his 'duty' to stand as an alternative to Mrs Thatcher, posed for photographs washing dishes in his shirtsleeves. Later that day he appeared in top hat and tails at the wedding of insurance broker James Graham and Miss Serena Kershaw.

On Thursday February 6, the ailing multi-millionaire Aristotle Onassis was flown from Athens to Paris for hospital treatment for myasthenia gravis. During the flight, he was wrapped in a blanket given him a few months earlier by his old friend Maria Callas, also in poor health. At Orly airport he refused the offer of a stretcher and insisted on going to his apartment on the Avenue Foch.

The following morning, with his wife Jackie at his side, Mr Onassis entered the American Hospital at Neuilly by the back door.

On Saturday February 8, the two main rivals for the Conservative Party leadership, Mrs Thatcher and Mr Whitelaw, kissed each other at the Young Conservatives Conference at Eastbourne. 'I don't know what all the fuss is about,' said Mr Whitelaw. 'After all, we've done it before lots of times, in hotels and halls, on staircases and in the streets.'

The same weekend, the volatile relationship between Richard Burton and Princess Elizabeth of Yugoslavia broke up in the South of France when the Princess suddenly returned to London said to be suffering from a 'surfeit of Burton'.

On Monday February 10, it was revealed that John Stonehouse had written to the Swedish Prime Minister pleading for Swedish citizenship to avoid persecution by the British press.

The same day in Paris, Mr Aristotle Onassis underwent a gall bladder operation from which he was never again to regain full consciousness. Shortly afterwards he was placed on a respirator.

On Tuesday February 11, Margaret Thatcher was voted leader of the Conservative Party after beating Mr Whitelaw in the second ballot by 146 votes to 79. In a statement from his house in Wilton Street, Belgravia, Mr Heath also quickly offered the new leader his 'warm congratulations' and wished her 'every success'.

Meanwhile, Mrs Thatcher's husband, Denis, had told reporters 'They say I am the most shadowy husband of all time. I intend staying that way.'

That night, Mrs Thatcher was present at a reception at Buckingham Palace for members of the Press. Among those who attended were Bernard Levin, Vere Harmsworth, Jocelyn Stevens, society columnist Betty Kenward and assorted TV executives and news-readers.

The following day in the House of Commons, Mr Wilson congratulated Mrs Thatcher on her victory before going on to ask Parliament to increase the Queen's Civil List to £1,400,000 a year in view of the grave economic situation. Willie Hamilton MP shouted angrily, 'We know that the Prime Minister is a member of the Establishment but he need not go down on all fours to prove it!'

The same afternoon, the Queen visited a nursery centre in Bloomsbury and was given ten pence by a four-year-old child. 'Here you are, Queen. I want to help you with your palace.' The Queen appeared astonished but nevertheless took the coin.

That evening, Mrs Thatcher visited ousted leader Mr Heath at his Belgravia home to discuss the possibility of a post in the Shadow Cabinet for the former Prime Minister. Mrs Thatcher left the house after only twelve minutes and was said to have spent less than five minutes with Mr Heath himself.

Meanwhile, 28-year-old Mrs Sheila Buckley had arrived in Australia, where her reunion with her former employer Mr Stonehouse was marred by a scuffle with a press photographer at Perth Airport. Mrs Buckley explained that she had made the journey 'to confer with Mr Stonehouse regarding certain documents concerning his company activities in Britain'.

On Thursday February 13, Prime Minister Harold Wilson arrived in Moscow for talks with Mr Brezhnev. Before their discussions got underway, the two leaders met for a highly informal drinks party at the Kremlin at which Mr Brezhnev snatched Foreign Secretary Jim Callaghan's red despatch box and pretended to make off with it, declaring that he now had 'all the British secrets'.

Back in Britain that night, the Queen Mother dined with her old friend Maureen

Marchioness of Dufferin and Ava at the latter's white-painted house in Knights-bridge. Among those present was the ebullient public relations man Billy Hamilton, who gave his impersonation of Mr Whitelaw for the royal guest.

Back in Moscow, on Friday February 14, Mr Wilson attended a seven course luncheon in the Kremlin's gold-and-white Hall of Catherine the Great, after which he spoke of the menace of thermo-nuclear warfare.

Meanwhile, hints from Mr Brezhnev that he would have liked a pair of Purdey guns as a present from the visiting Prime Minister had been ignored.

On Monday February 17, the marriage took place at Caxton Hall between 23-year-old Nicky Waymouth and American jewellery designer Kenneth Lane. The vivacious bride was given away by Lord Goodman and wedding guests included Lord Brooke, Paloma Picasso and the ageless Lady Diana Cooper.

The following morning, the new Conservative leader Mrs Thatcher, wearing tweeds and sensible shoes, breakfasted off scrambled eggs, brioches and muffins with Dr Henry Kissinger at Claridge's Hotel, where Kissinger's forty strong retinue had taken over the entire second floor. Later that day, Dr Kissinger lunched in Zurich with the Shah of Iran and dined in Paris with French Foreign Minister M. Sauvagnargues.

The same day, it was estimated that the Royal Family and their friends had shot more than 12,000 pheasants during the recent pheasant shooting season on the Sandringham estate.

Meanwhile, Prince Charles had been hunting with the Beaufort Hunt accompanied by Princess Anne. 'He seemed to enjoy himself. Why shouldn't he?' said his host, the 74-year-old Duke of Beaufort. The chairman of the League Against Cruel Sports said later, 'Prince Charles seems like so many members of the Royal Family to be hooked on killing animals for kicks.'

On Wednesday February 19, it was announced in Paris that an enquiry into the recent death of the Bishop of Montauban in a Montmartre brothel had cleared him of any wrong-doing. The 56-year-old Bishop, who had been wearing his bishop's ring and pectoral cross at the time, had only entered the building because he had been taken ill.

Back in London, on Thursday February 20, a complicated web of inter-company borrowing was disclosed when three more of Mr Stonehouse's companies went into voluntary liquidation. The same day, in the High Court, writs were issued claiming more than £100,000 from the absent MP.

Over in Washington on Friday February 21, the principal Watergate conspirators were sentenced to up to eight years in prison. Said former Attorney-General John Mitchell, now likely to spend a minimum of thirty months in custody, 'It could have been worse. He could have sentenced me to spend the rest of my life with Martha Mitchell.'

The following night, in a suburb of Santa Barbara, 57-year-old tycoon Henry Ford was arrested and charged with drunken driving after flunking a roadside sobriety test. 'He was a real gentleman, just as congenial as he could be,' said the highway patrolman who effected the arrest.

On Monday February 24, the world's attention turned momentarily to the remote kingdom of Nepal for the enthronement of Old Etonian King Birendra. Representatives of fifty-eight nations included the vivacious, unpredictable Madame Marcos of the Philippines and Britain's Prince Charles, who had stopped off en route in Tehran to inspect the Persian royal jewels.

Meanwhile in Australia, the Minister of Immigration had ruled that illegal immigrant John Stonehouse would be deported from the country within seventy-two hours of his ceasing to be an MP. On Thursday February 27, John Stonehouse expressed his deep disappointment at this ruling and insisted that he would not return to England. 'A psychiatrist's report has said that by returning to Britain I would do myself irreparable psychiatric damage,' he explained.

Back in London that weekend, Lord Goodman's Mercedes broke down in Wigmore Street.

On Monday March 3, the sleek new American Ambassador, Mr Elliot Richardson, arrived in Britain. Over a cup of tea at Heathrow airport he spoke of financial worries connected with the job and said he had obtained assurances from Washington that there would be 'an increase in the representational allowance'.

The following day, 85-year-old Charles Chaplin was wheeled forward at Buckingham Palace to receive his knighthood from the Queen. After this ceremony, he celebrated privately with a small party at the Savoy Hotel attended by Harold Wilson and Lady Falkender.

Meanwhile in New York, John Lennon and his estranged wife Yoko Ono had been reunited after eighteen months apart. 'Our separation was a failure,' said Lennon on Thursday March 6. 'We knew we would get back together. It was just a matter of time. Thank God it happened.'

The following day in Washington, it was revealed that 72-year-old Senator Strom Thurmond had now had his frizzy transplanted hair dyed a shade called 'chocolate kiss' in the Senate beauty shop.

Back in Britain, on Saturday March 8, the upper-classes flocked to the wedding of the bouffant-haired Earl of Lichfield and Lady Leonora Grosvenor, 25-year-old daughter of the Duke of Westminster, which took place in Chester Cathedral. After the ceremony a reception was held at the home of the bride's father which was attended by Nigel Dempster, the Queen, the Hon Michael Pearson, Norman St John-Stevas, Earl Mountbatten of Burma, the young Viscount Lewisham, Maureen Marchioness of Dufferin and Ava and the bridegroom's chauffeur Mr Percy Hancy.

The Earl of Lichfield and his bride. The group includes Her Majesty the Queen, Princess Margaret, the Duke of Westminster (in bow tie) and Earl Mountbatten of Burma

Afterwards, the happy couple flew to London by helicopter and spent their wedding night at the Connaught Hotel. The following day they were to fly off to Mustique where Princess Margaret had lent them her villa for the first part of their honeymoon.

On Tuesday March 11, 24-year-old Lord Hesketh who had been losing £100,000 a year on his racing team, said 'This is make or break year for the Hesketh racing team. We have got to win some races and money – or else.'

On Saturday March 15, multi-millionaire Aristotle Onassis died in the American Hospital in Paris with his daughter Christina at his bedside. His wife Jackie arrived from New York on the first available flight the next day and issued a formal statement: 'Aristotle Onassis rescued me at a time when my life was engulfed in shadows. We lived through many beautiful experiences together which cannot be forgotten and for which I will be eternally grateful.'

On Sunday March 16, in London, celebrities flocked to the opening of a new film *A Bigger Splash* describing a year in the life of David Hockney and the break up of his relationship with a favourite male model, Peter Schlesinger. 26-year-old Schlesinger later commented, 'I was never a kept boy with an allowance. It was a claustrophobic relationship which I had to break out of.'

On Monday March 17, David Frost was fined £22 for driving his Bentley at over 87 m.p.h. down the A1.

Meanwhile, the body of multi-millionaire Aristotle Onassis, which had weighed only 80 pounds at the time of his death, had been flown to Greece, accompanied by his daughter, his widow, Senator Edward Kennedy and others. On Tuesday March 18, the funeral service took place under an overcast sky on the private island of Skorpios where Onassis and Jackie had got married six years earlier. Among the floral tributes was a wreath tied with a violet ribbon and inscribed 'From Jackie to Ari'.

After the funeral, Mrs Onassis flew back to Paris with her children amidst speculation about the size of her new fortune. It was now thought that she might inherit as much as $200 million. On arrival at her luxury penthouse, a US Secret Service agent assigned to protect her son, John John, grappled with photographers attempting to enter the building.

Meanwhile, back in London, Harold Wilson's personal secretary 43-year-old Lady Falkender had been found enjoying a late night drink at Annabel's in Berkeley Square, inner sanctum of capitalism. She had been accompanied by 'a rather good looking chap' later identified as Mr Eric Miller, chairman of the Peachey Property Corporation.

On Thursday March 20, elderly billionaire Paul Getty announced that he must reluctantly postpone his retirement to California on account of his North Sea Oil interests. 'I just can't get away until I am absolutely satisfied how things are doing. To retire to California now would make me unhappy. It's a race between me and the undertaker.'

Meanwhile, the newly married Earl and Countess of Lichfield, who had spent the first part of their honeymoon staying at Princess Margaret's villa on Mustique, had been found stranded at Kingston, Jamaica, toying with a fried egg sandwich in the airport cafeteria.

On Friday March 21, Detective Chief Superintendent Kenneth Etheridge, deputy head of Scotland Yard's Fraud Squad, arrived back in Australia this time armed with a warrant for the arrest of Labour MP John Stonehouse on fifteen charges of forgery and theft. Later that day the arrest was effected and Stonehouse

Jackie Onassis and her step-daughter Christina accompany the body of shipping magnate Aristotle Onassis to Skorpios. Senator Edward Kennedy is in the background

appeared before Melbourne Magistrates Court dressed in a brown corduroy jacket. 'I will fight this extradition with every power at my disposal,' he said after being released on bail. 'Scotland Yard detectives have been conducting a vendetta against me.'

Back in London's dockland the following night, artist Andrew Logan held another of his mock, largely transvestite, 'Miss World' contests. The evening was marked by incidents. A contestant dressed as the Statue of Liberty caught fire and the co-hostess, author Molly Parkin, was thrown into a pool by the previous year's winner.

On Tuesday March 25, 69-year-old King Faisal of Saudi Arabia, leader of the world's richest oil-producing country, was shot dead in the ante-room of his palace in Riyadh. His assassin, his mentally deranged nephew Prince Faisal, was immediately overpowered and the King's brother Crown Prince Khaled was swiftly elected the new ruler.

Back in London, this tragic event was marked by the Saudi flag flying at half mast at Harrods department store, where the late king had been a lavish spender.

The following day in Australia, Mrs Sheila Buckley was arrested and charged with fraud involving thousands of pounds. After her appearance in Melbourne

Magistrates Court, her former employer John Stonehouse said, 'Mrs Buckley is being subjected to a police vendetta similar to that being pursued against me.'

Meanwhile, a romance had blossomed between actress Britt Ekland and millionaire pop singer Rod Stewart, who had met for the first time the previous summer at Mick Jagger's birthday party. On Sunday March 30, the couple flew off together to California in high spirits. 'I am in heaven,' said Rod. 'I have been looking for someone like Britt for years and years.'

On Tuesday April 1, Lady Churchill celebrated her ninetieth birthday with a family lunch party at Claridge's.

Pop star Rod Stewart and actress Britt Ekland at the beginning of their romance. 'I have been looking for someone like Britt for years and years,' said Rod

On Thursday April 3, trade union leader Clive Jenkins presented the awards to the year's best wine writers. 'I enjoy the good things in life,' he explained. 'And I particularly like a fine claret.'

On Saturday April 5, Princess Anne got an icy ducking when she was thrown off her horse into the River Avon at the Rushall Horse Trials in Wiltshire. She escaped unhurt, covered in mud.

Meanwhile, 40-year-old Lord Brooke, son and heir to the Earl of Warwick and owner of Warwick Castle, had joined his father in tax exile. He had taken a small flat in Paris where he was now obliged to stay for the next twelve months to establish a new tax position. 'He's rather miserable,' said a friend, 'although he's invited out a lot by French hostesses who want to marry their daughters off.'

Back in London, on Wednesday April 9, Margaret Duchess of Argyll coped with the worsening economic climate by throwing open her Mayfair home to the public. That evening she gave a party to publicize the event which was attended by the former Minister for the Arts Norman St John-Stevas, Norman Hartnell, Lord Duncan-Sandys and several ambassadors. It was noted that visitors to the Queen Anne house, where the Duchess had lived since before the War, would be charged £7.50 per head and shown most of the house including the duchess's pink lavatory with built-in arm rests.

The following Monday, April 14, 73-year-old authoress Barbara Cartland arrived in a white Rolls-Royce at the International Health Food Fair. She then toured the show, enthusiastically endorsing herbal tonics, balms, cleansers and her new discovery, propilis, 'the resin which the bees use to seal the hive'.

The same day, the Queen Mother flew off to Tehran for five days holiday as a guest of the Shah of Iran. She was accompanied by Ruth, Lady Fermoy, whose 14-year-old granddaughter Diana Spencer was completing her education at Riddlesworth Hall in Norfolk.

The following morning, police were called to examine a suspicious package on a Foreign Office windowsill. It turned out to be a staff food parcel.

Later that day, in the House of Commons, Chancellor of the Exchequer Denis Healey's budget increased both direct and indirect taxation and was described by Opposition leader Mrs Thatcher as 'equal shares of misery for all'.

That night in Paris, the opening of a new exhibition of paintings by David Hockney was celebrated with a dinner at the Moulin de la Galette in Montmartre, which was attended by playwright Tom Stoppard, artist Patrick Procktor and Bianca Jagger, now emerging as a personality in her own right.

Back in London, on Monday April 21, the popular Earl of Mar fell to his death from his fifth floor Knightsbridge flat. It was noted that the 60-year-old peer, Scotland's premier Earl, had listed 'pigeon-kicking' as one of his recreations.

On Wednesday April 23, a new play by Harold Pinter, *No Man's Land* opened at the Old Vic. Among celebrities who attended the opening night was the beautiful Lady Antonia Fraser. Missing from the event was the playwright's wife, actress Vivien Merchant.

The following day in Moscow, 23-year-old Anatoly Karpov, an economic student at Leningrad University, was officially enthroned as the new world chess champion. The ceremony was followed by a reception at the city's swish Hotel Metropole at which the new champion, who was soon to be seen driving around in a chauffeur-driven Mercedes, had a long chat with Harry Golombek, chess correspondent of *The Times*. Asked if Bobby Fischer had been invited an official replied, 'How could we? We have no address.'

Back in London, on Sunday April 27, Employment Secretary Michael Foot entered the Royal Free Hospital for a minor operation and said he had read the new unemployment figures 'with horror and with shame'.

The following Wednesday, April 30, the engagement was announced between 28-year-old Dai Llewellyn, elder brother of Princess Margaret's friend Roddy, and 22-year-old Miss Isobel Richli, daughter of the late Paul Richli, who was said to have been one of Europe's richest men. It was noted that Mr Llewellyn had recently been working as social secretary at the Clermont Club in Berkeley Square.

On Monday May 5, it was revealed that oil heiress Olga Deterding and television personality Jonathan Routh had finally parted after six years together. 'I'm fed up with everything,' said 46-year-old Olga at her Mayfair penthouse. 'Some friends have a small boat and are planning to sail around the world. I'm going with them and will be away for a year.'

The same day in Melbourne, Australia, Labour MP John Stonehouse tore up a High Court writ demanding £41,000. He later picked up the pieces and put them in his pocket.

The following day in London, a group of Mr Stonehouse's colleagues voted to expel him from the House of Commons.

On Wednesday May 7, Mrs Barbara Stonehouse issued a staunch defence of her husband. 'What has happened to my husband is a tragedy,' she said. 'He has lost everything in his life. He has lost his career, his family and his health.'

The following day, the Queen arrived at Tokyo's Haneda Airport and was whisked away in a black Rolls-Royce to the state guest house. That night she appeared at a banquet at the Imperial Palace wearing a thick white silk evening dress adorned with bands of gold embroidery.

Back in London the same evening, Olga Deterding was stopped while driving her black Rolls-Royce in Curzon Street and spent the night in a cell in Mayfair's Vine Street police station. 'I had to sleep on a concrete shelf and the blanket smelt of urine,' she said afterwards. 'I've never been in Holloway but I imagine that it must be infinitely superior.'

On Saturday May 10, Mr Heath's fourth racing yacht to bear the name *Morning Cloud* was lowered into the water after being named by the former Prime Minister's step-mother, Mrs Mary Heath.

On Sunday May 11, Prime Minister Harold Wilson returned to England after two weeks absence at the Commonwealth Conference in Jamaica. That night he appeared on television, puffing at his pipe, comfortably seated in a pink and white armchair and accused the aristocracy and others of 'rushing around like wet hens as though some devastating crisis had hit the country'.

On Tuesday May 13, the opening of the King Faisal Medical City on the outskirts of Riyadh was celebrated. It was said that the enterprise, where patients would be provided with five star hotel accommodation, had cost £100 million and had been built along basic lines originally laid down by international architect John Poulson, now in prison on corruption charges.

Back in London, on Thursday May 15, a dinner party at 10 Downing Street in honour of the Prime Minister of Fiji was disturbed when Lady Falkender left the table before the guest of honour had made his speech. She returned three-quarters of an hour later with Mr Frank Sinatra and his constant companion Mrs Barbara Marx. Mr Sinatra had arrived in London a few days earlier to bring a successful libel action against the BBC which had suggested he had links with the mafia.

The same night, at a charity ball to raise money for the preservation of rural England, gossip columnist Nigel Dempster was placed in the stocks and pelted with pies and eggs by eager socialites.

On Friday May 16, the former chairman of the extreme Right Wing British Movement, Mr Colin Jordan, was fined £30 after being found guilty of stealing a box of chocolates and three pairs of women's pink knickers from a supermarket in Leamington Spa.

Later that day in Washington, the Shah of Iran was guest of honour at a white tie dinner at the White House, described as the grandest social function yet during the Ford administration. 'We are proud of being a good and trusted friend of the United States of America,' said the Shah. 'It is a friendship based on permanent, durable reasons.'

The following day in New York, it was disclosed that Fabergé cosmetics company would be signing up 20-year-old Margaux Hemingway, highly publicized granddaughter of Ernest Hemingway, as a spokesman for its products.

Back in Britain, on Monday May 19, a helicopter carrying infra-red cameras capable of detecting human and animal remains began searching the Sussex coast near Newhaven for the possible remains of the missing Earl of Lucan.

On Tuesday May 20, sculptress Dame Barbara Hepworth died in a fire at her Cornish home. Her nurse said later, 'She was on fire, the whole bed was on fire; I could get to the telephone but that was also on fire. I couldn't get near her.' It was noted that 72-year-old Dame Barbara had designed her own tombstone several years earlier.

The same day in California, it was revealed that banker's daughter Sabrina Guinness, who had spent the last ten months looking after precocious child-star Tatum O'Neal, had now begun working as girl friday to rock star David Bowie.

The following day, a jet carrying the Osmond family was refused permission to land at Heathrow by airport officials fearing a repetition of the last year's dangerous scenes. The group were eventually permitted to land at Gatwick and were taken to 11 Eaton Square, which had been rented at £2,500 a week from Saudi Arabian businessman Adnan Khashoggi.

Princess Margaret and Lord Snowdon arrive at a film première amidst rumours that their marriage is on the rocks

On Thursday May 22, it was revealed that Sir Cecil Beaton, who had suffered a severe stroke the previous summer, was to sell the house in Pelham Place, Knightsbridge, which had been his London home for the past thirty-six years. 'The house bears the unmistakable imprint of its owner,' said estate agents Hillier Parker.

On Monday May 26, police were called to 11 Eaton Square after fans of the Osmonds had discovered their secret address and laid siege to the imposing five-storey house. When the famous family appeared on a balcony ten girls were carried away in a state of collapse.

The following day, it was announced that an exhaustive search of the Sussex coast for the body of the missing Earl of Lucan using a helicopter equipped with infra-red cameras had proved fruitless. They had identified the bodies of many rodents and other animals but discovered no trace of any human remains.

Meanwhile, the Emir of Kuwait had arrived in Paris for a simple medical check up and booked an entire floor of the Crillon Hotel.

On Sunday June 1, the Queen Mother dropped her handbag into the sea as she stepped from the royal barge onto a pontoon at Portsmouth. It was retrieved by Lieutenant Hugh Slade of the Royal Navy.

The same day, President Ford tripped on the gangway of his aircraft at Salzburg airport, fell three steps and crashed onto the tarmac on all fours.

Later that day, the President stumbled on the steep staircase of the nearby Schloss Fuschl and had to fling up his arm to keep his balance. Members of his entourage explained that he had a 'football' knee which sometimes troubled him when he was tired.

On Monday June 2, President Ford began talks in Salzburg with President Sadat about the Middle East situation. Missing from the scene was Sadat's attractive wife, Jehan, who was studying hard for a degree at the University of Cairo.

Back in London, on Tuesday June 3, 43-year-old Dominic Elwes, friend of the missing Earl of Lucan, presided over the opening of a new ladies' hairdressing salon in Pont Street, Belgravia.

The following day, gossip columnist Nigel Dempster told British television viewers, 'I am paid a certain sum of money to spy for my readers, to seek out the curious lives, the mistakes and the unhappiness of those who have got a privileged position.'

Gossip columnist Nigel Dempster, who emerged as more famous than many of the people he wrote about

Meanwhile in California, Bernard Cornfeld had been charged with making free overseas phone calls by means of a gadget known as 'the blue box' which had been discovered at his Beverly Hills home earlier in the year.

Back in London on Thursday June 5, former whizz kid Jim Slater told his shareholders to expect 'a very low level of profits indeed' and explained that he was still selling off the company's assets. An observer commented that the once mighty company was retreating to 'financial suburbia'.

The same day, the British people voted in favour of staying in the Common Market by a 2 to 1 majority. In a statement from the steps of 10 Downing Street Harold Wilson stated that fourteen years of national argument were over.

On Friday June 6, the death occurred in Paris of 54-year-old Paul Picasso who had squandered some 800,000 francs since the death of his famous father two years earlier. Among his many extravagances was the purchase of a Rolls-Royce upholstered in leopard skins.

On Sunday June 8, it was revealed that Aristotle Onassis, whose total fortune was thought to be worth between £300 and £400 million, had left his wife Jackie a modest annuity of $250,000 a year.

Back in Britain the following day, the death occurred of the 83-year-old Earl Spencer. A great patron of the arts and keen embroiderer, it was noted that the late Earl had repaired many of the tapestry armchairs at his stately home, Althorp in Northamptonshire with his own hands.

The same day in Australia, John Stonehouse was seized by detectives at Melbourne Airport as he tried to board a jumbo jet for London with his suits slung over his arm in plastic bags. He was taken to the city's Pentridge Prison where he immediately went on a hunger strike.

On Saturday June 14, the Queen's birthday honours included a CBE for former War Minister John Profumo in acknowledgement of his work in the East End of London among drug addicts, alcoholics, immigrants and ex-convicts.

On Monday June 16, the inquest on Lord Lucan's nanny opened in a small coroner's court in Pimlico. On the first day of the hearing, the Countess of Lucan told the court that the man who had attacked her on the night of the murder was her husband.

On Tuesday June 17, top-hatted race-goers, who included the Aga Khan, the Earl of Lichfield and hairdresser Teazy Weazy Raymond, attending the opening day of Royal Ascot, were picketed by striking stable lads, whose dispute over pay was now in its seventh week.

The following day, in a central square in Riyadh, Saudi Arabia, the execution took place of the American-educated Prince Faisal, who had murdered his uncle, King Faisal, weeks earlier. The Prince's head was sheared off with a clean sweep by a gold-handled sword and then displayed for fifteen minutes on a wooden spike.

Back in London, on Thursday June 19, the inquest on Lord Lucan's nanny ended with the coroner issuing a warrant committing the missing peer for trial at the Central Criminal Court on a charge of murder. Immediately afterwards, a senior Scotland Yard detective stated, 'We now have positive evidence that he is living under an assumed name and with a completely different appearance in a country I am not prepared to disclose.'

On Saturday June 21 in Paris, the marriage took place between Margaux Hemingway and hamburger baron Errol Wetson. After the ceremony, at which the bride wore a ruffled cotton Victorian-style gown and a wide brimmed straw hat, there was a party at the Paris Ritz, once the stomping ground of Margaux's grandfather, Ernest Hemingway.

Back in London, on Monday June 23, it was disclosed that 36-year-old millionaire bachelor Henry Keswick, who had recently returned to England after heading his family's trading business in Hong Kong, had purchased the weekly magazine the *Spectator*. 'My own politics are not particularly developed,' he said, 'but I do believe in freedom of choice.'

The following day, Detective Chief Inspector Roy Ransom and his colleague Detective Chief Inspector David Gerring flew to France to take statements from people in Cherbourg who claimed to have seen Lord Lucan. Staff at the town's Grand Hotel were convinced that he had stayed there, speaking fluent French. Said Mrs Maxwell-Scott, who had seen the missing Earl on the night of the murder, 'I think it is inherently unlikely that he is living in northern France. I hope he is still alive but I do not think he is there.' Said another friend, stockbroker Stephen Raphael. 'I doubt if he can manage half a dozen words in French.'

Over in New York, on Wednesday June 25, author Clifford Irving, still embroiled in legal troubles over his Howard Hughes biography hoax, filed a suit for bankruptcy claiming that he had debts of $55 million. He listed among his assets a $35 typewriter and a $50 tape-recorder.

Meanwhile, the Rolling Stones were giving a series of concerts in Madison Square Gardens. 'I love New York,' said Bianca Jagger in an interview at her hotel, during which she wore a red and white candy striped cotton dress designed by Emmanuelle Kahn.

Ernest Hemingway's 20-year-old granddaughter Margaux and her husband film producer Errol Wetson celebrate their marriage at the Paris Ritz

Back in London, on Thursday June 26, Lady Falkender won substantial libel damages from the *Evening Standard* which had published an unfounded report the previous year linking her with the forgery of Harold Wilson's signature and accusing her of misusing her position as his personal secretary.

On Friday June 27, Mr Edward Heath issued a statement referring to 'monstrous allegations' that he had been rude to Mrs Thatcher during her visit to his Belgravia home after she had won the Tory leadership. 'I must state categorically that there was no discourtesy of any kind at any time.'

The same day in Paris, the death of two counter-espionage agents in a gun battle in an apartment on the Left Bank was followed by a manhunt for South American terrorist Carlos Martinez, a well-educated man noted for his surface charm and arrogance.

On Monday June 30, Harold and Mary Wilson were photographed eating strawberries and cream at the Royal Agricultural Show in Warwickshire, a few minutes after Mr Wilson had made a speech describing the world's current economic crisis as 'the biggest recession since 1931'.

The same day, the new Archbishop of Canterbury, Dr Donald Coggan, laid down guidelines for the use of exorcism by the Church of England. He insisted that this should be carried out only 'in collaboration with medical treatment and with the minimum of publicity'.

That night in London, Mrs Henry Ford threw a party at Mark's Club in Mayfair in honour of Wendy, Carol and Melinda Rockefeller, step-daughters of the new American Vice-President. Among those present were Prince Charles, Lady Jane Wellesley, now working as a journalist on the *Radio Times*, the rangy Duke of Marlborough, American Ambassador Elliot Richardson and David Frost and his current girl-friend Mrs Caroline Cushing. Police and security men with explosive sniffing dogs mounted guard outside.

On Tuesday July 1, the French police hunting terrorist Carlos Martinez discovered an arsenal of weapons in a Paris flat. Included in the haul were sub-machine guns, pistols, grenades, dynamite, plastic explosives, detonators and home-made bombs.

Over in New York the same day, dustmen went on strike. By afternoon over 30,000 tons of rubbish had accumulated on the sidewalks and Sanitation Commissioner Mr Robert Groh said the city faced 'a health emergency'.

On Sunday July 6, President Ford showed his sporting prowess when he put on a pair of navy blue swimming trunks and dived into his sparkling new White House swimming-pool and quickly swum five lengths watched by seventy press men and photographers.

Meanwhile in Paris, leading socialite Mrs Rita Lachman, heiress to the Revlon cosmetics fortune, had been robbed of £1.8 million worth of jewellery. 'I now feel quite undressed,' she said. 'I have to go out night and day without a single piece on.'

Back in London, on Tuesday July 8, police spent five hours at Heathrow trying to locate a woman who they believed could be carrying money to the missing Earl of Lucan. They had received a tip-off that the woman was trying to board a South African Airways jumbo jet for Johannesburg with a bag of cash.

On Saturday July 12, many of the old-fashioned British aristocracy were present at a private party given by the Duke and Duchess of Buccleuch at their seventeenth-century Northamptonshire home, Boughton House.

On Tuesday July 15, the 83-year-old Duke of Leinster took his seat in the House of Lords for the first time. The white haired old peer had been prevented from taking his seat earlier because he was an undischarged bankrupt. 'I look forward to a new political career and the attendance allowance will come in useful,' he said.

The same day, the Earl of Snowdon returned to London after six months continuous travelling and separation from his wife, Princess Margaret.

On Friday July 18, Labour MP John Stonehouse and his former secretary, Mrs Sheila Buckley, at last arrived in London after a long delayed flight from Melbourne, during which the former minister and his secretary had drunk red wine, enjoyed a steak casserole and watched a new Walt Disney film *The Island on Top of The World*. From Heathrow Airport the couple were taken in a convoy of three cars to Bow Street Court, where they were to spend the night in the cells. A dozen pieces of luggage which they had with them were carefully listed as 'prisoners' possessions'.

The following morning, they appeared before a magistrate to face charges of conspiracy, forgery, fraud and theft. Mrs Buckley was released on bail but Mr Stonehouse was remanded in custody and driven to Brixton Prison where he immediately went on a fast. 'This is nothing personal,' he told prison officers, 'but every now and then I *do* go on a fast.'

On Monday July 21, it was revealed that a romance had now blossomed between

29-year-old Dai Llewellyn and beautiful Beatrice Welles, daughter of Orson Welles. 'I love her and I hope she loves me,' said Dai, whose engagement to Miss Isobel Richli had been broken off a few weeks earlier.

The following day in Greece, the marriage took place between 24-year-old Christina Onassis and 30-year-old shipping magnate's son Alexander Andreadis, after an eight day whirlwind romance. At the simple ceremony at a church outside Athens, the bride's step-mother Mrs Jackie Onassis stole the show in a full length black skirt and long sleeved white blouse. 'I do so love that child,' she said. 'I am so happy she has found him at last. I can see happy days ahead for her.'

The same day in London, Prime Minister Harold Wilson looked in for a quick glass of campari and soda before a luncheon at the Savoy Hotel in honour of singer Vera Lynn. At the lunch that followed Mr Wilson's personal secretary, Lady Falkender, sat between comedians Harry Secombe and Alfred Marks and was said to shed a tear when Vera Lynn sang 'We'll meet again' and 'The White Cliffs of Dover' at the end of the meal.

The following night, the beautiful Mrs Patricia Wolfson, who had featured in the controversial Love Gifts case four years earlier, gave a party at her house on Cheyne Walk, attended by Lord Drogheda's son photographer Viscount Moore and other celebrities.

On Saturday July 26, Prince Charles and Princess Elizabeth of Yugoslavia, former fiancée of Richard Burton, were found weekending at Earl Mountbatten's stately home in Hampshire. During an outing to Cowdray Park that afternoon the Princess was perched on the side of the Prince's open-topped Aston Martin.

The following morning, it was disclosed that Harley Street hair specialist Leonard Pountney had written to the Duke of Edinburgh offering him free advice about his thinning hair. 'I am 67 now and I plan to retire shortly. I would like Prince Philip to be my last client. It would be the greatest job I have ever done and I would expect no reward financial or otherwise,' said Mr Pountney, an expert on hair transplanting.

On Monday July 28, it was disclosed that actress Vivien Merchant was suing her husband playwright Harold Pinter for divorce, naming as 'the other woman' 42-year-old Lady Antonia Fraser, whom she accused of having 'cast a spell' on her husband. Lady Antonia's father 70-year-old Lord Longford had no comment to make. 'As far as I am concerned there is nothing else I can say,' he said.

Later that day, Mr John Stonehouse made another unsuccessful application for bail, this time offering to live at the House of Commons if it were granted. The former minister protested his innocence at Bow Street Court dressed in an immaculate grey charcoal suit with a red silk handkerchief tumbling out of his top pocket.

On Tuesday July 29, Princess Anne's father-in-law Major Peter Phillips began his premature retirement. It was noted that his colleagues at the Walls ice-cream and pork pie firm had clubbed together to present him with a desk blotter, cigarette box and a coffee mug.

The following day in New Delhi, the beautiful Rajmata of Jaipur, subject of a celebrated painting by Annigoni, was thrown into gaol. Her political opponents had falsely accused her of smuggling and currency manipulation after a mass of jewels and gold had been discovered at one of her family palaces.

On Friday August 1, attention turned to Helsinki where representatives of thirty-five nations laughed and joked as they queued to sign a document on security and co-operation. This agreement was a diplomatic triumph for Soviet leader Mr Brezhnev who had attended the talks surrounded by eleven car-loads of KGB men.

Later that day in Washington, a new scandal erupted when the Lockheed Air-craft Corporation stated that it had made payments totalling millions of dollars to foreign government officials and foreign political organizations to secure con-tracts.

On Sunday August 3, Prince Charles arrived in Iceland for a fishing holiday with the Hon. Anthony Tryon and his attractive Australian wife.

The following day, as the temperature in London hit 84°F, a spectator at Lord's Cricket Ground removed all his clothes and 'streaked' across the pitch in front of the television cameras and jumped over both sets of stumps. He was later fined £20 by the chairman of Marylebone Magistrates and told, 'Please moderate your behaviour in future.'

That night, about eighty close friends and relations of the Queen Mother sat down to a dinner in the Throne Room at Buckingham Palace to celebrate her seventy-fifth birthday. The band of the Welsh Guards played string music throughout the meal which ended with a three tier cake crowned with a single pink candle being produced.

On Tuesday August 5, it was reported that two major American television networks had turned down the offer of ex-President Nixon's memoirs. Both net-works said they were opposed to 'checkbook journalism'.

On Wednesday August 6, it was revealed that London socialite Mrs Davina Phillips had sold her London mansion, 10 The Boltons, to Sheikh Zayid of Abu Dhabi for £300,000. Already living in this exclusive backwater was Sheikh Isa Bin Sulman of Bahrein. Limousines were to keep up a twenty-four hour vigil outside their gates.

Later that day, creditors of the missing Earl of Lucan, who had disappeared owing £45,000, gathered to make their claims. Among them were Ladbrokes Casinos, who claimed £11,500 for unmet cheques for gaming chips and Cartier of Bond Street, from whom the missing peer had purchased a £9 crocodile skin watch-strap shortly before he disappeared.

That evening, Mrs Barbara Stonehouse visited her husband in Brixton Prison bringing him extra food and taking away his 'smalls' wrapped in a towel.

On Friday August 8, it was disclosed that the Dutch shipyard of Van Lent was working on a new £12 million yacht for King Khaled of Saudi Arabia. The vessel of 650 tons, would be 212 feet long and would include eight guest rooms and three state rooms.

Over in New York, on Saturday August 9, 21-year-old Samuel Bronfman, son and heir of Seagrams heir Edgar Bronfman, was kidnapped on his way to a party in a fashionable suburb. His captors announced that they had buried him with only ten days' water supply and demanded $4.5 million in ransom.

The same day at San Clemente, California, Mr Nixon spent the anniversary of his resignation as President of the United States closeted with his literary agent Swifty Lazar and television personality David Frost. At the end of six hours of discussion a cheque for $200,000 passed hands.

The following day, Mr Frost gave a press conference at the Beverly Hills Hilton at which he announced he had bought the exclusive rights to Mr Nixon's TV memoirs. 'I should make it clear,' he said, 'that the former President has neither requested nor has he received any editorial control.'

Meanwhile, President Amin's former Foreign Minister, Girton-educated Princess Elizabeth of Toro, had slipped into London and gone into hiding in a flat near Victoria Station.

On Thursday August 14, the temperature in London again hit the 80s. That afternoon 74-year-old novelist Barbara Cartland was found promoting health products and signing copies of her books at Woolworth's in Oxford Street. She was dressed in a pink silk suit and examined herself in a small mirror every ten minutes. 'I'll keep going till my face falls off,' she said.

The following Saturday, August 16, only fourteen months after their divorce Richard Burton and Elizabeth Taylor were reunited at a villa in Switzerland.

On Sunday August 17, kidnapped Samuel Bronfman was found gagged and blindfolded in an apartment in Brooklyn. He was flown by helicopter to his family's estate at Yorktown Heights, for a family reunion, amidst rumours that $2.3 million had been paid for his release. 'Sam is here and he looks fine,' said the family's public relations man. 'There will be no interviews, no pictures, no statements and that's it.'

Back in Britain, on Monday August 18, the engagement between Orson Welles's daughter Beatrice and 29-year-old playboy Dai Llewellyn was announced. 'This is the real thing,' said Llewellyn. 'Beatrice is the best thing that has ever happened to me.'

On Wednesday August 20, it was announced in Switzerland that Richard Burton and Elizabeth Taylor were to get married again.

The following day, Miss Taylor's old friend Henry Wynberg left London for Los Angeles wearing a beige safari jacket and grey slacks and accompanied by eight suitcases. 'I have nothing to say to anyone, d'you hear me, anyone,' he snapped.

On Thursday August 22, a row erupted in London over the revelation that MPs had ordered £12,000 worth of crockery from a West German firm, Rosenthal. 'In the present economic situation it is incredible that the Commons should place an order for pottery with a foreign firm, especially when in Britain we make the finest pottery in the world,' said Labour MP for Stoke on Trent John Forrester.

The following day, the Biba department store closed down only two years after opening. As bargain hunters picked through tinselled heaps of tee-shirts and tights and trays of gaudy plastic tat, it was said that this was 'the definitive death of Swinging London'.

On Wednesday August 27, Richard Burton and Elizabeth Taylor flew from Zurich to Tel Aviv by jumbo jet. Burton, now on the wagon, sipped iced water and said, 'I want to live with Liz for ever. This time it's for keeps.'

That night in London, Labour MP John Stonehouse was unexpectedly released from Brixton Prison on bail. After being reunited with his family in South London, he issued a statement criticising 'the ugly charade of the bail system'.

On Friday August 29, a telephone engineer admitted listening to calls to Princess Anne's home at Sandhurst and resigned his job. 'The Post Office has made me the scapegoat' he said angrily. 'They have made me take all the blame. I have only listened in on her line a few times.'

On Wednesday September 3, a diplomatic incident arose when an Ilyushin 62 Soviet airliner arrived at Heathrow with a dead man in its first class section. It was revealed that he had shot himself in the head during the flight from New York to Moscow.

On Friday September 5, anti-pornography campaigner Raymond Blackburn appeared before West London Magistrates Court and was fined £2 for being drunk and disorderly.

Later that day, Lord Lucan's friend, 44-year-old Dominic Elwes, was found dead in his Chelsea flat. An article from *The Times* prophesying economic doom written by Peter Jay was pinned to the wall.

Meanwhile in Sacramento, California, there had been an attempt on President Ford's life. As the President had walked towards the State Capitol building, 26-year-old Miss Lynn Fromme, a former follower of Charles Manson, had pointed a semi-automatic 45 calibre pistol at him. Secret service men had quickly grabbed Mr Ford's jacket and forced him to bend double to reduce the possibility of him becoming a target while the girl was disarmed. The President said later that the incident would not stop him meeting and mingling with the American people.

Back in Britain, on Saturday September 6, Harold and Mary Wilson arrived to spend the weekend with the Queen at Balmoral Castle.

Meanwhile, President Amin of Uganda was on a short visit to Italy. On Wednesday September 10, he arrived twenty minutes late for an audience with Pope Paul at Castel Gandolfo, blaming traffic conditions. Vatican officials said that it was the first time in living memory that the Pope had been kept waiting.

Over in Washington, on Friday September 12, a Senate Committee heard that in order to procure orders in Saudi Arabia, the Lockheed Aircraft Corporation had paid more than $106 million to Triad, a company owned by businessman Adnan Khashoggi. The payments had been made through Swiss and Liechtenstein banks. Mr Khashoggi said he would not comment on this 'stream of allegations made by Lockheed and others until there is an appropriate time and place to set the record straight formally'.

The world's richest man: arms dealer Adnan Khashoggi who was said to have an easy and continual access to world leaders

On Thursday September 18, the long hunt for missing heiress Patty Hearst ended when she was arrested in San Francisco looking, according to one commentator, like 'someone who might stand unnoticed at an all-night cafeteria'. A few hours later, she sent out a message from her prison cell saying, 'Tell my brothers and sisters that my revolutionary zeal remains undimmed.'

Back in London, on Friday September 19, it was announced that 29-year-old Dai Llewellyn had broken off his engagement to Beatrice Welles and switched his affections to Tessa Dahl, daughter of author Roald Dahl. 'I just couldn't be happier about it,' said Beatrice. 'I feel as if I had got rid of a large stone from around my neck.'

Meanwhile in New York, Mrs Jackie Onassis had taken a job as a consulting editor at the Viking Press at a salary of $10,000 a year. On Monday September 22, the sidewalks of Madison Avenue were jammed with reporters, photographers and television news cameramen as she arrived for her first day's work.

Later that day, in San Francisco, a shot was fired at President Ford as he emerged from a hotel in the city centre and a 45-year-old woman, Sara Jane Moore, was arrested. Ford returned to the White House, where that night he declared that he would not hide himself away from the people. 'We are going to stand tall and strong,' he said.

On Tuesday September 23, the American Immigration authorities announced that they had delayed the deportation of John Lennon on humanitarian grounds because his wife Yoko Ono was now expecting a baby.

Back in San Francisco the same day, a judge appointed three psychiatrists to examine heiress Patty Hearst and delayed making a decision on bail until he had heard from them.

In Europe, on Thursday September 25, Saudi Arabia's oil minister Sheikh Yamani stormed out of an OPEC meeting in Vienna after the conference had failed to accept a lower price structure. The Harvard-educated Sheikh then flew to London in his private jet for the night in order to make a telephone call to his government. He explained that he could not contact his government from Vienna.

On Tuesday September 30, MP John Stonehouse caused much embarrassment when he turned up at the Labour Party Conference at Blackpool. He was immediately isolated, surrounded by empty seats and generally ignored by his former friends and colleagues, with the notable exception of Mrs Mary Wilson who went up to him and shook his hand.

Meanwhile in Manila, Muhammad Ali had regained the world heavyweight championship title when his opponent Joe Frazier failed to answer the bell for the fifteenth round. After being pronouced winner, Ali collapsed with exhaustion.

On Wednesday October 1, 17-year-old Caroline Kennedy began an arts training course at Sotheby's in London where she would be working alongside a breed of girl recently branded 'Sloane Rangers'.

Meanwhile, the Prime Minister's secretary, Lady Falkender, yet to make her debut in the House of Lords, had again been discovered at Annabel's. This time her escort was her old friend Sir George Weidenfeld, who declared that they were discussing 'business'.

On Monday October 6, an admission by President Ford's 23-year-old son Jack that he had occasionally smoked pot made headline news.

On Tuesday October 7, John Lennon won his long fight to stay in the United States when the Court of Appeals reversed the deportation order originally made because of his 1968 conviction in the UK for possessing marijuana.

Two days later, Lennon's wife, Yoko Ono, was to give birth to a baby boy.

Back in Britain, on Wednesday October 8, Margaret Thatcher and Edward Heath publicly shook hands to the visible relief of all those attending the Conservative Party Conference. It was noted that Mrs Thatcher was wearing a turquoise dress made of linen and rayon slubbed fabric.

The following day, the re-opening of the Savoy Grill was celebrated with a special luncheon attended by Princess Margaret, Mr and Mrs Jocelyn Stevens, Tommy Sopwith, impresario Sir Emile Littler, society columnist Mrs Betty Kenward and others. Guests were served with quenelles and sole followed by roast partridges and fresh raspberries and coffee.

A few hours later, an IRA bomb exploded outside the Ritz Hotel, shattering the hotel's swing doors and killing an unemployed man standing at a bus stop. At the nearby Coq d'Or restaurant in Stratton Street windows were smashed and a doorman was blown back by the blast. 'We carried on eating and drinking because there seemed no point in doing anything else,' said one of the customers.

On Friday October 10, the re-marriage of Richard Burton and Elizabeth Taylor took place in a mud hut village in Botswana and was performed by the local district commissioner. Burton wore white trousers, white shoes and a red open-necked shirt. Miss Taylor wore a green dress, edged with lace and adorned with guinea fowl feathers.

Back in London, on Monday October 13, a 20 pound bomb was discovered in a black hold-all outside Locket's restaurant in Westminster, a favoured haunt of many MPs, celebrated for amongst others its nursery dishes. Among the fifty people in the restaurant at the time was Mr Heath's former private secretary Sir Timothy Kitson.

18-year-old Caroline Kennedy, whose every move was now being followed by the world's press

On Tuesday October 14, Mr Heath visited a bring and buy sale in aid of the Conservative Party at the Naval and Military Club and purchased a set of silver decanter labels, a thermos jug and a navy blue woollen jersey. 'This *is* a pleasant occasion,' he said.

On Wednesday October 15, the new Archbishop of Canterbury Dr Coggan appealed to the British nation to renew its sense of moral purpose. 'Guzzling does not satisfy. Grabbing and getting is a poor creed. Envy is a cancer,' he said.

That night in London, the 'glitterati' gathered to celebrate the publication of a new novel, *Dead Babies*, by 25-year-old Martin Amis. Among those present were Lady Antonia Fraser, now living with her friend Harold Pinter, Clay Felker, editor of *New York* magazine, critic Kenneth Tynan, up and coming journalist Tina Brown and the author's father, 53-year-old Kingsley Amis.

On Monday October 20, Prime Minister Harold Wilson hurried to Heathrow Airport to welcome Crown Prince Fahd of Saudi Arabia to the country. After bowing low, Mr Wilson escorted the Prince to Claridge's Hotel.

That afternoon, proceedings against Labour MP John Stonehouse at the Horseferry Magistrates Court were temporarily halted to enable him to make his long-awaited statement to the House of Commons. Mr Wilson and Mrs Thatcher both left the chamber before the former minister was called. During the thirteen minute speech that followed, Mr Stonehouse spoke of the collapse of his ideals and his 'psychiatric suicide' and was warned five times by the Speaker not to deviate from the agreed text. Watching in the gallery was Mrs Sheila Buckley, who wore a high-necked flowered blouse.

That night, Mr Wilson gave a dinner at 10 Downing Street in honour of Crown Prince Fahd of Saudi Arabia, which was attended by, among others, Lady Falkender and Conservative MP Hugh Fraser, estranged husband of Lady Antonia.

On Tuesday October 21, it was announced in Madrid that the elderly General Franco had 'suffered a crisis of acute coronary insufficiency' and been close to death. The crisis was now 'resolving itself satisfactorily'.

Back in London the following night, the fashionable crowd gathered to view Zandra Rhodes's new collection. Among those present was indefatigable party-goer 83-year-old Lady Charlotte Bonham Carter.

The upstairs drawing-room at Sir Cecil Beaton's country home where he took up permanent residence after suffering a stroke

Early the following morning, an IRA bomb exploded outside the London home of Conservative MP Hugh Fraser, killing leading cancer specialist Professor Hamilton Fairley, who happened to be passing. 18-year-old Caroline Kennedy was in the house at the time and was thought to have escaped death by seconds. 'There is no doubt that it was meant for me,' said Mr Fraser. 'Somebody obviously wants to blow me up.'

Later that day, Crown Prince Fahd of Saudi Arabia lunched with the Queen at Buckingham Palace.

On Friday October 24, the Prince left London for Venice, where he was to spend a few days at the Gritti Palace Hotel before returning to Saudi Arabia.

Back in London that evening, the City career of former whizz kid Jim Slater came to a halt when he resigned as chairman of Slater Walker after a day of spectacular dealing in the company's shares, which at one moment had slumped to as low as 35p. In a statement 46-year-old Mr Slater said he wished to devote more time to his family and other interests. 'During the last few days I have been advised to take things easier,' he said. His resignation was followed immediately by an announcement that his close friend Jimmy Goldsmith, chairman of the Cavenham Group, would take over as chairman of Slater Walker.

Later that night, in the wilds of Exmoor, a 35-year-old former male model, Norman Scott, was found weeping beside the body of his great dane, Rinka, which had been shot dead.

On Saturday October 25, it was announced in Madrid that General Franco had suffered 'a new episode of coronary insufficiency' but had again pulled through the crisis. Doctors attending him at El Pardo palace said, 'The state of his cardio-vascular system continues unchanged.'

On Monday October 27, it was revealed that interior decorator Colonel Algernon Asprey had secured a £1 million contract to decorate the Royal Palace in Jeddah. It was noted that Colonel 'Algie' had already furnished the Al Nassurua Palace in Riyadh.

On Tuesday October 28, it was disclosed that the marriage of Jimmy Goldsmith's daughter Isabel and photographer Baron Arnaud de Rosnay was being brought to an end. 'It is by mutual consent and the proceedings will be in France,' said Arnaud in New York, where he was currently trying to promote a new game he had invented called *Petropolis*.

The following day in Spain, where General Franco was now gravely ill and being attended by nineteen specialists, Prince Juan Carlos assumed power for the second time.

Over in Florida, on Sunday November 2, President Ford dived into a swimming pool at the residence where he was staying with President Sadat and hit his head. A spokesman explained that his injuries were not serious.

The following day in Aberdeen, the Queen pressed a button and inaugurated the trickle of North Sea oil into the British economy.

On the night of Tuesday November 4, at their Regent's Park home, Lord and Lady Lambton threw a party in honour of Andy Warhol, who had become a close friend of their daughter Anne. 'I haven't seen so many freaks in five years,' he remarked casting his eye over Bianca Jagger, Caroline Kennedy, Lord Hesketh, Hugh Fraser MP, Lady Diana Cooper, pop star Keith Moon, Little Nell and other members of the champagne-drinking fun set who were present.

On Wednesday November 5, John Stonehouse and his secretary Mrs Buckley were committed for trial at the Old Bailey on a variety of charges. The former

Labour minister then made a speech to the court in which he attacked his political colleagues, the press, Scotland Yard and 'the Establishment'. 'I state with absolute certainty that I am not a criminal,' he said.

Later that day at a meeting of the Institute of Journalists, the editor of *The Times* Mr William Rees-Mogg attacked gossip columnists, describing their activities as 'straight scandal-mongering' and accusing them of 'exploiting private suffering for higher circulation'.

On Thursday November 6, it was revealed that Elizabeth Taylor had refused a present of a $1 million pink diamond from her husband Richard Burton and had decided that they should spend the money instead on a hospital for the Botswana village where they had got married. 'I certainly don't need another ring,' she said.

Meanwhile in Madrid, General Franco had been moved from his palace to La Paz medical centre. Here on Friday November 7 he underwent a major operation during which most of his stomach was removed.

Late the following night in London, an IRA bomb containing $6\frac{1}{2}$ pounds of gelignite was found in a blue duffle bag outside Mr Heath's Belgravia home. The former Prime Minister was in Hampshire at the time, attending the annual dance of the Royal Lymington Yacht Club. He later took refuge with the 81-year-old Dowager Duchess of Rutland, Field Marshal Sir Gerald Templer, Lady Moyra Browne and other neighbours while the bomb was defused.

The following day, Mr Heath attended the Remembrance Day service at the Cenotaph with his war medals clinking on his overcoat.

Richard Burton and Elizabeth Taylor arrive at London's Dorchester Hotel after their second marriage

On November 11 in Madrid, General Franco, who had now had most of his stomach removed, sat up in a chair beside his bed. 'The Caudillo sat for an hour and a half in an armchair,' said Lieutenant-General Angel Campano, head of the Civil Guard.

Meanwhile in London, a new edition of *Woman's Own* had been published carrying an interview with Prince Charles, now approaching his twenty-seventh birthday. 'I have fallen in love with all sorts of girls and I fully intend to go on doing so. I personally feel that a good age for a man to get married is around thirty.'

On Wednesday November 12, an IRA bomb was hurled through the window of Scott's Oyster Bar in Mayfair, killing one customer and injuring fifteen. 'Dinner was being served to a large number of people including many titled customers when there was a large bang,' said a waiter.

The following day in Paris, it was revealed that the 79-year-old Duchess of Windsor had had a major stomach haemorrhage and been rushed to the American Hospital for treatment.

Back in Madrid, on Friday November 14, General Franco underwent an emergency operation to repair the ruptured stitches from his stomach operation seven days earlier. The General's daughter, the Marquesa de Villaverde pleaded with the doctors to 'take pity on him' and let him die.

Back in Britain, on Tuesday November 18, it was announced that playboy Dai Llewellyn's plans to marry Tessa Dahl had fallen through. 'Dai is incredibly charming,' said Tessa, 'but that is not enough. Looking back I wouldn't go through it all again.' Said 29-year-old Llewellyn, 'After all this, I'm into a lonely winter of baked beans on toast in front of the television. At this rate, I'll never make a decent marriage.'

That night, a 3 pound bomb packed with metal nuts was hurled through the window of Waltons restaurant in Knightsbridge where eighty people were having dinner. Two people were killed and twenty-nine injured. 'This bomb was designed to kill and injure,' said Detective Chief Superintendent Jim Neville of Scotland Yard. Victims were treated on the pavement and given succour by the nearby fashionable restaurant Ma Cuisine.

Meanwhile in Madrid, a high government official stated that the 82-year-old General Franco's brain activity had virtually ceased. Early in the morning of Thursday November 20, it was announced that he was dead. While his body was returned to El Pardo palace to lie in state a deathbed announcement was issued on his behalf in which he forgave his enemies and asked them to forgive him.

On Friday November 21, it was announced that young Lord Hesketh had lost the battle to keep his grand prix motor racing team going.

Over in Louisville that weekend, the gentle ex-Governor of Georgia, peanut farmer Jimmy Carter, emerged as one of ten possible Democratic candidates for the American Presidency.

Back in Britain, on Monday November 24, there was much excitement over some new photographs of the supposed Loch Ness Monster taken by researchers for the Boston Academy of Applied Sciences. 'There is no question of a hoax,' said Alan Charig, head of the palaeontology section at the Natural History Museum. 'I have seen the pictures and they are very interesting.'

The same day, David Frost left London for Tehran accompanied by his girlfriend Mrs Caroline Cushing, whose luggage required securing with a piece of string.

The following day, friends of the late Dominic Elwes who gathered for a memorial service at Mayfair's Farm Street Church included journalist Peter Jay, Nicholas Soames, Lady Charlotte Curzon, Lord Charles Spencer-Churchill, Kenneth Tynan and zoo owner John Aspinall. At the end of the service there was an ugly scene when Dominic Elwes's cousin, Tremayne Rodd, lunged out at John Aspinall and punched him in the face. 'I'm used to wild animals pawing me,' said Aspinall afterwards 'and have learned to roll with the punches.'

Zoo owner and gambler John Aspinall nurses his jaw after the memorial service for playboy Dominic Elwes

Meanwhile, President Gerald Ford had begun an official visit to China. On Monday December 1, he was welcomed to Peking with a banquet in the Great Hall of the People at which he used chopsticks to tackle shark's fins, crisp fried chicken and other delicacies.

The same day in Paris, it was announced that the Duchess of Windsor was leaving hospital where she had been treated for a serious stomach ulcer, and was returning to her home in the Bois de Boulogne to be looked after by nurses. 'I fear that her days of entertaining and being entertained are over,' said her secretary John Utter.

Meanwhile, the Loch Ness Monster controversy had divided scientists. On Wednesday December 3, Dr Gordon Sheals, Keeper of the Zoology Department at the Natural History Museum, expressed his doubts about the existence of a monster. 'The only incontrovertible evidence must be a body, skeleton or really detailed photographs,' he said.

On Wednesday December 10, there was a Foyle's Literary Luncheon at the Dorchester Hotel, in honour of former Prime Minister Edward Heath whose book *Sailing*, published a few weeks earlier, had already sold 76,000 copies. Mr Heath told the assembled company, 'I wrote the book because *Morning Cloud* has meant so much to me and my crew and because sailing has become an essential part of my life.' It was noted the menu included lemon sorbet in a boat-shaped pastry case with a puff of spun sugar to represent a morning cloud. Among those present was Earl Mountbatten of Burma, who chided Mr Heath on one point: 'An admiral's boat is not a yacht, it is a barge.'

Later that day, Princess Anne raced down the M1 motorway from Scotland in her new Reliant Scimitar, breaking the speed limit and losing her police escort. A report on the incident was later submitted to the Chief Constable of the relevant county.

Meanwhile Waltons restaurant, which had been devastated by an IRA bomb three weeks earlier, was back in business. On Thursday December 11, Margaret Duchess of Argyll and other celebrities crowded into the restaurant for an after-dinner party to celebrate the publication of a new book by Alistair Maclean.

On Friday December 12, in Paris, it was announced that Picasso's heirs would share a fortune valued at 3,000 million francs. It was said that Picasso's huge collection of paintings and drawings was now deposited in the safes of various banks across the world.

Back in London, on Wednesday December 17, trade union leader Hugh Scanlon was found lunching at Claridge's alongside Lady d'Avigdor-Goldsmid, the elderly Earl and Countess Fitzwilliam and the Duchess of Windsor's old friend Grace, Countess of Dudley.

The following day, Prime Minister Harold Wilson issued a writ for libel against gossip columnist Nigel Dempster who had stated two days earlier that the Prime Minister was feeling the strains of office. In response, Mr Dempster said, 'I have the utmost respect for the Prime Minister and would in no way wish to bring his personal life into disrepute. With the pressure of the Chrysler and other crises he is being over-sensitive to press comment.'

The same day, Chancellor of the Exchequer Denis Healey stated that the proposed wealth tax would not be introduced for at least another year. 'The great Socialist pipe dream of milking the rich could be dead for all time,' commented the *Daily Express*.

Meanwhile, the 70-year-old Earl of Longford had been found jogging on a dangerous bend on the A21 main road near his Sussex home, contravening the Highway Code by presenting his back to oncoming traffic.

On Sunday December 21, five pro-Palestinian terrorists demanding a renunciation of the recent Sinai agreement, entered the OPEC Headquarters in Vienna and seized eleven oil ministers, including Sheikh Yamani of Saudi Arabia. A few hours later the guerrillas and their hostages were permitted to fly out of the country on board an Austrian Airlines DC9.

The following day, the oil ministers of the non-Arab states were released at Tripoli Airport in Libya.

On Tuesday December 23, it was revealed in Britain that the repair of some of the Royal Navy's fighting ships was being held back at Portsmouth Naval dock-yard to enable work to be finished on the royal yacht *Britannia*, which was being refitted at the cost of £2.25 million.

Later that day in Algiers, the oil minister drama ended when Sheikh Yamani and the last of his captive colleagues were released. The guerrillas, under the control of the arrogant Venezuelan assassin Carlos Martinez, nicknamed 'The Jackal', then flew off to an unspecified destination.

On Christmas Day, Pope Paul addressed the 100,000 gathered in St Peter's Square in Rome and spoke of the 'emptiness of modern society' which he said was turning youth away from materialism and back to religion.

On Saturday December 27, President Ford had a widely publicized spill while skiing in the Colorado mountains.

The following day, President Ford's press officer Ron Nessen criticized the press for presenting the President as clumsy and unable to co-ordinate his movements. 'The President is healthy, he is graceful and he is by far the most athletic President within memory,' he said.

Back in London, on Monday December 29, the Sex Discrimination Act came into force and was immediately put to the test when journalist Maggie Brittain attempted to order a drink at El Vino's wine bar in Fleet Street. On being refused service, she left the premises in a huff, saying she would take the matter to a county court and claim damages. 'This has been a ludicrous, pathetic and pitiful exhibition of mindless prejudice,' she said. 'I am extremely insulted.'

1976

The next twelve months see Iranian ambassadors dispensing magnificent hospitality on both sides of the Atlantic. The suave Sheikh Yamani visits Mustique on board Mr Khashoggi's yacht and later in the year invites the island's owner, Colin Tennant, back to Saudi Arabia. In England, Arabs purchase the Dorchester Hotel, Fort Belvedere, Douglas Fairbanks's London home and become honoured customers in Savile Row. Early in the year, Mr Wilson suddenly resigns as Prime Minister – some say he times his departure to deflect attention away from the break-up of Princess Margaret's marriage – and is followed at 10 Downing Street by the avuncular and complacent Jim Callaghan. Mr Wilson stays in the headlines when a scandal breaks over his retirement honours list. Another grave scandal meanwhile breaks slowly over the head of the Liberal leader Jeremy Thorpe and Mr Wilson's former colleague Mr Stonehouse begins a seven year sentence for fraud. Throughout the year, Mrs Thatcher campaigns against a Marxist future for Britain, with only the partial support of her old leader Mr Heath, who has now been seriously bitten with the book signing bug. In the worsening economic climate, fallen tycoon Jim Slater describes himself as 'a minus millionaire' while his old friend Sir James Goldsmith throws his weight around, slapping sixty-three writs on the satirical magazine Private Eye and tries to get its editor gaoled for criminal libel. Mrs Mary Whitehouse fights a losing battle against the worsening moral climate: she starts a prosecution against Gay News but fails to get Danish film maker Thorsen banned from the country. By the end of the year, the controversial Sex Pistols punk group have made their outrageous TV debut, two lesbian couples have been blessed in a church and homosexual policemen have been officially accepted in San Francisco. Meanwhile, Bianca Jagger and other members of the élite fly Concorde to pursue an even more vigorous social life. In London, Langan's Brasserie opens: eccentric oil heiress Olga Deterding, who makes a bid for the ailing Observer this year, helps put this new meeting place on the map.

The New Year found Jimmy Goldsmith celebrating in Gstaad at a party given by film director Roman Polanski. During the evening, the 42-year-old millionaire snatched a camera out of the hands of fellow guest Lyndall Hobbs and tore out the film saying he did not wish to be photographed 'in this company'.

Later that day in London, it was revealed that Goldsmith had purchased his friend Jim Slater's shares in the ailing Slater Walker company for a total of £460,000.

On Friday January 2, the RMS *Windsor Castle* set off from Southampton for Cape Town in a force 9 gale. Among those on board was 62-year-old Lord Goodman, who was on a business trip to South Africa and had been advised to go by sea in order to get a much needed rest.

The following day, the worst gales recorded in Britain for thirty years gave way to floods, as swollen tides surged over Britain's sea defences.

On Sunday January 4, the controversial Bishop of Kingston, Dr Montefiore, flew off to Washington to take part in a public enquiry protesting against the introduction of the Concorde. 'I regard my action as patriotic,' he said. 'I will have done Britain a great service if Concorde is stopped.'

On Thursday January 8, Harold Wilson had a working dinner at the Knightsbridge home of David Frost to discuss a new television series he was to make entitled *The Prime Ministers*.

On Saturday January 10, Concorde stewardesses protested about their uniform, designed by Hardy Amies. 'Synthetics are too hot to work in and the skirt is bound to drag in the plane's narrow aisles,' said stewardess Sheila Mansbridge.

The same weekend, Saudi Arabian businessman Adnan Khashoggi put in an appearance at the christening in Marbella of Prince Alfonso Hohenlohe's daughter, giving the infant a Gucci leather bag containing fifty uncut diamonds, then flew to Gstaad where he gave a party for fifty friends at the Palace Hotel, at which a whole lamb was roasted.

On Monday January 12, it was revealed that Margaret Duchess of Argyll had annoyed her landlords, the Grosvenor Estate, by showing members of the public around her Mayfair home for £7.50 a head. 'I'm off on Concorde next week so everything will be in abeyance,' said the 65-year-old Duchess.

Superstar Liza Minnelli clasps the hand of Margaret Duchess of Argyll at a party in London

Later that day, Jimmy Goldsmith issued sixty-three writs against the satirical magazine *Private Eye* and its distributors and applied to the High Court to bring proceedings for criminal libel against the magazine following the publication of an article alleging that he had taken part in a criminal conspiracy to protect the missing Earl of Lucan.

Meanwhile, television personality David Frost had been spotted at Heathrow Airport pushing his own luggage trolley.

On Wednesday January 14, Sir Cecil Beaton celebrated his seventy-second birthday by going to see *No Man's Land* at Wyndham's Theatre. It was his first London outing since his stroke eighteen months earlier.

On Friday January 16, the funeral of 85-year-old Agatha Christie took place at Cholsey near Wallingford in Berkshire. The mourners were led by Dame Agatha's husband Sir Max Mallowan, who carried a black silk top hat and supported himself with a stick. As the coffin was carried to the grave, the yew trees in the churchyard whispered in the bitterly cold wind.

On Saturday January 17, the Earl of Snowdon protested at the refusal of the Royal Horticultural Society to permit blind people to attend the Chelsea Flower Show with their dogs. 'I can hardly believe that the kind of arrogant fascist attitude shown by the RHS still exists in this country. I hate to see some official dictating to a blind person what they can or cannot do.'

The following Monday, January 19, former Hollywood star Rita Hayworth, who was in London to appear on the Russell Harty TV show, refused to leave a TWA jet at Heathrow Airport and had to be half-lifted down the steps in a dishevelled state. She was later taken off to the Savoy Hotel without passing through Customs or Immigration control, while a friend explained, 'She doesn't like flying and was very tired.'

On Wednesday January 21, Concorde services to Rio de Janeiro and Bahrein were simultaneously inaugurated. Among fare-paying passengers on board the British Airways service to Bahrein was Margaret Duchess of Argyll, who was spotted thumping a speedometer gauge that wasn't working during the flight. Also on board was 50-year-old Bob Ingham, manager of a plant hire firm from Trowbridge in Wiltshire, who had dressed up in white and purple and painted his face silver, explaining that he represented the Age of Aquarius.

On Saturday January 24, it was revealed that flamboyant entrepreneur Adnan Khashoggi had taken delivery of a new £3,500,000 yacht *Mohamedia*. The vessel included fourteen guest suites, a cinema, a barber's shop and ten separate safes or strong rooms, but Mr Khashoggi said, 'A yacht is just a yacht.'

That weekend, a raucous crowd of youngsters at Annabel's in Berkeley Square, including 18-year-old Rebecca Fraser, Jasper Guinness and Clarissa Baring caused an older person present to remark, 'People like that should do National Service.'

Over in San Francisco on Tuesday January 27, the trial began of 21-year-old Patty Hearst. The newspaper heiress was in chains but was dressed like a debutante and looked as though she was about to be sick.

Back in London on Wednesday January 28, the publisher of the autobiography of Miss Linda Lovelace was acquitted at the Old Bailey of publishing an obscene article. 'There is in the world today a growing sense of freedom and this is reflected in the verdict,' said 66-year-old Mr Heinrich Hanau. Mrs Mary Whitehouse described the result as 'an absolute tragedy as a result of which children will suffer'.

The following day, in court at Barnstaple in Devon, 39-year-old former male model Norman Scott blurted out that he was being 'hounded because of my sexual relationship with Jeremy Thorpe'. After consulting his solicitor, Mr Thorpe issued a statement. 'It is well over twelve years since I last saw or spoke to Mr Scott. There is no truth in Mr Scott's wild allegations.'

The same day, the Department of Trade published its report on the collapse of the London and Counties Securities Bank of which Mr Thorpe had been a director. The Liberal leader was cleared of any wrong doing but the report stated that the saga was 'a cautionary tale for any leading politician'.

The following Monday, February 2, the British Airways Concorde left Heathrow for Bahrein less than half full, with only thirty-nine passengers on board.

Later that day in California, former Liberal MP Peter Bessell, who had been missing for the past two years, re-emerged to explain why he had made certain payments to Norman Scott. Fondling his three dachshunds, Heidi, Fritz and Thurston, he said, 'The idea that I paid him to keep quiet is rubbish, absolute rubbish. It was purely an act of charity. I felt sorry for him. He was so pathetic.'

Two days later in Washington, Transportation Secretary William T. Coleman caused dismay and anger in conservation circles when he ruled that France and Britain could operate a limited Concorde service to New York and Washington on a trial basis.

Back in Britain, on Friday February 6, public interest in the Norman Scott affair heightened when former airline pilot Andrew Newton appeared in court at Minehead in Somerset to face charges in connection with the incident the previous October when Scott's great dane, Rinka, was shot dead on Exmoor.

A few miles away the same day, Mr Jeremy Thorpe was given a rousing reception when he returned to his North Devon constituency. 'I want to thank you for the confidence you have shown in me which, if I may say so, I believe I still deserve,' he told his supporters.

Earlier that week, Princess Margaret had flown to Mustique, saving half the normal fare by travelling via Luxembourg to Barbados and then on via St Vincent to Mustique where she was soon joined by her friend 28-year-old Roddy Llewellyn. Also on Mustique was journalist Ross Waby, who was visiting the island with the sole purpose of getting a compromising photograph of the couple together.

On Monday February 9, British Prime Minister Harold Wilson spoke in the House of Commons about the sustained campaign of innuendo now being mounted against Mr Jeremy Thorpe. 'What is particularly nauseating,' he said, 'is the sanctimonious spirit in which this has been done.'

The following day, it was learnt that the ailing 79-year-old Duchess of Windsor had suffered a 'recurrent spell of weakness' and was being treated in the American Hospital in Paris where she was occupying the same room, number 282, where Aristotle Onassis had died the previous year.

On Wednesday February 11, the British Airways Concorde left for Bahrein less than a third full, with only thirty passengers on board.

On Thursday February 12, eccentric multi-millionaire Howard Hughes left his penthouse floor of the Acapulco Princess Hotel in the Bahamas and flew to a new hideaway in Mexico.

Back in London, on Monday February 16, a pile of bricks went on show at the Tate Gallery, exciting considerable controversy. 'We realize that some of our purchases are bound to cause contention,' said the gallery's director Sir Norman Reid, 'but I like the bricks. In fact, I was the one who bought them.'

That night in New York, Richard Burton returned to Broadway after many years absence when he took over a leading role in *Equus*. His wife Elizabeth Taylor had flown in to witness his debut and the famous couple dined together afterwards at Sardi's.

The following day, in San Francisco, Patty Hearst told the court how she had been raped by two of her kidnappers in a cupboard shortly after her abduction.

Over in New York, on Wednesday February 18, it was announced that Princess Lee Radziwill had founded her own interior design company. Her first big commission was to come from the Americana Hotels.

On Friday February 20, Richard Nixon came out of his exile in San Clemente, California, and made his way to a remote cargo section of Los Angeles Airport, where he boarded a specially fitted Boeing 707 airliner and flew to Peking as a guest of the Chinese government. He was accompanied on this mischievous trip by his wife Pat and his residual retinue of Secret Service bodyguards. It was noted that it was the fourth anniversary of his trail-blazing journey to China as President.

Back in Britain, on Sunday February 22, the *News of the World* published a blurred photograph of Princess Margaret and Roddy Llewellyn sitting in the bar in Mustique, taken by roving photographer Ross Waby. Roddy wore a stud in his ear and the union jack bathing costume which he had purchased in Edinburgh two and a half years earlier. The photograph caused an immediate outcry in England and Labour MP Willie Hamilton demanded that Princess Margaret should be 'sacked'.

On Monday February 23, nine peers gathered in a Committee Room at the House of Lords to consider which of two claimants to the Barony of Ampthill was the rightful heir. Representing Mr Geoffrey Russell was Old Etonian bachelor Sir John Foster, a flamboyant man of the world said to have residences in London, Paris and New York.

Later that day, the controversial Tate Gallery bricks were sprayed with food colouring and removed from display. 'They will not be on display for a while with people in their present mood,' said Sir Norman Reid who had been inundated with other 'works of art' during the past few days, including old vacuum cleaners, paper clips and bits of string.

On Wednesday February 25, it was confirmed in New York that Richard Burton and Elizabeth Taylor had agreed to a new separation. Miss Taylor was reported to have flown to her mother's home in Palm Springs while Burton was barricaded in his hotel with Suzy Hunt, estranged wife of racing motorist James Hunt. 'James and I have discussed divorce. The situation is very delicate,' she said.

Meanwhile, Russian author Alexander Solzhenitsyn had arrived in Britain for the first time since leaving Moscow two years earlier. On Monday March 1 he gave a television interview at a country house in Northamptonshire during which he expressed fears of the sudden and imminent fall of the West. 'The West is on the verge of a collapse created by its own hands,' he said.

The following day, Princess Margaret returned from the Caribbean and flew into Gatwick Airport to find public opinion had been stirred up against her by the publication of the photograph of her and Roddy Llewellyn in the *News of the World*.

Later that day, Lord George-Brown announced his resignation from the Labour Party declaring that it was the saddest night of his life. Leaving the House of Lords after this announcement, the former deputy Prime Minister tripped and fell and was helped to his feet by a journalist. The former Foreign Secretary blamed the mishap on his bi-focal spectacles and the pressmen's flash-bulbs.

On Wednesday March 3, the London scene was enriched by the arrival of the new American Ambassador, wealthy Southern belle Mrs Anne Armstrong.

The next day in Los Angeles, Dr Armand Hammer, chairman of the Occidental Petroleum Corporation, pleaded guilty to secretly contributing $54,000 to the former President Nixon's campaign fund. During the hearing, Dr Hammer was seated in a wheelchair with a portable heart-monitoring device in the adjoining room in case he became ill.

Back in Britain, on Friday March 5, there was a dramatic development in the Thorpe affair when merchant banker David Holmes, former Liberal Party Deputy Treasurer and a close friend of Mr Thorpe, admitted paying male model Norman Scott £2,500 in return for certain letters in his possession. Mr Thorpe was travelling on a train between Cheshire and London at the time of this statement and when told by a journalist who boarded the train at Watford about this development, said, 'This is completely new to me.'

That weekend, the London scene was enriched by the presence of Mrs Jackie Onassis who arrived in London to visit her daughter Caroline and booked into the Ritz Hotel. On Sunday March 7, mother and daughter went out for a stroll through the snow-covered streets. It was noted that Mrs Onassis was clutching a bottle of Robinson's Lemon Barley Water.

The following day, the 83-year-old Duke of Leinster committed suicide in his Pimlico bedsitter. The unfortunate old Duke had been made bankrupt three times in his life and the recent efforts of a public relations man had failed to restore his morale. 'He was under a dreadful amount of pressure,' said his fourth wife. 'He was deeply depressed about his life.'

On Tuesday March 9, Jimmy Goldsmith and his old friend Jim Slater were to be found on holiday together in Barbados. 'Obviously Jim Slater and I discuss things of mutual interest when we're together,' said Goldsmith, 'but that's not the purpose of his visit. He's here purely as a friend and we've been playing tennis.' Also in the party were Goldsmith's old friends Lady Annabel Birley and John Aspinall.

Two days later in London, Sir George Weidenfeld threw a party at his Chelsea riverside apartment to celebrate the sixtieth birthday of Prime Minister Harold Wilson. Half way through the evening Mr Wilson left the party to listen to a speech by Mr Healey in the House of Commons but returned to the jollifications later.

On Friday March 12, Mr Adnan Khashoggi's new Boeing 707 touched down at Le Bourget Airport near Paris. It was said that Mr Khashoggi had lavished £2 million on its interior, installing gold-plated toilet fittings, four TVs in the main cabin and wardrobes containing both Western and Arab dress. It was noted that Mr Khashoggi had recently taken over two floors of the luxury Olympic Tower skyscraper built by Aristotle Onassis two years earlier.

On Saturday March 13, senior detectives searching for the missing Earl of Lucan said they believed he was in South Africa or Rhodesia. 'I am convinced he is still alive,' said Detective Chief Inspector David Gerring. 'I firmly believe that he is in Africa. He knows South Africa well and had 25,000 Rhodesian dollars in his account at the Bulawayo branch of Barclay's International Bank. Lord Lucan has many friends in South Africa and it is very easy for him to blend into the type of life that can be found there.'

On Sunday March 14, racing motorist James Hunt flew to New York to discuss his marital situation with his wife Suzy. 'I'm going to talk to Suzy but I really don't know what the outcome will be,' he said. Early on Monday March 15, the couple spent an hour or two together and Hunt then flew on to the West Coast.

Back in Britain on Tuesday March 16, 60-year-old Harold Wilson suddenly announced his resignation as Prime Minister. This shock announcement wiped £1,000 million off the price of shares and was followed by intense speculation about what scandal was to break. According to one source, he was resigning to please his wife Mary who was said to have 'loathed every minute of Harold's time in office'.

The same day, at Exeter Crown Court, former airline pilot Andrew Newton stood trial accused of possessing a firearm with intent to endanger life. Chief prosecution witness former male model Norman Scott, wept in court as he described how his great dane, Rinka, had been shot dead the previous autumn and again claimed to have had a homosexual relationship with Liberal leader Jeremy Thorpe. A few hours later it was stated that a police investigation had discovered there was no link between the Liberal Party and this strange case.

Meanwhile, the state of Princess Margaret's marriage was making headline news across the world and on Wednesday March 17, Lord Snowdon was closely questioned by journalists when he stopped in Hong Kong on his way to open an exhibition of his photographs in Australia. 'I have never, over the past fifteen years, made any comment about my private life and I have no intention of doing so now,' he said.

The same day in San Francisco, the evidence in the trial of Patty Hearst was completed when the heiress's mother testified on oath that her daughter had been 'a very warm and loving girl' before being kidnapped two years earlier.

Back in London, on Thursday March 18, Madame Prunier presided over the closure of her famous restaurant in St James's Street, now protected by sandbags against a possible IRA bomb.

On Friday March 19, there came an official announcement that Princess Margaret and Lord Snowdon were to live apart. A few hours later, Lord Snowdon arrived at Sydney International Airport after 12,500 miles of jet travel. He was taken to a secret address and left strict instructions that he was not to be disturbed.

The following day, he issued an emotional statement saying that he was 'desperately sad' about the break-up of his marriage and wished Princess Margaret 'every happiness for the future'.

Meanwhile in San Francisco, Patty Hearst had been found guilty of armed robbery and ordered to undergo psychiatric tests before being sentenced. Back in Britain psychiatrist Dr William Sargant who had interviewed the 22-year-old heiress said he was 'absolutely convinced' of her innocence.

On Monday March 22, United Arab Emirates Ambassador Mr Sayed Mohamed al-Tajir, owner of Mereworth Castle, Dropmore and several other spectacular properties in and around London, said he was still backing Britain. 'I have done my homework and I know what is going on. I know that there will be a good recovery. I am not worried about sterling despite the way it has been falling,' he said at his Embassy overlooking Hyde Park.

On Tuesday March 23, President Amin of Uganda issued a public message to Lord Snowdon saying that the breakdown of his marriage would be 'a lesson to all of us men to be very careful not to marry ladies in very high positions'.

That night, the Queen dined with retiring Prime Minister Harold Wilson at 10 Downing Street. Among those present on this historic occasion were Sir George Weidenfeld, Michael Foot, who wore a dinner jacket no one had seen before, press officer Joe Haines, Lady Melchett and 44-year-old Lady Falkender who executed a superb curtsey to the Queen. In a speech, Wilson recalled that the Queen had last dined at 10 Downing Street on the occasion of the retirement of Sir Winston Churchill.

Retiring Prime Minister Harold Wilson welcomes the Queen to his official residence: the first time the Queen had dined at 10 Downing Street since the resignation of Sir Winston Churchill

The following day, Roddy Llewellyn broke his silence and issued a statement from his parents' home in Wales, refusing to comment on 'any of the events of last week', and expressing his regret at 'any embarrassment caused to Her Majesty the Queen, for whom I wish to express the greatest respect, admiration and loyalty'.

Later that day in London, Princess Margaret emerged for the first time since 'the great divide' to watch the Scottish Ballet at Sadlers Wells and look in afterwards at a party in Eaton Square given by the Hon Vere and Mrs Pat Harmsworth where other guests included Lady Jane Wellesley, the portly Lord Hesketh, the young Earl Grosvenor and three fun-loving daughters of Lord Lambton, Anne, Rose and Beatrix.

On Thursday March 25, it was disclosed that Lord Patrick Beresford, polo-playing friend of the Duke of Edinburgh, had joined the staff of Saudi Arabian oil minister Sheikh Yamani and was currently relaxing in the West Indies on board the £3.5 million yacht *Mohamedia*, which Yamani had borrowed from Mr Adnan Khashoggi.

Back in London that weekend, self-made businessman Victor Matthews celebrated his acquisition of the Ritz Hotel which his company, Trafalgar House, had purchased for £2.7 million. 'Of course this is an investment,' he said. 'But there's more to it than that. The name Ritz conjures up a whole life-style of luxury and glamour.'

On Monday March 29, there was a surprise party for Harold Wilson at 10 Downing Street, mainly attended by members of the entertainment profession, including David Frost and comedians Morecambe and Wise, and financed by his friend Eric Miller chairman of the Peachey Property Corporation. £3,304 worth of champagne was consumed and the retiring Prime Minister sang a duet with Eric Morecambe.

On Tuesday March 30, Princess Margaret dined at the Mirabelle restaurant in Curzon Street with 27-year-old Lord Buckhurst and went on afterwards to dance at Ronnie Scott's jazz club where the star attraction was Oscar Peterson.

Two days later, Princess Anne and Captain Mark Phillips were interviewed about their hunting activities. 'The fox is a pest in the country, as the pigeon is,' said Captain Phillips. 'I have seen pigeons with a handful of corn in their crops. It is a wonder that there is any left for the farmer at all.'

On Saturday April 3, it was disclosed that United Arab Emirates Ambassador Mr al-Tajir had spent £30,000 at Savile Row tailors Kilgour, French and Stanbury, during the past two years. His purchases included five overcoats made of vicuna, costing £1,800 each, several cashmere mink coats and several suits made of pure Italian silk. 'I personally deal with all al-Tajir's orders,' said the firm's managing director Mr Edward Tremble. 'He is just crazy on clothes. London is the Mecca for these things.'

On the following day, Sunday April 4, Lord Snowdon returned to London from Australia to find journalists crowding round the steps of his aircraft. He was driven off in a royal blue chauffeur-driven Volvo to the Kensington home of his mother, Lady Rosse.

That night in Washington, celebrities gathered for the première of *All the President's Men*. It was noted that President Ford had given his tickets to Mrs Katharine Graham, owner of the *Washington Post* which had helped to bring about the downfall of the Nixon regime.

On Monday April 5, eccentric multi-millionaire Howard Hughes died in a jet ambulance somewhere above South Texas. An autopsy later carried out at the Houston Methodist Hospital revealed that he had weighed only 90 pounds at the time of his death and had died of acute renal failure. Pilots of the jet ambulance said that their celebrated passenger had looked 'like a tired worn-out old person'.

The following day in London, former Prime Minister Harold Wilson took Sir Winston Churchill's old seat in the House of Commons to watch his successor, 64-year-old Jim Callaghan, make his debut as Prime Minister. Opposition leader Mrs Thatcher and Liberal leader Jeremy Thorpe offered their congratulations to the new premier.

On Wednesday April 7, the Queen Mother and the Empress of Iran suddenly popped up in the Royal Box at the Albert Hall to watch the London Symphony Orchestra rehearsing Tchaikovsky's *Pathétique*. It was noted that the Empress was on a short visit to England and was staying with the Queen Mother at Clarence House.

The same day, Mr Stonehouse announced that he was resigning the Labour whip and was to throw in his lot with the 5,000 strong English National Party, who were intent on putting the 'merrie' back into England.

The following weekend, Sheikh Yamani visited Mustique on board the 500 ton yacht *Mohamedia*. It was noted that fresh food was being flown to the yacht each day from Paris.

Back in London, on Monday April 12, the Privileges Committee of the House of Lords ruled that the Hon. Geoffrey Russell was the rightful heir to the late Lord Ampthill. 'I had no choice but to fight the case,' he said afterwards. 'Above all it was a question of defending my mother's honour.'

On Tuesday April 13, Princess Margaret and Lord Snowdon were together again at a luncheon at Windsor Castle following the confirmation of their son, 14-year-old Lord Linley, in St George's Chapel.

Later that afternoon, MP John Stonehouse was ordered to withdraw from the House of Commons while he was making a speech on political corruption. He was later escorted from the precincts of the Palace of Westminster by a Chief Inspector of the Police. 'I am going to protest most strongly about this unwarranted breach of a member's privilege,' he said afterwards.

Meanwhile, Jimmy Goldsmith's application to bring proceedings for criminal libel against *Private Eye* had begun in the High Court. On Wednesday April 14, Mr Justice Wien ruled that there was a case to answer and proceedings were duly instituted which could end in a two year prison sentence for the magazine's editor Richard Ingrams.

The Earl and Countess of Lichfield meet artist Andy Warhol during one of his many visits to London

On Thursday April 15, the marriage took place in Bavaria of Gert Rudolf Flick, co-heir to the Mercedes Benz fortune and known to his friends as 'Muck', and Princess Johanna zu Sayn-Wittgenstein.

The following day, Good Friday, found Christina Onassis relaxing in Switzerland with her new husband Alexander Andreadis. It was noted that she had recently taken delivery of a new £1 million Lear jet.

On Easter day in California, San Francisco police chief Charles Gain stated that there were twenty homosexuals in his force. He promised them his full support and urged them to 'come out of the closet' and show that homosexuals could be good police officers.

Over in New York, on Monday April 19, Richard Burton and Suzy Hunt dined at Sardi's after the Tony Awards presentations during which Burton had received a special 'Welcome back to Broadway' medal for his part in *Equus*.

Back in Britain, on Tuesday April 20, Lord Snowdon and Princess Margaret were both present at the Queen's fiftieth birthday dance in the ballroom of Windsor Castle. Others present included Mr and Mrs Harold Wilson, who had specially returned from the Scillies for the event, Mr and Mrs Denis Thatcher and Mr and Mrs Jeremy Thorpe. A notable absentee was the new Prime Minister Jim Callaghan, who remained 'deep in papers' at his Sussex farm and said he was 'too busy' to attend the party.

The following day, Princess Anne, who had left the party at 3 a.m. fell from her horse at the Portman Horse Trials in Dorset and was knocked unconscious when her mount Candlewick, weighing half a ton, rolled on top of her. She was taken seventeen miles to Poole Hospital where it was discovered that she had suffered a hairline fracture of the vertebrae.

The same day in Malaga, Spain, James and Suzy Hunt discussed the future of their marriage over coffee. 'What people will not realize,' said Suzy, 'is that we are all very happy doing what we are doing. James is happy living as he does and concentrating on racing. Richard is happy and so am I.'

Back in Britain, on Thursday April 22, it was announced that Harold Wilson had been appointed a Knight of the Garter. The former socialist Prime Minister's acceptance of this honour distressed certain members of the Labour movement. Said Labour MP Sydney Bidwell, 'If that is the sort of thing he wants as the crowning glory of his career, then that is it.'

On Saturday April 24, it was revealed that 46-year-old Lady Dartmouth had left her husband and was spending the weekend with 52-year-old Earl Spencer at his Northamptonshire stately home, Althorp. The Earl's 21-year-old daughter Lady Sarah Spencer explained, 'She is helping my father open the house on a commercial basis.' Lady Dartmouth's mother, novelist Barbara Cartland, refused to comment on this turn of events. 'I can say nothing, nothing, nothing,' she said. 'To speak about a family matter would be very vulgar.'

On Tuesday April 27, the trial of Sir Harold's old colleague, John Stonehouse and his secretary Sheila Buckley at last opened at Court number one at the Old Bailey. Stonehouse arrived at the court wearing a stern blue suit and crisp mauve shirt and Mrs Buckley was a-jangle with gold bracelets, ear-rings and rings.

On Wednesday April 28, the Queen Mother left England for a four day private visit to Burgundy where she was to stay at the Château de Sully with her old friend, the Duchess of Magenta. She visited local cathedrals and châteaux and was said to be 'drinking it all in'.

Over in California, on Thursday April 29, a handwritten will apparently penned by the late Howard Hughes was found by officials of the Mormon Church in Las Vegas. The will left one-sixteenth of his $1,000 million estate to service station operator Melvin Dumar. Among those to doubt the authenticity of this document was hoaxer Clifford Irving.

Back in Britain, on Sunday May 2, it was claimed that Sir Harold Wilson's retirement honours list had run into difficulties and honours for a city financier businessman, an impresario and a minor businessman had been withdrawn after questions from the official honours scrutiny committee. Sir Harold dismissed this suggestion as 'totally untrue'.

On Monday May 3, Madame Marcos and her husband, the President of the Philippines, had tea with the Queen at Buckingham Palace.

On Tuesday May 4, Queen Charlotte's Birthday Ball, which had originally launched the debutante season, was held for the last time and was poorly attended. 'I think the deb season as I knew it has long gone,' said 63-year-old Margaret Duchess of Argyll. 'I just don't think the girl of today wants to do that sort of thing anymore. They prefer to live on their own and take a job.'

The following day in California, former Liberal MP Peter Bessell changed his story about the Norman Scott affair. 'Scott never attempted to blackmail me,' he confessed. 'The whole idea was to make Scott shut his mouth. I have told lies, demonstrably. What I am saying now is the truth. I kept quiet before out of a deep sense of loyalty.'

That night in London, Mr Thorpe attended the Royal Academy dinner, dressed in white tie and tails. Also there, similarly dressed, was gossip columnist Nigel Dempster who questioned the Liberal leader about the latest developments.

Early in the morning of Sunday May 9, Ulrike Meinhof hung herself in her cell in Stuttgart prison. A former journalist and once glamorous figure in West Germany's left wing circles, Frau Meinhof had branched out into terrorist activities several years earlier.

Later that day in Britain, two affectionate letters written by Mr Thorpe to Norman Scott over twelve years earlier were published for the first time. 'I am sick and tired of the mystery being whipped up around these two letters so I am making them available,' said Mr Thorpe.

The following day, Mr Thorpe resigned as leader of the Liberal Party. 'No man can effectively lead a party if the greater part of his time has to be devoted to answering allegations and countering continuous plots and intrigues,' he said. 'I never wanted this to happen,' said Mr Norman Scott at a hotel in Exeter, 'I never expected it.'

That night in Marbella, Prince Alfonso Hohenlohe gave a party to celebrate James Hunt's victory in the Spanish Grand Prix.

Back in London, on Wednesday May 12, socialites gathered at a huge cocktail party at the Cadogan Square home of art connoisseur Charles Harding. Among those present were the Earl and Countess of Lichfield, Mrs Drue Heinz, the elderly Viscount Rothermere, Mr David Hicks and society columnist Mrs Betty Kenward.

A rare photograph of society columnist Mrs Betty Kenward, who once flew from London to Caracas for a dinner party

The following Friday, the indomitable Mrs Kenward flew to Caracas on Concorde for a dinner party given by British businessman Sir Raymond Smith.

The same day, Elizabeth Taylor flew on an inaugural flight of Iran Air from New York to Tehran, accompanied by Ambassador Zahedi's nephew and her hairdresser Arthur, to live it up at the 'caviare court'.

Back in California that weekend, author Truman Capote threw a party at his Malibu Beach home where he was planning to spend the summer. Guests included writer Christopher Isherwood, pop star Alice Cooper, artist David Hockney and his old friend Peter Schlesinger.

Meanwhile, the Rolling Stones were involved in a strenuous tour of Britain. On Monday May 17, the group appeared at Stafford and Mick Jagger and wife Bianca and their daughter Jade were put up for the night at the nearby stately home of the Earl of Lichfield, Shugborough Hall.

The same day, President Giscard d'Estaing arrived in Washington on board Concorde and was welcomed to the White House with a dinner also attended by film star Marisa Berenson, who wore a body stocking and several silk scarves.

Meanwhile in New York, Mrs Jackie Onassis had been spotted lunching at Mortimer's on 3rd Avenue with 24-year-old Mark Shand, a friend of her daughter Caroline.

Back in Britain, on Wednesday May 19, it was claimed that businessman Jimmy Goldsmith, a long term supporter of the Tory Party, had accepted a peerage from the retiring Prime Minister Harold Wilson. This revelation was followed by a top-level enquiry into how names on the honours list had been leaked.

On Friday May 21, *Private Eye* editor Richard Ingrams visited the Countess of Lucan at her house in Lower Belgrave Street to try and obtain evidence against Jimmy Goldsmith who was suing the magazine for criminal libel. He was entertained in the first floor drawing-room, now dominated by a portrait of the missing Earl by the late Dominic Elwes.

The following day, there were great festivities at Mentmore Towers in Buckinghamshire following the wedding of Mr Charles Garton and Lady Lucy Primrose, granddaughter of the late Earl of Rosebery.

On Saturday May 22, record tycoon Ahmet Ertegun threw a party in London in honour of the Rolling Stones who had concluded their British tour with three appearances at Earl's Court. Among those present were Princess Margaret, Sir George Weidenfeld, Caroline Kennedy and other socialites. Mick Jagger arrived at 2 a.m. wearing purple shades and held court outside the men's lavatory.

The following day, transatlantic supersonic services began when British Airways and Air France Concordes landed simultaneously at Dulles Airport, Washington.

Over in Washington on Wednesday May 26, Iranian Ambassador Ardeshir Zahedi threw a lavish party at which Dom Perignon flowed like water and there was limitless caviar. 'What a bore,' said one guest. 'Ardeshir really ought to change the menu.'

The same night in New York, gossip columnist Nigel Dempster was found chatting with his fellow countryman Sir Charles Clore at Regine's new club on Park Avenue.

Back in Britain, on Thursday May 27, Sir Harold Wilson's resignation honours was at last officially announced. Honours included peerages for Sir Joseph Kagan, Sir Bernard Delfont, Sir Lew Grade and Sir George Weidenfeld, and knighthoods for Eric Miller, chairman of the Peachey Property Corporation and the controversial

Jimmy Goldsmith. Among those to attack this list was John Junor, editor of the *Sunday Express*, who stated in a broadcast that the list 'stinks like a sewer lorry'.

The following day, the 28-year-old marriage of the Earl and Countess of Dartmouth ended in the Divorce Court. The 52-year-old Earl had sued his wife for divorce citing as co-respondent Earl Spencer, former equerry to the Queen, but the divorce was granted because of Lady Dartmouth's adultery 'with a man against whom the charge is not proved'.

On Monday May 31, a long and emotional letter from Lady Falkender was published in *The Times* denying any responsibility for the names on the Honours List. 'It was Sir Harold's list and his alone,' she wrote, accusing critics of the list of anti-semitism.

Later that day, Elizabeth Taylor flew into London from Tehran in a cheerful mood. Skipping and dancing in a white trouser suit at Heathrow she said, 'It's great to be a single girl. I have no future plans at all.'

The same day in New York, 57-year-old protocol-shattering Martha Mitchell, estranged wife of former Attorney-General John Mitchell, and one of the first people to call for Nixon's resignation, died in hospital. She had been suffering from cancer of the bone marrow and was said to have been 'desperate – without funds and without friends'.

On Wednesday June 2, Lester Piggott had his seventh Derby win when he romped home on Empery, owned by portly American tycoon Nelson Bunker Hunt. Among spectators was Sayed Sharaf, senior steward of the Bahrain jockey club who was over for the day on Concorde.

That night, Sir Harold Wilson issued a statement attempting to 'nail the lies' about his resignation honours list. 'The list was mine and mine from the beginning,' he said.

On Friday June 4, the outgoing Iranian Ambassador to Britain Dr Reza Amirteymour was found dead in his small flat near his old Embassy. 'It could have been an accident or it could have been self-inflicted,' said his successor Mr Parviz Radji. 'There was no sign of any foul play and no blood was spilt.'

The following night, 83-year-old multi-millionaire Paul Getty died at Sutton Place with his son Gordon at his bedside. As preparations began to fly his body to California, his close friend 43-year-old Mrs Rosabella Burch commented, 'I said goodbye to him two months ago. Since January he has not been going out and people could not get very close to him.'

Meanwhile, Suzy Hunt and Richard Burton had arrived in Haiti to try and obtain quickie divorces from their respective spouses. They were put up at the luxurious El Raco Hotel and on Monday June 7 were received by the country's young dictator, Jean Claude Duvalier who loaned them a helicopter to explore the island.

That night in London 28-year-old Roddy Llewellyn spent five hours at a dinner party at Kensington Palace given by Princess Margaret.

On Tuesday June 8, 83-year-old Lady Diana Cooper and Dr Roy Strong were among guests at the private view of paintings and water-colours by Sir Cecil Beaton at the Parkin Gallery in Belgravia. 'I feel very vulnerable looking at it all,' said Sir Cecil. 'It dates terribly. But some of them bear witness to times worth remembering.'

The following day, the Labour government won a No Confidence vote by a narrow margin. After his slender victory, Prime Minister Callaghan chided Opposition leader Mrs Thatcher in the House of Commons. 'Now, now, little lady,' he said, 'you don't want to believe all those things you read in the newspapers about crisis and upheavals and the end of civilization as we know it. Dearie me, not at all.'

Later that day, the neatly typed will of Paul Getty was filed in Los Angeles. The foxy old man, who was said to have been worth between $2,000 and $4,000 million left substantial sums to twelve women friends and left strict orders that the control of his estate was not to pass into the hands of his 19-year-old grandson, Paul Getty III. Among the women who benefited were Robina Lund, Lady Ursula d'Abo, Penelope Kitson, Mrs Rosabella Burch and other women who had comforted him in old age.

The following day, Thursday June 10, the multi-millionaire's grandson Paul said in his London hotel, 'I don't begrudge the ladies a penny. Not all the Getty family are interested in becoming billionaires.'

On Monday June 14, the former socialist Prime Minister Sir Harold Wilson was officially installed as a Knight of the Garter dressed in a floppy hat with ostrich feathers plume, mantle and other accoutrements which had been specially made for some £650.

On Tuesday June 15, the Royal Ascot crowds were enriched by the presence of Dame Edna Everage, who wore a hat depicting the Sydney Opera House and harbour. During the afternoon, Dame Edna clashed with Mrs Gertrude Shilling, a member of whose party shouted, 'Will you please get out of the way? We are not here for cheap publicity.'

Meanwhile in California, two rabbis had officiated at the marriage between tycoon Bernie Cornfeld, now said to be down to his last £1 million, and his glamorous girl-friend Lorraine Ambruster.

On Sunday June 20, Prince Charles and 25-year-old Davina Sheffield were together again after a long break during which Davina had worked in Vietnam

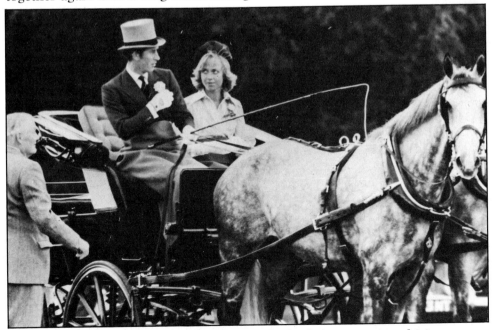

25-year-old Davina Sheffield sits beside Prince Charles during a carriage-driving competition at Smith's Lawn, Windsor

and elsewhere. That afternoon they appeared at Smith's Lawn, Windsor, in Charles's 140 mph Aston Martin Volante. It was noted that the Prince had turned down an invitation to attend the King of Sweden's wedding the same weekend.

On Monday June 21, staff at the Dorchester Hotel in Park Lane wept when they were told that the hotel had been acquired by an Arab consortium for £9 million. 'It was very touching,' said the chairman of the new board. 'The staff are obviously a very fine and loyal group of people.'

Close by the Dorchester the same day, a memorial service for the late Paul Getty was held at the American Church, North Audley Street. Among those present were Bianca Jagger, who was escorted by Paul Getty II, Lady Diana Cooper, Margaret Duchess of Argyll, the Duke of Bedford and the multi-millionaire's grandson, Paul Getty III. A tribute from President Ford was read out and the 59-year-old Duke of Bedford gave an address. 'His first love was business,' he said. 'He just had an allergy to money badly spent or invested or lying idle.'

On Wednesday June 23, it was announced that the Coq d'Or restaurant off Piccadilly had been sold by Grand Metropolitan Hotels to Irishman Peter Langan. 'I am confident that I shall make it pay,' he said.

The same day, President Giscard d'Estaing began an official visit to London during which he was to find time to visit 91-year-old Baroness Spencer-Churchill at her Knightsbridge flat.

On Thursday June 24, it was announced that the Queen had bought Gatcombe Park in Gloucestershire, for her daughter Princess Anne. The 530 acre estate, once considered for use as a lunatic asylum, had cost the Queen £700,000. Said Labour MP Ronald Thomas, 'In view of the economic crisis, I find this flaunting of wealth appalling, indeed almost obscene.'

That night, in London, there was a white tie and tails dinner at the French Embassy in honour of the visiting President. Ignoring this dress stipulation was

Princess Anne's new country home, Gatcombe Park, once considered for use as a lunatic asylum

union leader Clive Jenkins who wore a plain lounge suit; during the evening he was spotted chatting with the Conservative leader, Mrs Thatcher.

Meanwhile in Northamptonshire, Earl Spencer had announced that he was to take in paying guests at his stately home, Althorp. 'Our guests will stay in the eight state bedrooms', he explained. 'I'm turning to this venture because I want to be sure the house stays viable.'

On Friday June 25, the temperature in London hit 92° F in the shade. At Heathrow Airport officials scattered sand to prevent the Queen, Prince Philip and President Giscard d'Estaing sinking into the tarmac as they boarded a plane for Edinburgh.

Two days later, Palestine extremists hijacked a French airbus bound from Athens to Paris with 216 people on board. The plane later landed at Entebbe airport, Uganda.

On Thursday July 1, former Labour Minister John Stonehouse began his defence at the Old Bailey. He claimed that the twenty-one charges against him were not real crimes at all and that he was the victim of press and political hysteria. 'The key to these charges can now be found in the monumental blunders made by the police,' he said.

Meanwhile, 20-year-old Bjorn Borg had battled his way through to the Wimbledon men's finals. On Saturday July 3, he became Wimbledon's youngest champion since 1931 when he beat temperamental Romanian Ilie Nastase in one hour, fifty-five minutes. Between sets, Borg was observed spraying his torn groin muscles with an aerosol spray. After this victory, he flew back to Monte Carlo, where he was now living in order to avoid a ninety per cent Swedish income tax.

Later that night, in Uganda, airborne Israeli troops stormed Entebbe airport and freed the hijack victims in a daring forty-five second operation.

On Tuesday July 6, in Paris, M. Hervé de Vathaire, director of the Dassault Aircraft Company, visited a bank in the Avenue Grande Armée, withdrew 8 million francs in two suitcases and disappeared without trace.

Later the same day in Washington, the Queen was welcomed to the White House wearing a yellow chiffon evening dress. After a banquet in her honour the Queen danced a quickstep with President Ford, who wore white tie and tails, to the tune 'That's why the lady is a tramp'. The only man not in a white tie and tails on this occasion was British Foreign Secretary Anthony Crosland. 'It's Tony's personal crusade and I admire him for it,' said Dr Henry Kissinger.

Back in Britain, on Wednesday July 7, an off-duty policeman caught a glimpse of a man he believed to be the missing Earl of Lucan driving a green Citroen or Renault near Hailsham in Sussex. A police spokesman said, 'We are treating this sighting seriously.' Later, a local man resembling the Earl reported to the police.

Meanwhile in Uganda, a controversy had erupted over the whereabouts of 74-year-old Mrs Dora Bloch, who had been left behind in Kampala hospital at the time of the Entebbe raid. The authorities claimed that she had disappeared from hospital while more serious stories circulated that she had been dragged screaming from her bed and murdered by Amin's thugs.

Back in Washington, on Thursday July 8, the Queen presided over a state dinner at the British Embassy wearing a diamond tiara and crystal-embroidered sea green silk dress designed by Norman Hartnell. The occasion was marred by the Foreign Secretary's wife Mrs Susan Crosland slipping on the marble floor and breaking her jaw at the start of the banquet. It was noted that a similar accident had befallen Sir Harold Wilson on the same spot a few years earlier.

Later that night, there was a midnight drink-and-snack garden party at the embassy which was attended by Mr and Mrs Bob Hope, Miss Elizabeth Taylor and her new friend Senator John Warner, Mr Muhammad Ali and many others. President Ford sat beside the Queen wearing white tie and tails, semi-transparent silk socks and dancing shoes with black bows.

On Friday July 9, the Queen and Prince Philip flew to New Jersey where they boarded the royal yacht *Britannia* and sailed into New York harbour to a ticker-tape welcome. In a speech on her arrival, the Queen spoke of 'the magical and audacious skyline of Manhattan'.

Back in Britain, the same day, the Queen Mother visited the Thames Water Authority at Datchet, and inaugurated a new reservoir. After performing this duty, she visited the new staff club house and played the fruit machine in the bar.

The following day, fierce fighting broke out in Essex between members of the extreme Right Wing National Front and militant International Socialists. National Front speaker and Norfolk squire Andrew Fountaine was jostled and punched.

On Monday July 12, the marriage took place between singer Frank Sinatra and Mrs Barbara Marx in the drawing-room of Mr Walter Annenberg's 1,000 acre ranch at Palm Springs. The house was filled for the occasion with thousands of white hot-house orchids, roses, gardenias and chrysanthemums. Among the 130 guests were former Vice-President Agnew and Republican Presidential candidate Ronald Reagan.

The following day, the Queen sailed into the harbour of Halifax, Nova Scotia, on board the royal yacht *Britannia*. Among those welcoming her to Canada was the Governor-General's wife Madame Léger, whose Order of Canada decoration fell off her black chiffon dress into the sea as she stepped on board the royal yacht. Security frogmen were to spend a fruitless evening searching for it.

Wednesday July 14 saw the nomination of 51-year-old Jimmy Carter as Democratic presidential candidate. Mr Carter's 8-year-old daughter Amy cashed in on her father's new found fame by selling lemonade to reporters congregated outside the family home in Georgia.

Later the same day at Regine's in New York, Elizabeth Taylor danced the night away with her new flame, handsome, eligible, silver-haired Senator John Warner.

Meanwhile in London, the marriage had taken place between Lady Dartmouth and her friend Earl Spencer. 'It was such a quiet wedding that even *I* didn't go,' said Lady Dartmouth's mother, novelist Barbara Cartland who was interrupted writing *Look, Love and Listen* to be told of the nuptials.

On Friday July 16, a new sensation rocked London's art world when *The Times* announced that experts were in serious doubt about the authenticity of thirteen previously unknown Samuel Palmer drawings which had recently come onto the market, one of which had been sold for £15,000.

The following day in Montreal, there was wild cheering when the Queen opened the Olympic Games wearing a bright pink crêpe dress and matching hat with dangling pom-poms.

On Wednesday July 21, Britain's new Ambassador to Dublin, monocled 54-year-old Mr Christopher Ewart-Biggs was assassinated when a land-mine exploded under his car just 400 yards from his official residence. 'When will this senseless killing stop?' asked Mr Callaghan later in the House of Commons.

On Thursday July 22, Prince Charles became godfather to the infant son of the Hon. Anthony and Dale Tryon in a ceremony at Salisbury, Wiltshire.

The following day, Prince Charles became godfather to the infant son of Lord and Lady Tollemache in a ceremony at Helmingham in Suffolk.

That weekend in Britain, new legislation came into force to cope with the worst drought for 250 years and citizens now faced fines of up to £400 if they watered their gardens.

On Tuesday July 27, at breakfast time, ex-premier Tanaka was arrested and taken to Tokyo Prison for questioning about bribes he was alleged to have received from the Lockheed Aircraft Company. 'The political situation has entered a grave phase,' said the new Prime Minister Mr Miki.

Later that day, 45-year-old Soviet chess player Viktor Korchnoi applied for asylum in the Netherlands where he had been competing in the IBM chess tournament. It was said that his life in Russia had become intolerable after he had criticized world champion Anatoly Karpov.

On Wednesday July 28, the marriage took place in Chelsea between 20-year-old Dido Goldsmith, who had adorned London and Paris for the past two years and her Brazilian boy friend Roberto Shorto. 'We are planning a proper ceremony in Siena, Italy, in September,' said Dido. 'Hopefully all the family will be there.'

The following day, Dido's uncle Sir James Goldsmith stepped into the witness box at Bow Street Magistrates Court and gave evidence against *Private Eye*. Watched by his friends John Aspinall and Lady Annabel Birley, the 43-year-old millionaire paced up and down as he dismissed ideas of a Lucan set as 'a total nonsense and fabrication' and was asked by the magistrate to behave 'a little less theatrically'. The proceedings ended with *Private Eye* editor Richard Ingrams being committed for trial for criminal libel at the Old Bailey.

On Friday August 6, Sir James Goldsmith made a fresh attempt to get *Private Eye* editor Richard Ingrams and contributor Michael Gillard gaoled for contempt of court. During these proceedings which ended in a £250 fine for each of the defendants, it emerged that private investigators working for Goldsmith had raided the magazine's dustbins.

The same day at the Old Bailey, the long saga of John Stonehouse came to an end when he was found guilty of fraud, theft and deception. Sentencing the former Postmaster General to seven years' imprisonment, the judge said, 'You are not an ill-fated idealist. You committed these offences when you intended to provide for your future comfort.' Stonehouse's faithful secretary Mrs Sheila Buckley was given a two year suspended sentence for theft and conspiracy.

That weekend, Lady Antonia Fraser and her friend Harold Pinter were staying in Dorset. Lady Antonia played tennis wearing a white knee-length Jaeger dress and Jackie Onassis style sun-glasses, while Mr Pinter played cricket dressed in open-weave sandals and a blue and white check shirt and slacks.

On Tuesday August 10, it was revealed that the thirteen Samuel Palmer drawings which had recently come onto the market were the work of a talented picture restorer, Tom Keating, who was said to bear a grudge against the art establishment.

On Wednesday August 11, it was revealed that Fort Belvedere, former home of the late King Edward VIII, had been sold to an Arab businessman. 'I am selling the house for personal reasons,' said the Queen's cousin Gerald Lascelles, 'but it is a great wrench as I devoted twenty years of my life to it.' Said a spokesman for Aylesfords, the estate agents, 'These big houses certainly appeal to the Middle Easterners and they are among the few people who can afford to run them these days.'

The following weekend, while panic raged through London art dealing circles over the authenticity of works by Samuel Palmer and other masters, elusive white-bearded artist Tom Keating was on a bicycling holiday in the West of England, travelling on a red 50 cc moped.

On Wednesday August 18, an announcement that Prime Minister Callaghan

Cockney playwright and cricketer Harold Pinter and authoress Lady Antonia Fraser arrive at London's Heathrow Airport

was summoning his ministers to London to discuss the drought problems coincided with a statement from the Potato Marketing Board that the bulk of their crop was now 'under severe stress'.

On Thursday August 19, Tom Keating admitted flooding the art market with bogus paintings. In a letter to *The Times* he explained that he had done so 'as a protest against merchants who make capital out of those I am proud to call my brother artists, both living and dead'.

Over in Arlington, Virginia, on Saturday August 21, the marriage took place between Richard Burton and Suzy Hunt. The ceremony was conducted by the same judge who had married Dr Henry Kissinger and his bride two years earlier. 'Susan didn't say a heck of a lot,' said the judge afterwards, 'but she was very sweet and beautiful.' Among those to wish the couple well was Burton's ex-wife Elizabeth Taylor, who said, 'I'll give them a wedding present and wish them happiness.'

The same weekend in England, 150,000 fans of the Rolling Stones gathered for a special concert at Knebworth House in Hertfordshire. Among those present was 28-year-old Roddy Llewellyn, who said, 'I am footloose and fancy-free now. There is no one in my life. What I would like to do is a course in horticulture.'

The same night, Bianca Jagger flew in from New York and was reunited with her husband at the Ritz Hotel after the concert.

On Thursday August 26, Sheikh Zayid, ruler of Abu Dhabi, moved into 28 The Boltons, which he had bought from Douglas Fairbanks Jnr. earlier in the year for £300,000.

The same day in London, Mr John Stonehouse, now in Wormwood Scrubs beginning his seven year sentence for fraud, at last resigned as an MP. 'It has been an honour to work with this brilliant and much misunderstood man,' said Mr Frank Hansford-Miller, chairman of the English National Party, which Mr Stonehouse had joined after leaving the Labour Party four months earlier.

On Saturday August 28, Prince Talal of Saudi Arabia chartered a Middle Eastern Airlines Boeing to fly sixteen friends from London to the South of France for a night's gambling in Monte Carlo. The whole trip, including gambling losses, was said to set the Prince back by £500,000.

On Thursday September 2 there was a tea party at Lambeth Palace, London home of the Archbishop of Canterbury, to launch a biography of Dr Coggan's wife, Jean. Canvas-seated, stackable steel chairs had been provided to supplement the usual chairs and sofas and journalists were offered shortcake, lemon iced sponge cake and dainty watercress sandwiches.

On Monday September 6, it was announced that Pakistan was asking Britain to return the Koh-i-Noor diamond which had come into British possession in 1849 and was now the most famous of all the Crown Jewels and had been valued at £2 million a hundred years earlier. 'The Prime Minister and the Queen will discuss the matter,' said a Buckingham Palace spokesman.

On Wednesday September 8 at Orly Airport, businessman Hervé de Vathaire who had disappeared with 8 million francs two months earlier was arrested when he stepped off a scheduled flight from Athens. After three hours of questioning he was charged with embezzlement and taken handcuffed to the Santé Prison.

Early the next day in California, David Frost arrived by helicopter at the San Clemente home of ex-President Nixon to try and persuade him to fix an early date for the recording of his TV memoirs. The visit was a brief one as Frost had to catch a 1 p.m. flight to Chicago where he was due to give a lecture to the University of North Illinois.

On Friday September 10, it was reported that Prince Charles's old chum, Lady Jane Wellesley, had been elected 'Mother' of the National Union of Journalists chapel at the *Radio Times* where she was now working as a £5,000 a year planning assistant.

On Tuesday September 14, theatre critic Kenneth Tynan said he was leaving London for California. 'The English scene is stagnant,' he said. 'I feel a change in climate would be welcome. I'm thoroughly depressed with the state of affairs now.'

On Wednesday September 15, a Buckingham Palace spokesman said that the Queen found the proposal by a Dutch film maker to make a film on the sex life of Jesus Christ 'obnoxious'.

The same day, Roddy Llewellyn who had now begun a course at Merrist Wood Agricultural College near Guildford said he would not be joining Princess Margaret on a winter holiday in Mustique this year. 'I shall be working. I have taken up horticulture. I shall be too busy.'

On Saturday September 18, Prince Charles's 25-year-old friend Davina Sheffield hid in a lavatory at Heathrow Airport for half an hour to avoid reporters on her return from a week's holiday in the Outer Hebrides.

Meanwhile in America, there was much excitement over would-be President Jimmy Carter's interview with *Playboy* magazine. 'I'm a sinner,' he had confessed. 'I've looked on a lot of women with lust. I've committed adultery in my heart many times.' On Monday September 20, Mrs Carter said she had not read the article but insisted that she had a good marriage. 'He's a good husband. I trust him completely, absolutely.'

On Wednesday September 22, the Singapore government finally applied for the extradition of 47-year-old Jim Slater to stand trial over the affairs of Haw Par Brothers International, in which Slater had bought a large stake three years earlier and fifteen summonses were issued at the Mansion House.

The following day, Mr Slater visited his solicitors in the City of London and then sauntered nonchalantly to a taxi with his hands in his pockets.

Meanwhile, Peachey Corporation Chairman Sir Eric Miller had withdrawn his son Robert from Harrow School alleging that he had been submitted to anti-semitic persecution. On Friday September 24, the headmaster of the school denied the charges and said, 'For many generations Jewish boys have had perfectly happy school lives with us at Harrow.' Harrow governor Mr Evelyn de Rothschild declared, 'I was there thirty years ago and everything was fine.'

The same day, it was revealed that Prime Minister Jim Callaghan had refused to return the Koh-i-Noor diamond to Pakistan. He assured the Pakistan government that there was no question of the famous gem being handed over to any other government.

Later that day in San Francisco, a judge ruled that newspaper heiress Patty Hearst must serve a seven year sentence for the robbery for which she had been convicted earlier in the year. 'I do not think you are likely to be a future danger to society. Nevertheless the violent nature of your conduct cannot be condoned.'

Back in Britain, on Saturday September 25, Lord and Lady Spencer celebrated their recent wedding by giving a dance for a thousand friends at the Northamptonshire stately home, Althorp.

The following Monday, former whizz kid Jim Slater stated that he was now a 'minus-millionaire' owing approximately £1,000,000. 'I have a prospect of paying it back if I am given a chance,' he said. In reference to the attempts to get him extradited to Singapore, he said, 'I haven't a hope in hell of getting a fair trial there.'

On Tuesday September 28, new best selling author Shirley Conran threw a dinner party at her London home attended by her publisher Lord Longford, the newly ennobled Lord Kagan and other leading luminaries. The unruffled hostess said that she had prepared the entire meal – including octopus and squid salad, and lemon chiffon pie – in less than two hours.

Meanwhile, the Hon. Colin and Lady Anne Tennant had flown off for a holiday in Saudi Arabia. 'We are staying with Sheikh Yamani, who came out to Mustique this year,' Mr Tennant told a reporter. 'Don't ask me what one does in Saudi Arabia. We will have to find out.'

Over in California, on Thursday September 30, Richard Burton and his new wife Suzy were found enjoying hot fudge sundaes in the Pink Turtle Coffee Shop at the Beverly Wilshire Hotel. In the same hotel, chronic invalid Barbara Hutton, now 63 years old, was living in isolation seeing only her doctors.

On Friday October 1, it was announced that Christina Onassis was seeking a divorce from her second husband Alexander Andreadis, after only fifteen months of marriage.

Back in London, on Monday October 4, Mrs Mary Whitehouse delivered a script of the proposed film on the sex life of Jesus Christ to the Home Secretary Merlyn Rees. She described the script as 'more obscene, decadent and blasphemous than any normal, healthy mind should have conceived' and demanded that film-maker Jens Thorsen should be banned from Britain.

The following day in Denmark, Mr Thorsen commented, 'She is capable of reading pornography into the Holy Bible.'

On Friday October 8, Mrs Thatcher addressed her party conference at Brighton and called for Conservatives to crusade against 'a Marxist future for Britain'.

Later that weekend in America, Elizabeth Taylor announced her engagement to Senator John Warner, pipe-smoking former U.S. Secretary of the Navy, formerly married to a daughter of multi-millionaire Paul Mellon.

On Wednesday October 13 in France, the ailing Duchess of Windsor was awarded 80,000 francs in damages for the invasion of her privacy after photographs had been published showing her on the verandah of her Paris home being helped along by a nurse and two others.

Meanwhile in London, artist David Hockney was putting the finishing touches to a portrait of Irish chef Peter Langan which was to hang in his new restaurant which had just opened on the site of the old Coq d'Or off Piccadilly. On Friday October 15, Hockney returned to his home in Paris explaining 'It's boredom not the Inland Revenue which makes me live outside Britain.'

That night, patrons at the new Langan's Brasserie included the eccentric millionairess Olga Deterding whose triplex penthouse apartment was only a few yards away down Piccadilly overlooking Green Park.

Irish-born Peter Langan drinking champagne in his new London restaurant

The following day, 25-year-old Davina Sheffield was found weekending at Balmoral Castle as a guest of Prince Charles, sparking off further speculation that she could be a possible future Queen.

Over in New York, on Monday October 18, the funeral took place of 72-year-old Carlo Gambino, a mafia leader on whom the figure of 'The Godfather' had apparently been modelled. Members of his family arrived at the church in Brooklyn in a fleet of black Cadillacs and the dead man, who had suffered from a poor heart condition for many years, was buried in a $7,000 bronze coffin amidst speculation about who would succeed him.

Back in Britain on Wednesday October 20, 82-year-old Harold Macmillan stepped back into the limelight and called for a government of national unity to cope with the country's current problems. 'After my retirement and illness, I scrupulously kept out of politics of all kinds for thirteen years. Now I feel impelled to make some contribution to the solution of our problems.'

Three days later, on Saturday October 23, the Battle of Britain spirit was revived at a party given by Lord Montagu of Beaulieu to celebrate his fiftieth birthday at his Hampshire home. Search-lights raked the sky, air raid sirens were played and most of the guests were in khaki uniform. Among those present was 49-year-old Olga Deterding who came dressed as a nun, carried a Mauser sub-machine gun and attempted to drop in on the proceedings by parachute.

The following day, 8,000 miles away, James Hunt clinched the world motor racing championship when he won the Japanese Grand Prix in his Marlboro McLaren. 'I am going to get absolutely legless on beer,' he said afterwards. 'Champagne gives you a hangover.'

The same day in Los Angeles, details were revealed of the new 747 jumbo jet being built for King Khaled of Saudi Arabia. This new plane would be adorned with tapestries and tables of mother-of-pearl and would include an operating theatre in which the King's doctors could perform an open heart operation in mid-air should this be necessary. Plans to include a microwave oven large enough to roast an entire sheep had been regretfully abandoned by the plane's designers.

On Monday October 25, the Queen Mother arrived in Paris on a three day visit during which she stayed at the British Embassy where a pie, composed of quails stuffed with apples and raisins and laced with cognac and madeira, was served in her honour.

Back in London, on Tuesday October 26, Jim Slater appeared in the dock at Bow Street magistrates Court to face six charges of illegal share dealing brought by the Singapore government. He was ordered to surrender his passport and was remanded on bail of £45,000.

The following day, Slater's friend Jimmy Goldsmith was knighted by the Queen at Buckingham Palace. After the ceremony he hurried to the High Court where he was bringing a further contempt of court action against *Private Eye*.

That night, at a church in Essex, the Rev. Peter Elers, who had recently been elected president of Gay Christian Movement conducted a service of blessing for two lesbian couples. 'We entirely disassociate ourselves from this action,' said the Bishops of Chelmsford and Colchester. 'Mr Elers has given us a solemn undertaking not to conduct such a service in the future.'

On Tuesday November 2, peanut farmer Jimmy Carter was elected the new President of the United States of America. Celebrating later at his home in Georgia, he said, 'The dawn is rising on a beautiful new day, a beautiful new spirit in this country and a beautiful new commitment to the future.'

Back in Britain, on Thursday November 4, Sir James Goldsmith made a £3 million bid for the left wing Sunday newspaper the *Observer*, which was in serious financial difficulties.

The following Monday, November 8, the Queen and Prince Philip arrived in Luxembourg on an official visit. The Queen wore a mink coat and cherry-coloured beret – somewhat upstaging the Grand Duchess of Luxembourg and her daughter Princess Marie Astrid, who were in more sombre attire.

On Sunday November 14, it was disclosed in New York that Christina Onassis had paid her step-mother Mrs Jackie Onassis $8 million as a final settlement in return for her share of the luxury yacht *Christina* and the island of Skorpios.

On Wednesday November 17, Olga Deterding entered the fray for the *Observer*, 'I've got enough money to buy the *Observer* and have already contacted them with a view to making a bid,' she said. 'I would like to take an active part in running the paper and I do not want it as a hobby or a toy.'

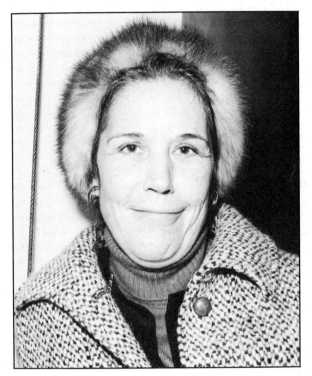

A formal portrait of oil heiress Olga Deterding at the time of her bid to buy the *Observer* newspaper

The same night, a London taxi driver refused to carry former fascist leader, 80-year-old Sir Oswald Mosley back to the Ritz Hotel after he had appeared on television denouncing the new biography by David Pryce-Jones of his sister-in-law Unity Mitford.

Two days later in California, 22-year-old newspaper heiress Patty Hearst was released on bail after the payment of a $1¼ million bail bond pending her appeal against conviction on bank robbery charges and seven year gaol sentence. She was driven to her parents' new apartment in the Nob Hill district of San Francisco where she scampered around, hugging friends, trying on old clothes and eating heartily. 'She's very pleased to be here and we're tickled to death to have her home,' said her mother, Mrs Randolph Hearst.

On Sunday November 12, it was announced that the City of New York was facing a new financial crisis and was obliged to raise a further $1,000 million to keep afloat. Mayor Abraham Beame had broken off a visit to Israel to hold talks with city and state officials.

The following day in Beverly Hills, the marriage of superstar Marisa Berenson and 35-year-old James Randall was celebrated with a $150,000 party attended by Andy Warhol, Linda Blair, star of *The Exorcist*, Liza Minnelli and her husband Jack Haley Jnr. and the fun-loving Mrs Vere Harmsworth, now established as a 'bi-coastal' personality, equally at home in New York and California. 'It was fabulous and fun,' said the 29-year-old bride. 'I went through the whole thing oblivious.'

Heathfield-educated Marisa Berenson, one of the world's most beautiful women

Meanwhile, back in Britain, new author superstar Edward Heath had spent the day signing copies of his new book *Music: A Joy for Life* at Hatchard's in Piccadilly. It was the first of thirty-three signing sessions booked for the next three weeks. 'He does 300 an hour,' whispered a representative of his publishers Sidgwick and Jackson.

On Saturday November 27, Princess Anne was stopped for speeding on the M1 in a Rover saloon. It was the fourth time she had been stopped for speeding in the past four years. 'What happens now is up to the police,' said a Buckingham Palace spokesman.

Meanwhile on Mustique, celebrations had begun to mark the fiftieth birthday of the island's owner Colin Tennant. Among those on the island were Princess Margaret, the Earl and Countess of Lichfield, Bianca Jagger and Mrs Pat Harmsworth. The festivities culminated in a Gold Ball on Wednesday December 1, at which Princess Margaret arrived in the heavily jewelled costume of a sultana and chatted with top American male model, Kalani Durdan, who wore a gold sarong.

Back in Britain the same evening, a new punk rock group The Sex Pistols, led by an ex-sewage worker calling himself Johnny Rotten, appeared on television and used 'some of the dirtiest language ever heard'. Their interviewer Bill Grundy was suspended and others concerned with the programme were told that they had made 'a gross error of judgement'. A representative of EMI records, with whom the group had signed a contract three months earlier, was more cheerful. 'After this row, it's anybody's guess how big they could be.'

Two days later, on Friday December 3, Mrs Mary Whitehouse sought permission in the High Court to bring criminal libel proceedings against *Gay News* and its editor Denis Lemon following the publication of 'an obscene poem and illustration vilifying Christ in his life and crucifixion'.

Back in America, on Saturday December 4, the marriage took place between Elizabeth Taylor and Senator John Warner at the bridegroom's estate at Middleburg, Virginia and was attended by only a few friends and some estate workers. 44-year-old Miss Taylor said afterwards that she planned to spend most of her time in the future as 'a housewife'.

On Tuesday December 7, an exhibition glorifying Russian costume opened at New York's Metropolitan Museum organized by *Vogue* editor Diana Vreeland assisted by Mrs Jackie Onassis. At the preview that night were the vivacious Madame Marcos, who arrived with Cristina Ford, Vicomtesse Jacqueline de Ribes, fashion designer Halston, Bianca Jagger and spry octogenarian Colonel Serge Obolensky.

On Saturday December 11, Elizabeth Taylor and her new husband John Warner arrived in London and booked into the film star's old haunt, the Dorchester Hotel, now owned by an Arab consortium.

The following day, Richard Burton and his new wife Suzy Hunt arrived in London and booked into the same hotel. During an interview soon after his arrival, Burton referred to his new wife as 'Elizabeth' and said of his former spouse, 'I'm very fond of the old girl'. Said Suzy, 'Elizabeth has her new happy marriage and Richard and I have each other.'

Mustique's owner Colin Tennant celebrates his fiftieth birthday flanked by his wife Lady Anne and Bianca Jagger

On Wednesday December 15, the 20-year-old marriage between Conservative MP Hugh Fraser and his glamorous wife Lady Antonia Fraser was dissolved in the Divorce Court.

The same day, Prince Charles's five years with the Royal Navy ended when he was pushed along the dockside at Rosyth Naval Base in a wheel-chair with a lavatory seat hung round his neck.

The following day in London, the Prince opened an extension of the Nightingale House Home for Aged Jews wearing a cap on his head.

On Saturday December 18, 60-year-old Mr Heath signed copies of his book *Music* at Broadstairs, amidst comment that there was now not a single hamlet that had not now been visited by the former Prime Minister on his book signing tour.

On Wednesday December 22, it was announced in Moscow that Mr Brezhnev's son Yuri had been appointed a deputy Minister of Foreign Trade.

On Friday December 24, the Royal Family congregated at Windsor Castle for the Christmas holiday. On Christmas Day itself, Prince Charles and 16-year-old Prince Andrew emerged from the castle to fill three or four plastic sacks with rubbish strewn about in Windsor Great Park.

The following Monday, December 27, Mrs Soraya Khashoggi returned to her home in Paris after spending Christmas in Switzerland with her ex-husband Adnan Khashoggi who had given her a superb emerald ring surrounded by forty-seven diamonds.

On Thursday December 30, singer Rod Stewart and his girl-friend Britt Ekland arrived in Glasgow to see in the New Year in the pop star's native land. 'Scotland is the only place to be at this time of year,' he said.

Back in London the following night, millionairess Olga Deterding, who had failed in her bid to buy the *Observer* newspaper, gave a New Year's Eve party with Yorkshire-born Ron Hall, down-to-earth editor of the *Sunday Times* colour magazine.

Richard Burton and his new wife Suzy Hunt, former wife of the racing driver

1977

The next twelve months see the Arab property-buying boom begin to slow down but the British aristocracy continue to part with their homes and possessions to anyone who will pay enough. In a memorable sale, the contents of Lord Rosebery's old home, Mentmore Towers, are sold for over £6 million. From his tax exile in Paris, Lord Brooke gives instructions that the contents of Warwick Castle should be slowly disposed of. A chapter in the life of the jet set ends when playboy Michael Pearson sells his London mansion and settles down with a nice German wife. After seventeen years popularizing Mustique, Colin Tennant sells the Caribbean island to some businessmen, though Princess Margaret keeps on her house there and continues to entertain her friend Roddy Llewellyn. In America, a new no hard liquor regime begins at the White House under the deeply religious President Carter, while in New York a new disco set suddenly blossoms around Studio 54 and the dynamic personality of Bianca Jagger, whose six-year-old marriage is now thought to be in difficulties. Meanwhile in Britain, where the Queen's Silver Jubilee is celebrated with gusto, Marcia-baiting has become a popular sport. Lady Falkender's friend Sir Eric Miller dies in tragic circumstances and gossip columnist Nigel Dempster consolidates his position by marrying the daughter of a duke. Still unmarried at the end of the year is balding 29-year-old Prince Charles, in spite of considerable efforts by the press to marry him off to a European Princess.

On New Year's Day, Mrs Soraya Khashoggi, ex-wife of multi-millionaire Adnan Khashoggi, flew into London from Paris. On arrival at her Eaton Square home, she claimed that her red cash box had been tampered with and the emerald ring her ex-husband had given her at Christmas was missing along with other jewellery valued at £145,000.

On Monday January 3, 16-year-old Prince Andrew passed briefly through Heathrow Airport on his way to Canada to spend the next two school terms at Lakefield College where he was to acquire the somewhat unsavoury nickname 'Randy Andy'.

On Tuesday January 4, the controversial Sex Pistols punk group caused confusion when they passed through the same airport on their way to Amsterdam. Said a KLM check-in girl, 'They called us filthy names and insulted everyone in sight. One of them was sick in a corridor leading to the aircraft.'

Following these incidents, it was announced that the group's contract with EMI had been terminated. 'They are afraid of us,' commented Johnny Rotten in Amsterdam. 'In a couple of years they'll regret this.'

On Thursday January 6, attention turned to Jamaica when thieves broke into the home of the Duke of Marlborough's sister 55-year-old Lady Sarah Spencer-Churchill and held her captive for several hours. One of her house guests, fabric designer Michael Szell, was shot in the arm and rushed to Kingston for emergency hospital treatment.

On Monday January 10, it was announced in New York that the long feud between three ex-Beatles and their former manager Allen Klein had ended with an out-of-court settlement. Said Mr Klein, 'This agreement would not have been realized without the tireless efforts and Kissinger-like negotiating brilliance of Yoko Ono Lennon.'

On Thursday January 13, at Aylesbury in Buckinghamshire, Rolling Stone Keith Richard was found guilty of possessing a few grains of cocaine and fined £750 by Old Harrovian Judge Lawrence Verney. Teenagers crowded into the gallery hissed with disbelief at the verdict.

On Wednesday January 19, the new Earl of Rosebery announced that his family's famous gothic extravaganza stately home Mentmore Towers in Buckinghamshire must be sold and its contents auctioned. 'The house is really a white elephant,' he said. 'I'm sorry the government did not feel able to take over the house but I can understand that the upkeep would be too expensive. We pay several thousand pounds a year to rent fire and burglar alarms alone.'

The following day in Washington, the official inauguration of Jimmy Carter as 39th President of the United States of America was marked by yawns from his 8-year-old daughter Amy and grumbles from his younger brother Billy, who said afterwards, 'One day in Washington is enough.'

Back in Britain, on Friday January 21, Princess Anne was fined £40 for doing just over 96 mph on the M1 motorway the previous November. 'Her Royal Highness wishes to express her regret for this matter having occurred and apologises,' said her lawyers. It was the first time in living memory that a child of a reigning sovereign had been brought before a criminal court.

On Monday January 24, 32-year-old Michael Pearson, heir to one of Britain's biggest fortunes, threw a party for his German-born fiancée Ellen 'Fritzi' Erhardt at his house in The Boltons. He chose the occasion to announce that he was to live abroad for tax reasons. 'I never wanted to make this move,' he said, 'but I am leaving because it is no use any more trying to build a business in Britain. There is no encouragement from the Chancellor and I shall be gone until the position changes.'

After the party, Pearson went on to the opening of a new London nightclub named Dial 9.

The following evening in Paris, social leader Ghislaine de Polignac gave a dinner party at Regine's which was attended by Princess Caroline of Monaco and her new boyfriend, man-about-town Philippe Junot.

Back in London, on Wednesday January 26, former whizz kid Jim Slater won his battle against extradition to Singapore and went off to celebrate at a party at David Frost's house in Egerton Crescent, also attended by his friend Sir James Goldsmith.

On Thursday January 27, the Dowager Lady Rosebery took photographers and reporters on a conducted tour of Mentmore Towers, the contents of which were now to be auctioned by Sotheby's. 'We won't talk about valuation because that makes it rather horrid,' she said.

The Grand Hall at Mentmore Towers, home of the late Earl of Rosebery, showing Gobelin tapestries, a very rare two-faced Louis XVI clock, and an important pair of Venetian gilt thrones, reputedly from the Doge's palace

That evening at 10 Downing Street, Prime Minister Jim Callaghan was host at an informal dinner in honour of the new American Vice-President Walter Mondale. Château Mouton Rothschild claret, and Graham's Port, originally laid down by Winston Churchill, were served and the meal ended with the teetotal Prime Minister giving his rendering of the famous hymn 'Jerusalem'.

Over in Washington, on Sunday January 30, President Carter said that his usual lunch at the White House would be a sandwich at his desk.

On Thursday February 3, the marriage took place at St Paul's Church, Knightsbridge, between 31-year-old Lord Douro, son and heir to the Duke of Wellington and Princess Antonia of Prussia, great-granddaughter of the Kaiser. Among those who witnessed the ceremony were the Queen Mother, Prince Charles and Princess Margaret.

The same day in the Guildhall Justice Room, Jim Slater was cleared of further charges that he had misused £4 million of his company's money. 'I am happy,' he said afterwards. 'I would love a holiday and now I am free to take one.' Asked how he would pay his lawyers' bills he said, 'I have got good friends who happen to believe in me.'

Over in Washington, on Friday February 4, it was revealed that a convicted black murderess, Mary Fitzpatrick, an old friend of the Carter family, had been reprieved in order to take up a post at the White House, looking after the President's daughter Amy.

The following day, President Carter declared that nine blizzard-torn counties of New York State were a 'disaster area' following the death of more than a hundred people in sub-zero temperatures.

On Sunday February 6, 8-year-old Amy Carter was baptized by immersion in a Baptist church near the White House. Among the 1,000 people present were President Carter, who described himself as a 'born again Christian', and Amy's nurse-maid Mary Fitzpatrick. Dressed in white baptismal robes, Amy stood in a large tank of water and was kept under the water for one second.

Back in Britain the same weekend, a row erupted over the Silver Jubilee hymn written by Poet Laureate Sir John Betjeman. 'It is absolutely pathetic,' said Tory MP Nicholas Fairbairn. 'It is the most banal, ninth-rate piece of child's verse.' These remarks greatly upset the Poet Laureate who explained next day, 'The words were meant for singing, not reading and therefore have plentiful long vowels.'

Meanwhile, further controversy over Sir Harold Wilson's resignation honours list had been stirred up by the publication of the memoirs of the former Prime Minister's press secretary, Joe Haines, who had claimed that the original list had been drawn up by Lady Falkender on lavender note paper. On Monday February 7, Sir Harold spent forty-five minutes with Lady Falkender at her house in Wyndham Mews, Marylebone, where she was in bed with a slipped disc, and then issued a powerfully worded statement referring to the 'farrago of twisted facts' and denying again that Lady Falkender had anything to do with the list. Also voicing his opinion on the matter was Lord Kagan, who had been raised to the peerage in the famous list. 'Lady Falkender is a competent and brilliant woman but it seems very odd to me to say that she drew up this list.'

The following day, the Earl of Longford plunged into the controversy with a plea published in *The Times* that the sneering at Lady Falkender should stop though he pointed out that he himself had 'never been intimate at Number 10'.

Meanwhile, 28-year-old Prince Charles had begun a short refresher flying course at the RAF in Cranwell and was put up nearby at Belton House, home of Lord Brownlow, whose 23-year-old granddaughter Fiona Watson, who had posed nude in *Penthouse* magazine three years earlier, was to entertain him during his off-duty hours.

On Wednesday February 9, it was disclosed that Lord Charles Spencer-Churchill, younger brother of the Duke of Marlborough, was to promote a new line of 'Lord Churchill' clothes in department stores across America. 'The retail chain I have gone with are ordering fabrics only from England and have already spent $2.5 million in places like Huddersfield,' he explained.

The following day, it was announced in America that former Secretary of State

Dr Henry Kissinger had signed a $2 million contract with Little Brown and Co to publish his memoirs.

Back in London, on Friday February 11, gossip columnist Nigel Dempster lost a gold money clip in St James's Square, containing all his credit cards and forms of identification and tickets for a forthcoming Rugby International match.

Over in Washington, on Monday February 14, President Carter's dinner for the Mexican President and Mrs Portillo was described as a quiet affair – with no hard liquor offered and no after-dinner dancing. It was noted that Mr Carter had also dispensed with the trumpets which in the past had heralded the arrival of the President at State dinners.

On Wednesday February 17, Harold Pinter and Lady Antonia Fraser flew into London on a night flight from New York. Questioned at Heathrow about her nomination as one of the world's most fashionable women, Lady Antonia replied, 'Do you mind? I've been up all night.'

The same day, an announcement came from President Amin that he would be attending the Commonwealth Conference in London later, causing dismay at the Foreign Office.

That night, Harold Pinter and Lady Antonia Fraser had recovered sufficiently from their flight to put in an appearance at a party given by 22-year-old Jane Bonham Carter at her Kensington home. Other fashionable people present included Princess Margaret, 26-year-old Lord Hesketh, Mark Shand and Clio Goldsmith.

On Saturday February 19, the tragic sudden death of Foreign Secretary Anthony Crosland shocked his colleagues and drew the public's attention to the enormous work load imposed upon cabinet ministers.

On Sunday February 20, details of Sir Harold Wilson's coat of arms were revealed in the *Sunday Telegraph*. These included a golden gryphon and winged lion as supporters and had cost the former Labour Prime Minister £480 in fees for the College of Arms.

The next day, it was announced that 91-year-old Lady Spencer-Churchill was selling paintings, furniture, silver and other heirlooms to pay her living costs. 'I'm sure my grandfather felt he was leaving her in comfortable circumstances,' said her grandson Winston Churchill MP, 'but no one could foresee the rate of inflation and taxation and the decline in the purchasing power of money. She is having to do this because of the increased cost of everything and in addition she requires to have paid nursing, which is not cheap.'

On Tuesday February 22, Lady Churchill said she would decline all offers to ease her financial plight. Her secretary said that Sir Winston's widow would 'greatly deplore any appeal initiated on her behalf'.

Over in Toronto, on Sunday February 27, Royal Canadian Mounted police raided the hotel bedroom occupied by Rolling Stone Keith Richard and found a quantity of heroin valued at $4,000. Richard was arrested and charged with possessing the drug for the purpose of trafficking.

Back in London, on Monday February 28, Frank Sinatra's opening concert at the Albert Hall was witnessed by a bunch of celebrities including Princess Margaret and the newly married Earl and Countess Spencer. 'I loathe this song,' said Sinatra before eventually singing his famous hit 'My Way'. It was noted that the entertainer's grey transplanted hair gleamed like steel.

On Wednesday March 2, Prime Minister Jim Callaghan wore an enormous white military-style belted raincoat when he visited Essex University, where Tory front bench spokesman Sir Keith Joseph had been pelted with flour bombs three weeks earlier. 'When I know I am coming near Essex University I wear my anti-demonstration gear,' he explained.

On Friday March 4, Lady Churchill's financial problems were solved when five paintings by her late husband were sold at Christie's for £86,300, four times more than they were expected to fetch. Among those present at the sale was Lady Churchill's old friend Lady Diana Cooper, who wore a big purple sombrero.

Frank Sinatra and his wife Barbara Marx during a visit to London's Mayfair

Back in Canada that weekend, Mrs Margaret Trudeau attended two concerts given by the Rolling Stones in Toronto, after which she travelled on to New York with her heroes Ronnie Wood and Mick Jagger amidst rumours that she was having a romance with the latter. On Wednesday March 9, Jagger said, 'Really this whole thing is ridiculous. Margaret Trudeau is a very attractive person but we are not having an affair.' Asked if she was having an affair with Jagger, Mrs Trudeau replied, 'Heavens no!'

On Thursday March 10, Prime Minister Jim Callaghan flew into Washington in Concorde and had an effusive, jocular first meeting with President Carter in front of a blazing log fire in the Oval Office.

The following day, it was reported that Lady Antonia Fraser's 19-year-old daughter Rebecca had moved out of the New York apartment of Mrs Jackie Onassis into the flat of 22-year-old Michael Zilkha, whose father had created the Mothercare chain of shops. 'There are just two of us in my flat but there is no romance,' said Michael.

Later that day in Los Angeles, film director Roman Polanski was arrested in the lobby of the Beverly Wilshire Hotel and charged with rape, sodomy, child molesting and furnishing drugs to a minor and taken to Los Angeles police station.

Meanwhile, at the nearby Beverly Hilton Hotel, David Frost and his team had begun making final arrangements for Frost's series of interviews with ex-President Nixon.

On Saturday March 12, Margaret Trudeau suddenly returned to Ottawa from New York in time for a dinner in honour of British Prime Minister Jim Callaghan.

Back in Britain, on Thursday March 17, it was announced that A & M Records had terminated their contract with the notorious punk group the Sex Pistols, following a controversy over the group's scandalous new record 'God Save the Queen', and handed over £75,000 in compensation. 'The Sex Pistols are like some contagious disease – untouchable,' said their manager, Malcolm MacLaren. 'It's crazy.'

Back in California on Friday March 18, preparations for the Nixon interviews were complicated when David Frost was struck down by severe toothache. An operation was swiftly performed by the distinguished endodontist Dr Dudley Glick which went off well but left Frost's face swollen up like a balloon for the next few days.

The following Wednesday, ex-President Richard Nixon arrived in a white Lincoln Continental at a house near his San Clemente home to begin taping his interviews with David Frost. Frost's first question was, 'Why didn't you burn the tapes?' to which Nixon gave an evasive and rambling reply which went on for over twenty minutes.

Ex-president Richard Nixon poses with TV interviewer David Frost during a break in their monumental series of talks. Note the two men's physical similarities

On Thursday March 24, film director Roman Polanski was indicted by a Los Angeles County grand jury on charges of unlawful sexual intercourse, furnishing Qaaludes to a minor and other offences.

The following night, Polanski refused to go into hiding and appeared that night in Hollywood's fashionable Ma Maison restaurant. 'I am not guilty, so why should I act guilty?' he said.

On Sunday March 27, former White House official John Dean, who had served only four months of his sentence for his part in the Watergate cover-up, arrived in London to preside over the publication of his 400 page book of memoirs, *Blind Ambition*.

Back in California, on Tuesday March 29, film director Roman Polanski appeared before Santa Monica Superior Court dressed in a rumpled blazer and open neck shirt and pleaded innocent to all the charges against him. Getting into his car later, he said, 'I am used to grief. This is just a trifle,' but as his car pulled away from the kerb he turned to reporters and shouted, 'Fucking animals! All of you!'

Back in Britain, on Wednesday March 30, Sir Eric Miller, close friend of Lady Falkender and Sir Harold Wilson, stepped down as chairman of the Peachey Property Corporation which he had built up, blaming 'the flood of unwelcome publicity' which he had received over the past two years.

On Thursday March 31, London's 'bright young things' gathered for the opening of a new nightclub on the site of the old Aretusa club in the King's Road, named Wedgies. 25-year-old Lord Burghersh had been recruited to welcome the guests who included Sir James Goldsmith's niece Clio Goldsmith and her new friend Lorenzo Ripoli, 31-year-old Dai Llewellyn and society columnist Betty Kenward, who wore her usual waitress-style black bow in her hair.

On Saturday April 2, 12-year-old wonder horse Red Rum won the Grand National for the third time. Said Irish jockey Tommy Stack afterwards, 'This horse is incredible. He just seems to love it out there.' Said an admirer, 'I love this bloody horse. If he was a woman, I'd leave home for him.'

The same day, 64-year-old King Khaled of Saudi Arabia left London's Wellington Hospital where he had had a steel pin inserted in his left leg. It was said later that the King had left tips for nursing staff totalling £20,000 and the total stay had cost him over £1 million.

On Thursday April 7, Opposition leader Mrs Thatcher was treated like a head of state when she arrived in Peking wearing a neatly tailored light blue overcoat. At a banquet that night in the Great Hall of the People, Mrs Thatcher identified the Soviet Union as the main threat to world peace.

Back in Britain, on Saturday April 9, Princess Anne made her first public appearance since the announcement that she was expecting a baby. Dressed in jeans and a casual light brown coat, she sat in a Range Rover at the Brigstock Horse Trials in Northamptonshire, where her husband was competing. After completing a clear round, Captain Phillips grinned at reporters and said, 'It's nice to know I can do something right sometimes.'

On Tuesday April 12, another chapter in the life of the jet set ended when Colin Tennant left Mustique. He had now sold the Caribbean island to Venezuelan paint manufacturer Hans Neumann and Canadian printer John McLaren. 'I don't even have a house on Mustique any longer,' he said on his return to England. 'After slogging away for seventeen years establishing the place, it's nice to be able to take a back seat at last.'

On Wednesday April 13, Mrs Thatcher flew from China to Japan, where she was again welcomed like a visiting head of state. Touring the Nissan car factory near Tokyo two days later, she remarked 'It was so refreshing to see everyone working. No one was standing around doing nothing.'

That night, Mrs Thatcher appeared at a reception given by the Liberal Democratic Party wearing a flowing Yuki gown.

Meanwhile, at the Cedars of Lebanon Hospital in Los Angeles, Paul Getty III had been provided with a new ear to replace the one he had lost at the hands of his kidnappers four years earlier. A series of delicate operations involving rib cartilage grafts had been performed.

The following weekend, there was panic on board the British warship HMS *Danae* currently anchored near Rio de Janeiro when escaped train robber Ronnie Biggs was brought on board by a group of sailors who had met him in a bar. 'There was a bit of fuss,' said Biggs afterwards, 'but I got back to the shore OK.' Rear-Admiral Martin Wemyss called for an immediate enquiry.

Back in London, on Monday April 18, it was revealed that playboy Michael Pearson had sold his house in The Boltons, featuring outdoor swimming-pool, shooting range and other trendy facilities, to an Arab purchaser for £1.2 million and was now based at a two bedroom flat in Monte Carlo.

That night, Prince Charles dined at Chequers with Prime Minister Jim Callaghan and a few members of the cabinet. At the end of the meal, the heir to the throne declared that he had a 'rotten, boring job', prompting one of those present to tweak him on the cheek and say, 'Well, you shouldn't have taken the job then, should you?'

The following day, Opposition leader Mrs Thatcher arrived back in London after a gruelling twenty-one hour flight from Hong Kong. At Heathrow Airport she was met by her husband Denis who said, 'Wonderful to see you darling, welcome home.' After a quick cup of coffee in a VIP lounge, Mrs Thatcher drove straight to the House of Commons.

On Wednesday April 20, author Clifford Irving flew into London from Mexico City to launch his book about the Howard Hughes affair, *Project Octavia*, and showing no trace of prison pallor. Accompanied by a beautiful new German girl-friend, he booked into a small hotel near the British Museum and languidly declared, 'I've paid my dues.'

That night, the seventieth birthday of Maureen Marchioness of Dufferin and Ava was celebrated with a party at the Savoy Hotel, at which the men wore white tie and tails and decorations and many of the women wore tiaras. Among those present were the 84-year-old Lady Diana Cooper, the Duke of Marlborough, the Earl and Countess of Lichfield and television personality Derek Nimmo.

Meanwhile, Roddy Llewellyn had completed his horticultural course and had begun accepting commissions to lay out people's gardens. 'I am delighted that Roddy has succeeded in establishing himself,' said his father Colonel Harry Llewellyn on Thursday April 21, 'I believe he has great talent.'

On Wednesday April 27, 84-year-old Lady Diana Cooper presided over a charity evening at her home in Warwick Avenue, dressed in gold lamé trousers, at which extracts from her autobiography were read to a specially invited audience.

Two days later in Monte Carlo, Prince Charles was placed opposite Princess Caroline of Monaco at a dinner in honour of Dr Henry Kissinger: a glittering event also attended by multi-millionaire Stavros Niarchos, Prince Charles's uncle Earl Mountbatten of Burma and actor David Niven, whose autobiography had now sold over 4 million copies in paperback. During his short stay in the principality, the Prince was also to meet the celebrated nightclub proprietor Regine but declined an offer to dance with her.

Back in London, on Saturday April 30, the social scene was enriched by the presence of film director Roman Polanski who had flown in from Los Angeles where he was now on bail. He lunched that day at San Lorenzo in Beauchamp Place and in the evening he put in an appearance at Tramp in Jermyn Street.

On Sunday May 1, Polanski flew to Paris where he was to sign a contract to make a movie based on Thomas Hardy's classic *Tess of the D'Urbervilles*.

Two days later in New York, Elizabeth Taylor, Jackie Onassis, Liza Minnelli, Margaux Hemingway and other international socialites were present at Bianca Jagger's birthday party in the new Studio 54 discothèque which had opened the previous week with much excitement. Bianca made a spectacular entrance mounted on a white horse. Later in the evening, her husband Mick was photographed licking a huge chunk of birthday cake and then sprawling on the shoulder of ballet dancer Mikhail Baryshnikov.

On Wednesday May 4, the first of the historic Frost – Nixon interviews was broadcast drawing scornful comments from politicians and other leading figures. 'He's *still* covering up,' said Senator Sam Ervin, who had chaired the first Watergate investigation.

On Thursday May 5, President Carter arrived in London for an economic summit. He was met at Heathrow Airport by Prime Minister Callaghan, who wore his familiar white belted mackintosh, and was then driven through the drizzle to the residence of the American Ambassador in a specially built bullet-proof Cadillac.

Two days later, on Saturday May 7, there was a state dinner at Buckingham Palace in honour of the seven world leaders gathered in London. Princess Margaret sat between Mr Callaghan and Mr Carter, who wore an old fashioned double-breasted dinner jacket and outsize bow tie. Guests dined off the 200 piece Royal Rockingham service originally made for William IV's coronation in 1830. The main dish on the menu was mousse de volaille à la crème with green beans, carrots and new potatoes.

On Wednesday May 11, the appointment of the Prime Minister's son-in-law, cigarillo-smoking journalist Peter Jay as Ambassador to Washington caused an outcry. 'This is nepotism at its most blatant,' said Tory MP Nigel Lawson.

Meanwhile, another diplomatic rumpus had erupted over the high rate of cancer among Americans serving at the American Embassy in Moscow and the appointment of a State Department investigation into whether the disease could be caused by micro-wave radiation beamed at the building. On Thursday May 12, it was reported that Dr E. Cuyler Hammond of the American Cancer Society had dismissed this idea as 'poppycock'.

Back in Britain, on Friday May 13, 67-year-old former architect John Poulson tottered out of Lincoln Gaol after serving three years of his six year sentence for corruption. 'We have no plans to go away,' said his wife. 'We feel that home will be the best place until he is stronger.'

Later that day in London, a bitter and chaotic annual general meeting of the Peachey Corporation ended with 49-year-old Sir Eric Miller, who had been accused of using the company's assets for his own purposes, being kicked off the board. Miller sat through the meeting with a sour deadpan expression on his face and finally strode out. 'I expected the meeting to be rough,' said the chairman Lord Mais later, 'but not so unpleasant and partisan as it was.'

Meanwhile, the long and complicated legal battle between Sir James Goldsmith and *Private Eye* magazine had been settled out of court. On Monday May 16, editor Richard Ingrams and contributor Patrick Marnham entered the dock in the Old Bailey's famous Number One Court to hear Sir James's barrister explain that the magazine had apologized. The two defendants were then formally pronounced not guilty.

On Wednesday May 18, the sale of the contents at Mentmore Towers began with the new Lord Rosebery, a former professional electrician, perching on top of a piece of scaffolding adjusting the lights. The first item sold was a battered Louis XVI console, which fetched £17,500.

The sale of the century in progress: Eva Lady Rosebery consults a catalogue listing the Mentmore heirlooms. Her granddaughter's husband, Charles Garton, goes over the contents with her

That night, the Society for the Preservation of Rural England gave a fund raising ball at which 31-year-old Dai Llewellyn made a rare appearance in drag, dressed as Alice in Wonderland.

On Thursday May 19, a chapter in European life ended when the Orient Express left Paris for Istanbul for what was said to be the last time. Champagne flowed at the Gare de Lyon as the train set off, but those on board were soon experiencing severe hardship. 'For one and a half days we had no water,' recalled one passenger later. 'And of course there was no food on the train. At each stop we had to rush off to the station cafeteria and forage for food. Whatever we got, we all shared.'

Meanwhile in Washington, President Carter's brother Billy had spent his first night in the White House, occupying the Lincoln bed.

Over in California on Friday May 20, film director Roman Polanski sat through another pre-trial hearing dressed in a stylish new suit and looking refreshed and confident after his trip to Europe. During the hearing, his lawyers sought to introduce evidence about the previous sexual experience of the teenage girl Polanski was accused of raping.

That night in New York, the 700 patrons at the exclusive Studio 54 included Mick Jagger, Polanski's friend Jack Nicholson, Margaux Hemingway and her husband Errol Wetson when the club was raided by about a dozen plain clothes policemen asking to see the club's liquor licence. 'It's all a big misunderstanding,' said co-owner Steve Rubell. 'Our attorneys will have all this cleared up in no time.'

Back in Britain, on Saturday May 21, the marriage took place between motor-racing peer Lord Hesketh and Miss Clair Watson, sister of Prince Charles's new friend Fiona Watson. After the ceremony in Yorkshire, the happy couple flew to Monte Carlo for the Grand Prix. Already at this resort were multi-millionaire tax exile Michael Pearson and his fiancée Fritzi Erhardt and close friend Dr Tony Greenburgh who were relaxing together on a rented yacht, *The Thism*.

The following week, the Heskeths flew on to Rome where on Wednesday May 25 they watched Liverpool win the European Cup. Later that week they appeared at the Cipriani Hotel in Venice where Lord Hesketh's new trim figure was noted by a poolside admirer. 'He must have lost nearly a stone. He looks quite dishy.'

Back in Britain, on Thursday May 26, the Mentmore sale went into its final phase with the disposal of coat-hangers, bootjacks, coal scuttles, fire irons, horse-hair mattresses, sewing machines, buckets and pails. The following day the sale ended after fetching a total of £6,389,933 and was followed by a party, at which champagne flowed and a vast cake in the shape of Mentmore Towers was wheeled in to the sound of bagpipes.

Later that day in Ottowa, Canadian Prime Minister Pierre Trudeau and his wife Margaret announced that their marriage was over. 'Margaret relinquishes all privileges as wife of the Prime Minister and wishes to leave the marriage and pursue an independent career,' said the joint statement.

Back in Britain, on Saturday May 28, a confrontation took place after a Silver Jubilee concert at Windsor between the Queen and Dame Edna Everage, who wore a diamond tiara and silver lamé gloves.

The historic encounter between Her Majesty the Queen and 'housewife-superstar' Dame Edna Everage

On Monday May 30, there was another Silver Jubilee gala at Covent Garden, which was attended by sixteen members of the Royal Family, including 94-year-old Princess Alice, Countess of Athlone, who wore the Order of Victoria and Albert, which her grandmother had given her as long ago as 1898. Prime Minister Jim Callaghan was in white tie and tails and was seen intoning the National Anthem with gusto.

On Thursday June 2, the 22-year-old Duke of Roxburghe, owner of Floors Castle in Scotland, lunched at San Lorenzo in Beauchamp Place with his fiancée Lady Jane Grosvenor, younger daughter of the Duke of Westminster.

That night, Princess Margaret joined the new young Foreign Secretary David Owen, Lady Melchett and other celebrities at the world première of Rudolf Nureyev's new production of *Romeo and Juliet* at the London Coliseum. The Princess was attended by Mrs Jocelyn Stevens, whose husband had recently survived an attempt to get him removed from the board of Beaverbrook Newspapers.

The following Sunday, June 5, thieves broke into the Hyde Park Crescent home of Princess Fatima, sister of the Shah of Iran, and made off with £100,000 worth of cash and jewels while the Princess was taking her son out for the day from Harrow School.

On Tuesday June 7, the Queen drove in the Gold State Coach drawn by eight greys to St Paul's Cathedral for a special Jubilee thanksgiving service. She wore the same bright pink crêpe dress and matching hat with dangling pom-poms which she had worn the previous summer at the opening of the Montreal Olympics.

Meanwhile, the whereabouts of President Amin of Uganda were unknown following an announcement that he was 'on the high seas' on his way to London to participate in the celebrations, and the sighting of a Boeing 707 above Nice thought to be heading for Britain. A spokesman at 10 Downing Street refused to say what arrangements had been made in the event of his arrival.

On Friday June 10, the world was informed that 28-year-old Prince Charles was going bald, after a bare patch the size of a duck's egg had been spotted on the crown of his head when he was playing polo at Cirencester. Hair-transplant expert Leonard Pountney immediately offered him a hair graft. 'I am a staunch royalist and of course there would be no charge for the Prince of Wales,' he said.

The following Tuesday, June 14, Prince Charles's escort on the opening day of Royal Ascot was 22-year-old Lady Sarah Spencer, daughter of Earl Spencer, whose vivid green costume struck a bright note on an otherwise cold, grey day.

On Wednesday June 15, *The Times*'s suggestion that the late Donald Beves, a wealthy Cambridge don who had died in 1961, was the Fourth Man in the Philby, Burgess, Maclean saga caused widespread indignation. 'For reasons that I cannot disclose the suggestion that Beves was the fourth man is wildly off the mark,' said author Andrew Boyle who was writing a definitive book on the period and claimed to know the identity of the fourth man, who he said was still alive and much better known than Beves.

The following day, a special luncheon of fresh, rare ingredients was served at London's Neal Street restaurant to celebrate the publication of *Cuisine Minceur* by French chef Michel Guerard. Presiding over the meal was the restaurant's portly manager, Old Harrovian Charles Campbell.

Later that day in Washington, retiring British Ambassador Sir Peter Ramsbotham threw a tea party in the garden of the British Embassy at which over 1,500 guests tucked into ripe strawberries, frothing bowls of real whipped cream and tiny sandwiches. A spokesman explained that owing to rising costs this would be 'the last big bash' to be held at the Embassy and future celebrations would be on a more modest scale.

Back in Britain, on Friday June 17, another major journalistic blunder occurred when the *Daily Express* announced that Prince Charles was to marry Princess Marie Astrid of Luxembourg. A statement was quickly issued from Buckingham Palace to say that there was no truth in the report. Royal press officer Ronald Allison stated that the Prince 'has either never met Princess Marie Astrid or if he has it has been no more than a formal handshake at official functions'.

On Wednesday June 22, Soviet leader Leonid Brezhnev left France after an official visit during which he had been presented with two more cars, a sports and station wagon model of the Metro Rancho Bagheer to add to his already impressive collection. It was said that the Soviet leader had not been pleased with the interior colour of the station-wagon and it had been quickly re-painted and re-upholstered to suit him.

Later that day in Alabama, former Attorney-General John Mitchell arrived in a private jet to begin his two and a half year gaol sentence in an open prison for his part in the Watergate cover-up. Entering the prison compound, he remarked: 'It's great to be back in Alabama.'

Back in Britain, on Friday June 24, at Blenheim Palace, over a thousand people attended a ball given by the Duke of Marlborough to celebrate the coming of age of his son Jamie, Marquess of Blandford.

On Tuesday June 21, the ugliest slanging match in the history of Wimbledon took place when Ilie Nastase was defeated by Bjorn Borg's relentless power play. Nastase hurled a ball at an umpire who had offended him and flew off to Paris cursing and raging.

Over in Berlin, on Friday July 1, it was revealed that the elderly Rudolf Hess had had a colour TV delivered to his cell in Spandau Gaol.

On Saturday July 2, Bjorn Borg retained the men's championship after an exciting final with Jimmy Connors, said to have 'more twists and turns than an Agatha Christie thriller'.

On Sunday July 3, attention turned to Marbella on the Costa del Sol where Bianca Jagger and David Bowie were frolicking together after attending the Paris première of Bowie's film *The Man Who Fell to Earth*.

Back in London, on Monday July 4, the trial began at the Old Bailey of Denis Lemon, editor of the homosexual newspaper *Gay News*, who had been accused by Mrs Mary Whitehouse of publishing a blasphemous libel by printing a poem depicting Christ as a promiscuous homosexual. During the trial that followed journalist Bernard Levin gave evidence that the newspaper was 'run by men of complete integrity' and Judge King-Hamilton was to remark, 'This is all beyond me.'

On Thursday July 7, Mr and Mrs Henry J. Heinz gave a party at their Mayfair mews home in honour of the new American Ambassador Mr Kingman Brewster. Among those present were publisher Lord Weidenfeld, the Marquess of Tavistock, dress-designer Hardy Amies and society columnist Mrs Betty Kenward.

Later that evening, Mr and Mrs Heinz were present at the open-air Berkeley Square Ball, which was attended by the Earl of Lichfield, Mick Jagger, Olga Deterding, Princess Margaret and other 'fun people'. Princess Margaret stayed till 2.00 in the morning and left with a ship in a glass bottle that she had won in a tombola.

The following weekend, multi-millionaire Gianni Agnelli and Adnan Khashoggi were found relaxing on their yachts near Cap Ferrat. Mr Agnelli, president of Fiat, was photographed jumping stark naked off his yacht *Capricia* into the sea, holding his nose.

Back in London, on Tuesday July 12, *Gay News* editor Denis Lemon was found guilty of publishing a blasphemous libel and fined £500 and given a suspended nine month prison sentence. Judge King-Hamilton said, 'It is possible to hope that by this verdict the pendulum of public opinion is beginning to swing back to a more healthy climate.'

Later that day in Washington, President Carter announced that he had decided to go ahead with the scientific development of the dreaded neutron bomb.

On Wednesday July 13, it was announced that England's former soccer manager

Don Revie had signed a £340,000 contract with the United Arab Emirates, where a £25 million soccer stadium was now being built.

On Thursday July 14, it was reported that the fun-loving twenty-year-old Rebecca Fraser had returned to London from New York and was now trying to become a model. 'I want to enjoy this nice free age where no one minds what anyone else does any more,' she said.

On Saturday July 16, Mick Jagger was found dancing in London's Dial 9 disco with a new friend, Texan model Jerry Hall, former girl-friend of pop star Bryan Ferry.

On Tuesday July 19, a battle began between the Duke of Rutland and the National Coal Board who were anxious to begin mining beneath the Duke's famous stately home Belvoir Castle. The Duke described the proposed operation as 'staggeringly expensive and unnecessary'.

Meanwhile, a row had erupted at London's famous Reform Club over the membership of *Gay News* editor Denis Lemon, who had recently been convicted of criminal blasphemy. Lord Arwyn, 80-year-old Welsh peer said to believe in the castration of homosexuals, demanded Mr Lemon's expulsion from the club while Labour minister Roy Hattersley said he would resign if the controversial editor was thrown out.

On Thursday July 21, the new British Ambassador to Washington, Peter Jay, flew into Washington on board a British Airways Boeing 747 wearing a crumpled white suit. 'I think there is no necessity for Concorde, when she's pretty well booked up, to fly government officials unless they have to get across the Atlantic in three and a half hours,' he said.

A few days earlier, Mr Jay had delivered a long diatribe about the inevitability of Britain's collapse at a private dinner at his Ealing home in honour of Mrs Katharine Graham, proprietor of the *Washington Post*.

On Saturday July 23, race-goers at Ascot included Sheikh Essa al-Kalifa of Bahrein, who was said to have fourteen horses in training in Britain. During the afternoon, he was invited into the Royal Box to take tea with the Queen, who had a large house party that weekend at Windsor Castle.

On Tuesday July 26, the tragic death of ex-debutante Jayne Harries made head-line news. It was revealed that she had died the previous week after injecting herself with heroin in a public lavatory in Cranleigh, Surrey. 'The pushers knew she had money and obviously they milked her as much as they could,' said her step-father. 'She became a victim of drugs at the age of fifteen. She went to one of those silly jet-set parties and began sniffing cocaine. Like so many people, I suppose she thought it was clever.'

The following night in London, the retiring French Ambassador Monsieur Jacques de Beaumarchais gave a farewell party attended by Princess Margaret in a pink beaded dress, trade union leader Len Murray, cartoonists Mark Boxer and Sir Osbert Lancaster, former Prime Minister Edward Heath, Mr Jeremy Thorpe, the vivacious Mrs Vere Harmsworth, Lord Goodman and other members of the beau monde.

On Friday July 28, 60-year-old artist Tom Keating gave himself up at the West End Central Police Station and was charged with conspiracy and criminal deception. He was granted bail in the sum of £5,000.

Later that day, 59-year-old Defence Secretary Fred Mulley fell asleep while watching a Jubilee flying display with the Queen. 'There was a momentary lapse of attention on his part,' said a Defence Ministry spokesman later. 'He very much enjoyed the impressive display.' It was noted that Mr Mulley had 'nodded off' only fifteen minutes after the flypast of V Bombers, Phantoms, Harrier Jump jets began.

On Saturday July 30, the marriage took place at Chelsea Registry Office between 38-year-old gossip columnist Nigel Dempster and 27-year-old Lady Camilla Harris, heiress daughter of the late Duke of Leeds. 'What's all this?' said Dempster to the crowd of journalists gathered outside. 'I can't think what possible interest my marriage could be to anyone.'

Meanwhile, 100 homosexuals had marched through the streets of Chelsea protesting about the recent *Gay News* blasphemy conviction.

On Friday August 5, Princess Marie Astrid of Luxembourg was among spectators at her brother Prince Jean's passing out parade at Sandhurst. Prince Jean dismissed rumours of the engagement between his sister and Prince Charles as complete nonsense. 'The stories are a joke in our family,' he said.

Over in California, on Tuesday August 9, film director Roman Polanski appeared in a packed Santa Monica courtroom to plead guilty to unlawful intercourse. Judge Rittenband accepted the plea, dismissed the other charges against him and cancelled the trial. Polanski was ordered to undergo psychiatric examination at the California State Prison but in the meantime was once again released on bail.

The following morning, Polanski was disturbed by a photographer as he placed a wreath on the grave of his wife, Sharon Tate. After a violent struggle, he managed to grab the man's camera and kick it thirty yards across the cemetery.

Three days later, on Saturday August 13, it was stated that President Carter had booted his son Chip out of the White House on learning that he wanted to separate from his wife Caron who had given birth to a baby boy six months earlier.

On Tuesday August 16, 42-year-old Elvis Presley was found dying on his bathroom floor at Memphis, Tennessee.

Two days later, nineteen-year-old Caroline Kennedy was among thousands of fans of the late pop star permitted to file past his open coffin, while outside his mansion a day and night vigil by a further 80,000 mourners was disrupted when a car crashed into the crowd killing two people.

On Sunday August 21, the Sultan of Oman was among passengers held up in familiar delays at Heathrow Airport. On being refused permission to depart in his private jet, the Sandhurst-educated potentate jokingly offered to buy the air control centre.

The following day, attention turned to the tiny Greek island of Hydra where Mick Jagger and his wife were staying, attempting to patch up their marital difficulties.

Meanwhile, troubles had also hit the relationship between Britt Ekland and Rod Stewart. On Tuesday August 23, it was announced in Santa Monica, California, that Britt was suing Rod for up to $20 million claiming half his assets on the grounds that he had only become a 'superstar' with her aid.

On Thursday August 25, the engagement of twenty-year-old Princess Caroline of Monaco and middle-aged jet-setter Philippe Junot was announced in Monte Carlo. It was said that Prince Rainier had agreed to the engagement with some reluctance.

Back in London, on Saturday August 27, it was said that former whizz kid Jim Slater was now easing his way back into the City via several private property companies and an association with the controversial Mr 'Tiny' Rowland.

On Monday August 29, a village fête at Wonersh in Surrey was officially opened by the new Lord of the Manor, wealthy Kuwaiti Muhammad Qabazard, who wore elegantly cut Arab robes and arrived in a silver Rolls-Royce. 'I am having a lovely time,' he said. 'I get on well with all the villagers.'

Back in Memphis, Tennessee, on Monday August 29, four men were arrested as they tried to steal the body of the late Elvis Presley now buried in a flower decked mausoleum. Police had been tipped off in advance and were hiding at the grave-yard when the men broke in.

Over in Britain, on Friday September 2, it was revealed that the Chancellor of the Exchequer Mr Denis Healey had paid £65,000 for a country property at Alfriston in Sussex. The house had eight bedrooms, four bathrooms and a swimming pool and was situated only a few miles from Prime Minister Callaghan's farm.

On Sunday September 4, a helicopter carrying Captain Mark Phillips to a show-jumping event was forced to do an emergency landing. 'My old ticker started fluttering a bit,' said Phillips afterwards, 'but the pilot was first class.'

On Wednesday September 7, Mick and Bianca Jagger made a brief appearance at San Lorenzo's restaurant in Beauchamp Place at which the revellers included 20-year-old Rebecca Fraser, 26-year-old Lord Burghersh and the Earl of Pembroke. 'I thought this was a restaurant not a fashion show,' said Mick as they quickly left the premises.

Meanwhile, Opposition leader Mrs Thatcher had begun a nine-day tour of America. On Thursday September 8, she entered the world of American high finance dining in New York with banker David Rockefeller, who was noted for his pumping handshake and fixed smile.

On Saturday September 10, Mrs Thatcher arrived in Houston and was given a VIP tour of the Space Center. Squeezing through a small door into a mock-up of the space shuttle, she remarked, 'One tries not to be inelegant about these things.'

The same day in Kenya, a former servant of General Amin revealed that the Ugandan President kept the severed heads of several of his victims in a refrigerator at one of his homes believing that they warded off the 'evil eye'. The President's wife Sarah had been horrified to find the head of her former lover in the fridge.

In the early hours of Tuesday September 13, violence erupted on the Côte d'Azur when a Rolls-Royce carrying the Shah of Iran's twin sister, Princess Ashraf, back to her villa after playing roulette in a Cannes casino was ambushed. Shots were fired and the Princess's woman companion was killed.

Later that day in Washington, Mrs Margaret Thatcher and President Jimmy Carter met in the Oval Office at the White House. During their forty-five minute chat, Mrs Thatcher told the President to prepare to deal with her as Britain's future Prime Minister.

That night in New York, leading British fashion designer Zandra Rhodes ap-peared at a party at the 21 Club with her hair dyed green and black and wearing a punk rock dress with a large hole ripped out of the front to give a peek-a-boo of her thighs.

Back in Britain, on Wednesday September 14, Mick Jagger said he was looking for a school for his five-year-old daughter Jade. 'We're studying a list of places she might go,' he said. 'She's been attending a nursery school in New York and now we are just looking for an ordinary day school for her.'

Two days later in Paris, singer Maria Callas collapsed and died in her apartment, leaving her relatives to squabble over her $12 million fortune.

On Saturday September 17, the Earl of Lichfield, young tycoon John Bentley, gossip columnist Nigel Dempster and other friends left London by bus for Southend Airport where they boarded a private plane to fly them to Germany for the marriage of 33-year-old multi-millionaire Michael Pearson and 26-year-old Ellen 'Fritzi' Erhardt, which took place at a picturesque Bavarian lakeside resort. The bride-groom's father Lord Cowdray said he was glad his son's hedonistic bachelorhood was over, 'he has had some lively times but I'm sure he'll make Ellen a good steady husband.'

Lord Cowdray's son Michael Pearson and his 26-year-old bride Ellen 'Fritzi' Erhardt are all smiles after their wedding in Bavaria

The following day, it was revealed that legendary big spender Mrs Jackie Onassis had obtained a $20 million settlement from her late husband's family in return for abandoning all further claims to his estate.

On Monday September 19 in California, Judge Rittenband gave film director Roman Polanski a further ninety days freedom to work on his film *Hurricane* in the South Pacific before he need submit to psychiatric evaluation. Commentators wondered if the judge was going 'soft in the head' or had been swayed by the influence of the film industry.

Back in London, on Thursday September 22, Sir Eric Miller, whose career was now being investigated by the Director of Public Prosecutions, shot himself dead in the garden of his home in the Little Boltons, Chelsea. At his funeral the following day at Willesden Jewish Cemetery, few of his famous friends were present and Rabbi Unterman spoke of the crumbling of his 'larger than life ambience'.

Meanwhile, American beauty queen Joyce McKinney and her friend Keith May had appeared at Epsom Magistrates Court accused of kidnapping Mormon mission-ary Kirk Anderson and holding him prisoner in a cottage in Devon. During the committal hearings, 27-year-old Miss McKinney denied the charges and declared, 'For the love of Kirk, I'd have skied down Everest in the nude with a carnation up my nose.'

On Monday September 26, former Conservative Minister Reggie Maudling ad-mitted he had been to the late Sir Eric Miller's home 'seventy or eighty times' and had eaten caviare. 'Who wouldn't eat caviare if it was offered?' he asked.

The same day Freddie Laker's Skytrain took off at last for New York. On this inaugural flight, Mr Laker travelled on the flight deck and gave a commentary during take off. He later stated he had made an £11,500 profit on the first flight.

Meanwhile, the *New York Times* had stated that there were now more than 100 homosexual discothèques in Manhattan.

On Thursday September 29, a bottle of 1808 Château Lafite was sold at Christie's for £8,300 to American wine merchant Mr Addy Bassi, who later flew back to Washington with the precious bottle in his hand luggage, wrapped in towels.

Meanwhile in California, much indignation had been felt over the publication of a photograph showing Roman Polanski relaxing in a nightclub in Munich with fifteen-year-old Natassia Kinski who was to star in his new film, *Tess of the d'Urbervilles* instead of working in the South Pacific on *Hurricane*. On Friday September 30, Judge Rittenband angrily called a special court hearing 'to get some facts straight' about what the film-director was doing in Europe.

On Friday October 7, Concorde left London for Bahrein without a single passenger on board. 'We never expected the Concorde Bahrein service to make a profit,' said a British Airways spokesman. 'The service must be evaluated as a whole.'

Meanwhile in America, Billy Carter had claimed that he was earning more money by his publicity stunts than his brother was making as President. 'Ah campaigned for Jim all through the South and ah figure it's all even,' he said.

Back in London, on Tuesday October 11, Princess Margaret gave a black tie dinner party at Kensington Palace to celebrate her friend Roddy Llewellyn's recent thirtieth birthday. Among those present were the Earl and Countess of Lichfield, 26-year-old Lord Buckhurst and Mr and Mrs John Nutting. Fifty more mutual friends were invited in after dinner.

On Thursday October 13, the death occurred in a mental hospital in Northamptonshire of the 97-year-old Gladys, Duchess of Marlborough, a once celebrated figure who had spent the last forty years in total obscurity.

The following day in New York, Mrs Jackie Onassis resigned her post as consulting editor at the Viking Press in protest at the firm publishing a novel by Jeffrey Archer about a plot to assassinate her brother-in-law Edward Kennedy.

That weekend found 85-year-old President Tito of Yugoslavia installed at a luxury hotel in south-western France run by Michel Guerard, high priest of *cuisine minceur*. Tito was accompanied by his doctor, two nurses, his butler and thirty bodyguards – and ran up a £4,000 bill in three days.

On Tuesday October 18, police investigations into the Thorpe–Scott affair were reopened following the publication in the *Evening News* of allegations by former airline pilot Andrew Newton, now released from prison, that he had been hired by a prominent member of the Liberal Party to kill former male model Norman Scott.

The following day in Chicago, Prince Charles addressed a banquet at the start of his official American tour. 'I must have shaken a thousand hands,' he said 'I also received numerous delicious kisses. I've never come across such astonishing friendliness. It's truly marvellous.'

On Sunday October 23, the Queen's jubilee voyage round the Caribbean on board the royal yacht *Britannia* was enlivened when a nine-foot shark was found basking near the ship while it was moored off the island called Iguana. The Queen was not in the water at the time but ventured in bravely later.

The following night in New York, a party thrown by Lally Waymouth, daughter of *Washington Post* proprietor Mrs Graham, in honour of Lord Weidenfeld was enlivened when literary giants Norman Mailer and Gore Vidal came to blows. Wine was thrown and according to Gore Vidal, Mailer 'threw his tiny fist in my face'. Other illustrious figures present at the party included Jackie Onassis, and the new British Ambassador Peter Jay.

Meanwhile in India the new Prime Minister, 81-year-old Mr Morarji Desai, had revealed that he was a firm believer in the health-giving properties of urine and drank a glass of his own every morning with beneficial effects. In defence of his habit he quoted the scriptures, 'Drink waters out of thine own cistern and running waters out of thine own well.'

Back in London, on Wednesday October 26, the Shah of Iran's birthday was celebrated with a party at the Iranian Embassy in Prince's Gate hosted by 40-year-old bachelor Parviz Radji who had now emerged as London's most generous host. The event was attended by representatives of almost every country in the world, including the Chinese Ambassador, Mr Sung Chih Kuan, who wore a Mao suit.

Later that day it was revealed that a unique quartet of Canalettos from Warwick Castle were to be sold. The paintings had been quietly packaged up and sent to London, and two of them were thought to have already been purchased by American racehorse owner, Paul Mellon.

On Thursday October 27, Jeremy Thorpe gave a press conference in the library of the National Liberal Club, at which he once again denied that he had ever been involved in any plot to kill or harm Mr Norman Scott and declared that he had no intention of resigning his seat in parliament. He was attended by his wife Marion, his parliamentary colleague Clement Freud and a partner of the Goodman Derrick solicitors firm, who interrupted the conference to disallow the question when Thorpe was asked if he had ever had a homosexual relationship.

Later that day in Hollywood, Prince Charles dined with actress Farrah Fawcett-Majors and other stars at a charity dinner at the Beverly Hilton.

On Saturday October 29, it was noted that President Carter was already looking tired and strikingly older and new wrinkles had been spotted on his face.

The following day on Mustique, Princess Margaret welcomed the Queen and Prince Philip to her holiday home, Les Jolies Eaux, where they stayed for lunch and dinner before returning to the royal yacht *Britannia*. A plane-load of photographers were there to cover the visit.

Meanwhile, Roddy Llewellyn was also on his way to Mustique and on Wednesday November 2, was spotted at Barbados Airport, where the Queen was about to get onto Concorde for the flight home, and was unfairly accused of 'trying to get in on the royal act'.

Back in London the following morning, the Queen opened parliament, dressed in a gold embroidered white dress, ermine-trimmed velvet train and the imperial crown. In order to read the Speech from the Throne, the Queen took out a pair of half-moon spectacles from her white handbag.

On Friday November 4, it was reported that Dido Goldsmith's twelve month old marriage was being quietly dissolved. 'I hope to have my decree absolute by Christmas,' she said. 'I haven't been put off marriage though. It has taught me not to be so rash. I was too young.'

The following Monday November 7, Tatum O'Neal's fourteenth birthday celebrations ended at Tramp discothèque in Jermyn Street, where she did an exotic waltz with Bianca Jagger. 'God, how awful,' said an onlooker.

The following evening in Melbourne, Australia, Prince Charles danced the night away at a party given by publisher Barry Harper, father of Charles's friend Lady Tryon, who was also present.

The next day, Wednesday November 9, the Prince kissed a 28-year-old girl in a crowd in Adelaide. 'I feel terrific,' said the girl. 'I would have liked to ask the Prince home to tea but I didn't get the chance.'

On Sunday November 13, Prince Charles arrived back in England suffering from suspected food poisoning and was unable to attend the Remembrance Day service in Whitehall.

The following day, he had recovered sufficiently to go out hunting with the Middleton Hunt at Garrowby in Yorkshire, where he was staying with the 65-year-old Earl of Halifax and his son Lord Irwin. A few days later, Prince Charles was to dine at Althorp, Northamptonshire home of Lord and Lady Spencer and was to meet 16-year-old Lady Diana Spencer, attractive younger sister of his close friend Lady Sarah Spencer.

Back in London, on Tuesday November 15, Princess Anne gave birth to a baby boy in the private Lindo Wing of St Mary's Hospital, Paddington. 'How charming,' commented Labour MP Willie Hamilton. 'Another one for the payroll.'

Later that day in Washington, the Shah of Iran was welcomed to the White House by President Carter, who was counting on him to keep oil prices down. The welcoming ceremony on the lawn of the White House was disturbed by noisy demonstrations by opponents of the Shah, who wielded sticks, chanted slogans and released tear gas.

Meanwhile in California it had been revealed that Patty Hearst, still out on bail, was now accompanied everywhere by a team of security guards armed with pistols, rifles and semi-automatic machine guns. When she visited a beauty parlour in San Francisco she was accompanied by twenty people and a two-year-old German shepherd dog.

On Monday November 21, it was announced in Virginia that beer endorsed by President Carter's brother Billy had been banned on the grounds that it was 'downgrading to the office of president'.

Back in London, on Wednesday November 23, it was stated that the Arab property boom was ending. Estate Agent Andrew Langton explained that the Arabs had bought while the market was low and had done brilliantly well.

On Monday November 28, socialite Mrs Rita Lachman flew into Paris on board the transatlantic Concorde and was met at the airport by a blue station-wagon belonging to the invalid Duchess of Windsor and whisked into 'the city of light'.

Meanwhile, Paris society had been disturbed by a disagreement between the beautiful Madame Dewi Sukarno and the city's reigning nightclub queen, Regine, who now owned two nightclubs in Paris and others in Monte Carlo and New York.

Back in London, on Tuesday November 29, Colonel Harry Llewellyn, 66-year-old father of the controversial brothers Roddy and Dai, received his knighthood from the Queen for his services to Welsh sport and equestrianism. 'I'm allowed two guests and I'm taking my wife and daughter,' he said before setting off for Buckingham Palace.

On Wednesday November 30, Sex Pistol Sid Vicious and his American girl friend Nancy Spungeon were arrested after the discovery of certain substances in their room at the Ambassador Hotel in Lancaster Gate, which the police had raided after reports that the punk star had damaged hotel property.

Meanwhile in Saudi Arabia, 23-year-old Princess Misha had been beheaded in the market place in Jeddah for committing adultery.

On Thursday December 1, it was revealed that 42-year-old Adnan Khashoggi had lent his private DC 9 'plane to ferry medical supplies to Madras to aid cyclone victims. 'Mr Khashoggi is one of the most generous men in the world, but he is very discreet about it,' said his London representative Charles Riachi. 'He gives huge amounts to under-privileged people every year.'

Sid Vicious, bass guitarist with the Sex Pistols punk rock group, and his girl-friend Nancy Spungeon

On Friday December 2, the Queen's car broke down with a blown gasket near Thruxton in Hampshire and she was obliged to continue her journey in an accompanying car.

On Sunday December 4, attention turned to the Central African Empire and the $22 million coronation of Jean Bedel Bokassa as Emperor. The self-made monarch wore robes made by the Paris firm of Guiselin, who had made Napoleon's uniforms, and a crown studded with $500,000 worth of diamonds. He travelled to the ceremony in a green and gold carriage drawn by eight horses imported from Normandy.

Back in Britain the following day much excitement attended former Prime Minister Edward Heath's departure from London in a special blue and white train for a whistle-stop tour of Britain signing copies of his new book *Travels* and other publications. He was seen off at Paddington Station by his publisher Lord Longford, who had presented Mr Heath with a Cartier gold pen after his one-hundredth signing session.

On Wednesday December 7, the special train reached Manchester, where journalists poured on board and helped themselves from a bar stocked with Bollinger champagne and Glenfiddich malt whisky, while Mr Heath, seated at a Queen Anne desk, went on signing.

Over in New York the following day, Liza Minnelli was forced to cancel a performance of her Broadway extravaganza *The Act* after inhaling smoke during a fire at her apartment on Central Park South. Her publicist said it was the first time in her career that she had missed a performance.

A few days later, she had completely recovered from her indisposition and was found dancing at Studio 54 in white satin disco pants at a party in honour of Bianca Jagger.

Over in California, on Sunday December 11, the Los Angeles scene was enriched by the presence of Detective Chief Superintendent Michael Challes and his colleague Detective Superintendent David Greenaugh who had arrived in Los Angeles to interview former Liberal MP Peter Bessell about the alleged plot to murder Mr Norman Scott.

The following day in London, a chapter in international life closed when 93-year-old Baroness Spencer-Churchill died suddenly while lunching in her flat overlooking Hyde Park. In a glowing tribute Prime Minister Callaghan declared, 'Her character, dignity and charm made her deeply beloved.'

On Tuesday December 13, 43-year-old tax-exile Lord Brooke slipped quietly into Britain, where he was now under criticism for selling a cascade of treasures from his family home, Warwick Castle.

The following day, Lord Brooke was not present at Sotheby's when the famous Warwick Castle portrait of Elizabeth I went under the hammer for £35,000. It was purchased by art dealer Hugh Leggatt, one of Lord Brooke's fiercest critics who had expressed fears that Warwick Castle would end up an empty shell like most of the great châteaux of France.

Back in California, on Thursday December 15, film director Roman Polanski showed up at Chino prison to submit to the long-awaited psychiatric evaluation. He was in an outwardly cheerful mood and joked with reporters present but on entering the gaol was immediately placed in solitary confinement where he was to remain throughout the Christmas period.

The following night in New York, Bianca Jagger was again found boogy-ing in Studio 54, dressed in black satin jacket and white harem pants. 'I can't dance with all these flash bulbs popping,' she protested. 'Why can't people leave me alone?'

Back in London, on Monday December 19, 38-year-old Germaine Greer, former high priestess of the Women's Lib movement, entered the London Clinic for a four hour abdominal operation designed to increase her chances of having a baby. 'Ironic isn't it, with so many girls terrified of becoming pregnant?' she said.

Meanwhile, 23-year-old Bobby Kennedy, second son of the late Senator Kennedy had been enrolled as a student at the London School of Economics. A lively young man, he had already bounced onto the city's social scene, appearing at a party given by Lord John Cholmondeley at his home in Hyde Park Gardens.

On Tuesday December 20, Mrs Thatcher's husband Denis dismissed as 'completely untrue' a story that he had been troubled by fleas at his hotel during the recent Conservative Party Conference at Blackpool.

Later that day, many flights out of Heathrow Airport were delayed by fog causing fights to break out between passengers trying to get the remaining seats on a flight to New York.

On Thursday December 22, there was excitement at Heathrow Airport when pop star Rod Stewart stepped off a British Airways airliner from Los Angeles with a glass of brandy in his hand, after a chaotic flight from Los Angeles with thirteen friends during which the first class cabin of the airliner had been littered with empty bottles and other rubbish, the sheepskin covers caked with food. Said Rod's music arranger, Dave Horowitz, 'I took a valium and went to sleep and when I woke up, Rod had smeared jam and mustard all over my face. I couldn't let him get away with that so I filled his shoes with jam.'

The same day in the Music Room at Buckingham Palace, 94-year-old Princess Alice, Countess of Athlone was present at the christening of six-week-old Master Peter Phillips by the Archbishop of Canterbury, Dr Donald Coggan. During this remarkable event, attended by five generations of the Royal Family, the Queen's first grandchild gave piercing screams said to be heard throughout the palace.

Meanwhile, seventeen-year-old Prince Andrew had been refused admission to

Annabel's in Berkeley Square for not wearing a tie. A tie was quickly found and the Prince was allowed to enter the club with a party of young friends, one of whom said later, 'He is a bit of a flirt, but the most charming person you could hope to meet.'

Christmas Eve found Mick Jagger installed at the Savoy Hotel with his new friend model Jerry Hall, while his wife Bianca stayed at his house in Cheyne Walk, Chelsea.

Early the following morning, Sir Charles Chaplin died in his eighteen bedroom home in Switzerland. His death at the age of eighty-eight generated tributes from all over the world. The Soviet News Agency Tass stated that he had 'glorified ordinary people', while in England, the *Daily Express* declared 'Charlie Chaplin will never die'.

On Thursday December 29, President Carter left Washington on the first leg of a nine day six nations overseas shuttle. He was accompanied in his blue and silver presidential airliner by his wife Rosalyn, who he described as 'my best political weapon', and his National Security Affairs adviser 'Ziggy' Brzezinski.

On Friday December 30, Bianca Jagger flew from London to New York on Concorde, explaining, 'I'm going to spend the New Year in America with some friends.'

The same day, the U.S. State Department reversed an earlier decision to forbid the controversial punk rock group, the Sex Pistols, to enter America for a nineteen day tour. 'We are delighted,' said a spokesman for the giant American record company, Warner Brothers. 'The Pistols will take the country by storm.'

On Saturday December 31, President Carter arrived in Tehran. 'Iran is an island of stability in one of the most unstable parts of the world,' he said, adding special words of praise for the 58-year-old Shah. 'There is no leader for whom I have a deeper gratitude and a greater friendship.'

1978

The fashionable world now seems full of cocaine-snorting disco-dancing celebrities and punk weirdos attended by waiters in satin jock straps. In the next few months, London succumbs to ultra disco, Roddy Llewellyn tries to become a pop-singer, and self-confessed homosexual Quentin Crisp emerges as an international hero. In the midst of this confusion, Lady Falkender consolidates her position as a leading socialite, begins to appear in couture gowns and hob-nobs with Sir James Goldsmith; Prince Charles sees more of the sensible Lady Sarah Spencer and Adnan Khashoggi buys himself a country home in Buckinghamshire. Striking out in a new direction altogether is Christina Onassis, who marries a Russian and settles in a flat overlooking the botanic garden in Moscow. A graver note is struck by the stabbing of Bulgarian defector Georgi Markov with a poisoned umbrella and the arrest of former Liberal leader Jeremy Thorpe on charges of conspiracy and incitement to murder. By the end of the year, the new punk aristocracy has not flourished. The Sex Pistols do not destroy America but themselves and the fashionable and much talked about Studio 54 is in serious trouble.

New Year's Day found Mick Jagger and his new friend 22-year-old model Jerry Hall installed at a cottage near the Greensleeves Hotel in Barbados. 'People are always asking me if my marriage is over or not,' said Jagger, who had seen in the New Year with old friends Penelope Tree, *Monty Python* star Eric Idle and recording mogul Clive Davis.

The following night in New York, Bianca Jagger was found dancing at Studio 54 with the club's owner Steve Rubell and superstar Andy Warhol, but she refused to talk about her marriage. 'Wow, what a woman,' said an admirer. 'She's like someone with a built in super-charger.'

On Tuesday January 3, the New York scene was enriched by the arrival of the Sex Pistols, who were to start a fourteen day tour of the United States. During their eventful flight from London, outraged passengers had protested, 'What are we flying with – animals?'

On Thursday January 5, at Norfolk, Virginia, 45-year-old Elizabeth Taylor, now said to weigh 11 stone 7 pounds, began a campaign to get her sixth husband, John Warner, re-elected to the Senate. 'This is the proudest moment in my life,' she told a cheering crowd.

On Saturday January 7, the Sex Pistols' tour began with a riotous concert at Randy's Rodeo in San Antonio, Texas, during which fireworks and animals' entrails were hurled onto the stage. Singer Sid Vicious, dressed in black leather, chains and padlocks, clubbed a fan with his guitar, while his colleague Johnny Rotten screamed, 'Give us a chance and we will destroy America.'

Earlier that day in Britain, 29-year-old Prince Charles had been out hunting with the Belvoir in Leicestershire and was seen taking swigs from a hip-flask offered him by the Marchioness of Cholmondeley.

On Tuesday January 10, it was annouced in London that Roddy Llewellyn was to embark on a career as a singer and had already signed a contract with Claude Wolff, husband of singer Petula Clark. 'I consulted Princess Margaret before taking up the offer to make records and she had no objections,' he said. 'I know I've been quite a fickle character in the past. Hopefully, I can settle down to singing.'

On Wednesday January 11, the long mystery over the whereabouts of a controversial portrait of Sir Winston Churchill by Graham Sutherland ended when it was revealed that it had been destroyed by the late Lady Churchill. 'I am not distressed,' said 74-year-old Mr Sutherland, now living in the South of France. 'I think it is an odd sort of thing to happen but these things do happen.'

On Saturday January 14, former President Richard Nixon returned to Washington for the first time since his ignominious departure three and a half years earlier. The following day, he attended a memorial service for the late Hubert Humphrey and shook hands with President Carter, who had recently been elected the world's best dressed statesman.

Back in London the same day, ousted Tory leader Edward Heath appeared to have got over his difficulties with Mrs Thatcher when he spent forty-five minutes at her Chelsea home. It was said to be their first big reconciliation since the battle for the Tory leadership three years earlier.

On Monday January 16, pop star David Bowie announced that he was now suing his wife Angie for divorce. 'I blame the life style we have both led for the state of our marriage,' he said.

On Tuesday January 17, Mrs Ann West, mother of one of the victims of murderess Myra Hindley presented a petition to the Home Secretary bearing 27,000 signatures against the possibility of her release on parole as a result of efforts by

Singer David Bowie who described
the life of a rock star as hateful

Lord Longford, whom she described as a 'misguided do-gooder'.

Over in New York, on Thursday January 19, troubles hit the Sex Pistols' tour of America. Sid Vicious was taken from a plane at Kennedy Airport suffering from drugs and alcohol and his colleague Johnny Rotten announced that he was leaving the group and returning to England.

The following day in Gstaad, the marriage took place between 26-year-old Andrea de Partago and 34-year-old multi-millionaire Mick Flick, co-heir to the Mercedes Benz empire. Armed bodyguards attended the service in a local parish church and the choir stalls were checked for bombs.

On Saturday January 21 in Peking a dinner was given in the Palace of the Popular Assembly in honour of the French Prime Minister M. Raymond Barre who was visiting China with a group of leading industrialists. On the menu were foie gras au poivre vert, lobster soup and canard à l'orange accompanied by Dom Perignon 1970 and Mersault 1975.

On Tuesday January 24, the marriage took place in the chapel of Limerick Prison between 37-year-old Dr Rose Dugdale and IRA terrorist Eddie Gallagher, the father of Dr Dugdale's three-year-old son. Army helicopters hovered above the prison as the bride and groom exchanged gold rings.

Meanwhile in London, a bankruptcy court had heard how 39-year-old Kitty Milinaire, glamorous Iranian-born daughter-in-law of the Duchess of Bedford, had lost more than £3 million gambling. 'I lost control. I didn't know what I was doing. It was like a disease,' said Mrs Milinaire, now said to be in debt to the tune of £500,000.

The following day, Thursday January 26, this unfortunate lady's troubles were increased when she was arrested and charged with the theft of two rings from Cartier, said to be worth £200,000. On being bailed to stand trial in March she declared, 'I am innocent. I shall be pleading not guilty.'

On Friday January 27 in California, Roman Polanski was released from prison, where his incarceration had been enlivened by visits from his friend Jack Nicholson and ex-Beatle John Lennon. He was to spend the weekend at a rented house in Los Angeles where a party was given for him on the Saturday night.

Back in London, on Monday January 30, the eccentric homosexual, 69-year-old Quentin Crisp, opened in a one man show at the Duke of York's theatre. Among those present in the audience was oil heiress Olga Deterding, who after the show threw a party in Mr Crisp's honour at her triplex penthouse apartment on Piccadilly.

Self-proclaimed homosexual Quentin Crisp who suddenly emerged as an international celebrity

On Tuesday January 31, former Sex Pistol Johnny Rotten left London for Miami, dressed in a torn mackintosh. 'I'm going shark fishing,' he said.

Meanwhile, Roman Polanski had fled from American justice and bought the last available ticket on a British Airways flight to London. He arrived at Heathrow before lunch on Wednesday February 1 and then flew on to Paris, where he explained that he could no longer put his fate 'in the hands of a judge who was prejudiced against him'.

The same day Prince Charles flew off in a twin-engined Andover of the Queen's Flight for Klosters, where he was to spend a ten day skiing holiday with Lady Sarah Spencer at a seven bedroom chalet rented by the Duke of Gloucester.

On Thursday February 2, a joint statement was issued in New York on behalf of Mick and Bianca Jagger denying widespread rumours that their marriage was on the rocks. 'We are not getting divorced nor are we taking any steps to dissolve our marriage. There is no disagreement between us about our child or any other subject.'

On Monday February 6, Princess Marie Astrid of Luxembourg, still thought of as a possible bride for Prince Charles, arrived in England to continue her English studies at a language school in Cambridge.

Later that day in Klosters, Lady Sarah Spencer and Prince Charles travelled up a ski-lift together. 'There is really nothing between us,' Lady Sarah told reporters.

The following night in Moscow, master spy Kim Philby popped up in the audience of the Bolshoi production of *Othello*, looking slimmer and slightly shrunken. 'I don't drink as much as I did in the Beirut days,' he said. 'I'm fighting the battle of the waist.' He was accompanied by his fourth wife, Nina, who was smartly dressed in a black velvet skirt.

On Wednesday February 8 in London, 20-year-old Sex Pistol Sid Vicious and his 19-year-old girl friend Nancy Spungeon appeared at Marylebone Magistrates Court on a drugs charge and were remanded on bail. It was noted that Vicious wore pencil thin trousers at the hearing and a jacket with broad padded shoulders and his girl-friend wore a sweater with plunging V-neck.

On Friday February 10, the young Marchioness of Tavistock said how unhappy she was living at Woburn Abbey. 'I'm my own gaoler,' she said, jangling an enormous bunch of keys. 'I'd be quite happy to live in a three bedroom council house. I'd pack up and leave tomorrow if it wasn't that I love my husband and he wants to stay.' She accused her in-laws the Duke and Duchess of Bedford of being 'extremely selfish' for leaving the famous stately home.

On Sunday February 12, an employee on the Chartwell estate, 62-year-old Ted Miles, confessed that many years earlier he had burnt the controversial portrait of Sir Winston Churchill by Graham Sutherland, on the orders of the late Lady Churchill. At his villa in the South of France, Mr Sutherland spoke of the destruction of the portrait as 'an act of vandalism unequalled in the history of art'.

The following day in New York, Mrs Jackie Onassis began a new job in publishing, working as an editorial adviser for the Doubleday firm where she was soon to be praised by her colleagues for being bright, efficient and understanding.

On Wednesday February 15, at the Palace Hotel in Gstaad, the Duke of Bedford replied to recent criticisms by his daughter-in-law Lady Tavistock. 'Henrietta really can't start complaining now,' he said. 'If you marry some guy with a title you have a duty and responsibility to carry on what his ancestors had in the past. She was perfectly aware what she was getting into.'

On Thursday February 16, Britt Ekland flew into London from Los Angeles and confirmed that she had come to a financial agreement with her former boy-friend Rod Stewart. 'I'm not saying if it's one million dollars, one million pounds or twelve million pounds. We worked out a settlement two months ago. I'm not at liberty to say what it is.'

The same day in Paris, 44-year-old Roman Polanski was interrupted while sipping coffee in a café near his apartment in the Champs Elysées. 'I only want one thing. That people should leave me alone,' he said.

On Friday February 17, Lady Sarah Spencer gave in to press pestering and spoke frankly of her relationship with Prince Charles. 'I am not in love with him,' she said. 'I can assure you that if there was to be any engagement between Prince Charles and myself, it would have happened by now. I wouldn't marry anyone I didn't love – whether it was the dustman or the King of England. If he asked me I would turn him down.'

Meanwhile in Rio de Janeiro, escaped train robber Ronnie Biggs had appeared on stage with the Sex Pistols and read some poetry.

Back in Britain, on Wednesday February 22, it was announced that Adnan Khashoggi, supposedly the world's richest man, had offered £1 million for the Woodlands Park estate in Buckinghamshire, former home of film producer Harry Saltzman, which he wanted for his private use.

The following day in Paris, Roddy Llewellyn gulped down two cognacs and two glasses of champagne before tele-recording a duet with singer Petula Clark, who said afterwards, 'We have spent a lot of time together and he really is a sweet boy. His voice is certainly good enough to get him a Number One but everyone needs the right material.'

Two days later, on Saturday February 25, Roddy flew off to the Caribbean on a scheduled flight for another holiday with Princess Margaret at her villa on Mustique, where the following day he took to his bed feeling very ill.

Back in London, on Tuesday February 28, Bobby Kennedy Jnr. denied there was romance between him and 21-year-old Rebecca Fraser, eldest daughter of authoress Lady Antonia Fraser. 'Take it from me it's all a load of ———,' he said. 'Our families are great friends. That's all there is to it.'

On Wednesday March 1, the Queen Mother attended a performance of *Don Giovanni* at the London Coliseum, during which she shared the Royal Box with solicitor Lord Goodman and celebrated art historian 70-year-old Sir Anthony Blunt.

Later that night in Switzerland, the body of Sir Charles Chaplin was stolen from a churchyard overlooking Lake Geneva. 'The grave is empty, the coffin has gone,' said a bewildered village policeman.

On Thursday March 2, it was revealed that 35-year-old Prince Michael of Kent and Baroness Marie-Christine von Reibnitz, former wife of admiral's son Tom Troubridge, had been to see the Archbishop of Canterbury at Lambeth Palace. 'It was a private visit and we are not prepared to discuss it further,' said a spokesman for the Archbishop.

On Friday March 3, Roddy Llewellyn was said to be seriously ill and was flown to a private clinic in Barbados where it was discovered he was suffering from upper gastro-intestinal haemorrhage and was quickly given five pints of blood.

Meanwhile, union leader Hugh Scanlon had left Barbados after a fortnight's holiday at the luxury Sandridge Hotel, where he had occupied an air-conditioned suite.

Back in Britain, on Saturday March 4, art historian Sir Anthony Blunt, the Earl of Inchcape and Lord Butler of Saffron Walden were among the congregation at a memorial service at Trinity College Cambridge for the veteran classics don Andrew Gow who had died earlier in the year.

On Sunday March 5, two senior police officers left London for Los Angeles to interview former Liberal MP Peter Bessell about the Norman Scott affair for the second time.

Over in New York, on Monday March 6, Elizabeth Taylor celebrated her recent forty-sixth birthday at Studio 54, dressed in a mauve sequinned trouser suit. Her husband John Warner stayed in the background and at 1.30 a.m. began smothering yawns. 'I'm a politician,' he explained. 'I've got to get up in the morning and *work*.'

The following day in Barbados, a crowd of 100 people cheered Princess Margaret when she arrived at the clinic where her friend Roddy was being treated for an intestinal haemorrhage.

On Wednesday March 8 in Washington, 85-year-old President Tito explained why his 54-year-old wife had been missing from his side for the past few months. 'To speak quite frankly, it is easier for me to be without her. If she is with me, I have to care about her too. I have so many responsibilities.'

Back in Barbados, on Thursday March 9, Roddy Llewellyn gave a press conference at his hospital, dressed in a maroon dressing-gown. 'I have been advised by my doctors to have no unnecessary excitement as it could trigger off my complaint again,' he said.

That night in Rio de Janeiro, 29-year-old Prince Charles danced with a young black samba dancer at a party given by the local mayor and was cheered on by a thousand dinner guests.

Back in Britain, on Friday March 10, the famous 1,800 year old Warwick Vase was removed from a conservatory in the grounds of Warwick Castle and a notice was put up saying that the building was 'closed for repairs'.

The next weekend, there was further controversy over the decision of Lord Brooke to sell off his family's entire collection of archives. The 43-year-old heir to the Earl of Warwick had already caused dismay by selling four Canalettos for £1 million.

On Wednesday March 22, the British première of *Saturday Night Fever* was celebrated with a party attended by leading luminaries such as 69-year-old Quentin Crisp, Bianca Jagger, Mark Shand, Philip Niarchos, David Frost, punk star Jordan and the controversial Joyce McKinney who was still awaiting trial on abduction charges. The film's star John Travolta arrived late and left early.

On Thursday March 23, Captain Mark Phillips left the army after eleven years' service. 'I think he felt there was no future for him in it,' said his father Major Peter Phillips.

The same day in the House of Commons, Labour MP Dennis Canavan, raged at Princess Margaret's visits to the bedside of her friend Roddy Llewellyn and asked the Chancellor of the Exchequer to 'stop all unnecessary spending on the over-privileged including the £1,000 a week we give a parasite like Princess Margaret', and demanded that the Queen's sister should retire gracefully from public life. He was later to apologize for these remarks.

The following day, Good Friday, Russian cellist Rostropovich who had been stripped of his Soviet citizenship the previous week, arrived in Britain. 'We heard the news on television in France,' he said.

On Easter Day, Roddy Llewellyn was back in London. 'I shall go on seeing Princess Margaret when and where I want,' he said at Heathrow. 'Let them all criticize – I don't mind.'

Meanwhile, the Conservative Party had been taking steps to improve its image and, on Wednesday March 29, it was announced that leading London advertising agency, Saatchi and Saatchi, had been hired to put together a multi-million pound campaign designed to bring down the Labour government.

The same day it was revealed that 45-year-old Lady Falkender was now buying her gowns from a couturier in Belgravia, Viennese-born Baroness Inga Sprawson. 'Lady Falkender buys most of her things from me,' this lady explained. 'I suppose they're more chic. She has become a very good customer.'

On Friday March 31, pop star Elton John showed off his new hair transplant, performed the previous September in Paris and hidden by a flat cap since the operation. 'It's been very successful,' he said. 'My hair has started to grow. It will be ready soon and I can give up wearing a hat.'

That weekend, the Bishop of Truro, Dr Graham Leonard, joined critics of Princess Margaret when he described her recent holiday with Roddy Llewellyn as 'foolish' and called for her to resign from public life. The Bishop of Southwark, Dr Stockwood, immediately leapt to the Princess's defence stating that public recognition of her achievements was 'of far greater importance than the censoring of her private life, whatever that might be'.

On Monday April 3, a mentally disturbed man entered the National Gallery and slashed Poussin's *Adoration of the Golden Calf* causing several strips of the masterpiece to fall to the floor.

In the early hours of the following morning, Jeremy Thorpe's friend David Holmes, former deputy treasurer of the Liberal Party, was driven from London to Bristol to be interviewed about an alleged plot to murder former male model Norman Scott.

Meanwhile, Princess Margaret had been struck down by 'red' flu and retired to bed at Windsor Castle. On Wednesday April 5, she was not well enough to attend the confirmation of her daughter, Sarah Armstrong-Jones, but was able to attend a lunch after the service, at which her estranged husband Lord Snowdon was also present.

On Thursday April 6, it was officially announced that the Princess would remain in public life.

On Friday April 7, American actress Farrah Fawcett-Majors flew into Heathrow wearing an unflattering two-piece woollen suit to protect her from the rigours of the English spring.

The following day, the famous Warwick Vase, which had been removed from Warwick Castle the previous month, was found in a warehouse in Wimbledon. 'I am not going to waste your time,' the Castle's owner Lord Brooke told a reporter who phoned his Paris home, 'so I'll just say goodbye to you, thank you very much.'

On Sunday April 9, Farrah Fawcett-Majors compèred a charity show at the London Palladium with Prince Charles, whom she had met in Hollywood six months earlier, and Earl Mountbatten of Burma in the audience. After the show, the actress renewed her acquaintance with Prince Charles over dinner at the Dorchester Hotel.

The following morning, a survey of England's motorway catering was published by Egon Ronay, whose inspectors said they had discovered 'inedible gravy under stale pastry' and 'processed peas in lurid green liquor'.

Meanwhile in London, the staff at Claridge's Hotel had gone on strike for the first time in 163 years when chefs, chambermaids and floor waiters had walked out in protest at the dismissal of a 19-year-old kitchen trainee, Richard Elvidge. On Tuesday April 11, patrons at the hotel had to make do with a limited menu of steak and kidney pie, Irish stew, poached salmon or 'anything from the grill'. 'We are living in a new world,' said the assistant restaurant manager. 'I hope you will forgive us.' Among those lunching at the hotel that day was Lady Falkender, who said afterwards, 'I had soup and steak and thoroughly enjoyed it. I thought the service was very good.'

That night, ultra disco at last hit London when the Embassy Club in Bond Street was reopened as a discothèque with 37-year-old former men's outfitter Michael Fish acting as Master of Ceremonies. Joining in the celebrations that evening was 70-year-old Maureen Marchioness of Dufferin and Ava, who had been a habitué at the club forty years earlier. Mr Fish denied that the club would be exclusively homosexual but admitted that it would be 'the sort of place where a bloke can dance with a bloke without stares'.

The same night bubbly blonde Joyce McKinney, who was still on bail on kidnap charges, arrived at the première of *The Stud* in a chocolate-coloured Rolls-Royce.

The following day, Miss McKinney and her friend Keith May jumped bail and fled to America, passing through Heathrow Airport disguised as deaf mutes. They carried sixty pounds of excess baggage which they claimed was full of costumes for a mime show.

Back at the reopened Embassy Club that weekend, top photographers Lord Snowdon, who was accompanied by his friend Lucy Lindsay-Hogg, the Earl of Lichfield and David Bailey attended a male fashion show which ended with a scantily clad male model cracking a whip on the cat walk.

Back in New York, on Monday April 17, Jackie Onassis led a demonstration to plead for the preservation of Grand Central Station.

The following day at Americus, Georgia, Billy Carter was admitted to hospital in order to undergo 'a general check-up and health maintenance procedures'.

Meanwhile in London, Energy Secretary Tony Benn had fallen down a staircase at his Ministry, chipping an ankle bone. 'I wasn't pushed, I fell,' he insisted afterwards. On Thursday April 20, he hobbled into a cabinet meeting at 10 Downing Street on crutches.

The same day, the Queen was present at the marriage in the Guards Chapel between 21-year-old Lady Jane Spencer and Mr Robert Fellowes. Among those who acted as bridesmaids was the bride's younger sister 16-year-old Lady Diana Spencer who wore a pinafore dress of patterned lawn and cream-coloured silk.

16-year-old Lady Diana Spencer as a bridesmaid at the wedding of her older sister Jane to Mr Robert Fellowes. In the foreground are Miss Laura Polk and Master James Duckworth-Chad

The following night in Paris, celebrities gathered for a masked ball given by international socialite Lou Lou de la Falaise to celebrate the safe return of the Right Wing to the National Assembly. The most oustanding costume was that of 37-year-old Madame Dewi Sukarno, who was dressed as a pink fairy godmother and carried a magic silver wand.

On Saturday April 22, superstar Bianca Jagger left London on Concorde for New York, where she was to stay with her friend dress designer Halston at his apartment on the upper East Side.

Back in London, on Monday April 24, the strike at Claridge's Hotel collapsed as 120 kitchen staff, chambermaids and floor waiters went back to work after failing to achieve any of their stated objectives.

On Wednesday April 26, Liberal MP Jeremy Thorpe broke his silence about the Norman Scott affair now being re-investigated by the West Country Police. 'All this will be over very shortly,' he said.

That night in New York, Studio 54 celebrated its first anniversary with a huge bash.

The following day, Mick and Bianca Jagger lunched together quietly at Quo Vadis on East 63rd Street. Their tête-à-tête ended abruptly when they were spotted by a lurking photographer and they made separate exits. Bianca ran down the street to the apartment of her friend Halston.

Back in Britain the following weekend, the crème de la crème of the jet set and Arab world gathered at a big party given by Mr Adnan Khashoggi at his newly acquired estate in Buckinghamshire. Among those present was Princess Caroline of Monaco's fiancé Philippe Junot who was found dancing with actress Jacqueline Bisset.

On Tuesday May 2, novelist Barbara Cartland announced that she was looking for a new chauffeur for her white Rolls-Royce. 'My last man is off to drive the London buses for £130 a week,' she explained.

On Thursday May 4, Princess Margaret was admitted to King Edward VII's Hospital for Officers in a state of exhaustion. Her official spokesman Major John Griffin said, 'She has been very much under the weather recently, feeling very ill. The doctors hope she will not be in hospital too long.'

The same day in Western Germany, Soviet leader Leonid Brezhnev arrived fifteen minutes late for a meeting with President Scheel and Herr Schmidt after his specially fitted Mercedes 600 had had a puncture on the Cologne–Koblenz autobahn.

That night in New York, Bianca Jagger celebrated her thirty-third birthday dancing at Studio 54 in a white satin pant suit and attended by waiters in satin jock straps. Joining in the fun were singer actress Liza Minnelli, whose husband had now filed a petition for divorce, TV star David Frost, Truman Capote and actor Ryan O'Neal.

On Friday May 5, the marriage took place in Paris between 25-year-old Paloma Picasso and 29-year-old Spanish playwright Rafael Lopez Sanchez. After the ceremony in a Left Bank registry office, there was a dinner party given by German fashion designer Karl Lagerfeld, who had created the bride's wedding dress, followed by dancing at the capital's newest nightclub Le Palace where there was a floor show combining a series of circus acts in a ring decorated as a white wedding cake.

Back in Britain on Wednesday May 10, it was announced that Princess Margaret and Lord Snowdon were to be divorced. The announcement was followed a few hours later by statements from Lord Snowdon and Roddy Llewellyn. Lord Snowdon called for 'support and encouragement for Princess Margaret when she comes out of hospital and goes about her duties again' and Roddy Llewellyn, now in Tangiers, stated: 'I am saying categorically that I will never marry Princess Margaret. Circumstances, personal reasons, would prevent it.'

Picasso's daughter Paloma and
Argentine playwright Rafael
Lopez Sanchez celebrate their
wedding at Le Palace nightclub
in Paris

The following day, the Princess left hospital, though she was still suffering from hepatitis and gastro-enteritis and was now forbidden to touch alcohol for a period of up to one year.

On Monday May 15, months of speculation over the Jagger marriage ended when Bianca launched divorce proceedings against her husband in London.

On Tuesday May 16, police were called to a new Battersea nightclub, Bennetts, after a disturbance had been caused by four friends of Mrs Thatcher's Old Harrovian son Mark. 'Mark had already left the club when this happened,' said a spokesman for Mrs Thatcher's office the following day. 'But things seem to have got out of hand and I gather police were called. It's very unfortunate.'

On Wednesday May 17, the body of the late Sir Charles Chaplin, which had been stolen from its grave months earlier, was found in a maize field near Lausanne. Two men were arrested and charged with disturbing the peace of the dead and trying to extort a ransom. 'The family is very happy and relieved that this ordeal is finished,' said a spokesman at Lady Chaplin's home overlooking Geneva.

Back in London, on Saturday May 20, a fire broke out in the kitchen of the fashionable Langan's Brasserie. Patrons fled into the street, and the restaurant's jovial proprietor Peter Langan sprayed the flames with champagne while awaiting the arrival of the Fire Brigade.

The following Monday, the Queen arrived in West Germany on a State Visit and that night slept in the same bed in Schloss Gynich which had been occupied by the Russian leader Mr Brezhnev earlier in the month.

Meanwhile, a plane carrying Prince Charles, Sir Harold Wilson and Lord Home back from the funeral of Australian statesman Sir Robert Menzies was unable to land for refuelling at Perth Airport because of an escaped bull on the runway.

On Tuesday May 23, 19-year-old trainee chef Richard Elvidge whose dismissal from the staff at Claridge's had caused a strike the previous month, accepted a £1,050 peace offering from the hotel and promptly ordered a slap up lunch at the hotel's Causerie Restaurant. 'Despite all that has happened, Claridge's is still a great hotel with fine restaurants and excellent food. I'm sorry I had to leave,' he said. 'He has sold us down the river,' commented angry Union colleagues.

On Wednesday May 24, the 18-year-old marriage of Princess Margaret and Lord Snowdon was formally dissolved in the divorce court. The proceedings took less than two minutes. 'I pronounce decree nisi in accordance with respective registrar certificates,' declared 71-year-old Judge Roger Willis, who later refused to discuss the matter.

Meanwhile at Cannes, crowds at the annual film festival had been enriched by the presence of Sir Harold Wilson and his personal secretary Lady Falkender who were on a two day visit to see how the British film industry was faring.

On Thursday May 25, it was announced in Washington that 10-year-old Amy Carter was to be fitted with contact lenses.

Over in Deauville, on Saturday May 27, in the early hours, a group of gangsters lead by France's Public Enemy Number One, Jacques Mesrine, who had recently escaped from gaol, entered a casino, stole 60,000 francs and shot British dentist Laurence Reilly in the leg.

On Tuesday May 30, headlines blazed the news that a diamond as big as a hen's egg had been unearthed near Pretoria, South Africa. 'It's not only the size of it,' said a de Beers spokesman. 'It has exceptional quality and colour. This diamond has singular beauty.' The diamond, thought to be worth about £6.5 million, had been picked up during the standard 'grease belt' sorting procedure.

Back in Britain, the following day, a lemonade bottle was thrown at a Rolls-Royce carrying Prince Charles near Newcastle. Within hours of the incident, a new pane of glass had been cut and polished at the Rolls-Royce service station at Neasden and was on its way north.

On Thursday June 1, the Queen and Prince Philip were guests of honour at a dinner party at Goldsmiths' Hall in London to celebrate the sixtieth birthday of Lord Astor of Hever. Among others present was the vivacious Mrs Brooke Astor who had flown in from America for the celebrations.

The following day, the twenty-fifth anniversary of the Queen's coronation was celebrated with a gigantic fireworks display in Green Park. Among those watching the event was Olga Deterding who threw a party at her three-storey penthouse overlooking the park which was attended by Lady Diana Cooper, Margaret Duchess of Argyll, professional cook Jennifer Paterson, eccentric homosexual Quentin Crisp, David and Lady Pamela Hicks, Arabella Churchill and assorted journalists including Yorkshire born Ron Hall of the *Sunday Times*.

The following day, Miss Deterding attended the Trooping the Colour ceremony escorted by young writer Peter York and dressed in a white three-piece suit made of mattress ticking, Kurt Geiger shoes and carrying a vintage pair of binoculars.

The same day, Chief Superintendent Challes and Detective Superintendent Greenaugh, whose enquiries into the Norman Scott affair were now nearing their conclusion, had a long interview with Mr Jeremy Thorpe.

On Tuesday June 6, Bianca Jagger joined Mark Shand, Dido Goldsmith and other fashionable young people at a twentieth birthday party for Lord Brooke's daughter, Charlotte Greville. It was noted that Charlotte's father had given her a double rope of black pearls.

The following day, the Derby was won by Shirley Heights, owned by the Earl of Halifax and his son Lord Irwin. 'It's the first time for fifteen years that a gentleman has won the Derby,' said Old Etonian commodity broker Jake Morley as the winning owners made their way to the Royal Box. Among others present was miners' leader Joe Gormley, who wore a sky blue pin-striped suit and dark blue trilby.

Back in London, on Thursday June 7, Lord and Lady Harlech threw a party at their house in Notting Hill, which was attended by Princess Margaret and Roddy Llewellyn, Mrs Jackie Onassis, dazzlingly dressed in white, Hugh Fraser MP, Shadow Education Minister Norman St John-Stevas, Lord Weidenfeld, Lord Goodman and many more.

That weekend in New York, panic hit the fashionable Studio 54 discothèque after the arrest of two of its regulars on drug charges. Club officials feared that the premises had been packed with undercover agents in preparation for a massive 'coke' witch-hunt.

Meanwhile in California, 48-year-old financial wizard Bernie Cornfeld had begun a ninety day sentence for defrauding the Pacific Telephone Company to the tune of $1,000 a month by means of a little blue box. It was noted that Cornfeld still faced charges in Switzerland in connection with the operations of his former firm, IOS.

Back in Paris, on Wednesday June 14, the contents of the home of the late Maria Callas came up for sale in a crowded auction room in the Hotel George V. Articles being disposed of included carpets, paintings, objets d'art, saucepans, a washing machine and three vacuum cleaners.

The following night in London, tireless socialite Roddy Llewellyn, dressed in a satin-collared dinner jacket, was escorted by Moroccan born Naima Feth-Eddine at a charity ball at the Royal Academy. Others present included Lord and Lady Drogheda, Mr and Mrs Jack Heinz, Princess Joan Aly Khan and the legendary party-goer Lady Charlotte Bonham Carter.

Back in California the following weekend, these celebrations were thrown into perspective by a party given by Sheikh Shamsuddu al-Fassi at his mansion on Sunset Boulevard, which had now been redecorated at a cost of $7 million, and featured a red billiard room, clam-shaped bath tub, peach-coloured music room and twelve crib nursery. Security guards mingled with guests as they consumed caviare, champagne and Middle Eastern delicacies.

Back in London on Monday June 19, self-confessed gambler and bankrupt, 39-year-old Kitty Milinaire appeared before Knightsbridge Crown Court accused of stealing £200,000 worth of Cartier jewellery. Her lawyer told the court, 'She comes from a background of such money that you and I cannot get to terms with it.'

The following evening at Sotheby's, there was a casino-like atmosphere when the sale began of the collection of German industrialist Robert von Hirsch, who had died the previous year. On the first day items on sale fetched a total of £2,777,100.

On Wednesday June 21, the Queen and Prince Philip drove down the course at Ascot accompanied by 17-year-old Crown Prince Reza of Iran, who was staying as their guest at Windsor Castle.

On Thursday June 22, there was another party in honour of Andy Warhol, this time held at the Institute for Contemporary Arts in the Mall. Among those present were punk star Jordan, now described as 'the girl who introduced rubber to England', fellow punk Polly Styrene, artist David Hockney, Mrs Vere Harmsworth, veteran fashion editor Diana Vreeland and Margaret Trudeau, estranged wife of the Canadian Premier, who stormed out when an inebriate spilt wine down her dress.

Sotheby's Chairman Peter Wilson auctions a twelfth-century enamel medallion from the von Hirsch collection. This item was purchased by the Staatliche Museum in Berlin for $2.2 million

Christie's Chairman Joe Floyd auctions Coco Chanel's famous 'little black dress'. This item was purchased by Baroness David de Rothschild for $3,000

Later that night in Paris, Princess Caroline of Monaco and her fiancé Philippe Junot mingled with multi-millionaire Stavros Niarchos, Princess Ferial of Jordan and the Duke and Duchess of Bedford at a party at Maxim's given by Mr and Mrs Oscar Wyatt from Texas. Dinner began with baby boiled lobsters and ended with an iced raspberry sorbet.

Missing from this party was 27-year-old Christina Onassis who was now on her way to Moscow by train. On Sunday June 25, she arrived in the Russian capital surrounded by rumours that she was to marry Soviet shipping official Sergei Kauzov.

The same day, it was stated that international swindler Robert Vesco who had been expelled from Costa Rica was now trying to bargain with the authorities in the Bahamas so that he might settle there.

Back in London the following Tuesday, June 27, it was revealed that Olga Deterding had been banned from Langan's Brasserie, a few minutes walk from her Mayfair penthouse. 'Her visits have become too disruptive,' said chef Richard Shepherd. 'The other day she even invaded my kitchen.'

That evening the von Hirsch sale ended at Sotheby's, having netted a total of £18,468,300. After the last lot had been disposed of, dinner-jacketed auctioneer Peter Wilson received a round of applause.

Later that night, the fashion crowd gathered at Olympia to see Zandra Rhodes' new collection, at which models paraded in satin cami-knickers. Among those present were Diana Vreeland, Bianca Jagger, who had looked in earlier on the von Hirsch sale, and the indestructible 85-year-old Lady Charlotte Bonham Carter.

The legendary Lady Charlotte Bonham Carter: farmer, art patron, philanthropist, and international party-goer

The same night in Monte Carlo, Prince Rainier and Princess Grace gave a ball at their palace to celebrate the forthcoming marriage of their daughter Princess Caroline and ageing playboy Philippe Junot. Late arrivals included Frank Sinatra and David Niven, who had had their own party earlier in the evening.

Back in London on Wednesday June 28, Iranian-born former gambler Kitty Milinaire was found not guilty of stealing jewellery from Cartier and went home 'numb with joy' after an eight day trial.

That night saw the gala opening of a new casino in the basement of the London Ritz. Among those present were 85-year-old Lady Diana Cooper, Nigel Dempster and his wife Lady Camilla, multi-millionaire Sir Charles Clore, Olga Deterding who was escorted by art critic Bevis Hillier, and restaurateur Peter Langan, who said he had already drunk six bottles of champagne that day. It was noted that 600 books of gold leaf had been used to re-decorate the premises.

Artist David Hockney enters the fashionable Langan's Brasserie

On Thursday June 29, the marriage took place of the beautiful Princess Caroline of Monaco in a chapel in the Royal Palace at Monte Carlo. The Princess wore a white organdie dress and veil designed by Marc Bohan at Christian Dior. Later, two doves were released from a gilded cage inside the wedding cake.

The following day in Vienna Town Hall, the marriage took place between Prince Michael of Kent and the sophisticated and soignée Baroness Marie-Christine von Reibnitz. After the ceremony, guests who included Princess Anne and Earl Mountbatten of Burma left for a reception at the British Embassy in a cavalcade of gleaming Mercedes.

Meanwhile, a world tour by 31-year-old David Bowie had reached London with a series of concerts at the Earl's Court stadium. In an interview on this occasion, Bowie, his hair now a natural colour, described the life of a rock star as 'hateful' and declared that he had even considered committing suicide.

On Saturday July 1, 85-year-old Lady Diana Cooper donned her famous nun's costume for a fancy dress ball given by Mrs Diana Phipps at Buscot, near Faringdon. During the evening, she was photographed chatting with Lord Goodman, who was dressed in a monk's habit.

On Tuesday July 4, Richard Burton and his new wife Suzy arrived in London. Suzy wore blue boots and a shocking pink plastic mac and explained, 'This is my summer outfit for England.' Said Burton, 'It's costing me a fortune in dresses for the wife.'

The same day, a report on the alleged conspiracy to murder former male model

Liberal MP Jeremy Thorpe and his wife Marion leave a memorial service for the late Lord Selwyn-Lloyd

Norman Scott was sent to the Director of Public Prosecutions.

Meanwhile, at Christie's auction rooms, jewellery belonging to the late Gladys, Duchess of Marlborough, who had died in total obscurity in a mental hospital the previous year aged 97, had fetched a total of £452,755.

On Thursday July 6, three bags of horse manure were hurled into the chamber of the House of Commons, narrowly missing the leader of the house, Michael Foot. 'I take a serious view of this,' said the Speaker, ordering a twenty minute adjournment while brushes, dustpans and disinfectants were brought in to clear up the mess.

On Friday July 7 in New York, Mrs William 'Babe' Paley, a leader of the city's 'beautiful people' and wife of the CBS tycoon, died of cancer. It was noted that she had never given up the fight and had continued giving dinner parties until the end.

Meanwhile Liza Minnelli, whose marriage was now in the process of dissolution, had acquired the spectacular Manhattan home formerly occupied by jewellery designer Ken Lane, and his vivacious wife Nicky.

Back at Wimbledon, on Saturday July 8, Bjorn Borg became men's champion for the third time, falling to his knees after beating American Jimmy Connors. 'I'll follow Borg to the ends of the earth,' said Connors afterwards. 'I'll stay with the son of a bitch till I beat him.'

The following day, the Iron Butterfly, Madame Marcos, alighted briefly in London and, decked in emeralds, threw a party at the Philippines Embassy which was attended by Sir James Goldsmith and his constant companion Lady Annabel Birley, Stavros Niarchos and Princess Ferial of Jordan, Princess Elizabeth of Yugoslavia, banker Mario d'Urso and other celebrated figures.

On Tuesday July 11, 80-year-old newspaper proprietor Lord Rothermere died at his Mayfair home. His title passed to his son, the Hon. Vere Harmsworth, whose wife Bubbles had long been one of the most active social figures on both sides of the Atlantic.

That evening, Mrs Angie Bowie arrived at the West End première of *Thank God It's Friday* escorted by punk musician Drew Blood and admitted that her marriage was over. 'It's in legal hands now. It was a lovely period of my life, but if it's over, it's over.'

Over in New York, on Thursday July 13, it was disclosed that Elizabeth Taylor was selling the giant pear-shaped 69 carat diamond which her ex-husband Richard Burton had given her nine years earlier. 'Politics can be expensive,' said the jeweller handling the sale. 'Miss Taylor and her husband have a big estate to maintain. The money probably looks better than the stone at the moment.'

The same day, Mrs Jackie Onassis posed graciously for photographers and chatted with the hoi polloi at the opening of a new bookstore on 5th Avenue run by Doubleday publishing firm.

On Monday July 17, the new world chess championship began in sweltering heat in the Philippines. Challenger Victor Korchnoi burst out laughing when the event began with a military band playing the 'Internationale' instead of the Soviet National Anthem and a Soviet functionary rushed to the bandstand in a panic.

Back in Britain the same day, relatives of Lord Brooke protested at the 'sacking' of Warwick Castle, the contents of which had been slowly disposed of over the past few months. Said Lord Brooke's cousin, Priscilla Greville, 'The Grevilles have guarded Warwick Castle since Elizabethan times but Warwick is no longer safe in the hands of the Grevilles.'

On Wednesday July 19, airline owner Freddie Laker was knighted by the Queen at Buckingham Palace. 'Given my background, this was an honour I would never have dared dream about,' he said afterwards.

Over in Washington the following day, President Carter's adviser on health and drug abuse, Dr Peter Bourne, resigned after admitting that he had prescribed methaqualone to one of his associates using a pseudonym for the patient's real name.

On Friday July 21, troubles hit the World Chess Championship in Manila, when challenger Viktor Korchnoi claimed that a yoghurt sent to the champion Anatoly Karpov was a coded message. Karpov dismissed the charge as ridiculous.

Back in America, on Sunday July 23, the Rolling Stones gave a concert at Arnaheim Stadium in California. Among the 55,000 spectators was film star Elizabeth Taylor, who had arrived at the stadium in a helicopter.

On Monday July 24, the world's richest man, Mr Adnan Khashoggi, celebrated his forty-third birthday on board his yacht near Cannes, surrounded by outlandish rumours that he had secretly married Mrs Jackie Onassis three months earlier.

Meanwhile, it had been disclosed that Italian industrialist Gianni Agnelli was going round with a cyanide pill embedded in one of his teeth for use in case he was kidnapped.

On Thursday July 27, there was further excitement in international society when Miss Christina Onassis, currently occupying a twelfth floor suite overlooking Moscow's Red Square, announced her engagement to Soviet shipping official Sergei

Kauzov. Miss Onassis had previously dismissed rumours of the engagement as 'preposterous'.

The same day, Princess Caroline of Monaco and her husband Philippe Junot were found relaxing on the Pacific island of Moorea, swimming in emerald green lagoons and enjoying the sparkling sand and surf.

Fiat president Gianni Agnelli, who was said to keep a cyanide capsule embedded in his tooth to swallow in the event of kidnapping

On Tuesday August 1, the marriage took place in Moscow between Christina Onassis and Sergei Kauzov. The bride arrived at the simple ceremony in the Central Palace of Marriages in a battered Chevrolet and wearing a simple lilac-coloured dress. The couple spent their wedding night in the bride's suite at the Intourist Hotel amidst rumours that Mr Kauzov was to change his name to Onassis.

Back in London, on Wednesday August 2, Liberal MP Jeremy Thorpe made a telling speech in the House of Commons during which he took the Tories to task over Rhodesia.

Over in New York the following morning, David Bowie and Liza Minnelli emerged from Studio 54 holding hands. 'She's the most exciting woman I've ever met,' Bowie declared.

Back in Britain on Friday August 4, Jeremy Thorpe, his friend David Holmes and two others were arrested and charged with conspiring to murder former male model Norman Scott. Released on bail after appearing in Minehead Magistrates Court, the former leader of the Liberal Party said, 'I plan to keep up my public engagements and the private ones.'

The same day, 38-year-old Norman Scott, now said to be charging £80 for a photograph, posed with his dogs for the cameras of the CBS American TV company at his Dartmoor home. 'The last thing I ever wanted to do was to create a national scandal,' he said

On Saturday August 5, the newly wed Christina Onassis arrived in Athens without her husband, surrounded by rumours that her marriage was already in difficulties. She explained that she had come home 'for urgent business reasons'.

On Sunday August 6, 80-year-old Pope Paul died at his summer palace at Castel Gandolfo outside Rome after suffering a heart attack during a mass at his bedside. On his death, all the lights in the house were immediately extinguished and bells began pealing.

The same day in America, Mrs Gertrude Vanderbilt, one of America's richest women, died leaving substantial sums to the family of the Duke of Marlborough, whose grandfather had married into the Vanderbilt family eighty years earlier.

Early the following week, new posters prepared by advertising agency Saatchi and Saatchi began to appear in England, promoting the Conservative Party. On Wednesday August 9, the Chancellor of the Exchequer, Denis Healey, dismissed the campaign as 'an attempt to sell Mrs Thatcher as if she was a soap powder'.

Meanwhile in Rome, tax exile the Earl of Warwick tried to explain why his son Lord Brooke had been selling the treasures of Warwick Castle. 'This year or next the entire south-west wall of the castle must be shored up and restored. The wall will require about two acres of scaffolding, which today costs the earth.'

On Monday August 14, Jeremy Thorpe was permitted to fly to Switzerland to attend a United Nations conference on racialism. He was to stay with his old friend Sir James Murray, British Ambassador to the United Nations.

On Wednesday August 16, multi-millionaire art collector, Dr Armand Hammer, flew into Edinburgh in his private jet, accompanied by an enormous Rembrandt painting entitled *Juno*, which had travelled in the jet's bedroom wrapped inside a mattress, and which was to go on show at the Scottish National Gallery. 'Some people call me lucky,' said 80-year-old Dr Hammer. 'But when you work between ten and fourteen hours a day, you get lucky.'

Multi-millionaire art collector Dr Armand Hammer, who had been wheeling and dealing in Russia since the 1920s

The next day, Dr Hammer flew on to Warsaw and Moscow to put the finishing touches to a deal in chemical fertilisers said to be worth $20,000 million a year.

On Friday August 18, 29-year-old Prince Charles arrived in Deauville for a short holiday as guest of 32-year-old art dealer Daniel Wildenstein. Among those in the royal party was Charles's old American girl friend, Laura-Jo Watkins.

Back in Central London, on Sunday August 20, a bus carrying twenty-one El Al air hostesses was ambushed by a Palestinian splinter group. The injured were rushed to Middlesex Hospital, where oil heiress Olga Deterding was being treated for a brain haemorrhage she had suffered a few days earlier.

On Tuesday August 22, the Queen briefly left Balmoral Castle and flew south to stay with the Earl of Halifax at his 18,000 acre Garrowby Hall estate. That day at York Races the Queen, Lord Halifax and his son Lord Irwin tucked into grouse shot on the nearby estate of the Earl of Swinton.

The same day, suave superstar Rex Harrison flew into London, carrying two umbrellas and accompanied by glamorous 40-year-old Mercia Tinker, who was soon to become his sixth wife.

The following Saturday August 26, 15,000 people in St Peter's Square, Rome, were informed by a plume of smoke from the chimney of the Vatican that a Pope had been selected. Cardinal Albino Luciani, Patriarch of Venice, said he was surprised to find himself the new Pope and chose the name John Paul I.

Meanwhile, actress Marisa Berenson, whose marriage to millionaire James Randall had collapsed, had arrived in Rome to continue work on the film *Greed* which had been interrupted by a serious car crash in South America earlier in the year. Marisa had undergone plastic surgery by the celebrated jet-set surgeon Dr Ivo Pitanguy and said, 'I'm surviving.'

On Thursday August 31, Princess Caroline of Monaco and her husband Philippe Junot flew into London and spent five hours shopping before flying on to Scotland 'to get away from it all'. The famous couple were offered VIP facilities at Heathrow Airport but refused to use them.

The following Sunday, September 3, saw the installation of the new Pope, John Paul I, in a simple ceremony at the Vatican. The Queen was represented at the ceremony by the new Duke of Norfolk, England's leading Roman Catholic layman.

On Tuesday September 5, Olga Deterding emerged from the Middlesex Hospital after receiving treatment for a brain haemorrhage. That night she threw a party at her Mayfair penthouse with her head completely shaved. 'People think I've become a punk rocker,' she said.

Later that day at Camp David, President Sadat of Egypt and Prime Minister Begin of Israel began peace talks organized by President Carter in a bid to establish himself as an international statesman rather than a White House flop.

Back in London, on Thursday September 7, rock star Keith Moon, drummer with The Who pop group noted for his wild behaviour, was found dead in bed with a massive overdose of the sedative drug, Heminevrin. He died in the same Mayfair flat in which singer Mama Cass had died four years earlier.

The same day, Bulgarian defector Georgi Markov was stabbed in the thigh by an umbrella as he waited for a bus on Waterloo Bridge. He was to die a few days later from the effects of a poison contained in the tip of the umbrella, said to be twice as powerful as cobra venom.

Meanwhile, 65-year-old Margaret Duchess of Argyll had sold the lease of her Mayfair house, where she had lived since before the War and moved into a three bedroom flat in nearby Grosvenor House, which she had rented for £30,000 a year. She took with her 200 pairs of shoes.

On Saturday September 9, at Colin Tennant's house in Scotland there was an extravagant fancy dress party at which Princess Margaret dressed up as Sophie

Tucker in a blonde wig, her friend Roddy appeared as a wizard, and Bianca Jagger and her six-year-old daughter Jade performed a sensitive ballet.

On Sunday September 10, President Carter telephoned the Shah of Iran from Camp David to express the hope that the violence in his country would soon end and to re-affirm the importance of Iran's alliance with the West.

The same day, superstar John Travolta flew into Britain from Deauville accompanied by four bodyguards to launch his new film *Grease*.

Three days later, there were chaotic scenes at the film's première in Leicester Square when 5,000 Travolta fans broke through a police barrier. A spokesman for the young superstar said, 'He is badly shaken and as white as a sheet.' Said the new Lady Rothermere, 'I was very frightened. It's just been mass hysteria. I've never seen anything like it since the days of Beatlemania.' Missing from these scenes was the film's co-producer Robert Stigwood, whose yacht *Sarina* had gone aground earlier in the day off the Isle of Corfu.

Early the following morning, Thursday September 14, Travolta left London for Milan in a private jet.

Later that day, Jeremy Thorpe arrived at the Liberal Conference at Southport in a red Alfa Romeo sports car and made a brief appearance on the platform to the embarrassment of many of those present. 'I'm fed up to the teeth with Thorpe,' said Liberal MP Cyril Smith later.

Back in London that weekend, Lady Rothermere threw a party at her Eaton Square flat in honour of Allen Carr, portly co-producer of the film *Grease*. Guests included 18-year-old Damian Elwes, whose father Dominic Elwes had died in tragic circumstances three years earlier, and Dai Llewellyn, who was escorted by 28-year-old Gunilla von Bismarck, great-granddaughter of the founder of the German Empire. It was noted that Miss von Bismarck wore skin-tight satin trousers and a revealing shirt.

On Sunday September 17, President Sadat and Prime Minister Begin emerged from their Camp David talks to sign peace documents under the glare of Washington's TV lights.

Meanwhile, guardian of public morals Mrs Mary Whitehouse had arrived in Australia. On Tuesday September 19, her audience at Brisbane pelted her with strawberry pies.

Back in London that afternoon, it was revealed that the eight bedroom Kensington house where Sir Eric Miller had shot himself the previous year had been purchased by Sheikh Hamad, ruler of one of the United Arab Emirates, for £500,000.

The following night, the London glitterati gathered once more, this time for a party by the proprietor of the *Spectator*, millionaire bachelor Henry Keswick, at the Lyceum Ballroom. Among the hundreds present was 46-year-old Lady Falkender, who was unable to join the Earl of Longford, Nigel Dempster and others on the dance floor on account of her bad back.

The next morning there was much excitement over a new interview with Opposition leader Mrs Thatcher in *Woman's World*. 'There are times when I get home at night and everything has got on top of me when I shed a few tears, silently, alone,' she had confessed.

Later that day in Australia, Mrs Mary Whitehouse was again assailed with foodstuffs. Lecturing in Sydney that afternoon she was pelted with pies and cream cakes.

On Sunday September 24, it was revealed that 77-year-old novelist Barbara Cartland was to make a record singing with the Royal Philharmonic Orchestra.

Songs would include 'A Nightingale sang in Berkeley Square' and 'If you were the only girl in the world'.

The following day, more troubles hit the world chess championship in the Philippines, now in its tenth week, when World Champion Karpov left his luxury hotel in Manila complaining of a noisy lawn mower outside his window.

On Friday September 29, attention turned suddenly to Rome where the new Pope had been found dead in his bed after only thirty-three days in office. The Vatican's well-oiled machinery immediately began the process of selecting his successor amidst calls for a post-mortem following sensational 'readings' of the death by certain leading Catholics.

The same day in the South Pacific, Princess Margaret was taken ill on board the frigate *Ortago* taking her to the Independence celebrations on the island of Tuvalu. The Princess's temperature soon rose to 104° and her advisers decided to fly her to hospital in Sydney, 2,500 miles away, travelling on a stretcher bed.

Back in Europe, on Sunday October 1, an illustrious crowd had gathered at Longchamps for the Prix de l'Arc de Triomphe. Among those who watched Lester Piggott romp home on Robert Sangster's Alleged for the second year running, were the 41-year-old Aga Khan, the Earl and Countess of Donoughmore, who had been kidnapped by the IRA four years earlier, Baron Heinrich Thyssen, and the massively built Mr Nelson Bunker Hunt, who was said to own a million acres of Texas and oil reserves worth £1 billion.

Two days later, at the Cleveland Clinic in New York, 65-year-old King Khaled of Saudi Arabia underwent open heart surgery.

Back in Britain the same day, the long saga of Warwick Castle ended when it was revealed that Lord Brooke had sold the ancient dwelling to Madame Tussaud's for £1,500,000. Lord Brooke's cousin Miss Priscilla Greville said she was 'absolutely horrified' by the sale and fellow stately home owner Lord Montagu of Beaulieu said, 'I think it is a very sad day when any great family is forced by circumstances to give up a great house like that.'

On Wednesday October 4, Captain Mark Phillips took his place among students at the Royal Agricultural College at Cirencester.

On Saturday October 7, the marriage took place at Luton Hoo in Bedfordshire of 26-year-old Earl Grosvenor, son and heir to the Duke of Westminster and 20-year-old Miss Natalia Phillips. Among the hundreds present at a reception afterwards at Luton Hoo were gardeners, cooks and nannies from the bride and bridegroom's homes. Missing was the bridegroom's father, who had been rushed to the intensive care unit of the Westminster Hospital the previous night with an asthma attack.

The same weekend in Tehran, riots broke out again and several banks were set on fire. At the official re-opening of Tehran University, hundreds of students clashed with police.

On Monday October 9, it was revealed that an application had been made to export the ten ton Warwick Vase, one of the last remaining chattels of Lord Brooke, valued at £250,000.

That night, at Tramp discothèque in Jermyn Street, would-be pop singer Roddy Llewellyn, with blown-dry hair, launched his first record album, entitled *Roddy* and sprayed champagne on assembled photographers. During the next two weeks the album was to sell only thirteen copies at London's biggest record store.

Meanwhile, 6,000 miles away, Princess Margaret had recovered from her illness and had arrived in Japan on a commercial airline's scheduled flight. On the same

Lady Llewellyn flanked by her sons Dai and Roddy at a party to launch Roddy's first record

day as Roddy's debut, she was received by the Emperor and Empress and bestowed upon the Emperor's sister-in-law Princess Chichibu the honour of Dame Grand Cross of the order of St Michael and St George.

Back in America, on Thursday October 12, Elizabeth Taylor was rushed to hospital after a chicken bone had got lodged in her throat at a political rally.

The same day at New York's Chelsea Hotel, dancer Nancy Spungeon was found dead with a knife wound in her stomach. Her boyfriend, former Sex Pistol Sid Vicious, was arrested and charged with murder. Also staying at the Chelsea at this time was 69-year-old homosexualist Quentin Crisp, now making his name in America.

On Monday October 16, a wisp of tell-tale white smoke from the chimney of the Sistine Chapel in Rome revealed that a new pope had been selected. He was Cardinal Karol Wojtyla, Archbishop of Cracow, the first non-Italian to be chosen for this high office for 450 years. Said a close friend, Monsignor Derek Worlock, Archbishop of Liverpool, 'He is a man of wonderfully exuberant good spirits.'

On Tuesday October 17, the world chess championship ended in Manila when challenger Viktor Korchnoi resigned in the thirty-second game. Exhausted champion Anatoly Karpov immediately retired to his bed.

Meanwhile in California, Princess Margaret was being fêted on her way home from the Far East. That day in Hollywood, she had luncheon with the stars of the TV series *Starsky and Hutch* and in the evening she was guest of honour at a party given by the Bloomingdale department store family, at which other guests included the former Governor of California, 67-year-old Ronald Reagan, and the globe-trotting Bianca Jagger.

The same day in New York, former Sex Pistol Sid Vicious, who had been accused of murdering his girl-friend, was released on $50,000 bail. He emerged from the court-room laughing and said, 'I'm longing for a slice of pizza.'

On Sunday October 22, British Foreign Secretary David Owen expressed strong support for the Shah of Iran in his present troubles. 'It would not be in the interest of this country or the West for the Shah to be toppled,' he explained.

Later that day in New York, Sid Vicious was placed in the psychiatric ward at Bellevue Hospital after attempting to commit suicide by slashing his wrists.

Two days later in Toronto, Rolling Stone Keith Richard was placed on a year's probation for possessing heroin. He was also ordered to give a performance for the benefit of blind people.

On Thursday October 26, the Shah of Iran celebrated his fifty-sixth birthday quietly at the Golestan Palace, near Tehran, where the same day a police chief was shot dead and a military commander was critically wounded by snipers.

Meanwhile, Prince Charles had arrived in Austria, where he was to pay a private visit to the estate of Prince Franz Josef of Liechtenstein, during which he shot five wild boar. On Monday October 30, he returned to England to be named 'Hooligan of the Year' by a member of the RSPCA, Mr John Bryant. 'Not content with fox hunting, he has killed five wild pigs, pheasants and hares while on a royal tour in Vienna,' said Mr Bryant.

On Tuesday October 31, a strike by oil workers in Iran demanding the release of all political prisoners caused a halt in the flow of oil from this troubled country.

The same day in Washington, the Shah's son, 18-year-old Crown Prince Reza, was welcomed to the White House by Jimmy Carter. 'Our friendship and alliance with Iran is one of the most important bases on which our entire foreign policy depends,' said the President. 'We wish the Shah our best and hope the problems will soon be resolved.'

Later that day in New York, there was a Halloween party at Studio 54. The club was washed with laser beams and at midnight 2,000 balloons dropped from the ceiling. Joining in the fun were Liza Minnelli, Truman Capote, Sidney Lumet and his former wife, the celebrated Miss Gloria Vanderbilt, who had recently started designing jeans.

Back in London on Thursday November 2, it was revealed that a thief had entered the five star Wellington Hotel and robbed Sheikh Salman Jassim al-Thani of Qatar of £150,000 worth of jewels and two Smith & Wesson revolvers which were in his bedside locker. 'We think this is just a case of a sneak thief who struck lucky,' said a police spokesman.

The following day, King Khaled of Saudi Arabia flew home after convalescing in Bermuda following open-heart surgery in New York.

On Sunday November 5, banks and offices were set on fire in Tehran and the British Embassy was invaded. 'It was all rather politely done,' said a British official. 'They just asked us to leave and then set the building on fire.'

A few hours later, at a villa in the suburbs of Paris, the exiled Ayatollah Khomeini commented on these developments. 'Only the departure of the Shah and the cleansing of the system can provide a way out of the present situation,' he said.

Back in London on Tuesday November 7, pop star Elton John was taken to the Harley Street clinic suffering from exhaustion and overwork and complaining of chest pains.

Over in Hollywood, on Wednesday November 8, 17 stone impresario Allan Carr entered the Cedars Sinai hospital to have his jaws wired. 'I've got to lose 80 pounds and every other way I've tried has failed,' he explained.

On Saturday November 11, the ranks of international invalids were joined by 54-year-old Earl Spencer who was now being treated in London's National Hospital after a cerebral haemorrhage.

On Tuesday November 14, former Liberal MP Peter Bessell arrived in England to give evidence in the forthcoming Magistrates Court proceedings against his old friend and colleague Jeremy Thorpe.

The following night, Prince Charles's thirtieth birthday was celebrated with a party at Buckingham Palace, at which disco-dancing took place to the music of the Three Degrees. Among the 300 guests were journalist Emma Soames, former jet-setter Patricia Wolfson, now studying for a degree at London University, Lord Burghersh, Mr and Mrs Boz Ferranti and Lord Vestey. One of the few women present to wear a tiara was Princess Margaret. 'I've been to a banquet at the Guildhall and I couldn't take the wretched thing off,' she explained.

Earlier that day in Paris, the marriage had taken place between Sir James Goldsmith and his longstanding companion Lady Annabel Birley, sister of the Marquess of Londonderry. On leaving his apartment Sir James clashed with a Fleet Street photographer who had tried to take his photo. 'I'm just one of the people who will not accept this kind of nonsense,' Sir James said later. 'Hickey and these people are diseases like flu and everybody is subject to them.'

On Monday November 20, attention turned to the seaside resort of Minehead in Somerset for the start of Magistrates Court proceedings against Mr Jeremy Thorpe and three others. The former Liberal leader arrived to fight the charges in a white Rover 3500 and wearing his familiar brown trilby.

The following day, it was revealed that Mentmore Towers, Buckinghamshire home of the late Lord Rosebery, had been sold to the followers of the Maharishi Mahesh Yogi for £240,000, for use as a centre for transcendental meditation. 'We hope that people who work on the estate, whom we will keep on, and others will be pleased that the house is being put to beneficial use,' said Mr Vesey Crighton, a director of the Age of Enlightenment, 'but we expect some local curiosity.'

Back at Minehead Magistrates Court, on Thursday November 23, former Liberal MP Peter Bessell admitted during cross-examination that he was being paid £50,000 by the *Sunday Telegraph* for his memoirs.

The following day in London, it was announced that 54-year-old Earl Spencer was 'critically ill' in the National Hospital where he had been admitted a few days earlier suffering from a cerebral haemorrhage.

On Saturday November 25, former President Richard Nixon arrived in Paris on the start of a European tour designed to re-establish him as an international statesman. He was greeted at Orly Airport by the American Ambassador and driven in a presidential style motorcade to his hotel.

The following day, Mr Nixon shook hands, laughed and waved and told reporters that his role in the Watergate affair was 'not a crime, it was a bloomer'.

That night in New York, Mrs Jackie Onassis threw a party in the city's oldest established disco, Le Club on East 55th Street, for her two children. 140 intimates, including Jackie's brother-in-law Senator Edward Kennedy, dined off seafood Newburg, moussaka and poulet aux raisins. It was noted that Mrs Onassis had asked for 'total and complete privacy' to surround the event.

Back in London, on Monday November 27, the Earl of Lichfield gave a party at the Hyde Park Hotel to celebrate the birth of his son and heir. Among those present dancing the night away together were Princess Margaret and Roddy Llewellyn.

On Tuesday November 28, former Liberal MP Peter Bessell left England for his home in California, wearing a camel-hair overcoat and Russian style white fur hat, after accusing his old friend Jeremy Thorpe of conspiracy and incitement to murder.

The following day at Minehead Magistrates Court, former male model Norman Scott entered the witness box and gave sensational evidence of how Thorpe had made love to him seventeen years earlier.

The same day, former President Richard Nixon arrived in London and was greeted at the Airport by the American Ambassador Kingman Brewster and Conservative MP Jonathan Aitken and driven to Claridge's Hotel. On arrival at his third floor suite, Mr Nixon ordered a Spanish omelette.

On Thursday November 30, the temporary closure of *The Times* newspaper group was marked by a party at Langan's Brasserie at which jazz and steel bands played and guests ranged from actor Jack Nicholson to former minister Mrs Barbara Castle, who wore a window pane check jacket.

On Friday December 1, the 72-year-old Earl of Longford gave a lunch party at the Hyde Park Hotel in honour of Mr Nixon. Among those present was Mrs Thatcher's husband Denis. It was noted that the last guests did not leave until 3.45 p.m.

The following day, the former President left London on a scheduled flight.

Richard Nixon, on his first European tour since his resignation as President of the United States, poses with his publisher, Lord Longford, at a luncheon at the Hyde Park Hotel

That night at Christie's, twelve TV networks covered the sale of Coco Chanel's personal wardrobe and costume jewellery. Among those present was Baroness David de Rothschild who paid £1,500 for Chanel's legendary 'little black dress'.

On Tuesday December 5, the London scene was enriched by the presence of Yoko Ono, who flew in wearing a floor-length white fur coat. 'I am only here for a few days on a business trip,' she explained.

That night, 46-year-old Lady Falkender was present at the opening of a new art gallery in Belgravia rubbing shoulders with biographer Michael Holroyd, television personality Robert Kee and other media workers.

The following evening, Lady Falkender was present at the Savile Row preview of old family photographs belonging to the Marquess of Londonderry and was shown round the exhibition by the Marquess's sister, Lady Annabel Goldsmith, whose new husband Sir James burst into the room wearing a blue city overcoat.

Two days later, at Minehead Magistrates Court, Mr Thorpe sat with his arms folded as a statement on his behalf was read to the court denying an affair with

Norman Scott and refuting any suggestion that he had been party to a conspiracy to kill or injure him.

On Friday December 8, Enoch Powell MP claimed that if Prince Charles were to marry a Roman Catholic it would signal the beginning of the end of British Monarchy. A Buckingham Palace spokesman said later, 'All I can say is that Prince Charles is not getting engaged to anyone, let alone a Roman Catholic, and to the best of anyone's knowledge he does not intend to.'

The following Monday in Iran, troops in armoured cars and lorries protected with mounted machine guns opened fire on anti-Shah demonstrators.

On Tuesday December 12, Sir Harold Wilson and his friend Lord Kagan were both present at the funeral of Mrs Golda Meir, in Jerusalem.

Back in Britain the following day, a warrant was issued for the arrest of Lord Kagan on control exchange offences.

The same day, the Minehead Magistrates ruled that former Liberal leader, Jeremy Thorpe, who had been charged with conspiracy and incitement to murder, had a prima facie case to answer and he was committed with his three co-defendants to stand trial at the Old Bailey. 'I plead not guilty and will vigorously defend this matter,' he said before being released on £5,000 bail and driven off in his white Rover to his North Devon home.

Over in New York early the following morning, the Federal authorities raided the ultra chic Studio 54 discothèque and seized two ounces of cocaine and large quantities of financial records.

On Friday December 15, the marriage took place at Kensington Registry Office in London between 48-year-old Lord Snowdon and his close companion for more than two years, 37-year-old Mrs Lucy Lindsay-Hogg. After the ceremony the happy couple drove off in an unwashed Volvo estate car.

The following night, Princess Margaret was at the Royal Opera House, Covent Garden, to watch Merle Park and David Wall dancing in *The Sleeping Beauty* and was said to be looking relaxed and happy.

Over in Washington on Thursday December 21, it was announced that President Carter was suffering from haemorrhoids and must cancel all his appointments for the day. His doctors stressed that there was no need for immediate surgery.

Back in Britain the following day, the Queen left London for Windsor Castle with a favourite Corgi occupying the back window of her car. In her message to the Commonwealth that Christmas the Queen was to insist, 'We must not let the difficulties of the present or the uncertainties of the future cause us to lose faith.'

Meanwhile in Iran, anti-Shah demonstrators clashed again with the police and oil production slumped to less than half a billion barrels a day. On Tuesday December 26, central Tehran was described as a battle-ground as police opened fire on anti-Shah demonstrators, killing ten people including a professor at Tehran Polytechnic who had staged a sit-in at the Ministry of Science.

Back in Britain, on Friday December 29, it was revealed that an intriguing friendship had blossomed between 86-year-old Lady Diana Cooper and the 99-year-old music lover Sir Robert Mayer. 'He is absolutely delightful,' said Lady Diana. 'So far he has taken me to the opera and has been to lunch in my house. He's a wonderful companion, very witty and handsome. He has lovely thick hair.'

Later that day, the Shah of Iran's 92-year-old mother arrived in Los Angeles on board a 747 jumbo of the Iran airforce. She was accompanied by a poodle and a pekinese and was expected to stay at the Beverly Hills home of her daughter, Princess Ashraf, while the troubles in Iran lasted.

1979

The final year of the decade begins with Britain facing another industrial crisis and the troops standing by to control supplies of fuel and food while the smiling Prime Minister Jim Callaghan attends summit talks on the sunbaked island of Guadeloupe with President Carter. During the weeks and months that follow, the Shah of Iran flees his country in tears, General Idi Amin's tyrannical rule ends in Uganda and grocer's daughter Mrs Margaret Thatcher becomes the first woman Prime Minister of any Western nation. Later in the year, the Queen's uncle Lord Mountbatten of Burma is murdered by the IRA and her former art adviser, Sir Anthony Blunt, is exposed as the Fourth Man. Much of the material that follows has a desperate new note of commercialism about it. In England, both Mark Thatcher and Captain Mark Phillips have their sporting activities sponsored by industry, impresario Lord Grade says he would like to 'sign up' the Pope, Lady Falkender appears at a meeting of the Institute of Directors, and playboy Dai Llewellyn sells his memoirs to the News of the World. In America, Mrs Soraya Khashoggi sues her former husband for a record $2,000 million while back at the Old Bailey trial of Mr Thorpe further prosecution witnesses admit that they have signed lucrative contracts with the press. This new jaded quality of public life is faithfully reflected in the gossip columns of the day and before the year is out Nigel Dempster has been told by his employer that his column has begun to have the taste of 'cold fried potato'.

The New Year's celebrations in London were marred by the death of oil heiress Olga Deterding, who collapsed on the stroke of midnight at a club near her Mayfair home. 'Olga was a marvellous woman,' said her old friend TV personality Alan Whicker. 'A giver who was out of her age.'

Later that day, the smooth and hospitable Iranian Ambassador to London Mr Parviz Radji, who said he had gone to bed at 11 p.m. the previous night, stated, 'I am not in touch directly with His Majesty but I am in contact with the Foreign Ministry. As far as my own arrangements are concerned I think it would be unwise for me to leave my post in the foreseeable future.'

On Tuesday January 2, the Shah sent a formal message to the Queen at Sandringham advising her to cancel her trip to his troubled kingdom.

Meanwhile, Britain's industrial troubles were worsening and millions of pounds worth of fresh fruit began rotting in the docks of Liverpool, Southampton and other ports. On Friday January 5, it was announced that the army was standing by to control supplies of food and fuel.

The same day, on the Caribbean island of Guadeloupe, the Prime Minister Jim Callaghan got down to summit talks with President Giscard d'Estaing, Chancellor Schmidt and President Carter. During breaks in the discussions, Presidents Carter and Giscard d'Estaing played tennis. A suggestion that Callaghan should be umpire and Chancellor Schmidt ball-boy was dismissed as frivolous.

Back in Britain, on Saturday January 6, the Duke and Duchess of Buccleuch threw a party at their home near Selkirk at which the champagne served had been cooled in snowdrifts outside the house.

On Monday January 8, Prince Charles had an unsuccessful day's hunting with the Quorn at Willoughby-on-the-Wolds in Leicestershire. 'Our foxes are right crafty,' said a local farmer.

A ride in the snow at Sandringham: the Queen (centre) with Lady Tollemache (right) and Lady Sarah Spencer, close friend of Prince Charles

The following night in crisis-stricken London, there was an illustrious gathering at the opening of Regine's new nightclub in Kensington. Among those present were Prince Charles's friend Lady Sarah Spencer, the Earl of Lichfield, Princess

Caroline of Monaco and her husband Philippe Junot, property tycoon Geoffrey James, Peter Cadbury and the celebrated Lady Rothermere.

Meanwhile in Los Angeles, singer Michelle Triola had begun a historic court action against her former lover Lee Marvin claiming half the $1 million he had earned during the six years they had lived together.

On Wednesday January 10, Mr Callaghan flew home from the Caribbean on board a Royal Air Force VC10. 'We've had strikes before. We've come close to the brink before. Please don't run down your country by talking about mounting chaos,' he snapped at the airport. Later that day in the House of Commons, Mrs Thatcher demanded that the suntanned Prime Minister declare a state of national emergency.

On Friday January 12, the Queen, Lady Sarah Spencer and Prince Edward went out riding at Sandringham warmly dressed against sub-zero temperatures. On another part of the 20,000 acre estate Prince Charles was out shooting, dressed in a belted Norfolk jacket, plus-two trousers and tweed cap.

The same day, the Prince's old friend, actress Farrah Fawcett-Majors, flew into London, remarking, 'It's lovely to see the snow. I hope it keeps snowing. I never get a chance to wear my fur coats in Los Angeles.'

Over in Washington on Saturday January 13, President Carter said he hoped the American people realized he had no control over his younger brother Billy, who had recently paid a controversial visit to Libya, wearing the same shirt for five days in temperatures of over 100°F.

The following day, it was revealed that a new pastry chef, 59-year-old Albert Kumin, had been appointed to head the White House bakery. It was noted that Mr Kumin had previously worked at the World Trade Center and the Four Seasons restaurant in New York and his repertoire included a special high-domed chocolate-ribboned fancy cake, tiny croissants that flaked at the touch as well as toasted peanut cake and other Southern specialities. Of his White House job he said, 'As far as my career is concerned, it is the icing on the cake.'

Back in London, on Monday January 15, there was another party at Regine's club attended by Britt Ekland, Georgie Fame, the Three Degrees and Roddy Llewellyn, who spent most of the evening sitting beside gossip columnist Nigel Dempster. Driving home afterwards Roddy's Ford Transit van hit a police car in Knightsbridge. He was taken to Kensington Police Station and not permitted to leave until 5 a.m.

The following afternoon, Roddy had tea with Princess Margaret in Kensington Palace.

The same day the Shah of Iran fled from his troubled country in tears. At Mehradad Airport, he boarded a pale blue Boeing with only the minimum of possessions and clothes and flew himself to Egypt where the Hotel Oberoi on the Upper Nile had been taken over for him.

That night in Washington, the Iranian Embassy was closed by diplomats as 'a gesture of solidarity with the people of Iran who are working for democracy'. Ambassador Zahedi, who was said to have spent over $2 million a year on entertaining was said to have taken the shut-down 'quite well'.

Over in Rome, on Wednesday January 17, Lord Grade spent twenty-five minutes with Pope John Paul II and was appointed a Commander of the Order of St Sylvester. 'His Holiness knows the great impact which my film *Jesus of Nazareth* has had,' said Grade afterwards. 'He's got great charisma. I'd like to sign him up.'

Two days later, it was revealed that 24-year-old Lord Jermyn, son and heir to the Marquess of Bristol, had gone into exile for a year in Monte Carlo to protect his family fortune. 'He's terribly sad,' said his solicitor. 'After all he has given everything up. It's going to be very hard for him to start with but he does know a few people in the South of France.'

On Sunday January 21, it was revealed that Captain Mark Phillips had spent £11 on practical jokes at a shop in Tetbury in Gloucestershire. 'This will certainly liven things up at Windsor,' he had said as he left the shop grinning. A Buckingham Palace spokesman commented, 'Captain Phillips has a lively sense of humour and enjoys a joke like anybody else. I have no idea if he played any of these tricks on members of the Royal Family.'

On Monday January 22, Twiggy left England stating 'This whole scene makes me sick. I'm British and proud of it but what the hell is happening over here?'

On Tuesday January 23, the worst gale for sixteen years dumped a foot of snow over most of Southern England. At the Old Bailey the trial of artist Tom Keating was delayed when one of the jurors was unable to reach the court.

That evening, former Prime Minister Harold Macmillan braved the weather to go to the Carlton Club and unveil a bust of Mrs Margaret Thatcher. After the ceremony, Mrs Thatcher sat on the floor at Mr Macmillan's feet.

On Friday January 26, the debonair Iranian Ambassador Mr Parviz Radji took his leave of the Court of St James and flew to Rome. 'He has been dismissed by the Foreign Office in Tehran,' explained his personal assistant. 'He spent the morning saying goodbye to people at the Embassy and his friends in London.'

Later that day in New York, multi-millionaire statesman Nelson Rockefeller was found dead in his town house in the company of a 25-year-old blonde research assistant Megan Marshack. A few hours later, his family tried to cover up this scandal by announcing that the former Vice-President had died in his office in the Rockefeller Center with only a bodyguard in attendance.

Back in Britain, on Monday January 29, the Earl of Longford visited John Stonehouse in Norwich Prison. A Home Office spokesman said that the 73-year-old 'dogooder' had made several applications to visit the former Postmaster-General but this was the first time that Stonehouse had agreed to see him.

That night in Washington, former President Richard Nixon returned to the White House for the first time since his departure five years earlier to attend a dinner in honour of the Chinese deputy premier Teng Hsaio-ping. Others present included Senator Edward Kennedy, who said of the former President, 'I think he is welcome here.'

On Thursday February 1, the fifteen year exile of the Ayatollah Khomeini ended when he drove into Tehran in a blue Cadillac. 'The Shah has destroyed everything in our country,' he said.

Later that day in San Francisco, 24-year-old Patricia Hearst was released from Pleasanton Prison after serving twenty-two months of a seven year sentence for armed bank robbery. She left the prison wearing a bullet-proof vest and escorted by three bodyguards.

The following day in New York, punk rock star Sid Vicious died of an overdose of heroin at an apartment in Greenwich Village. Back in London, his manager Malcolm MacLaren said, 'I'm totally bamboozled and angry and very upset.'

On Saturday February 3, the marriage took place in Philadelphia between 20-year-old Joseph Kennedy III, son of the late Bobby Kennedy, and Sheila Brewster Rauch, daughter of the head of the nation's largest savings bank. Among those who attended the ceremony were Senator Edward Kennedy and Mrs Jackie Onassis.

Newspaper heiress Patty Hearst
re-emerges as a sophisticated
socialite

Back in Britain that weekend, artist Tom Keating fell off his moped, causing a further delay of the Old Bailey trial the following week.

On Monday February 5, in Los Angeles, Bianca Jagger filed papers to divorce her husband and began a legal battle to obtain a share of his $20 million fortune. It was noted that she was now represented by top lawyer Marvin Mitchelson, currently embroiled on behalf of Michelle Triola in her controversial suit against actor Lee Marvin.

The following day, the Shah of Iran was found installed at the Jehane Kabir Palace near Marrakesh. 'I am in need of rest, much rest,' he said. 'I live from day to day.'

Back in London, on Thursday February 8, the Old Bailey trial of artist Tom Keating was again delayed, this time because a juror needed time off for emergency dental treatment and because Keating himself had bad bronchitis.

Over in New York, on Friday February 9, playboy Philippe Junot was found dancing without his wife, Princess Caroline of Monaco, at the new ultra-chic Xenon discothèque.

On Sunday February 11, a weekend of bloody fighting in Tehran ended with a shattering defeat for the West when Prime Minister Dr Shahpur Bakhtiar resigned and disappeared. Ayatollah Khomeini promptly seized power and put out a statement asking everyone to remain peaceful and not to attack buildings or embassies.

The following day, the Queen began a tour of the Arabian peninsula, flying into Kuwait on Concorde, dressed in an apricot sorbet coloured afternoon frock designed by Norman Hartnell, a pill box hat and long gloves. That night, at Kuwait's Salem Palace there was a state banquet in the Queen's honour at which lamb cooked in rich spices was served.

The same day in Tel Aviv, Lord Kagan said he would return to England to face tax and currency charges 'when the mood takes me'. He explained, 'I like it here. I like the climate. I find the people very interesting. I am also engaged in helping my firm in exports. I find it very agreeable.'

Back in Britain, on Wednesday February 14, it was reported that thousands of sheep had been marooned on isolated hills in West Wales where the roads had been blocked by fifteen-foot snowdrifts.

Meanwhile, Roddy Llewellyn's career as a pop singer had collapsed and, on Thursday February 15, he left London for his seventh holiday on Mustique with Princess Margaret. Brushing aside photographers who blocked his path at Heathrow Airport, he shouted, 'No photographs please.'

On Saturday February 17, the Queen arrived in Saudi Arabia wearing a full-length sapphire silk dress with long sleeves, but no veil, and was welcomed by King Khaled who supported himself with a stick.

The following day, the Queen watched a camel race and then visited Saudi Arabia's new military hospital where black-veiled mothers nursed their babies. In the evening there was a picnic in the desert at which fifty lambs were roasted over a spit and great silver dishes of lobster, roast turkey and beef were served. As a compliment to the Queen, a unicorn had been sculpted in butter.

Back in Britain, on Monday February 19, the elderly Duke of Westminster, owner of 300 acres in Belgravia and Mayfair, died leaving an estate worth an estimated £500 million. 'I realize the responsibility for the estates now falls entirely on my shoulders,' said his 27-year-old son Earl Grosvenor, 'but I am prepared for that and I accept it.'

On Tuesday February 20, Foreign Secretary David Owen told the House of Commons that the Shah of Iran had been informed through unofficial channels that he would not be welcome in England.

The following day, former trade union leader Hugh Scanlon, once described as the Wild Man of the Far Left, took his seat in the House of Lords, dressed in three cornered hat and heavy ermine-trimmed robes.

Two days later, Captain Mark Phillips took part in a students rag at the Royal Agricultural College at Cirencester and had a custard pie thrown in his face.

On Saturday February 24, the Queen sailed into Abu Dhabi on board the royal yacht *Britannia* wearing a silk-print dress of navy and mustard and a small mustard hat. She was welcomed by Sheikha Fatima wife of Sheikh Zayid of the United Arab Emirates, who presented her with an ornate necklace. In return, the Queen gave the Sheikha a photograph of herself saying apologetically, 'I'm afraid this is rather small.'

Back in London, on Monday February 26, the trial of self-confessed art faker Tom Keating was abandoned on the grounds of the defendant's poor health. After the Attorney-General had studied a hospital report, explaining that the defendant was suffering from heart, bronchial and chest complaints, Mr Keating left for a secret hideout well pleased with this turn of events.

On Wednesday February 28, the Queen arrived in Oman, where a breeze blew off her hat but she managed to catch it and hold onto it, until her lady-in-waiting, the Duchess of Grafton, slipped her a hat pin.

The following day, during a trip into the interior of Oman, Prince Philip was left sitting in a chauffeurless grey Cadillac in extreme heat. Later, a police car siren went off and he lost his temper. 'Switch that bloody thing off you silly bugger,' he shouted.

Two days later, 30-year-old Prince Charles stopped off in Hong Kong on his way to Australia. During his short stay in the colony he sampled curried snake meat, remarking, 'Boy, the things I do for England.'

Back in England, on Monday March 5, ex-Beatle George Harrison was pushed through Heathrow Airport in a wheelchair. It was revealed that he had been involved in an accident with a tractor on his Oxfordshire estate. 'I feel a right clot,' he said. 'For about two weeks I will have to hop everywhere.'

Meanwhile, Roddy Llewellyn had turned again to horticultural activities and had been commissioned to design the garden for gossip columnist Nigel Dempster's new South Kensington home.

On Thursday March 15, former Slater Walker director Richard Tarling was escorted from his Wimbledon home by Superintendent Roger Lim of the Singapore police and taken to Heathrow Airport for extradition to Singapore to face charges in connection with the affairs of Haw Par Brothers International. It was noted that Mr Tarling's arm was in a sling, he having recently broken his thumb after tripping over his dog.

Meanwhile the Queen Mother had given an informal interview with a reporter on the *Toronto Star*, during which she remarked, 'Things change so terribly fast these days. Look at the Shah of Iran, poor man.'

On Tuesday March 20, the Institute of Directors' annual meeting at the Albert Hall was adorned by the presence of 47-year-old Lady Falkender, who sat beside her new friend Lady Annabel Goldsmith, wearing brown velvet and long boots. Asked by a reporter why she was there, Lady Falkender replied, 'Anything I would say to you would be rude.' She later heard a powerful speech from Sir James Goldsmith, criticizing the Callaghan government.

That night, Dido and Clio Goldsmith represented the Goldsmith clan at another party to launch Regine's new premises. Others present included socialite Nicky Haslam, gossip columnist Nigel Dempster and Bianca Jagger, who wore an eighteenth-century Chinese jacket and was escorted by interior designer John Stephanides.

On Friday March 23, three High Court judges reversed a Magistrates Court decision and found former City tycoon Jim Slater guilty of misusing £4 million of his company's money. 'I am very disappointed. The case seems to have gone against me on a very fine point of law,' said Slater who was on a salmon-fishing holiday in Scotland. 'I do not consider I have done anything to be ashamed of.'

On Tuesday March 27, the eccentric 63-year-old Marquess of Bristol left England to join his son, Lord Jermyn, in Monte Carlo. 'I can see no future any more for living in this country, which is going Communist and which is controlled by a Left Wing government,' he explained. 'I suppose in essence my reason for quitting is the absolutely iniquitous, unfair and penal tax system.' It was noted that the Marquess was taking his chef and chauffeur into tax exile with him.

Later the following night in the House of Commons, Conservative MPs shouted and danced for joy when the government was defeated in a vote of no confidence. Prime Minister Jim Callaghan sat quietly amidst the turmoil.

The same evening a new nightclub named Edens opened in Mayfair with Margaret Duchess of Argyll, property tycoon Geoffrey James, Dai Llewellyn and others in attendance. When news of the Conservative victory came through, Llewellyn jumped onto a table and bellowed, 'We are free at last! The government has been beaten!'

Two days later, on Friday March 30, as the party leaders began their campaigns for a general election, the country was stunned by the murder of Conservative MP Airey Neave, whose car was blown up by an IRA bomb as he drove out of the House of Commons car park, the first MP to be assassinated within the precincts of Westminster since the shooting of Prime Minister Spencer Perceval in 1812. 'Some devil has got him,' said Mrs Margaret Thatcher.

That night on television Enoch Powell reacted in a bizarre manner to this tragedy. 'I am sure Airey Neave would have wished nothing better than to share the same end as so many of his innocent fellow victims for whom the House of Commons is responsible,' he said.

On Saturday March 31, Jeremy Thorpe, who had been asked to stand again as Liberal candidate for North Devon in spite of the forthcoming Old Bailey trial, said, 'This is my eighth election and I'm delighted to be back in the fray.' That weekend, he toured his constituency, kissing and embracing voters and saying 'Thank you m'dear' and 'Nice to see you again, m'darling' to middle-aged ladies.

Over in California, on Monday April 2, the marriage took place between 25-year-old Patty Hearst and 33-year-old policeman Bernard Shaw who had acted as one of her bodyguards before she began her jail sentence. Tight security surrounded the ceremony on the Treasure Island naval base which was attended by the bride's parents, Mr and Mrs Randolph Hearst and Mrs Bing Crosby and other celebrities.

The following day, the exiled Shah of Iran was found installed in a seventy room hotel on Paradise Island in the Bahamas with his wife and two sons, at an estimated cost of $50,000 a day. 'I am thoroughly enjoying my stay here,' he said. 'My family and I want to rest and enjoy the beautiful weather and the lovely islands.'

Back in Britain, on Wednesday April 4, witty journalist Auberon Waugh declared his candidature for the North Devon seat now being defended by Mr Jeremy Thorpe and explained that he would be standing for the Dog Lovers' Party. 'I intend to represent the canine aspects of the modern political scene,' he said.

Writer Auberon Waugh: dog-lovers party's candidate at the 1979 general election

The following weekend in London, Opposition leader Mrs Thatcher paid a highly publicized visit to her local butcher and spent £7.40 on a large chicken, 4½ lbs of minced meat and 1 lb of bacon.

On Wednesday April 11, President Amin fled from Kampala and Radio Uganda announced, 'From today the oppressive and illegal regime of Idi Amin is no longer in power.' A few hours later, Tanzanian troops marched unopposed into the capital and a new President was sworn in.

Early the following morning in New York, Studio 54's co-owner Steve Rubell and two others were arrested after a brawl at the famous discothèque over the filming of celebrities at the night-spot. Rubell was released thirty hours later at 10 a.m. on Good Friday, April 13, stating that he would sue the City of New York for $5 million damages for being falsely imprisoned.

Meanwhile in Europe, there had been great excitement over claims by British surgeon Hugh Thomas that the elderly man held in Berlin's Spandau Gaol was not Rudolf Hess but an imposter. This suggestion was quickly dismissed by Hess's wife, who said of Mr Thomas, 'This fellow hasn't got all his cups in his cupboard.'

Back in America on Wednesday April 18, Michelle Triola's historic action against her former boy-friend actor Lee Marvin ended after twelve weeks with the judge awarding her $104,000. Though this sum was only a fraction of what she had originally demanded, she hailed the judge's ruling as a victory for all women. 'If a man wants to leave his toothbrush in my house, he can bloody well marry me,' she said. Lee Marvin also appeared satisfied with the result, claiming that he won the case 'on all counts'.

Earlier that day in London, Roddy Llewellyn kissed his brother Dai at a party given by restaurant owner Viscount Newport to celebrate the re-opening of the Caviare Bar in Knightsbridge. It was noted that 33-year-old Dai Llewellyn was on crutches following a skiing mishap and was accompanied by a new girl friend, 20-year-old Vanessa Hubbard, niece of the Duke of Norfolk.

The following day, Mrs Thatcher went electioneering at the Cadbury's chocolate factory in Birmingham and tried to explain her policies against a background of bubbling and clattering machinery. Mr Denis Thatcher remained in the background remarking, 'Fascinating – but how do you get the walnut exactly in the middle of the fudge?'

On Saturday April 21, Mrs Thatcher's 25-year-old journalist daughter Carol flew home from Australia to participate in the run-up to the general election. In an interview, she revealed that her mother was 'the kind of woman who sobs at sentimental films, gets wobbly knees before important speeches and loves shopping for bargains'.

Meanwhile in California, President Carter's younger brother Billy had been undergoing treatment for alcohol addiction at Long Beach Naval Hospital. On Monday April 23, he emerged from the hospital vowing never to drink again. 'I feel as funny as hell without a beer can in my hand. But I still intend to be a good old boy,' he said.

Back in Uganda, reports that former President Idi Amin had been seen driving around near his home town of Arua in a black Mercedes Benz saloon fuelled rumours that the ousted dictator was still in the country.

On Friday April 27, it was revealed that the former Prime Minister Sir Harold Wilson had praised Mrs Thatcher's ability in an informal interview with a *Daily Mail* reporter and had declared that she might get the vote of his wife Mary in the forthcoming general election.

On Wednesday May 2, it was revealed that Lady Antonia Fraser's 22-year-old daughter Rebecca had now set up home in America with 25-year-old Bobby Kennedy Jnr. who had been her constant companion for the last year and a half. The couple had settled in a red-brick house in the cherry blossom country of Charlottesville, Virginia. 'It's the most unselfish love I've ever seen,' said a mutual friend. 'They are very much in love but no one thinks they will marry immediately.'

On Thursday May 3, the British people went to the polls and voted grocer's daughter Margaret Thatcher to power with a solid majority. Among those who lost their seats to the Conservatives was 50-year-old Mr Jeremy Thorpe, who

Following his brother's wedding in Boston, Bobby Kennedy Jnr visits New York's Studio 54

received a kiss after his defeat from the flamboyant Henrietta Rous, who had been fighting for the same seat as candidate of the Wessex Regionalist Party.

The following morning, Mrs Thatcher breakfasted off grapefruit segments, a boiled egg and coffee at her Chelsea home and set off via the Conservative headquarters and Buckingham Palace for 10 Downing Street. 'I shall strive unceasingly to fulfill the trust and confidence the British people have put in me,' she said on the doorstep of her new home.

On Saturday May 5, attention turned to the Philippines where Madame Imelda Marcos was celebrating her twenty-fifth wedding anniversary. Among those gathered at the Malacanan Palace in Manila that weekend were the Duchess of Cadiz, 27-year-old granddaughter of the late General Franco, ageing playboy Gunther Sachs, actor Sean Connery, banker Mario d'Urso, and gossip columnist Nigel Dempster, who left later for a jaunt on the presidential yacht *An Pangulo*.

Back in London, on Tuesday May 8, the trial of Jeremy Thorpe and three others charged with conspiracy to murder opened at the Old Bailey. Mr Thorpe arrived at the court in his lawyer's Rolls-Royce, wearing a velvet-collared overcoat and a black homburg instead of his more familiar brown trilby.

The following day, the Earl of Longford took tea with three London prostitutes at a flat in Shepherd's Market in Mayfair. It was later discovered that he had left his cheque book in the flat. 'I imagine it dropped out on the sofa,' he said.

Over in Hollywood on Friday May 11, 66-year-old Barbara Hutton collapsed in her penthouse suite at the Beverly Wilshire Hotel and died before she reached the Cedars Sinai Hospital. The much married Woolworth heiress, who had been ill for many years, weighed only 5 stone 8 pounds at the time of her death and had been living on Coca-Cola, cigarettes and a health drink called Metrecal.

Back in England, on Saturday May 12, Earl Spencer's return to health after his serious illness the previous winter was celebrated with a service of thanksgiving at All Saints Church, Northampton, conducted by the Bishop of Southwark, Dr Mervyn Stockwood. Among those present in the large congregation were the Earl's mother-in-law, 77-year-old Barbara Cartland, his 17-year-old daughter Lady Diana Spencer, and the new Minister for Arts Mr Norman St John-Stevas.

The following day in Iran, death sentences were passed on the absent Shah and his family. In a bloodthirsty statement, Ayatollah Khalkhali said that anyone who killed the Shah would be acting on the orders of the courts and would not be punished.

On Monday May 14, it was announced that the seven ton Warwick Vase, originally sold to the Metropolitan Museum of Art in New York, had now finally been acquired by the Glasgow City Museum for £250,000.

The same day at the Thorpe trial at the Old Bailey, chief prosecution witness Peter Bessell spoke of his addiction to tea and was told by the judge to shut up.

On Tuesday May 15, the Queen drove through London in the Irish State Coach to open the new parliament. Waiting for the Queen's speech in the House of Commons, the new Prime Minister, Mrs Thatcher, dressed in an off-white suit and peach-coloured straw hat, brushed a speck from the jacket of her colleague, Mr Norman St John-Stevas. Watching the proceedings from a side gallery was the Prime Minister's husband Denis, who wore impeccable morning dress. In the debate that followed, Mrs Thatcher snapped at the former Prime Minister, Jim Callaghan, 'You had your chance. Now it's our turn!'

New Prime Minister Margaret Thatcher brushes a mark off the shoulder of Mr Norman St John-Stevas at the State Opening of Parliament

On Thursday May 17, Norman Scott arrived at the Old Bailey to give evidence against the former Liberal leader. As he stepped from his car, his hair was caught by a gust of wind and blown haywire.

On Saturday May 19, it was revealed that miners' leader Joe Gormley had been provided with a £9,000 Vauxhall Royale by his union, fitted with stereo radio and cassette recorder, power steering, push button adjusting seats and windows and a sun roof, capable of a maximum speed of 125 mph.

That night in Jeddah, Saudi Arabia, British doctor Richard Arnot and his wife Penny gave a party at their sixth floor flat, which ended with the mysterious death of two of the guests and the host and hostess being arrested for serving alcohol.

Back in Britain, on Monday May 21, a new theory that Queen Victoria had married her great friend John Brown and had a child by him made headline news. 'The nettle must be firmly grasped,' said Dr Macdonald, curator of the Museum of Scottish Tartans in Perth.

The same day, the Queen admired the orchids at the Chelsea Flower show and appeared unruffled by this scandal about her great-great-grandmother.

The following day the Thorpe Trial at the Old Bailey took a new twist when Thorpe's barrister, Mr Carman, admitted that his client had had 'homosexual tendencies'.

Over in Paris, on Wednesday May 23, thieves entered the Avenue Foch home of Mr Mohamed al-Tajir, sampled his caviare and champagne and made off with porcelain, carpets and other works of art valued at £1.5 million.

Later that day in New York, Margaret Trudeau, estranged wife of Pierre Trudeau, was found dancing in Studio 54 wearing white disco pants a few hours after the defeat of her husband in the Canadian general election. 'He's the most wonderful man I know,' she said.

Back in Britain, on Sunday May 27, an encounter took place at Smith's Lawn, Windsor, between Prince Charles and a punk calling himself Phil Sick. 'Why do you wear those chains round your legs?' asked the heir to the throne.

The following Thursday, May 31, the Royal Première of *The Muppet Movie* at the Leicester Square Theatre was somewhat marred when Princess Anne, in a flowing red gown, refused to cuddle Kermit the Frog. 'I'm not Mrs Thatcher,' she snapped.

The next day in Zimbabwe, Rhodesia, eighty-nine years of white rule ended with the appointment of Bishop Muzorewa as the country's first black Prime Minister. Former Prime Minister Ian Smith said he would not be joining in the celebrations and went to bed early.

On Saturday June 2, Pope John Paul II arrived in Warsaw and knelt in scorching sunshine on the tarmac at the airport to kiss his native soil. He then celebrated mass in Warsaw's main square before 250,000 people amidst ominous warnings from the Kremlin that church leaders should not use the visit for 'anti-state purposes'.

Back in Britain, on Tuesday June 5, celebrities gathered at the Royal Festival Hall for a special concert to celebrate the hundredth birthday of music lover Sir Robert Mayer. During the evening, an odd encounter took place between the Queen and the short-sighted 86-year-old Lady Diana Cooper. 'I'm very sorry, ma'am, but I didn't recognize you without your crown on,' said Lady Diana, to which the Queen replied, 'It's Sir Robert's evening, I left it at home.'

On Wednesday June 6, the Queen watched her own horse, Milford, fail miserably in the 200th Epsom Derby. Along with other spectators was Jeremy Thorpe's sometime solicitor Lord Goodman, who was offered the assistance of two commissionaires to climb the steep slope up to a pavilion where he was to lunch with banker Evelyn de Rothschild.

The following day at the Old Bailey, barrister George Carman shocked the court by announcing that he would not be calling any evidence in defence of his client, Mr Thorpe.

That night, in Marbella, 31-year-old James Hunt announced that he was giving up motor-racing after suffering 'awful premonitions' at the recent Monte Carlo Grand Prix.

On Friday June 8, the parents of Miss Mary Jo Kopechne, who had drowned ten years earlier after spending the evening with Senator Edward Kennedy, announced that they would not 'interfere' if Mr Kennedy decided to run for the presidency. 'Maybe he'll make a great President,' they said. 'Everyone makes mistakes. We have no reason to bring up anything now.'

Meanwhile, Christina Onassis had returned to her seven room apartment overlooking the botanical gardens in Moscow, after spending the winter in Paris, Athens and Barcelona. It was noted that Miss Onassis was free to come and go as she pleased.

On Saturday June 9, a judge in Los Angeles ordered Mick Jagger to pay his estranged wife Bianca $3,000 a week maintenance while the divorce proceedings continued. 'That's what she needs, that's what she'll get,' said the judge.

On Sunday June 10, the Shah of Iran flew to Mexico and drove in a small motorcade to Cuernavaca where he had been provided with a temporary lodging place. In an interview soon after his arrival he said, 'My heart is bleeding. For twenty-seven years I toiled and sweated and shed tears to make my country something. Look what is happening now.'

Back in London, on Monday June 11, prosecuting counsel Peter Taylor told the Old Bailey jury that Jeremy Thorpe's involvement in the current case was 'a tragedy of truly Greek or Shakespearian proportions' but went on to inform the jury, 'Sympathy can have no part in your deliberations.'

On Tuesday June 12, Chancellor of the Exchequer Sir Geoffrey Howe's first budget, which cut income tax and reduced public spending by £4,000 million, was well received by tax exiles across the world. In Los Angeles, pop star Rod Stewart said, 'It's great for Britain. It's great for Show Business.' While in Paris the Duchess of Bedford declared, 'Oh marvellous. Does that mean we can go home now? I must get my husband out of the bath and tell him.'

The following day in Washington, President Carter astonished guests at a private dinner for sixty members of Congress by declaring, 'If Kennedy runs, I'll whip his arse.'

The same evening in New York, Mrs Jackie Onassis and Mrs Lally Waymouth gave a party for Arthur Schlesinger. 'Thank God, I didn't think anyone would come,' said Mrs Waymouth as New York gossip columnist Liz Smith made her entrance.

On Thursday June 14, it was announced that Mrs Margaret Jay, wife of the former British Ambassador to Washington and daughter of the former Prime Minister, was to have her own chat show on American television. 'It's true,' she said. 'I have been talking to ABC television. After all, I worked in television for sixteen years in Britain.'

On Saturday June 16, 86-year-old Lady Diana Cooper and 75-year-old Sir Cecil Beaton mingled with pop star Bryan Ferry, 27-year-old Mark Shand and other members of jeunesse dorée at a fancy dress party given by interior decorator Nicky Haslam at his Hampshire hunting lodge.

The same night at a château near Deauville, there was a jet set gathering to celebrate the marriage of Stavros Niarchos's daughter Maria and French pharmaceuticals heir Alexis Chevassu. Star guests at this celebration were King Constantine of Greece, Princess Caroline of Monaco, Christina Onassis and her Russian husband Sergei Kauzov.

Lady Rothermere as she appeared at Nicky Haslam's hunting party

On Monday June 18, the world's leaders gathered in Vienna to discuss the limitation of missiles in nuclear arsenals in Russia and the United States. During the talks, 72-year-old Leonid Brezhnev stumbled on the steps of the Soviet Embassy and was given a helping hand by President Carter.

The following day in London, Baron Enrico de Portanova, heir to an American oil fortune, said at Claridge's that he faced assassination by self-appointed representatives of Ayatollah Khomeini, following a false report that he had sold his house in Acapulco to the exiled Shah of Iran. 'The truth is that I have never met him nor have I ever had anything to do with him or his family,' he said.

On Wednesday June 20, the jury in the Thorpe trial retired to consider their verdict and the former Liberal leader and his three co-defendants were taken to Brixton prison for the night.

The following day at Ascot, the Queen was walking from the Royal Enclosure to the Paddock when she was pushed and jostled by a top-hatted racegoer, who thrust his way between the Queen and her companion, Lord Abergavenny. 'These incidents are very regrettable but often unavoidable,' said a Buckingham Palace spokesman afterwards.

On Friday June 22, the jury in the Thorpe trial returned after sixteen hours of deliberation and found Mr Thorpe and his co-defendants not guilty of all the charges against them. 'I am delighted with the result,' said the former Liberal leader as he left the court. 'I am glad that justice was done.'

Later that afternoon at his rented wooden bungalow in Devonshire, former male model Norman Scott said that he was disgusted by the verdicts.

The following morning, Mr and Mrs Thorpe posed for photographers on the lawn of their Bayswater home. 'I have nothing to add to my statement after the hearing,' said Mr Thorpe. 'Not even what I had for breakfast. Period.'

Later that day in Greece, a bishop was discharged after being found in bed with a colleague's wife.

On Tuesday June 26, the Prime Minister Mrs Thatcher left London for the Tokyo Summit. En route to Japan, her RAF VC10 paused for a brief refuelling stop at Moscow during which Soviet premier Mr Kosygin hosted a ninety minute champagne and caviare supper at the airport over which the two leaders discussed the world economy, strategic arms limitation, energy and the plight of the Vietnam refugees.

A few hours later, President Carter arrived in Tokyo with his 11-year-old daughter Amy, who yawned her head off at the airport and was then struck down with flu.

Over in New York, on Thursday June 28, Studio 54 owners Steve Rubell and Ian Schrager were indicted on twelve counts of systematically skimming off more than $2.5 million from the gross takings of their club during the past two years.

Back in Britain, on Friday June 29, Lord Rothermere, proprietor of the *Daily Mail*, sent a much publicized memo to the paper's gossip columnist Nigel Dempster complaining that his page was 'beginning to have the taste of an old, cold fried potato'.

On Sunday July 1, Mr and Mrs Jeremy Thorpe attended a special service of thanksgiving at the tiny eleventh-century church of Bratton Fleming on Exmoor. 'The darkness is now past and the true light shines,' said the portly Rev. John Hornby in his address to the congregation. 'This is the day which the Lord hath made!'

The following day, Prince Charles took 24-year-old Sabrina Guinness, former nanny to Tatum O'Neal and girl-friday to David Bowie, to see the brilliant Fats Waller musical *Ain't Misbehavin'* at Her Majesty's Theatre.

Meanwhile, superstar Bianca Jagger had abandoned the high life and flown to the war-torn country of Nicaragua in an attempt to make contact with members of her family whom she had not seen for years and also to report on conditions for the British charity Save the Children.

Back in Europe, on Friday July 6, the jet set gathered at Countess Bismarck's villa at Marbella for the baptism of the infant offspring of Count and Countess Rudolf Schoenburg. Guests included Queen Sofia of Spain, Prince Alfonso Hohenlohe and actress Deborah Kerr and were served with guacamole and salmon appetizers, sausages and veal-burgers.

On Saturday July 7, 23-year-old Bjorn Borg took the Wimbledon's men's single title for the fourth year running after a titanic centre court struggle with young American Roscoe Tanner. 'I was unbelievably nervous at the end,' said Borg. 'I almost couldn't hold my racket.'

That night a party at Longleat House, stately home of the Marquess of Bath, ended in tragedy when the peer's younger son, 41-year-old Lord Valentine Thynne, once described as 'the prince of the beatniks', was found hanged at his home a mile away.

The same weekend there was a twenty-five hour party at the Hertfordshire home of Playboy boss Victor Lowndes which was attended by 33-year-old Dai Llewellyn, TV newscaster Reggie Bosanquet, Jonathan Aitken MP, Princess Elizabeth of Yugoslavia, impresario Michael White, Dido Goldsmith and her current escort Sir William Pigott-Brown and portly pop star Gary Glitter.

On Wednesday July 11, 79-year-old Earl Mountbatten of Burma was guest of honour at the Berkeley Square ball at which rock and roll star Alvin Stardust did a set-piece on stage. Others present included Auberon Waugh, who was found chatting with Victor Lowndes, business man Jarvis Astaire and 33-year-old Dai Llewellyn, who auctioned off a 1924 Rolls-Royce.

Over in New York, on Thursday July 12, 70-year-old mafia boss Carmine Galante was shot dead with a machine-gun in the garden of a Brooklyn restaurant. He fell to the floor with his cigar still clenched grotesquely between his teeth.

On Saturday July 14, 23-year-old Lord Blandford, son and heir to the Duke of Marlborough, flew into Britain from America to attend a disco-dance at Haddon Hall in Derbyshire, given by Lady John Manners. Other young sprigs of the aristocracy present included Lord Mancroft's boy Benjamin and the Earl of Uxbridge, son and heir of the Marquess of Anglesey.

On Wednesday July 18, the new Countess of Snowdon gave birth to a baby girl in Westminster Hospital. Her husband attended the birth and a Buckingham Palace spokesman said later, 'The Queen has been informed and is glad all is well.'

The following day, the Queen, Prince Philip and Prince Andrew left for a tour of Africa. On Friday July 20, the royal party 'arrival celebrations' in Dar es Salaam were held up as garlands of flowers were placed round Prince Andrew's neck.

Meanwhile, English missionary Mary Hayward had fled from Uganda where she had spent her time recently looking after twelve children of the ousted President Amin. 'I don't know what happened to them,' she said on Saturday July 21. 'I've slippered many of them but they were such nice children.'

On Monday July 23, the Queen drove through the capital of Malawi in a deep red Rolls-Royce belonging to President Banda, who accompanied his royal guests, waving a fly whisk.

The previous day in Tanzania, a member of the Queen's staff had found a large black rat in his hotel bedroom.

Back in Britain, on Thursday July 26, 74-year-old multi-millionaire Sir Charles Clore died in the London Clinic after a long battle with cancer and leaving most of his £80 million fortune to charity. 'He was a lovely, lovely man,' said his old school-mate, Lord Grade.

The same day in the House of Commons, a Conservative MP asked the Minister of Health how many deaths could be attributed to jogging during the past five years. He said he believed the sport was 'potentially lethal', and felt it would be a good idea for track-suits to carry a government health warning.

Over at Hyannis Port, Massachusetts on Friday July 27, the recent eighty-ninth birthday of America's leading matriarch, Mrs Rose Kennedy, was celebrated with a party attended by her children Senator Edward Kennedy, Mrs Pat Lawford and Mrs Eunice Shriver.

The following day, Mrs Kennedy's former daughter-in-law Jackie Onassis celebrated her fiftieth birthday away from the glare of publicity, cruising off Maine on a friend's yacht.

The following day in Hollywood, actress Farrah Fawcett-Majors and her husband Lee Majors announced that they had agreed to a trial separation. The blonde television and movie star said that there was no third party involved and the couple's manager blamed the separation on stress caused by career conflicts.

On Wednesday August 1, it was reported that Mr Nixon's plans to buy a $750,000 nine room penthouse in a fashionable Madison Avenue block had been strongly opposed by other residents. 'I have no axe to grind politically or morally,' said Mrs Jane Maynard, 'but Nixon is very controversial and I think it would change the ambience of the building if he lived here.'

The following day in the South China Sea, it was thought that two flimsy boats carrying about 500 Vietnamese refugees had been lost in a typhoon.

On Sunday August 5, it was announced that 33-year-old Mrs Soraya Khashoggi was suing her ex-husband, reputed to be the world's richest man, for £2,000 million. The British-born Mrs Khashoggi claimed that she had helped him to make his fortune.

The glamorous Soraya Khashoggi who was to sue her husband Adnan for £2.000 million

On Tuesday August 7, 24-year-old Dido Goldsmith was found sunning herself on Mustique, declaring that she had left her £200 a week job at Regine's London club. 'I've not been to the club for months,' she said. 'I'll always be friends with Regine herself. But I'm no longer working full-time. I can't be bothered.'

Back in Britain, on Monday August 13, it was announced that Mr Jeremy Thorpe was planning a new career for himself in television and had had talks with impresario Lord Delfont about the possibility of hosting his own TV programme.

Early the following morning, former Labour Minister John Stonehouse was released from Norwich Prison after serving less than half his sentence for theft, fraud and deception. He jumped into a waiting green Volvo which sped off at high speed, chased by press cars.

Two days later, Mr Stonehouse's mother, Mrs Rosina Stonehouse, collapsed in a church in Southampton saying she was under terrible strain because her son had not telephoned her.

On Thursday August 16, New Wave stars intent on recreating the mod cult of the Sixties gathered at the première of a new film *Quadrophenia* featuring The Who pop group. 'It mystifies me completely,' said singer Roger Daltrey. 'Why should kids go back in time to find something new?'

On Monday August 20, Mrs Rosina Stonehouse stated that her son had telephoned her to say that he was safe and well. 'I don't know where the call came from. He didn't say and I didn't ask. I was just so pleased to hear from him.'

Over in New York, on Thursday August 23, it was revealed that former President Nixon's attempts to buy another $1 million twelve room apartment overlooking Central Park had also run into difficulties. 'Certain aspects are still to be clarified,' said the managers of the block, 'including the matter of security.'

The same day, Russian ballet star Alexander Godunov defected from the Bolshoi Ballet and was granted political asylum in the United States. A former classmate of Mikhail Baryshnikov, Godunov was said to feel imprisoned by the Bolshoi's seldom changing repertoire.

The following day, State Department officials refused to allow a Russian airliner with Godunov's wife ballerina Ludmilla Vlasova on board, to leave Kennedy Airport. Surrounding the airliner with police cars, officials explained that they were anxious to learn if the ballerina was returning to Moscow of her own free will. 'It is in the national interest of this country that we speak privately to Miss Vlasova,' explained an official.

On Monday August 27, 79-year-old Earl Mountbatten of Burma, his grandson and a boat boy were killed when an IRA bomb exploded on his fishing boat at Mullaghmore, County Sligo. Among many world leaders to express their horror was Pope John Paul II who declared, 'This act of shocking violence is an insult to human dignity.' At Balmoral Castle, it was announced that the Queen had heard of her husband's uncle's death 'with profound regret'.

The same day in Northern Ireland, fifteen members of the 2nd Battalion of the Parachute Regiment died when a mine exploded by remote control.

Meanwhile in New York, ballet star Ludmilla Vlasova had been permitted to fly home to Moscow after seventy hours on board a stranded Aeroflot airliner at Kennedy Airport, after satisfying American diplomats that she was not being forced to return against her will.

On Tuesday August 28, it was announced that Prince Charles's former girl-friend Lady Sarah Spencer was to marry 28-year-old farmer Neil McCorquodale. 'We met three years ago in London through mutual friends. Really, it's been a whirlwind romance for the last two or three months,' explained Lady Sarah, now working for Savills estate agency.

The following day, the Prime Minister, Mrs Thatcher, paid a surprise visit to the troubled province of Northern Ireland.

A week later on Wednesday September 5, the state funeral of Earl Mountbatten of Burma took place with full pageantry in Westminster Abbey and was attended by the Queen, Prince Philip, Lord Snowdon, Mr Denis Thatcher and the Irish Prime Minister Mr Lynch. After the service, the coffin was taken to Romsey in Hampshire on a special train decorated with red roses and pink carnations.

Later that day in New York, Bantam Books paid a record $3,208,875 for rights to *Princess Daisy* by Judith Krantz, exciting anger in certain quarters that publishers were now only interested in 'blockbusters'.

On Friday September 7, there was excitement in British ecclesiastical circles over the announcement that the Bishop of St Albans, Dr Robert Runcie, was to be the new Archbishop of Canterbury. An enthusiastic pig-breeder and former war hero, who had won the MC for rescuing a colleague from a blazing tank, he said, 'I was genuinely astonished when I was told of the choice.'

The following day, Mrs Margaret Thatcher and her husband Denis arrived at Balmoral Castle to spend the weekend with the Queen.

On Sunday September 9, former Rhodesian leader Mr Ian Smith arrived in England for talks about the future of his country. At Heathrow Airport, he had an unscheduled encounter with his old adversary Sir Harold Wilson, who was flying off the same day for a lecture tour in America.

On Monday September 10, the marriage took place in London between Lord Lovat's son Andrew Fraser and Lord Brooke's daughter Charlotte Greville. Among those who were present at a reception afterwards at the Turf Club were Baron Heinrich Thyssen, 28-year-old Lord Hesketh and his mother Kirsty Lady Hesketh, who wore a black eye-patch, and the glamorous Rajmata of Jaipur, who wore a green and gold sari.

On Wednesday September 12, 19-year-old Prince Andrew drove himself in a modest new Ford Escort to Dartmouth Naval College where he was to begin his training as a midshipman.

That night in Washington, 400 fashion-lovers gathered for a show by Zandra Rhodes at which models paraded in chiffon gowns, with pompom pigtails, and elegant satin and chiffon face-masks. At the end of the evening, Miss Rhodes appeared on stage to receive a standing ovation, with shocking pink hair and 'pagoda' eyebrows.

International fashion designer Zandra Rhodes, celebrated for her chiffon gowns, pom-pom pigtails and shocking pink hair

On Thursday September 13, the ailing and almost unconscious 83-year-old Duchess of Windsor was taken back to her home in the Bois de Boulogne after four months treatment at the American hospital in Paris.

Back in London, on Friday September 14, Sir James Goldsmith presided over a champagne and scrambled eggs breakfast at Claridge's to celebrate the publication of the first edition of his weekly news-magazine *Now!* 'I think it has an even chance of survival,' he said.

The following day in Shropshire the marriage took place between 31-year-old Viscount Newport, son and heir to the Earl of Bradford, and Miss Jo Miller, daughter of turf accountant Benjamin Miller. Guests at the reception afterwards at the bridegroom's home, Weston Park, were offered caviare and freshly made hot toast.

Later that day in America, President Carter collapsed while taking part in a six mile cross-country race near his Camp David retreat. The 54-year-old President was treated with smelling salts and then had a quart of salt water injected through a vein in his arm. His physician, Mr Lukash, later declared that the President's life had not been in danger.

Back in Britain, on Monday September 17, a controversy erupted over Mark Thatcher's departure for Tokyo carrying a Japan Airlines bag and wearing a jacket bearing advertisements for Marlborough cigarettes and Playboy Toiletries for Men. A Downing Street spokesman commented, 'He leads his own private life.'

On Thursday September 20, 25-year-old Sabrina Guinness arrived at Balmoral Castle to spend a long weekend with the Royal Family. 'Officially she is the guest of the Queen but really Prince Charles invited her,' said her father, banker James Guinness.

The following day in India, the auction of the jewels of the late Nizam of Hyderabad, which had excited worldwide interest, was called off at the last moment when the New Delhi Supreme Court declared that the jewels, worth an estimated £15 million, were a national treasure.

The same day in Africa, self-proclaimed Emperor Bokassa lost his throne and fled from his Central African Empire on board a sky blue Imperial Caravelle airliner. He arrived a few hours later at Evreux airport near Paris but was refused permission to leave his plane. He later flew on to exile on the Ivory Coast, surrounded by rumours that the remains of some thirty-seven people had been found at the bottom of the private pool where he had kept his pet crocodiles.

Meanwhile, senior statesman Harold Macmillan, now 85 years old, had flown to the Far East on Concorde. On Monday September 24, he walked along the Great Wall of China wearing a Mao cap. Offered a chair and a doctor after his exertions, he said he would prefer a bottle of brandy.

The same day in Geneva, the long-awaited trial began of financier Bernie Cornfeld, whose once vast company IOS was now in the hands of the liquidators. 'We believe we have a very good defence,' said one of the lawyers hired by the 52-year-old former multi-millionaire.

On Tuesday September 25, there were wild scenes at the troubled Studio 54 now equipped with fog machines, laser-lit chandeliers and a giant moving bridge high above the dance floor. 'It was reminiscent of scenes at the fall of the decadent Roman Empire,' said an onlooker.

The same night, the beautiful people flocked instead to the rival nightspot Xenon where there was a gala party to celebrate the Broadway opening of *Evita*.

Back in London, on Wednesday September 26, Sir John Betjeman read out a poem to celebrate the re-consecration of the tower of St Anne's church, Soho. 'It's not very good I'm afraid,' said the 73-year-old Poet Laureate.

The following day, Lady Lucan protested about a new television documentary being made about the murder of her nanny five years earlier, declaring that the actor playing her husband, the missing Earl of Lucan, was badly cast. 'My husband was a fantastically good-looking man,' she said. 'He had broad shoulders and he had the bearing of a gentleman.'

On Saturday September 29, Pope John Paul II flew into Dublin breakfasting on board an Aer Lingus Boeing 747 off Irish bacon, sausages, black and white puddings and soda bread. In a speech on his arrival, he pleaded with the gunmen and bombers of Northern Ireland. 'On my knees I beg you to turn away from the paths of violence and return to the ways of peace.'

Back in New York that night, Princess Caroline of Monaco and her husband Philippe Junot were found dancing at the new ultra-chic Xenon disco. The chain-smoking Princess was heavily made up with her blouse open to the mid-chest.

On Friday October 5, it was revealed that former President Richard Nixon, who had twice been thwarted in his attempts to buy an apartment in Manhattan had now settled for a twelve room four storey house on the upper East Side. His wife Pat was soon found shopping in the local late night supermarket, flanked by security guards.

The following day, Pope John Paul made history when he set foot in the White House where over 7,000 people were invited to a reception in his honour.

Back in London, on Tuesday October 9, Lord Weidenfeld gave a cocktail party at his Chelsea flat to celebrate the publication of a new biography of Prince Charles by journalist Anthony Holden. Among those present were TV personality Russell Harty, Sir Harold and Lady Wilson, Miss Edna O'Brien and eager young 'royalty watcher' Hugo Vickers.

Sir James Goldsmith leaves a party given by Lord Weidenfeld accompanied by his wife Lady Annabel and his new friend Lady Falkender

Meanwhile in France, there was considerable excitement over accusations that President Giscard d'Estaing had accepted gifts of £100,000 worth of diamonds from the former Emperor Bokassa, now exiled on the Ivory Coast. A curt statement from the Elysée Palace that there was nothing out of order about the gifts failed to silence the President's critics.

On Thursday October 11, Jeremy Thorpe announced that he would not be standing again as Liberal candidate for the North Devon constituency which he had represented for twenty years. He explained that he was 'not able to guarantee the time necessary to win back the seat'.

The same day, Princess Margaret left England on Concorde for a fund-raising tour of America on behalf of the Royal Ballet accompanied by the Earl of Drogheda and four other officials.

On Saturday October 13, Mrs Margaret Thatcher celebrated her fifty-fourth birthday wandering in the Rose Garden at Chequers after a triumphant week at the Conservative Party conference.

The following day a controversy erupted over an announcement that Captain Mark Phillips's equestrian activities were to be sponsored by British Leyland. 'We are a young couple with a mortgage,' said Captain Phillips. 'It costs about £3,000 a year to keep a horse in training.'

On Monday October 15, the final act in the long drawn out IOS saga took place in Geneva when 54-year-old former tycoon Bernie Cornfeld was acquitted on fraud charges. Mr Cornfeld wept with joy as spectators cheered and applauded the verdict.

Meanwhile in America, Princess Margaret's tour on behalf of the Royal Ballet had run into difficulties following an allegation by a Chicago columnist that the Princess had called the Irish 'pigs' at a private dinner party. A vigorous denial that the Princess had made any such remark by her personal secretary, Lord Napier, failed to calm the storm.

Back in Britain the following Friday, it was announced that Norman Scott had left his Dartmoor cottage for a trip to America.

On Saturday October 20, the Queen, Prince Charles and most of the Royal Family were present at the marriage of Lord Romsey, TV producer grandson of the late Lord Mountbatten and Miss Penelope Eastwood, daughter of the founder of the Angus Steak House chain. Intense but discreet security surrounded the ceremony in Romsey Abbey which was followed by a reception for 750 guests at Broadlands, Lord Mountbatten's former home, now open to the public.

The following day, Mrs Soraya Khashoggi's battle for a share in her husband's £2,000 million fortune hotted up when she arranged for his DC9 jet to be impounded at Heathrow Airport. 'I impounded the plane because Adnan refused to be judged by a court of law,' explained Mrs Khashoggi now being represented by American lawyer Marvin Mitchelson.

The same day at St James's Church, Piccadilly, the baby daughter of gossip columnist Nigel Dempster was christened Louisa by the theatrical parson, the Rev. William Baddeley. Godparents included literary agent Caroline Dawnay, Lady Montagu of Beaulieu and celebrated restaurateur Peter Langan.

On Monday October 22, the Shah of Iran, now said to be very sick and fighting for his life, was put on board a Gulf Stream jet at Mexico airport and flown to New York for emergency treatment at the Cornell Medical Center. The 59-year-old former monarch was said to be suffering from a malignant tumour and a blocked bile duct.

Meanwhile in Australia, police had arrested a man they believed to be the missing Earl of Lucan. Shown a photograph of the suspect, Lady Lucan commented, 'The police obviously haven't got a clue. My husband is a real aristocrat. He looks like a real Lord.'

Back in New York, on Wednesday October 24, the Shah of Iran was operated on for cancer. His gall bladder was removed and a biopsy was taken of the lymph nodes in his neck. 'Recovery is anticipated if there are no complications,' said the Shah's senior aide Mr Robert Armao.

Later that day in Los Angeles, police claimed to have uncovered an IRA plot to assassinate Princess Margaret as she opened a Rolls-Royce garage. 'We've established that the man we are looking for is a high-ranking IRA man,' said Captain Larry Kramer. 'I cannot identify him as the investigation is continuing.'

Back in England, on Saturday October 27, the upper classes put on their tiaras for a magnificent ball given by the Earl and Countess of Pembroke at their stately home in Wiltshire, Wilton House. 75-year-old Sir Cecil Beaton, who had recently been pronounced dead in the *Daily Telegraph*, his friend Lady Diana Cooper and other senior citizens mingled with Sabrina Guinness and other members of the jeunesse dorée. Prince Charles, who was staying nearby at the country home of Lord and Lady Tryon, put in a brief appearance and photographer David Bailey recorded the event for posterity.

Over in New York on Wednesday October 31, the glitterati turned out in force for a party at Maxwell's Plum in honour of Andy Warhol and his new book *Exposures*. Guests included Paloma Picasso, Shelly Duvall, the late Bobby Kennedy's daughter Karen and Studio 54 co-owner Steve Rubell.

Back in London on Friday November 2, Bianca Jagger was granted a divorce on the grounds of her husband's admitted adultery with model Jerry Hall. At the brief hearing in the High Court, Bianca wore a black costume, black pill box and short veil. 'I feel that when you are divorced you wouldn't like to be asked about it,' she said.

The same day, Bianca's old friend, 75-year-old Sir Cecil Beaton, was found painting in his Wiltshire garden wearing an outsize straw hat and vivid green silk scarf.

Two days later in Tehran militant students entered the American Embassy and seized a hundred hostages saying that they would not release them until the Shah, now recovering from his operation in New York, returned to the country to face trial.

Back in America on Wednesday November 7, Senator Edward Kennedy formally declared his candidacy for the Democratic Presidential nomination and spoke of the 'stark failure' of the current administration to provide the leadership the nation yearned for. His wife Joan, now living apart from the Senator, said 'I look forward very enthusiastically to my husband being the next President of the United States.'

On Thursday November 8, the Shah of Iran issued a statement from his hospital bed saying he was willing to leave the United States if this would bring about the freedom of the American hostages in Tehran.

On Sunday November 11, Princess Margaret returned to London after a two week holiday on Mustique with Roddy Llewellyn after her controversial tour of America.

Two days later in America, former Governor of California, 68-year-old Ronald Reagan announced his candidacy for the Republican Presidential nomination in a televised speech at a fund raising dinner in New York.

On Wednesday November 14, Mr Reagan said he supported President Carter's ruling that $5,000 million of Iranian assets held in American banks should be frozen.

Back in Britain, on Thursday November 15, many years of speculation ended when the Prime Minister Mrs Thatcher named 72-year-old bachelor Sir Anthony Blunt, celebrated art historian and former surveyor of the Queen's pictures, as 'the Fourth Man' in the Burgess–Maclean–Philby spy scandal. The statement was swiftly followed by an announcement from Buckingham Palace that Sir Anthony had been stripped of his knighthood.

On Friday November 16, in the midst of this drama, former Prime Minister Edward Heath, Lord Goodman and the Speaker of the House of Commons attended the marriage of the young Conservative MP for Thanet, Jonathan Aitken, and the glamorous Miss Lolicia Azucki.

On Saturday November 17, Professor Anthony Blunt broke his silence and issued a statement from a secret address. 'Of course I intend to stay in England and as soon as present uncertainties are resolved I look forward to resuming my work as an art historian,' he said. 'Meanwhile I would like to express my appreciation for the loyalty of all my friends.'

On Sunday November 18, a mass fund-raising jog in London's Hyde Park was boycotted by actor Robert Morley. 'I decided to refuse the invitation,' he said. 'I'd have thought that Carter fellow had given us sufficient warning about that sort of thing. Personally, I never break out of a slow walk.'

On Tuesday November 20, former Communist Anthony Blunt arrived at the offices of *The Times* in a white land-rover and was given a large whisky and soda before submitting to an eighty minute press conference, during which he appeared remarkably composed and expressed no word of regret about his spying activities. Asked if he had been treated leniently because he was a member of the so-called Establishment, he replied, 'I cannot say.' After the interview, a lunch of smoked trout, veal and fruit salad was served.

Professor Anthony Blunt gives a press conference following his exposure as the Fourth Man in the Burgess–Maclean–Philby spy scandal

The following Friday, the long drawn-out quarrel between Madame Dewi Sukarno and nightclub proprietor Regine came to a climax when Madame Sukarno sued Regine in a Paris court claiming 10,000 francs after being banned from one of her clubs the previous year. The court gave itself a month to consider its verdict.

On Wednesday November 28, fears that Senator Kennedy could be a target for a would-be assassin were re-awakened when a 58-year-old woman entered his office in Boston brandishing a hunting knife. 'The Secret Service have the whole situation in hand,' said the Senator afterwards, now accompanied everywhere by a highly skilled medical team capable of handling any emergency including gun or knife wounds.

The next day at his New York hospital, the Shah of Iran was said to be 'quite distressed' by a sudden decision of the Mexican authorities not to grant him a new visa.

On Saturday December 1, the Empress of Iran visited her husband wearing jeans and jogging shoes.

The following day, the Shah was flown to a United States airforce base near San Antonio in Texas. The Shah had had no contact with President Carter or any high US official during his recent illness but a statement was issued by the White House saying that the United States would provide 'a secure convalescence facility where he can recuperate pending further travel plans'.

Meanwhile back in Britain, a strike was now brewing in the steel industry. On Monday December 3, the leader of the biggest union involved, Mr Bill Sirs, flatly refused to accept the management's latest 2% pay offer. 'Our members are livid. They are not going to accept this sort of offer, which they regard as highly insulting,' he said.

On Wednesday December 5, it was revealed that actress Liza Minnelli had married Broadway producer Mark Gero in a private church ceremony attended by a few friends.

On Friday December 7, a 34-year-old nephew of the Shah of Iran, Prince Shahriar, was shot dead in a Paris street by an assassin on a motorcycle while carrying groceries in the fashionable Avenue Foch.

On Sunday December 9, the former Ugandan President Idi Amin was found living out his exile in a lonely beach house eighty-five miles east of Tripoli on the Libyan coast. It was noted that his weapons had been confiscated and his telephone disconnected.

Back in London, on Monday December 10, former Liberal leader Jeremy Thorpe re-emerged to make an impassioned plea for human rights from the pulpit of St Peter's church, Eaton Square. Distinguished members of the congregation included Lady Wilson and Sir John Gielgud.

Later that day, there was a big gathering at the Ritz Hotel to celebrate the new *Tatler* magazine, now edited by 26-year-old Tina Brown. David Frost, Lady Rothermere, Dido Goldsmith, Dai Llewellyn, former TV newsreader Reggie Bosanquet and Margaret Duchess of Argyll were among those present.

On Tuesday December 11, it was announced in Athens that Christina Onassis had instructed her lawyer to file a petition for divorce against her third husband, 38-year-old Soviet shipping official Sergei Kauzov, on the grounds of irreconcilable differences. 'She is still fond of him and she will want to provide for him well,' said a close friend.

Back in London, on Wednesday December 12, author Andrew Boyle, who had been responsible for the recent unmasking of Sir Anthony Blunt, told a Foyle's Literary luncheon that there were still about thirty 'moles' left. 'They have been cleansed, sanitized and made neutral,' he said, 'though perhaps not all of them.'

The same day, 59-year-old Lord Soames left England, dressed in a lounge suit and trilby hat, to take up his responsibilities as the new Governor of Zimbabwe. On arrival in the troubled country, he posed for photographers and cracked jokes with reporters and generally made light of the onerous tasks ahead.

Two days later, on Friday December 14, speculation about the identity of a well-known Conservative MP with whom Mrs Soraya Khashoggi was said to have had a long affair, ended when 39-year-old Winston Churchill, grandson of Sir Winston and nephew of Lord Soames, admitted that he was the man involved. His confession was followed by a statement from the vice-chairman of his local Conservative association. 'The people here have a very high opinion of Winston and we always back him in everything. I am sure we will support him through whatever crisis he is in now.'

On Saturday December 16, the Shah of Iran was flown from Texas to Panama where he had been assured a warm welcome by General Torrijos and a new home awaited him on the island of Contadora, some thirty miles from the coast commanding splendid views of the ocean. His senior aide Mr Robert Armao said, 'He needs rest and sun and good food during his convalescence.'

The same day in Northern Ireland, where 2,000 people had been killed in the past ten years, five more British soldiers died in two bomb explosions as the IRA began a new Christmas offensive.

The following day in London, a full Rhodesian cease-fire was agreed at the Lancaster House Conference.

That night in Washington, Mrs Margaret Thatcher arrived at a state banquet hosted by President Carter in an exuberant mood. 'I'm so excited to be in the White House,' she said, 'And it was a particularly exciting day, with the signing of the Rhodesia agreement and all.'

Back in New York on Tuesday December 18, drug pusher Johnny Conaghan confessed that he had sold Qaalude pills at several of the city's discos including the troubled Studio 54.

The following night at Manhattan's El Morocco Club, actress Margaux Hemingway celebrated her engagement to the three-times married Bernard Fucher. Joining in the fun were Norman Mailer, Justine Cushing, frock-designer Halston and other members of the city's élite.

Back in London on Thursday December 20, journalist Bernard Levin was robbed of his briefcase as he got into a taxi outside Fortnum and Mason's in Piccadilly. He revealed later that the case contained a portable tape-recorder and various giftwrapped Christmas presents.

That night in Paris there was a crowded black tie party at Regine's. 'This is a mess, I'm going crazy,' screamed Philippe Junot to his wife Princess Caroline of Monaco as he tried to make his way through the crush. Meanwhile frail Madame Gres, France's oldest surviving couturier, sailed through unmolested.

Early the following morning in New York, disco owner Steve Rubell, who, together with Ian Schrager, had now pleaded guilty to both private and corporate tax evasion, climbed into the disc jockey's pulpit at Studio 54 and announced that drinks were on the house.

On Friday December 21, it was revealed that 33-year-old Dai Llewellyn had joined the National Union of Journalists. 'I thought that being an NUJ member would help my career TV-wise,' he explained. 'I've carved myself a bit of a niche, being representative of the type of animal that goes out at night.'

Christmas Day found the British Prime Minister Mrs Thatcher at Chequers with her husband Denis and twin son and daughter Mark and Carol. It was noted that Mrs Thatcher's holiday reading matter would be the newly published *Unfinished History of the World* by Professor Hugh Thomas.

Meanwhile in Tehran, Ayatollah Khomeini had permitted clergymen to visit the American Embassy and hold services for the remaining hostages being held there. It was noted that six prisoners declined to attend these services.

On Friday December 28, President Carter used the 'hot line' to Moscow to protest about the sudden massive airlift of Soviet troops into Afghanistan. He

Princess Caroline of Monaco and her husband Philippe Junot meet famous nightclub owner Regine

demanded that the Russian authorities should order their immediate withdrawal or 'face very serious consequences'.

The same day in New York, it was revealed that John Lennon had started work on his first new album for seven years. The former Beatle and his wife Yoko Ono travelled from their apartment in the Dakota Building to a down-town recording studio under heavy disguise.

Back in London on Monday December 31, 32-year-old Roddy Llewellyn celebrated the end of the decade by giving a party in a basement Chelsea restaurant. During the course of the evening, his elder brother Dai, who had now sold his memoirs to the *News of the World*, looked in on the festivities.

SOURCES OF ILLUSTRATIONS

The illustrations are reproduced by kind permission of the following: The Associated Press Ltd., pages 29, 79, 94, 152; BBC Hulton Picture Library, pages 150, 162, 186, 200, 267, 270; Camera Press London, pages 18 (Bryan Campbell), 49 (Dalmas), 67 (Jane Brown), 74 (James Pickerell), 96 (Brian Aris), 101 (Patrick Lichfield), 106 (Felix Zeitlhofer), 120 & 124 (Alfred Strobel), 127 (Chris Smith), 139, 143 (Peter Kain), 149 (Colin Davey), 157 (Paul Spielman), 159 (Beryl Sokoloff), 178 (Dafydd Jones), 192 (Jerry Watson), 193 (Patrick Lichfield), 197 (Leonard Burt), 201 (John Bryson), 205 (Tom Blau), 216 (Tim Coleman), 222 (L. Cherrault), 227 (Ian Swift), 233 (Alan Davidson), 248 (Leslie C. Wilson), 251 (Jerry Watson); Keystone Press Agency Ltd., pages 12, 20, 23, 31, 36, 38, 48, 50, 57, 60, 62, 65, 71, 89, 91, 111, 120, 128, 132, 146, 164, 174, 181, 235, 237, 245, 256, 263; Popperfoto, pages 16, 25, 27, 35, 44, 54, 63, 93, 116, 145, 160, 194, 212, 229, 232, top and bottom, 257, 273; Press Association, page 206; Rex Features Ltd., pages 15, 85, 168, 176, 182, 234, 238, 242, 260; Robert Rosen, pages 102, 221, 265, *Sunday Times*, page 189; Universal Pictorial Press & Agency Ltd., page 191; Eric Hands, page 254.

INDEX